The Constitution Besieged

HOWARD GILLMAN

The Constitution Besieged

The Rise and Demise of Lochner Era

Police Powers Jurisprudence

DUKE UNIVERSITY PRESS

Durham and London   1993

Third printing in paperback, 2004
© 1993 Duke University Press
All rights reserved
Printed in the United States of America
on acid-free paper ∞
Library of Congress Cataloging-in-Publication Data
appear on the last printed page of this book.

To the memory of my parents,
Stan and Charlyne Gillman

Contents

Acknowledgments

In the early stages of this project I received invaluable support and guidance from Bob Gerstein, Doug Hobbs, and Joyce Appleby. Each of them read the initial drafts of the manuscript and shared with me their considerable expertise on judicial politics and American political (and legal) development. Willie Forbath, Bill Roy, and Bob Welsh also helped me clarify important features of the argument. Clyde Barrow took the time to read a later version of the manuscript; I am grateful that I was able to benefit from his thoughtful advice and familiarity with sources relating to the development of American political thought. At one point or another I also received helpful comments from Bob Gordon, Mark Tushnet, Rick Funston, Barbara Sinclair, and Lief Carter. Mindy Conner, from Duke University Press, did an extraordinary job copyediting the manuscript. I deeply appreciate the efforts of these friends, colleagues, and acquaintances to make this manuscript more coherent, relevant, and interesting. If their efforts are not always evident in the finished product it is because I was either too naive or too stubborn to appreciate what they were trying to tell me.

This book was completed as I began settling into my new home at the University of Southern California. I appreciate the support for this research that I have received from USC; in particular I would like to thank Michael Preston, Dean C. S. Whitaker, and Dean Gerald Segal. My most valuable resource at USC, however, has been Judith Grant, and I would like to extend a special thanks to her for overall support, advice, camaraderie, and friendship.

My deepest gratitude and appreciation goes to my best counselor and my best friend, my wife Ellen, who has sustained me through the long haul. Our daughter Arielle has been less specifically helpful, except insofar as her presence in our lives makes almost everything we do seem more meaningful.

Introduction

Political institutions appear to be "more than simple mirrors of social forces." They are themselves created by past human political decisions that were in some measure discretionary, and to some degree they are alterable by future ones. They also have a kind of life of their own. They influence . . . the senses of purpose and principle that political actors possess. And sometimes, at least, those purposes and principles may be better described as conceptions of duty or inherently meaningful action than as egoistic preferences. Correspondingly, the behavior they alter may serve other values than economic or systemic functionality.—
Rogers Smith[1]

When contemporary commentators decry the abuse of judicial power or the evils of "judicial activism" the historical examples that most readily come to mind are drawn from Supreme Court decision making around the turn of the century, a period often referred to as the *"Lochner* era." According to the long-standing common wisdom about this period, toward the end of the nineteenth century many conservative American judges began to aggressively disregard the proper boundaries of their authority in order to search out and destroy "social legislation" that was inconsistent with their personal belief in laissez-faire economics and social Darwinism. Prior to this period the postbellum judiciary had given some indication that it would be tolerant of innovative government interventions in the market. During the 1870s and 1880s, for example, the Supreme Court permitted states to set up slaughterhouse monopolies, regulate the rates that could be charged by the owners of grain elevators, and prohibit the sale of alcohol and foodstuffs such as oleomargarine.[2] However, this tolerance apparently diminished as industrial conflict intensified during the "Great Upheaval" of the 1880s and the depression of the early 1890s.[3] In 1895 alone the Court struck down the income tax, approved the use of the injunction against labor strikes and boycotts, and interfered with the administration of antitrust laws. Soon thereafter it began to nullify legislation designed to improve the dismal conditions of workers.[4]

The case that has come to represent the transgressions of an ostensibly activist judiciary is *Lochner v. New York* (1905). At issue in this case was a state law that made it unlawful for bakers to work more than ten hours a day or sixty hours a week. As the story goes, supporters of the legislation argued that this "maximum hours" law was necessary to protect these workers from unscrupulous employers who cared little about the effects of continuous work on the well-being of their employees; because the state had evidence that long working hours were having a detrimental effect on the health of bakers, it felt justified in imposing this constraint on the employment practices of bakery owners. However, opponents of this law argued that employers had a constitutional right to make contracts with their employees without government interference. Of course, the Constitution nowhere specifically mentions this "right" to make employment contracts, but nevertheless opponents pointed out that the due process clause of the fourteenth amendment prohibits state governments from taking away a person's "liberty" without "due process," and they insisted that one of the liberties protected by this amendment is the liberty to freely negotiate contracts with others. Translating their claim into the language of constitutional law, they advanced the position that the fourteenth amendment protects "liberty of contract," and that this liberty was infringed when the government prohibited employers and employees from agreeing on terms of employment that required workers to work more than the legislated "maximum hours." To the surprise and dismay of many, a majority of the justices on the Supreme Court agreed with those who challenged the law. In his opinion for the Court, Justice Rufus W. Peckham wrote, "The statute necessarily interferes with the right of contract between the employer and employes, concerning the number of hours in which the latter may labor in the bakery of the employer." Moreover, Peckham expressed the view that "a law like the one before us involves neither the safety, the morals nor the welfare of the public, and that the interest of the public is not in the slightest degree affected by such an act."[5]

Most Court scholars treat this case as an archetypical example of the corruption of judicial power for two reasons. First, they argue that in ruling that the statute was defective because it violated liberty of contract as protected by the due process clause of the fourteenth amendment, the justices in the majority were reading into the Constitution a prohibition on legislative power that could not be found in the text of the Constitution and was not supported by any previous interpretation of either the words of the text or the intent of the framers—in short, they view the majority's protection of a constitutional "right" to make contracts as a fraudulent interpretation of the Constitution, as an example of judges *making* law rather than *interpreting* it. Second, critics charge that in expressing the view that the legislation was not substantially related to legitimate concerns about public health and safety, the majority was assaulting the doctrine of separation of powers by substituting its conception of good, effective policymaking for that of the legislature, which had determined that maximum hours laws would in fact contribute to the physical well-being of workers. The upshot of this analysis is the conclusion that a majority on the Court simply made up a constitutional "right" as a cover for an illegitimate, unrestrained act of judicial legislation.

When critics have attempted to explain why the *Lochner* majority and other turn-of-the-century judges felt free to manufacture rights that did not exist and intrude into the legislature's sphere of authority, many followed Justice Oliver Wendell Holmes's suggestion in his *Lochner* dissent that the case was "decided upon an economic theory [laissez-faire] which a large part of the country does not entertain." In other words, members of the majority were basing their decision on their personal policy preferences in favor of laissez-faire economics instead of limiting themselves to a faithful interpretation of the fundamental law. And so, for example, six years after the constitutional revolution of 1937 and the abandonment of "liberty of contract," Carl Brent Swisher wrote about the turn-of-the-century Court's "rigid conservatism" where noninterference in "liberty of contract was involved," and linked this ethos to Justice Stephen J. Field's *Slaughterhouse* dissent, in which he "sought to read into the Constitution . . . a laissez-faire order in which he believed with all the depths of his being."[6] Others expanded upon this observation and claimed that the majority was interested in promoting the interests of capital during a period of unprecedented social turmoil and unpredictable democratic movements. A few years after Swisher's pronouncement Alfred H. Kelly and Winfred A. Harbison argued that the turn-of-the-century Court's laissez-faire orientation was the result of the postwar hegemony of the Republican party—"a party of big business"— and the appointment to the Court of corporate lawyers "concerned primarily with protecting the property rights and vested interests of big business." The particular manifestation of this class bias was the doctrine of "freedom of contract," a "conception introduced into constitutional law directly from *laissez-faire* economics. There is virtually no other explanation for its appearance, for it certainly rested neither upon any specific constitutional principle, nor upon any well-established precedent."[7] While the shadings on the story varied from account to account, until recently virtually all major discussions of *Lochner* followed these leads and took for granted that the case vividly illustrates the potential harm when activist judges turn away from important institutional norms and become more interested in making law than in interpreting it.[8] William M. Wiecek recently summed up the lore when he observed that "*Lochner* has become in modern times a sort of negative touchstone. Along with *Dred Scott*, it is our foremost reference case for describing the Court's malfunctioning. . . . We speak of 'lochnerizing' when we wish to imply that judges substitute their policy preferences for those of the legislature."[9]

But even as this common wisdom was being forged there were those who challenged the critics' emerging characterization of the Court's jurisprudence as essentially unprincipled or rooted in extraconstitutional policy preferences for laissez-faire economics. Not long after *Lochner v. New York* was decided, Charles Warren offered a number of impressive defenses of the Court that were designed to put into perspective the 557 of 560 state laws challenged under the due process or equal protection clauses that were upheld by the justices. In light of this evidence Warren argued that it was simply wrong to view the justices as preoccupied with minimizing government regulation of the economy.[10] Other contemporaries, such as Roscoe Pound, were critical of many of the Court's decisions but nevertheless rejected the legal realists' claim that "judges [were projecting] their personal, social and economic views into the law." As he saw it, "when a doctrine is announced with equal vigor and held with equal tenacity by courts of Pennsylvania and of Arkansas, of New York and California, of Illinois and of West Virginia, of Massachusetts and of Missouri, we may not dispose of [the question] so readily."[11] In time scholars began to provide more comprehensive reviews of nineteenth-century judicial decisions and opinions which indicated that judges were not singlemindedly dedicated to market liberty per se. For example, in the 1950s, James Willard Hurst argued that "the release of individual creative energy was the dominant value" in nineteenth-century legal culture, not laissez-faire, and "[w]here legal regulation or compulsion might promote the greater release of individual or group energies, we had no hesitancy in making affirmative use of law." Around the same time Leonard W. Levy attempted to show that a "theory of the general interest was common" in nineteenth-century America and that this "commonwealth idea precluded the laissez-faire state whose function was simply to keep peace and order, and then, like a little child, not be heard."[12] Explorations of how the legal concept of public rights has been used throughout American history to justify interventions in the market has also been a prominent feature of Harry N. Scheiber's work since the late 1960s.[13]

This work led some scholars to get out of the habit of exaggerating the turn-of-the-century judiciary's hostility to social legislation. When Robert McCloskey came out with his influential short history of the Supreme Court in 1960, he summarized the record by noting that there is "no doubt the pace of social change was moderated; a respectable number of 'excesses' were prevented; a respectable amount of money was saved for the businessman; a good many laborers were left a little hungrier than they might have been if the Court had not been there to defend economic liberty." But, he added, "it is highly questionable that the due process clause was a major factor in determining the drift of American economic policy during this period. Most of the important legislative measures that were really demanded by public opinion did pass and did manage to survive the gauntlet of judicial review."[14] However, the growing recognition that turn-of-the-century judges upheld a good deal of social legislation still left unexplained why some social legislation—such as the maximum hours law in *Lochner*—was declared unconstitutional. In the absence of any alternative conceptualization of the values embedded in nineteenth-century police powers jurisprudence, and in the presence of a realist-inspired skepticism of the explanations offered by the judges, many commentators continued to explain what was now seen as the occasional (but nevertheless conspicuous) judicial hostility toward market regulation by reverting back to the language of laissez-faire economics and illegitimate judicial activism. Typical was the analysis offered by Loren Beth in *The Development of the American Constitution*, in which he wrote that while there was "no plan or conspiracy with big business," and while the Court was not "wholeheartedly pro-business or pro–free enterprise," it was nevertheless the case that conservative justices felt that the "Constitution established a laissez-faire economic order" and that judicial invocations of words like *reasonableness* stood for "the proposition that courts can and should be willing to substitute their judgment as to what is desirable for that of other agencies of government."[15]

Two developments in the scholarship of the period have led to an erosion of this persistent neo-Holmesian conceptualization of the *Lochner* era. First, Eric Foner, Charles McCurdy, William Nelson, David M. Gold, and William Forbath, among others, have traced the origins of the "liberty of contract" doctrine not to the convenience of the robber barons, but rather to the ideology of the antislavery movement, the infant Republican party, and (by extension) the newly reconstructed Union.[16] In Forbath's paraphrase of Foner, "abolitionists talked about the freedom of the Northern worker in terms of self-ownership, that is, simply not being a slave, being free to sell his own labor."[17] On the basis of this work we have learned that, as a principle of political morality, the notion that government should leave workers free to contract a price for their labor was much more precedented, and had a much more noble origin, than the common wisdom about *Lochner* has led us to believe. In fact, liberty of contract was an important theme of the party responsible for the amendments to the Constitution that the *Lochner* Court was interpreting. Still, acknowledging that we can trace the tradition of "liberty of contract" at least to the antislavery movement explains only part of the story of the *Lochner* era. There were many circumstances in which judges allowed legislatures to interfere with market liberties, including relations between employers and employees. Judges certainly believed in liberty of contract, but their commitment to it was far from absolute; it may even be fair to say that using liberty of contract to trump legislation was the exception and not the rule. How, then, are we to make sense of why some interferences with market liberty were condemned while others were condoned? Unless we are satisfied with the realist-influenced belief that judges simply upheld laws they liked and voided laws they did not, or with the rather vague observation that judges "balanced" a concern with protecting market liberty against a concern with allowing legislatures to promote the "public welfare,"[18] we are still in need of a language which will help us uncover some principled basis for the distinctions the justices were making in their opinions and decisions.

This alternative language has been provided by a number of scholars who have examined the extent to which nineteenth-century courts were on guard against not all regulations of the economy but only a particular kind of government interference in market relations—what the justices considered "class" or "partial" legislation; that is, laws that (from their point of view) promoted only the narrow interests of particular groups or classes rather than the general welfare. Twenty years ago Alan Jones, in a number of important articles on the influential writings of Thomas Cooley, reported that Cooley's jurisprudence stressed not market liberty per se but rather a Jacksonian ethos that emphasized equal rights and the dangers of legislating special privileges for particular groups and classes. In his opinions and treatises Cooley attacked monopolies and incorporation laws because he opposed "arbitrary and unequal legislation, as well as the identification of legislation with the interests of privileged and powerful capitalists." The centerpiece of the legal tradition that Cooley embraced was the principle "that the state could have no favorites, and that its business was 'to protect the industry of all, and to give all the benefit of equal laws.'"[19] In the 1970s Charles W. McCurdy's reinterpretation of Justice Field's opinions contributed to the integration of Jones's analysis of the Jacksonian origins of Cooley's thinking into the discussion of late-nineteenth-century Supreme Court decision making. McCurdy rediscovered how Field—traditionally considered the prototype of a rigid, heartless, laissez-faire, social Darwinist ideologue—was more than willing to uphold statutes that prohibited certain businesses considered detrimental to the public welfare, prescribed standards of fitness for lawyers and doctors, required railroad corporations to erect cattle guards and eliminate grade crossings at their own expense, and regulated working hours or compelled hazardous businesses to compensate workers injured on the job. In sum, Field shared much of the Court's (forgotten) willingness to uphold legislative interventions in market relations.

Field did make it clear, however, that government's police regulations had to provide "general benefits." Under "the pretense of prescribing a police regulation," government could not create monopolies in the "ordinary trades"; solve unemployment problems by forbidding Chinese laborers to work for railroad companies; or provide dairy interests with a protective umbrella by proscribing the manufacture and sale of oleomargarine. Field contended that those laws . . . manifestly "discriminated against some [persons] and favored others." . . . In other words, Field imposed limitations on the police power, not to protect individuals from enactments designed to "promote . . . the general good," but rather to prevent powerful socioeconomic interests, through the use of corruption or the force of sheer numbers, from utilizing the legislative process as a weapon to improve their own position at the expense of other individual's "just rights."

As another scholar wrote a few years later, the Court as a whole in its police power decisions seemed preoccupied with applying "the general proposition that the mere preference of one group over another, that is, legislation based only on favoritism or on spite, is outside the scope of proper governmental activity."[20]

More recently Michael Les Benedict has argued that during the nineteenth century the dominant concept of appropriate state-society relations "mitigated only against certain kinds of government interferences in the economy, not against all interference. That concept was that the power of government could not legitimately be exercised to benefit one person or group at the expense of others." David M. Gold has concluded that judicial review of legislation in the nineteenth century "rested not on a wish to protect business from government, but on a desire to preserve 'the great principle upon which all popular governments rest—the equality of all before the law.' . . . It was [an] animus against 'special' or 'class' legislation . . . that underlay constitutional doctrine limiting legislative power to the enactment of laws that served a public purpose."[21] By 1988 William E. Nelson, in *The Fourteenth Amendment*, was prepared to assume the point made by Jones, McCurdy, Benedict, and Gold—that the late-nineteenth-century Supreme Court organized its police powers jurisprudence primarily around a distinction between legitimate general welfare legislation and illegitimate factional politics; he went so far as to argue that "the people who adopted the [fourteenth] amendment in the 1860s anticipated the distinction between public good and partisan interest that animated the Supreme Court's interpretation of the amendment less than a decade later." Without discounting contemporaneous concerns about market liberty and the ideology of free labor, Nelson demonstrated that by the 1830s "ideas about equality had become a staple of American political rhetoric"; that, during Reconstruction, Republicans rebutted critics who charged that the fourteenth amendment would infringe on states' rights by arguing that "[t]he only effect of the amendment was to prevent the states from discriminating arbitrarily between different classes of citizens"; that from the beginning the Supreme Court held that the "plain and manifest intention" of the fourteenth amendment "was to make all citizens of the United States equal before the law" and to ensure that "[s]pecial privileges can be conferred upon none, nor can exceptional burdens or restrictions be put upon any"; and that "[h]undreds of state cases reaffirmed the approach taken by the nation's highest court," with state judges "regularly declar[ing] unconstitutional regulatory legislation that contained unequal classifications or worked for the benefit of a narrow class rather than the community as a whole" while at the same time allowing state governments to "engage vigorously in activities promoting and regulating the economy."[22]

Some of this material relating to the judicial aversion to unequal legislation has begun to work its way into discussions of the period,[23] but nevertheless there is a good deal of work to be done before the Holmesian paradigm (of a runaway laissez-faire judiciary) is dislodged. We are still in need of a more thorough illustration and elaboration of the way nineteenth-century lawyers and judges conceptualized the differences between invalid class politics and valid public purposes. Most of the discussions wherein revisionists have identified these features of *Lochner* era jurisprudence have been in articles, and not infrequently these articles have focused on the writings of only a particular judge or legal scholar. The one book-length discussion of the period that takes full account of the political-legal culture's disdain for class politics has as its central focus not police powers jurisprudence per se, but rather the question of how the Republican party of 1866 could "have been committed simultaneously to federal protection of black rights and to preservation of the existing balance of federalism"; consequently, there is in that excellent work only a limited attempt to demonstrate the presence of an antifactional ethos in state and federal judicial decisions and legal commentary.[24] There is room, then, for more evidence of the late-nineteenth-century legal community's obsession with drawing distinctions between legitimate promotions of the public interest and illegitimate efforts to impose special burdens and benefits. Moreover, very little attention in the existing literature has been given to the question of why this highly precedented feature of police powers jurisprudence fell into disrepute around the turn of the century and how the assault against the tradition was articulated; answers require investigations that extend well beyond the decision of *Lochner v. New York*. We have also reached a point at which our understanding of the period would be sharpened by a few intramural discussions among revisionists relating to issues such as the origins of late-nineteenth-century police powers jurisprudence, the interpretations that have been offered of particular cases, and other features of the story which will help illuminate the ideas that animated judicial behavior at the turn of the century.[25]

It should be clear by now that my purpose in writing this book is to make a contribution to this developing revisionist reinterpretation of what turn-of-the-century jurists were saying and doing, and why they were saying and doing it. Specifically, it is my contention that the decisions and opinions that emerged from state and federal courts during the *Lochner* era represented a serious, principled effort to maintain one of the central distinctions in nineteenth-century constitutional law—the distinction between valid economic regulation, on the one hand, and invalid "class" legislation, on the other—during a period of unprecedented class conflict. Moreover, I hope to show that the standards used by these judges to evaluate exercises of legislative power were not illegitimate creations of unrestrained free-market ideologues, but rather had their roots in principles of political legitimacy that were forged at the time of the creation of the Constitution and were later elaborated by state court judges as they first addressed the nature and scope of legislative power in the era of Jacksonian democracy. These principles encouraged nineteenth-century judges to uphold legislation that (from their perspective) advanced the well-being of the community as a whole or promoted a true "public purpose" and to strike down legislation that (from their perspective) was designed to advance the special or partial interests of particular groups or classes. The prevailing standards governing the police powers were, of course, designed to place limits on government's ability to impose on people's liberty or property, but the boundaries of these limits had more to do with historically informed considerations of what constituted a valid public purpose than with concerns about maximizing an individual's freedom by narrowing state power to a few essential responsibilities. Once these features of *Lochner* era police powers jurisprudence are understood, the crisis in American constitutionalism that arose around the turn of the century becomes a story not of the sudden corruption of the law and the judicial function, but rather of how the judiciary's struggle to maintain the coherence and integrity of a constitutional ideology averse to class politics was complicated and ultimately derailed by the maturation of capitalist forms of production and the unprecedented efforts of legislatures to extend special protections to groups that considered themselves vulnerable to increasingly coercive market mechanisms.

It should be clear at the outset that, unlike others who have attempted to revive an interest in *Lochner* era jurisprudence,[26] I have no interest in resurrecting the ghost of *Lochner* by reciting some incantation about the importance in our constitutional tradition of rights to property and contract. While I agree with these conservative polemicists that the judiciary during the *Lochner* era was being faithful to a well-established constitutional tradition, for reasons that I hope to make clear it seems to me that the same forces that led to a collapse of this jurisprudence make calls for a return to first principles virtually indefensible. For this tradition was developed at a time when capitalist forms of production were in their infancy, and was grounded explicitly in the belief that commercial development in the New World would not lead to the kind of "European" conditions that might justify special government protections for dependent classes. This was an assumption that was meaningful at the beginning of the nineteenth century but much less so by the beginning of the twentieth. The crisis in American constitutionalism that we associate with the *Lochner* era was triggered by the judiciary's stubborn attachment to what historical participants perceived to be an increasingly anachronistic jurisprudence, one that had lost its moorings in the storm of industrialization.[27]

By focusing on the legal principles and standards invoked and applied by nineteenth-century jurists, I hope not only to correct some lingering misconceptions regarding the substance of *Lochner* era constitutional jurisprudence but also to encourage a renewed appreciation of the extent to which judicial behavior—that is, writing opinions and making decisions—may be motivated by a set of interests and concerns that are relatively distinct from the preferences of particular social groups, the policies prescribed by particular economic theories, or the personal social and political loyalties and sympathies of individual judges. It was the mischaracterization of turn-of-the-century constitutional jurisprudence that led political scientists to view judicial opinions as empty rhetoric designed to mask policy preferences rather than as principled explanations for legal decisions; a reexamination of the explanations offered by the justices in their opinions might help us uncover a pattern among decisions that would otherwise be incomprehensible. In what might be considered a return to what is sometimes derisively referred to as a "traditional" or "prerealist" analysis of judicial politics—more generously referred to as "postbehavioralist" analysis—this study rests primarily on an interpretation of legal texts and related materials in order to demonstrate how federal and state judges shared a common method of evaluating exercises of the police powers, and how their decisions were supported by arguments that represented something more than rationalizations of idiosyncratic policy preferences and something different from an ideological commitment to laissez-faire economics or social Darwinism.[28]

In addition to offering a better understanding of the institutional concerns of the legal community during the *Lochner* era, I also want to give an account of the conditions that gave rise to nineteenth-century police powers jurisprudence and the conditions that contributed to its demise. After all, if liberty of contract and the requirement that legislation had to be "reasonably related" to legitimate concerns about community health, safety, and morality were not empty and shameless inventions of unrestrained judges, then it is fair to ask, where did they come from, what did they mean, and why did they become so controversial? To the extent that the meanings associated with these doctrines were forged within the historical circumstances of their creation and elaboration, there is one (long) answer to these questions. As I show in chapter 1, the legal doctrines that informed the late-nineteenth-century judiciary's understanding of the nature and scope of the police powers were first articulated by state court judges during the period of Jacksonian democracy. Many of these largely unknown antebellum state court opinions and decisions became the most frequently cited cases of the *Lochner* era. An examination of some of the leading cases of the period is essential if we are to understand the legal context within which postbellum judges interpreted the legislation of their time. While frequently extolling the virtues of private property and market liberty, most of these cases demonstrated a superior judicial commitment to the familiar Jacksonian preoccupation with political equality or government neutrality, the belief that government power could not be used by particular groups to gain special privileges or to impose special burdens on competing groups. As we shall see, to the extent that a regulation was considered a valid promotion of the general welfare, and not an invalid attempt at unfair class legislation, nineteenth-century judges tended to uphold the law even if it interfered with property rights or market liberty. However, the decisions and opinions of judges during this formative period of nineteenth-century police powers jurisprudence were themselves influenced by the actions of an earlier generation, and so chapter 1 begins with the framing of the American Constitution and explores the concern of dominant classes to construct a republic that would effectively prevent "factions" from gaining control of legislative power.

There is another reason why it is important to begin this story at the beginning of the Republic, and it has to do with the reason why *Lochner* era jurisprudence came into disrepute around the beginning of this century. The aversion to factional politics that was built into the structure and ideology of the Constitution was premised on the assumption that a commercial republic would not pose a threat to a citizen's independence or autonomy by creating conditions of social dependency, conditions that might make it understandable for vulnerable classes (for example, debtors or wage earners) to ask the government for special protection against powerful and unavoidable market competitors (creditors or employers). In fact, the master principle that government should impose no special burdens or benefits explicitly rested on the (disputed) claim that the market was essentially harmonious and liberty loving; if pockets of social dependency should happen to arise in certain places (such as urban centers), the vast American frontier would provide an everlasting escape for those who were willing to take advantage of the freedom of the freehold. Within the context of infant capitalism these assumptions seemed consonant with the experiences of many, if not all, people, and to the extent that this depiction of the market continued to conform to people's experiences, the ethos of the faction-free republic remained relatively uncontroversial; if the promotion and protection of an individual's well-being could be accomplished without government intervention in disputes between competitors in a free market, then any such intervention could only be interpreted as either a corruption of public power or an unnecessary and essentially arbitrary interference in market relations. These assumptions animated and supported both the framers' conception of a faction-free republic and, maybe more importantly, the judiciary's initial characterization of the proper scope of state legislative powers. Still, as I show at the end of chapter 1, even as courts began to translate this vision of market liberty and political equality into a workable constitutional ideology, vulnerable classes were beginning to experience the coercive side of capitalist forms of production and challenge the founders' vision of a class-neutral polity. These early challenges were unsuccessful, but they foreshadowed—and therefore give us insight into—the crisis in American constitutionalism that would arise much later in the century.

After outlining the origins of nineteenth-century police powers jurisprudence and identifying the fragile foundation upon which it was constructed and accepted, I turn, in chapter 2, to a review of the decisions in which the justices of the postbellum Supreme Court, taking advantage of the expanded opportunity to review state exercises of the police power under the fourteenth amendment, adopted the rules and principles that had been devised and refined by their antebellum state court counterparts. Many of the familiar cases of this period—such as *Slaughterhouse, Munn, Butchers' Union, Barbier, Yick Wo,* and *Powell*—take on a new meaning once we appreciate the extent to which they represent a *continuation* of a tradition whereby judges attempted to define the boundaries of state power by drawing distinctions between legislation that legitimately promoted the general welfare and legislation that illegitimately promoted the special interests of particular groups and classes. These cases are also important insofar as they elaborate the standards with which justices later in the century would evaluate the unprecedented social legislation of the *Lochner* era. However, at the same time that the justices were nationalizing a constitutional ideology averse to special government burdens or benefits, changes were occurring in the structure of capitalist social relations that led increasing numbers of people to question whether their well-being could be protected by a formally neutral polity.[29] These changes triggered a proliferation of group and class activity as powerful interests began demanding special favors from government and vulnerable groups began demanding special protection from the coercive effects of a corporate industrial economy. These demands constituted a direct challenge to an established tenet of political legitimacy, and the legal community—state courts and legal commentators—responded accordingly in repeated condemnations of illegitimate "class" politics.[30]

In chapter 3 I look at the decade leading up to and following *Lochner,* a time when the justices on the Supreme Court were preoccupied with maintaining distinctions between legitimate health and safety regulations and illegitimate social and economic legislation; it was at this time that the justices and other legal elites began to disagree over the extent to which, in making these distinctions, judges should defer to reports drawn up by social reformers. Chapter 4 moves beyond the disputes over this "sociological jurisprudence" and examines the more fundamental challenges leveled at the principle of government neutrality by political and social elites who contemplated more innovative and unprecedented responses to the problems associated with industrialization. Among those responses was the minimum wage, and it was this issue that prompted some justices to question whether they should continue to defend what was increasingly perceived to be an untenable distinction between health and safety legislation, on the one hand, and illegitimate class favoritism, on the other. There was nothing inevitable about the outcome—the result was actually quite fateful—but in the end a majority found it difficult to abandon their defense of a Constitution besieged.

I refer to a "Constitution besieged" to emphasize the point that the controversies surrounding judicial decision making during the *Lochner* era represented much more than a set of disagreements between people with different policy preferences or different understandings of the proper role of the judiciary. The judiciary's persistent attachment to traditional limits on legislative power represented the final defense of a principle of political legitimacy that the framers sought to permanently enshrine in the fundamental law; when this principle made its way into constitutional ideology it helped shape state-society relations in the United States for a century and a half. The eventual collapse of this constitutional tradition signaled the rise of a new American Republic organized around a different understanding of the proper use of legislative power. This is not something to be bemoaned; it should simply be recognized if we are to understand and appreciate the significance of constitutional decision making and judicial politics during the *Lochner* era.

I would like to preempt at least one possible objection to my decision to focus on the jurisprudence and not the jurists, and that is the claim that legal materials do not determine legal results and therefore cannot be an adequate explanation of judicial behavior. To the extent that this postrealist assumption has informed most discussions of judicial politics, at least by political scientists, it might be helpful if I make explicit my own assumptions about the nature of judicial politics and the effect of legal ideology on judicial decision making.

As I see it, the kind of political conduct being observed when one examines the patterns of reasoning in legal discourse is the formulation and maintenance of an authoritative state ideology. By treating law as ideology I mean to imply that I consider legal materials to be more than a collection of words, ideas, and concepts that are used flexibly and haphazardly to justify the naked pursuit of material interests. Ideological structures represent what Peter L. Berger and Thomas Luckman referred to as a "social construction of reality,"[31] the normative models people use to impose order on disorder, to make events or structures comprehensible and behavior meaningful by identifying what is natural or anomalous, important or insignificant, valuable or worthless, legitimate or illegitimate.[32] Ideologies are social constructions of reality because they do not descend from the heavens and are not randomly generated—they are created and elaborated by particular groups or classes to support or oppose particular constellations of authority and to rationalize or undermine particular sets of social relations.[33] Legal principles and judicial opinions are ideological constructs in the sense that their function is to defend specific structures, processes, and practices by suggesting that they are good, natural, traditional, in the general interest, or a matter of common sense.[34] As Alan Hunt summarized it, treating law as a form of ideology "counsels us . . . to search out the resonances of the social, economic, and political struggles that reside behind the smooth surface of legal reasoning and judicial utterance." However, as we conduct this search, we must be mindful of the fact that "ideologies have their own distinctive characteristics, the most important of which are an internal discourse such that the elements of an ideology are not reducible to a mere reflection of economic and social relations."[35]

The fact that legal ideologies shape the way judges interpret their world makes them legitimate objects of study in their own right. (The law also provides lawyers and judges with a specialized vocabulary, but it would trivialize the significance of legal culture to suggest that the law is nothing more than a set of words that judges use to promote other unrelated agendas.) Making legal ideology or judicial opinions the object of serious inquiry need not imply a belief in the science of law or mechanical jurisprudence: modern hermeneutics and the deconstructionists have taught us that neither doctrinal formulations nor legal texts possess a singular, objective, determinable meaning. Meaning is extracted from these sources by interpreters, and interpreters cannot help but be influenced by their particular cultural, social, and political context.[36] It is often the case, however, that the meanings extracted from texts (or associated with certain principles) settle into consistent patterns which, for a time anyway, are considered relatively coherent and controlling by members of a particular "interpretive community": some interpretations and conclusions come to be seen as more valid than others; some disputes might appear clear-cut while others appear open-ended and indeterminate and still others are something in between.[37]

The phenomena whereby a particular interpretive community comes to treat (ostensibly indeterminate) texts and principles as meaningful and directive are evident, it seems to me, among legal elites.[38] Generally speaking, when judges decide cases they do not feel completely unencumbered by existing legal rules and doctrines. Sometimes they may feel as if they have no choice and at other times feel as if they have some discretion, but these different experiences are themselves governed by the prevailing assumptions and practices of the legal community. Judges, lawyers, law professors, even political scientists routinely make predictions about how certain cases or issues will be resolved, on the basis not only of the idiosyncratic attitudes of particular judges but also using standards or precedents that are perceived to be external to particular judges; if existing standards or precedents had no such force, there would be no reason for anyone to worry about what judges say in their opinions. At some level it may be possible to demonstrate that a judge's opinion is incoherent or that the standards or precedents invoked by a judge are essentially indeterminate; yet while the deconstruction of legal materials is important to the extent that it helps us think of these cultural artifacts as historically contingent and potentially unstable ideological constructs, it does not necessarily make them any less meaningful for participants.[39]

As Charles M. Yablon has observed, the postrealist claim of the indeterminate nature of legal rules and principles "need not at all deny the existence of predictive, or even causal relationships between legal doctrine and concrete legal results. Rather, the Critical claim of legal indeterminacy may be understood as a declaration that doctrine can never be an adequate *explanation* of legal results."[40] It seems to me that, in the end, the issue of whether a particular legal result at a particular time can best be explained as a matter of principle, policy, unmediated class interest,[41] perceived functional necessities,[42] or even bribery can only be clarified through the use of historical, reconstructive, and interpretive methods—methods that bring us closer both to the social and political contexts within which participants acted and to the webs of meaning embedded in those contexts. These methods are perfectly empirical;[43] they are also appropriate if not indispensable tools for social scientists, whose subjects are not objects.[44] To behavioralists troubled by the challenge of scientific verification involved in this kind of work I offer Clifford Geertz's advice to "measure the cogency of our explications . . . against the power of the scientific imagination to bring us in touch with the lives of strangers. It is not worth it, as Thoreau said, to go round the world to count the cats in Zanzibar."[45]

In studying the distinctive politics of the judiciary, political scientists may profit from the advice offered by E. P. Thompson about how best to conceptualize the law. He noted that while the law was often "devised and employed, directly and instrumentally, in the imposition of class power," at the same time

> it existed in its own right, as ideology; as an ideology which not only served, in most respects, but which also legitimized class power. . . . [But if] the law is evidently partial and unjust, then it will mask nothing, legitimize nothing, contribute nothing to any class's hegemony. The essential precondition for the effectiveness of law, in its function as ideology, is that it shall display an independence from gross manipulation and shall seem to be just. . . . [F]urthermore it is not often the case that a ruling ideology can be dismissed as mere hypocrisy; even rulers find a need to legitimize their power, to moralize their functions, to feel themselves to be useful and just. In the case of an ancient historical formation like the law, a discipline which requires years of exacting study to master, there will always be some men who actively believe in their own procedures and in the logic of justice. The law may be rhetoric, but it need not be empty rhetoric. Blackstone's *Commentaries* represent an intellectual exercise far more rigorous than could have come from an apologist's pen.[46]

Justice Peckham was no Blackstone, but neither was constitutional law during the *Lochner* era empty rhetoric. It represented a well-developed, albeit increasingly untenable, conception of the appropriate relationship between the state and society. In the following pages I hope to shed some new light on the nature of that jurisprudence, as well as on its social origins and the conditions that contributed to its demise.

CHAPTER ONE

The Origins of *Lochner* Era
Police Powers Jurisprudence

*The Constitution here referred to cannot be simply the document. It can only be
that Aristotelian conception of the constituting idea or body of ideas which lies
within the political system and, indeed, within the society generally and which by
its presence qualifies the society and its political system to become a cohesive
entity.—H. Mark Roelofs[1]*

The notoriety of *Lochner v. New York* (1905) rests on the widespread
assumption that the case represents the corruption of judicial power in at
least two respects. First, by invoking an ostensible right to liberty of
contract to trump a maximum hours law for bakers, the majority took
the unprecedented step of constitutionalizing an ethos of market freedom at a time when it was a matter of political dispute whether an
unregulated market was always the best policy. Second, in announcing
that laws interfering with liberty of contract would be upheld only if (in
the opinion of the Court) they were "reasonable and appropriate" attempts to promote "the morals, the health or the safety of the people,"
Justice Peckham promulgated a doctrine that illegitimately gave the
justices the authority to second-guess legislative conclusions regarding
effective public policy—an authority that the members of the majority
exercised with a vengeance when they gave their blessing to those sections of the Bakery Act that related to the conditions of the workplace as
"reasonable and appropriate exercises of the police power of the State"
but struck down those sections relating to working hours as merely
"labor laws," unrelated to "the interests of the public" and therefore
"unnecessary and arbitrary interferences" with personal liberty.

The implication of this characterization of the *Lochner* era is that the hostility exhibited toward certain types of legislation by turn-of-the-century jurists was a function of the idiosyncratic biases of unrestrained judges, and not a function of any standards or practices embedded in the American constitutional tradition. However, as I hope to show in this chapter, the essential elements of the *Lochner* Court's approach to the bakery law—the emphasis on market liberty, the belief that market liberty could be interfered with if legislation promoted a valid public purpose, and the suggestion that valid public-purpose legislation was distinct from laws that merely promoted the interests of some classes at the expense of others—were long-standing features of nineteenth-century police powers jurisprudence; these elements were inherited by *Lochner* era jurists, not invented by them. Maybe more fundamentally, the assumptions about the nature and scope of legitimate legislative authority that led the *Lochner* Court to void a maximum hours law were built into the structure and ideology of the Constitution itself at the time of the founding. In short, the judiciary at the turn of the century was, to a large extent, giving voice to the founders' conception of appropriate and inappropriate policymaking in a commercial republic, a conception that, over time, had been elaborated, clarified, and transformed into a workable set of doctrines by state court judges in the second quarter of the nineteenth century.

Looking back at the founding, and at the formative years of nineteenth-century police powers jurisprudence, will help reacquaint us with a political tradition that no longer governs the exercise of legislative power in American politics. Still, the language and preoccupations of that tradition shaped the contours of state-society relations for nearly a century and a half. It was a language that disdained "factional" politics, partial laws that represented the corrupt use of public power by certain groups seeking to advance purely private interests; it celebrated the value of state "neutrality," the principle that government should show no favoritism or hostility toward market competitors, but should exercise power only to advance a true public purpose. However, this language did not operate only at the level of flexible and indeterminate abstraction. Those who supported the Philadelphia Constitution used these concepts in the hope of delegitimizing certain kinds of laws passed by democratic state legislatures in the 1780s, laws such as debtor-relief legislation and wage and price controls. The framers insisted that their "more perfect union" would ensure that legislatures remained neutral with respect to the conflicts arising among and between social groups competing in the private economy. In the second quarter of the nineteenth century this language was used by Jacksonian Democrats to assault what they considered to be all sorts of unnecessary and illegitimate special privileges bestowed by legislatures. Over time, state courts began to use the language to distinguish legitimate exercises of state power from exercises of state power that did not, in their judgment, deserve to be called the "law of the land." Thus in history did this political tradition become meaningful rather than merely rhetorical. In order to appreciate the way this tradition shaped the nineteenth- and early-twentieth-century judiciary's understanding of the scope of legitimate legislative authority—including the *Lochner* Court's understanding—it is important to pay some attention to the historical evolution of this tradition.

One other lesson relevant to the *Lochner* era can be mined from these earlier events, and it has to do with the reason why this long-standing tradition came into disrepute around the turn of this century. When the master constitutional principle of formal equality or government impartiality was first elaborated by the framers in the 1780s, its legitimacy rested specifically on the assumption that a commercial republic would not create conditions of social dependency that could be used by vulnerable groups to justify requests for special government protection and assistance. If, as the framers argued, the market was essentially harmonious and liberty loving, and if the almost endless access to the freehold on the American frontier ensured that those who might happen to find themselves in pockets of dependency would always be able to escape these conditions and become free and independent citizens, then there was little justification for allowing the government to intervene in the conflicts that arose among groups competing in a free market. So long as people considered this depiction of the social implications of capitalism to be an accurate representation of their own experiences, the neutral state remained a relatively uncontroversial characterization of American first principles. However, at the same time the founding vision was being translated into political practice and constitutional law, capitalist forms of production were beginning to mature; and throughout the nineteenth century those who felt disadvantaged by these developments began increasingly to question the validity of the assumptions that sustained the founding vision, assumptions about social independence in a commercial republic. An appreciation of the foundations upon which the neutral polity was built will help us understand why this tradition was besieged toward the end of the century during a period of intensifying class conflict.

The Founders' Vision of a Republic Free of Factional Politics

A century before *Lochner* era judges worked to block certain kinds of government interference in the market, another group was directing its efforts toward the promotion and protection of commerce and the erad-ication of certain kinds of "factional" legislative practices designed to advance the special or partial interests of certain groups or classes. The story of the *Lochner* era should begin with these earlier efforts, for the distinctions *Lochner* era judges attempted to draw between valid public-purpose legislation, on the one hand, and invalid class legislation, on the other, had their origins in a similar set of distinctions elaborated by the framers of the Constitution as they struggled to promote their vision of the American Republic and to marginalize or delegitimize competing sets of political practices and traditions.

Setting aside for the moment the politics of slavery at the time of the founding, it is possible to see the Constitution as the product of the efforts of a coalition of groups that had banded together largely out of a shared commitment to the promotion and preservation of a harmonious and liberty-loving market against those who insisted that government had a responsibility to interfere in market relations on behalf of vulner-able classes such as wage earners, debtors, and small farmers. To say that the American founding represented (among other things) the protection of capitalist social relations is not to deny that many of the founders' contemporaries expressed hostility at the idea that government would be preoccupied with commerce. Many members of the landed aristocracy rooted their social vision and conception of good government in the tradition of civic humanism, in which the "Renaissance vocabulary of power, corruption, degeneration, virtue, stability, and balance" made reasonable their claim that a republican form of government would be preserved only if power rested with the independent, wise, talented, refined, and selfless proprietary class and if government resisted the temptations of the commercial spirit.[2] While not unanimously behind the notion of rule by a propertied elite, evangelical social reformers were also interested in returning society "to its ascetic beginnings, where civic virtue, spartan living, and a disdain for worldly things had prevailed."[3] However, support for this neoclassical tradition, which put great emphasis on the obligations of citizenship and popular deference to wise and virtuous leaders, had been eroding for some time as people began to experience the final breakdown of feudal authority and the liberating effects of an increasingly integrated economy, developments which "involved modes of behavior and political stances diametrically opposed to the constitutional ideal of the disinterested citizen living on his own, cultivating the public weal, and committing his virtue to the maintenance of a rightly-ordered constitutional monarchy."[4] As early as the late seventeenth century, commercial elites ("monied men but without estate"), buoyed by their faith that the general welfare of the community was best served by sound promotion of this commercial development, had begun to express their experiences in Whig ideology, which encouraged individuals to pursue their private interests in the market and the government to pursue policies that would contribute to the commercial expansion and trading interests of England.[5]

Still, at the time of the American Revolution, neither Whig ideology nor the tradition of civic humanism represented hegemonic and homogeneous idioms of politics; different classes drew on the rich and diverse languages of liberalism and republicanism differently, and in the process they constructed and elaborated ideologies meaningful for their particular experiences.[6] The urban gentry—men like Thomas Hutchinson of Boston and the import-export merchants, lawyers, physicians, and wealthy clergymen who supported him—"adhered to the canons of Whig political theory, including balanced government, the vital role of a legislature elected by propertyholders, and equal justice before the law"; they also "openly espoused the world of international trade and capitalist relations and in this sense they were 'modernizers.'" Yet they were profoundly conservative in their social philosophy, believing in hierarchy and order and expecting those who lacked "a sufficient stock of reason and knowledge" to defer to their political stewardship.[7] For others, the civic humanist and conservative Whig idea of "advancing the common good under the direction of those at the top of society was clearly seen as a mask for protecting the interests of the economically dominant."[8] Commercial middling classes—local traders, ship captains, unpedigreed lawyers, small manufacturers, mechanics, tradesmen, craftsmen, small farmers, and others who championed the virtues of the commercial life because they experienced greater opportunities for social advancement than could be expected in more rigid social structures—agitated throughout the eighteenth century for a greater role in politics. Their liberal Whig social vision not only accepted the legitimacy of private profit seeking but also "projected a future economic world in which men's energies, cut loose from age-old mercantilist controls instituted to promote the good of all, would produce a common good far better"; this prompted many of them to lead "the opposition to the new regulation of economic life by England" in the years leading up to independence. They also believed strongly that "liberty was essentially the condition of being secure in one's property, which they held in modest to substantial amounts, and they had little desire to share political power with the . . . growing mass of propertyless and impoverished city dwellers below them."[9]

An important variation on this petit bourgeois liberalism was embraced and promulgated by groups such as Philadelphia's artisan community, who attempted to nurture the liberating qualities of the new social order while mitigating the market's threat to communal and egalitarian traditions that had deep roots in "popular" English culture. They believed that the development of the private economy had enabled them to become independent, self-reliant producers and citizens—men who possessed the simple virtues that found expression in Benjamin Franklin's aphorisms (such as industriousness and frugality); it also made them fully capable of participating in public affairs, notwithstanding the conservatives' attempts to discredit them by referring to them as "mean" or "vulgar." But they also recognized that market freedom enabled selfish merchants to indulge their private greed at the expense of members of the community, particularly the laboring poor, who had limited aspirations for capital accumulation and whose well-being was vulnerable to market fluctuations in prices and wages. Because they had experienced the market as a mixed blessing, many artisans felt that the community had the responsibility to ensure that market mechanisms did not result in the establishment of conditions of social dependency such that one person's well-being was dependent on the actions of another. Should this occur, they argued, it would be appropriate for government to intervene on behalf of some groups competing in the marketplace— protecting debtors from creditors (through the passage of insolvency laws), workers from employers (by setting and protecting wage rates), and consumers from producers (by imposing price controls)—and to prevent the establishment of great divisions in wealth; for as Rousseau had argued, in a true republic, "no citizen [should be] rich enough to be able to buy another, and none so poor as to be forced to sell himself."[10]

The image of the self-reliant or autonomous individual was central to many different versions of republican ideology. Such independence had traditionally been considered a prerequisite for civic virtue, or at least for "responsible" participation in the political process, in that it provided the leisure with which to refine one's talents and the material security that enabled one to set aside purely private interests—to be "disinterested"—in the consideration of public policy. Historically, both the gentry and the merchant elite had used the fact of their wealth as justification for their ostensibly selfless stewardship of the general welfare. Liberal Whigs used their developing status as independent and autonomous producers to agitate for their participation in the polity. Still, at the time of the founding, most Whigs did not agree with artisan republicans that the preservation of a citizen's social independence necessitated entangling government in conflicts between competing groups or classes.[11] While some ambivalent American Whigs joined with the artisans in worrying that commercial development might create conditions of social dependency, many took faith in the belief that the problem could be handled without direct government interference in group or class conflict by simply improving access to the freehold for dependent laborers and promoting free-trade policies that would provide markets for industrious farmers and cheap goods for consumers. As Benjamin Franklin put it, "no man who can have a piece of land of his own, sufficient by his labour to subsist his family in plenty, is poor enough to . . . work for a master."[12]

Like Franklin and James Madison,[13] Thomas Jefferson worried that the development of manufacturing might threaten the well-being of republican citizens; he also believed that America's abundant supply of land could effectively combat the corrupting effects of commerce. While he was in Virginia Jefferson linked a proposal establishing a fifty-acre qualification for voting with an offer to give fifty acres to every landless adult white male, an act that reflected Jefferson's belief that governments "did not exist to protect property but rather to promote access to property, or more broadly speaking, opportunity."[14] Promoting access to land would make citizens self-reliant; by contrast, promoting manufacturing risked the political domination of the poor by the rich through the cultivation of ignorant and dependent labor. While an exclusive emphasis on manufacturing might be an appropriate path of economic development for Great Britain, Jefferson argued that such a policy was neither necessary nor appropriate in the United States. As he explained in his *Notes on the State of Virginia*:

In Europe the lands are either cultivated, or locked up against the cultivator. Manufacture must therefore be resorted to of necessity not of choice, to support the surplus of their people. But we have an immensity of land courting the industry of the husbandman. . . . Corruption of morals in the mass of cultivators is a phenomenon of which no age nor nation has furnished an example. . . . Dependence begets subservience and venality, suffocates the germ of virtue, and prepares fit tools for the designs of ambition. . . . [G]enerally speaking, the proportion which the aggregate of the other classes of citizens bears in any State to that of its husbandmen, is the proportion of its unsound to its healthy parts, and is a good enough barometer whereby to measure its degree of corruption.[15]

In promoting access to land, Jefferson believed that he would be promoting the interests of farmers and small producers or artisans. Workers in the cities could escape low wages by becoming independent farmers; this safety valve would help ensure that wages in the cities would be sufficient to support a self-sufficient standard of living for wage earners, and perhaps make it possible for them to become independent artisans.[16] His faith in the harmonizing qualities of the market and the liberating potential of a vast frontier led Jefferson to advocate a highly restrictive role for government in economic affairs, a role restricted to actions designed to broaden people's opportunities to find *their own* social independence and personal autonomy in a market that allowed even "the humblest person . . . to take care of himself."[17] Unlike many of Philadelphia's artisans, Jefferson and his followers believed that social independence could be guaranteed without government interfering directly in group or class conflicts on behalf of vulnerable groups. Access to land and markets and the dismantling of artificial economic privilege were offered as more harmonious alternatives to debtor relief, paper money, and wage and price schemes.[18] It was a vision that rested firmly on the faith that these alternative "class-neutral" policies were sufficient to ensure the self-reliance that was at the heart of republican citizenship. For Jefferson, the republican ideal had come to mean limiting "the capacity of special interests to interfere with that natural society created by human wants."[19]

Of course, this "natural society" was itself produced by a complex and politically charged system of legal rules and principles concerning property rights, contractual obligations, and tortious liabilities whose social effects were far from neutral.[20] The relations among and between individuals and groups in revolutionary America were largely constituted in terms of the privileges and duties and categories imposed by common-law rules and principles. The common law established a set of class identities and class interests linked to the ownership of different types of property (slaves, land, capital, the tools of one's trade, commodities) and the enjoyment of the rights and privileges associated with such ownership. It also established a set of social relations between or among different property owners (landed interests, bankers, manufacturers, merchants), those who owned property and those who did not, and those who acquired certain privileges and obligations as a result of their participation in a market economy governed by the ethos of freedom to contract (debtors and creditors, producers and consumers, landlords and tenants, artisans and apprentices)—an ethos that held people to the explicit or implicit terms of the bargains they made of their own "free will," defined in practice as the absence of some relatively exceptional circumstances, such as duress, fraud, incapacity, or unfair advantage.

Contrary to the more democratic and egalitarian vision of a commercial republic embraced by groups such as Philadelphia's artisan community, many at the time of the founding considered the exercise of public power illegitimate precisely to the extent that it was designed merely to advance the special interests of particular classes or to interfere with the common-law (natural and just) obligations imposed on competing participants in the market economy on behalf of favored classes. This sensibility was predicated on the assumption that the social relations constructed by the common-law regime of contract and property were essentially fair and liberty loving—or at least would be in the United States, with its expansive frontier—and that the enforcement of common-law obligations would not result in certain classes having to suffer under conditions of dependency or servitude vis-à-vis competing classes that might make reasonable requests for special government favors. The common law recognized that there were those who, because of their own weaknesses and deficiencies—and most certainly not because of the workings of a free market—could not, or should not be allowed to, take advantage of the opportunities that existed for self-advancement and personal autonomy; consequently, children, women, and "imbeciles" might deserve some special government protections or burdens (as might sailors in ships on the high seas, who lacked the options provided by the free market). But these were anomalies, the exceptions that dramatized the implications of not having one's natural rights and abilities fully respected. For those who viewed the society constructed by the regime of property and free contract as harmonious and liberating, and not hierarchical or oppressive (especially as compared to the social relations constituted by feudal law), it was natural to consider certain classes' use of public power to gain an unfair advantage over competing classes illegitimate—an acceptance of class politics invited a return of the kind of class oppression that was nowhere evident in market relations. For men like Alexander Hamilton and Jefferson, it was better that the government promote and protect the market and its attendant privileges and obligations, and adopt policies that nurtured these conditions without intruding into the conflicts that were a natural feature of the opportunities it had to offer.

Nevertheless, in the years after independence, the overtly class-based politics of price controls, debtor relief, and paper currency was evident in many of the newly created states, with farmers finding available coin scarce, urban consumers struggling against a war-fueled inflation (and profiteering merchants), and many individuals suffering under general indebtedness.[21] In 1777, the Continental Congress recommended that efforts be made "to regulate the prices of labour, manufacturing, [and] internal police," efforts that had "become necessary to supply the defect of public virtue, and to correct the vices of some of her sons."[22] In 1779, artisans, sailors, and militiamen in Philadelphia used the authorized power of popular committees to set and enforce price controls and wage rates; a year later, Philadelphia hosted a wage- and price-fixing convention. Workers whose wages were not keeping up with the wartime inflation supported these measures. "Philadelphia's master craftsmen estimated that prices of food and other commodities had risen twenty times while wages had increased only fourteen times over the prewar figures."[23] But in the 1780s these interventions began to provoke a response by those who suffered the burdens of these "partial" benefits (mostly merchants and creditors). Maybe more important, as the 1780s progressed, the practice of intervening explicitly on behalf of particular classes caused a split in the artisan and mechanic community: whereas journeymen, small producers, poor consumers, and others who lacked sufficient security in capital tended to remain loyal to the older tradition of the moral economy out of their shared experience with being vulnerable to unregulated market fluctuations, master craftsmen and the new breed of commercial artisans tended to embrace a more modern faith in an unregulated market because they believed they could prosper or at least remain independent in such an environment (at least so long as they had access to capital, which explains the bank wars of the 1780s and 1790s).[24]

The faith expressed by members of this latter group was neither insincere nor idealistic. In late-eighteenth-century America as many as four out of five freeborn men owned land or the tools of their trade, and workmen's wages were relatively high. At a time when capitalist forms of production (wage labor and the factory system) were still in their infancy, and when many independent producers could reasonably believe that the free market would provide personal autonomy and opportunities for self-improvement, the rationale underlying the need for communal control of prices and wages was becoming less persuasive to more people.[25] Even Thomas Paine, who initially supported the movement for price controls because of his disdain for profiteering merchants such as Robert Morris and Silas Deane, soon found himself extolling the virtues of hard money, a national bank, and "fiscal responsibility" on the grounds that there was an essential harmony of interests among individual producers operating in a market free of special privilege.[26]

The story of the 1780s is the story of how early attempts to place the operation of the market under the control of a democratized political system eventually led to an alliance among social elites, who had been traditionally fearful of the threats posed by unrestrained majorities to their property, and liberal Whigs or independent producers, who were interested in liberating commercial life from what they considered to be inequitable and unnecessary government intrusions. (They also believed that the harmonious market would be better served by a central government that was able to maintain a stable national currency, remove impediments to national and international markets, and guarantee government debt obligations.)[27] The concerns and visions of these classes differed in many respects, but they had a common interest in keeping the government *neutral* with respect to the conflicts that arose between or among market competitors. From this common interest was born an ideology that attempted to characterize any use of government to promote the special interests of certain classes as both an assault on people's rights and a violation of a basic principle of republicanism—the principle that public power could only be used disinterestedly to advance the general welfare of the community as a whole. In 1785 Madison wrote that "equality . . . ought to be the basis of every law," and this principle is violated when laws subject "some to peculiar burdens" or grant "to others peculiar exemptions."[28] In 1787 he wrote to Jefferson that the "vices" coming out of the state legislatures were "so frequent and so flagrant as to alarm the most steadfast friends of Republicanism, . . . [and] contributed more to that uneasiness which produced the Convention . . . than those which accrued to our national character and interest from the inadequacy of the Confederation to its immediate objects."[29] By the time the delegates met at Philadelphia they were fundamentally in agreement about what had to be done: they must delegitimize those conceptions of republicanism that encouraged class politics and create a truly "disinterested and dispassionate umpire in disputes between different passions and interests in the States."[30]

This goal can be clearly seen in what is easily the most familiar and recurring theme expressed by the supporters of the new order: good republican government required institutional structures that were popular yet still divorced from the corrupting influence of "factions," defined by Madison in *Federalist* no. 10 as a number of citizens, majority or minority, united by some common passion or interest (usually arising out of "the various and unequal distribution of property") that was adverse to the "permanent and aggregate interests of the community." While in the abstract this definition of *faction* could be used to challenge the legitimacy of many political structures and policies—including efforts to control popular majorities—Madison made it clear that his definition was inspired by recent events. This corrupting spirit was evident in state governments marked by "conflicts of rival parties," in which the "public good" was too often sacrificed to "the superior force of an interested and overbearing majority." As Madison told the story, an initial overenthusiasm with participatory politics had resulted in governments that were taking sides in disputes between competing factions—landed and manufacturing interests, mercantile and moneyed interests, debtors and creditors—instead of permitting "enlightened" republican statesmen dispassionately to adjust clashing interests to the public good. These historical references are intended to establish the central point that led Madison and his allies to Philadelphia: the use of public power to advance the interests of one class at the expense of a competing class was to be considered the most vivid and authoritative example of illegitimate and unrepublican government. The advertised virtue of the new constitutional structure was precisely that it was engineered to preempt this kind of factional politics: "To secure the public good and private rights against the danger of such a [majority] faction, and at the same time to preserve the spirit and form of popular government, is then the great object to which our inquiries our directed."[31]

The implications of this version of republicanism were spelled out quite clearly by Madison in his discussion of the representative logic of the Constitution in *Federalist* no. 10. Madison distinguished democracies from true republics on the grounds that in the latter the existence of a representative structure governing an enlarged territorial base (instead of direct popular participation in institutions close to the people) helped "refine and enlarge" the views of public officials and made it less likely that any one faction would be able to take control of the government. In contrast to the democratic state legislatures, the new national government would be run by republican statesmen "whose wisdom may best discern the true interest of their country, and whose patriotism and love of justice will be least likely to sacrifice it to temporary or partial considerations." Among other things, these men would have "a thorough knowledge of the principles of political economy," because "the man who understands those principles best will be least likely to resort to oppressive expedients, or to sacrifice any particular class of citizens to the procurement of revenue."[32] This last reference once again conjures up the image of corrupt state legislatures in the 1780s, caught up in the "rage for paper money, for an abolition of debts, for an equal division of property, or for any other improper or wicked project." In their place Madison offered, in the "proper structure of the Union" set out by the Federalists, a truly "republican remedy for the diseases most incident to republican government."

"If it be asked," Madison continued, "what is to restrain the [new government] from making legal discriminations in favor of themselves, and a particular class of the society? I answer, the genius of the whole system [and] the nature of just and constitutional laws."[33] As the Federalists explained it, the logic underlying virtually the entire constitutional structure derived from the basic goal of delegitimizing factional politics and encouraging the belief that legitimate government exercised power disinterestedly to advance a transcendent general welfare. The election of senators by state legislatures made it less likely that they would be "tainted by the spirit of faction, and more out of the reach of those occasional ill-humors . . . [which] beget injustice and oppression of a part of the community."[34] The electoral college "affords a moral certainty, that the office of President will never fall to the lot of any man who is not in an eminent degree endowed with the requisite qualifications" of republican statesmanship, because a candidate would have to possess a special kind of merit "to establish him in the esteem and confidence of the whole Union."[35] Once set up, power would be divided among these branches and among the national and state governments to further ensure that no single interest would be able to dominate, to "guard one part of the society against the injustice of the other part."[36] Even the courts had a role to play to preserve this faction-free polity. As Hamilton explained in *Federalist* no. 78, "it is not with a view to infraction of the Constitution only, that the independence of the judges may be an essential safeguard against the effects of occasional ill humors in the society. These sometimes extend no further than to the injury of the private rights of particular classes of citizens, by unjust and partial laws."[37] Contrary to the mistaken reading scholars still give the Federalist Papers as a pluralist tract that recognized the inevitability of interest groups and redefined the general welfare as the product of a healthy competition among them,[38] the founders' encouragement of "a multiplicity and interplay of interests" was designed "to *block them all*, so that, above their self-defeating squabble, the true interest of the entire body of the people may shine clear by contrast, for pursuit by virtuous men."[39]

What the country ended up with in 1787, in both the structure of its national institutions and in the ideology that supported that structure, was a representative style of government that was avowedly hostile to an overtly class-based politics, as illustrated by the (allegedly) unsavory behavior of overactive state legislatures in the decade following independence. The issue that brought together the Federalist coalition was *not* that government should never interfere in the market or regulate property but only that any such interference or regulation had to be justified in terms unrelated to the desire to service the "private" interests of groups engaged in economic competition. As Madison described it to Jefferson soon after the Constitutional Convention, the primary concern of the delegates was "to modify the sovereignty *as that it may be sufficiently neutral between different parts of the Society* to controul one part from invading the rights of another, and at the same time sufficiently controuled itself, from setting up an interest adverse to that of the entire society."[40]

The Constitution was not an "elitist" document in the sense that only social elites embraced it, even if it was the particular gravity of their concerns that constituted the driving force behind its creation and ratification. People had reasons to support the Constitution that were unrelated to their social class: Georgians wanted greater security from the

Indians; western settlers wanted the expulsion of the British from posts held in violation of the Treaty of 1783; New Yorkers were embroiled in local partisan conflicts.[41] Nevertheless, it was a document that embodied the social vision of some classes and not others: those who were more active in and optimistic about the commercial economy tended to favor it, while those who found themselves in a subsistence economy (particularly small farmers) or otherwise believed that commerce corrupted republican virtue tended to oppose it.[42] The Constitution set up a political structure specifically designed to nurture and protect the social relations produced by capitalism by preventing the state from taking sides in the disputes arising among or between competing classes.

Political Equality and Market Liberty in Jacksonian America

With their victory the framers of the Constitution established the boundaries of legitimate debate about state-society relations in the new commercial republic. Members of the Federalist coalition did not share a common understanding of the way public power should be used, but they did share a common understanding of which policies would be inappropriate in the new republic—namely, the factional policies adopted by many states in the 1780s. Eventually, as I intend to show in the next section, the founders' commitment to market liberty and their aversion to factional and class-based politics was transformed into constitutional ideology in early police powers jurisprudence; however, this did not happen until well into the nineteenth century, during the period of Jacksonian democracy. Before examining the judicial decisions and opinions that gave birth to nineteenth-century police powers jurisprudence it may be useful to examine the extent to which the founders' conception of legitimate state-society relations survived the transition to the nineteenth century, and how the dominant ideologies of the age of Jackson shaped the formative period of state constitutional lawmaking.

In the years after the creation of the Constitution, national leaders began the process of formulating and implementing political agendas that were consistent with the constitutional vision of a neutral polity. For example, in promoting his Treasury Plan, Hamilton argued that the national government would best serve the general welfare by assuming the revolutionary debt, incorporating a national bank, and encouraging American manufacturers. Hamilton insisted that these policies worked to the benefit of all classes: public creditors would benefit from the rise in the value of securities, which in turn would increase the supply of investment capital; merchants would expand and operate at lower profit margins, to the benefit of consumers; foreign trade would expand, benefiting manufacturers, merchants, artisans, mechanics, and agricultural interests; and land values (which had depreciated since the Revolution) would go up.[43] Jefferson's alternative plan flowed from his belief that the British model of economic development was inappropriate for the United States and from his concerns about having public power so closely linked to a "monied elite."[44] Once in office he repealed direct taxes, retired the national debt, dismantled the standing army and navy, dramatically increased the available freehold with the Louisiana Purchase, supported internal improvements that would help the domestic flow of commerce, and vigorously pursued free trade.[45]

Advocates of each agenda would continue to disagree among themselves as to whether the other side had violated the neutrality principle: Did incorporation represent the use of government power to advance the special interests of privileged groups at the expense of the rest of the community, or was it a contribution to the general welfare of a community? Did democratization of political institutions represent an invitation for factions to corrupt the legislative process through the reproduction of social conflicts in government, or was it a necessary device to prevent the privileged use of power by a corrupt elite? These debates could and did continue because they were the unresolved issues of the founding; Hamilton and Jefferson had simply specified the acceptable range of debate in American politics. But the founders had resolved that it would be inappropriate for public power to be used to advance the interests of certain groups or classes at the expense of others, and neither of the competing agendas required the government to intrude itself directly in existing disputes between competing factions.

These sensibilities continued to affect discourse and decision making in American politics even after the decline of the Federalists and Jeffersonian Republicans. Jacksonian democracy represented a rather heterogeneous coalition of social groups who shared a sense that they had been disadvantaged by the gradual return of a Federalist political economy during the Virginia Dynasty and sought to use innovative party structures to eradicate the privileged use of public power.[46] The reestablishment of Hamiltonian republicanism had begun, ironically, with the Embargo Act of 1807, in which Jefferson attempted to use the power of economic coercion (instead of war) to open foreign markets to American farmers, but which had the effect of setting American manufacturing on firm footing; it continued with the British blockade during the war of 1812, the erection of protective tariffs after the war, and the chartering of the Second Bank of the United States in 1816. Over time those members of the "thriving and vigorous" commercial classes who were not the direct beneficiaries of special manufacturing protection and promotion—or who suffered from having to compete with those who were—came to feel that the national government was "hostile to their needs and interests"; it was a "betrayal of the Jeffersonian promise of equal rights in favor of special benefits for a single class."[47] In Richard Hofstadter's words, "What is demanded is only the classic bourgeois ideal, equality before the law, the restriction of government to equal protection of its citizens. This is the philosophy of a rising middle class; its aim is not to throttle but to liberate business, to open every possible pathway for the creative enterprise of the people."[48]

Like the Jeffersonians before them, the Jacksonian coalition was bonded by the belief that it could hold its own in a political and economic system purged of the vestiges of special privilege; the members' common desire was to remove most "restrictions and privileges that had their origin in acts of government."[49] The coalition included businessmen who found it difficult to break into the existing order of mercantile privilege that took the form of special corporate charters; the heads of state banks, who resented the privileged position of the national bank; farmers who had once monopolized local markets and suddenly had to face competition from grain transported on government-subsidized canals; master mechanics who were losing out to merchant capitalists able to obtain credit from publicly chartered banks; and farmers and laborers hurt by the price inflation caused, in their minds, by the issue of currency from those banks.[50] The themes that energized these interests into a coherent political movement had been laid out and proven effective some thirty years earlier when the Jeffersonians organized against the Federalists— the democratization of politics in order to break up an established class of self-interested politicians (such as those who had conspired to steal the election from "the people" in the "Corrupt Bargain of 1824") and the eradication of illegitimate government-sponsored privilege in the economy in order to exorcise corruption in the polity and maximize or democratize opportunity for personal liberty, social independence, and self-improvement in the private economy. In short, it was an ideology of market freedom protected specifically by a core value of political equality.

The democratization of the political system was embodied in reforms such as white manhood suffrage, the paper ballot, small polling districts, the direct election of governors and other local officeholders (as well as presidential electors), short terms of office, and rotation in office.[51] In matters of political economy Jacksonian democracy was manifested in a brutal Indian removal program (which made western lands more available for white freeholding), a restructuring of the credit system so that it serviced more than just the interests of a financial and commercial elite, and a widespread attack on the neomercantilist Commonwealth tradition of using tax exemptions, franchises, subsidies, and other corporate privileges as a central tool in the promotion of commercial development.[52] The gradual diminishment of the practice of using special acts of incorporation in favor of general laws of incorporation represented the dual hostility toward political and market privilege: incorporation by special charter resulted not only in the monopolization of sectors of the economy but also in the corruption of legislatures through bribery or other schemes designed to protect this artificial privilege.[53] Contrary to the older Hamiltonian and developing Whig conceptions of political economy, Jacksonians argued that the belief that government should "operate directly or indirectly on the industry and prosperity of the community" was not only the advocacy of an unnecessary public responsibility but would lead, in the words of *The Democratic Review*, to "the most pernicious abuse."[54] As the *New York Evening Post* described it, "The common good, the interests of the many, have long been entirely neglected in a confused scramble for personal favors; and instead of leaving one business man to cope with another, on the fair and equitable principles which nature and the Constitution sanction, the Legislature . . . by means of chartered privileges, has been all along engaged in *siding* with some to the injury of others and in doing all that is possible to make the *unchartered* multitude 'poor indeed.' "[55]

Jackson's Bank Veto message illustrates the extent to which the values of political equality and economic liberty were inextricably linked in the second quarter of the nineteenth century. After explaining why he considered the Second Bank of the United States unconstitutional, Jackson went on to stress that its principal shortcoming was that it was a grant of special privilege whose stock was held by "a few hundred of our citizens, chiefly of the richest class." The remarks that followed summarized the organizing principles of his regime:

> It is to be regretted that the rich and powerful too often bend the acts of government to their selfish purposes. . . . In the full enjoyment of the gifts of Heaven and the fruits of superior industry, economy, and

virtue, every man is equally entitled to protection by law; but when the laws undertake to add to these natural and just advantages artificial distinctions, to grant titles, gratuities, and exclusive privileges, to make the rich richer and the potent more powerful, the humble members of society—the farmers, mechanics, and laborers—who have neither the time nor the means of securing like favors to themselves, have a right to complain of the injustice of their Government. There are not necessary evils in government. Its evils exist only in its abuses. If it would confine itself to equal protection, and, as Heaven does its rains, shower its favors alike on the high and the low, the rich and the poor, it would be an unqualified blessing. . . .

. . . Many of our rich men have not been content with equal protection and equal benefits, but have besought us to make them richer by act of Congress. By attempting to gratify their desires we have in the results of our legislation arrayed section against section, interest against interest, and man against man, in a fearful commotion which threatens to shake the foundations of our Union. It is time to pause in our career to review our principles, and if possible revive that devoted patriotism and spirit of compromise which distinguished the sages of the Revolution and the fathers of our Union.[56]

"After the destruction of the Bank," wrote another Democrat, "must come that of all monopolies, of all PRIVILEGE." The editor of the *New York Evening Post* defined liberty itself as "nothing more than the total absence of all MONOPOLIES of all kinds, whether of rank, wealth or privilege." Robert Remini has concluded that Jacksonians expected government "to refrain from exercising powers which might provide one group an advantage over the others. . . . [I]f Jacksonian Democracy means anything at all, the definition must begin with what the Democrats believed was a crusade against political and economic privilege." To be more specific, the Jacksonian crusade was against political privilege and *artificial* economic privilege, privilege that was a by-product of "corrupt" or "unrepublican" government policies, as opposed to those advantages that were the "fruits of superior industry, economy, and virtue." Jackson himself punctuated this theme in his farewell address when he echoed Washington's warnings of the spirit of faction by issuing his own warning to his generation: "[Unless you check the] spirit of monopoly and thirst for exclusive privileges you will in the end find that the most important powers of the Government have been given or bartered away."[57]

The Jacksonian "purification" of America's founding ideology found its purest expression in New York's "radical" antimonopoly party, the Locofoco Democrats, led by men such as George Bancroft, William Cullen Bryant, William Leggett, and Theodore Sedgwick, Jr.[58] This offshoot of mainstream Jacksonianism arose in response to what was perceived to be the betrayal of the principle of equal rights by conservative New York Democrats, whose policy of "judicious" opposition to monopoly allowed them to continue issuing bank charters to their compatriots. In 1834 Sedgwick had written a series of articles in New York (they were later compiled into a pamphlet entitled *What Is a Monopoly?*) in which he attacked the granting of virtually all special advantages from which the mass of people would be excluded, a practice that he claimed assaulted the founding "doctrine of equal rights."[59] He believed, in Schlesinger's words, that "commercial advantages could be more equitably secured under another system" which would let "all businesses, and banking among them, be thrown open to universal competition (except for railroads and turnpikes, where the object could not be attained without monopoly rights, but here the charters should have reservations of revocability). The antimonopoly party must smash the system of special charters, with its by-products of graft, log-rolling, lobbying and political dishonesty, and open the field to genuine free enterprise."[60] Similarly, in a statement that is as good a summary of the central propositions of what would become nineteenth-century police powers jurisprudence as one could find in contemporaneous courts, Leggett wrote that the "functions of government, when confined to their proper sphere of action, are . . . restricted to the making of general laws, uniform and universal in their operation. . . . [If the government is allowed the] power of intermeddling with the private pursuits and individual occupations of the citizen, a government may at pleasure elevate one class and depress another; it may one day legislate exclusively for the farmer, the next for the mechanic, and the third for the manufacturer, who all thus become the mere puppets of legislative cobbling and tinkering instead of independent citizens relying on their own resources for their prosperity."[61]

Before looking at how these sensibilities worked their way into judicial decision making during the formative years of the police powers, it is important to take special note of workers' early experiences with this ethos of market liberty and political equality. After all, propertyless workers made up the class that was least likely to enjoy social independence in a commercial republic. Artisan republicans in the 1770s and 1780s worried aloud whether they would be able to attract a wage sufficiently high to enable them to be self-sufficient and eventually to become independent producers; their concern led them to support government policies that protected vulnerable, dependent classes from more powerful market competitors. The framers' aversion to factional politics rested largely on the assumptions that these workers did not need special government benefits (in the form of debtor relief or wage and price schemes). Obviously, by the time of *Lochner v. New York*, there were many people who believed that it was important to pass laws specifically designed to promote the interests of workers. During the time of Jackson, however, this kind of labor legislation was not in evidence, despite the emergence of organizations dedicated to promoting the interests of wage earners. In order to understand the controversies at the end of the nineteenth century involving the constitutionality of labor legislation it is important to understand the fate of these early movements.

At the same time party leaders in the age of Jackson were maintaining the framers' class-neutral polity on the promise that commercial development or market opportunities were consistent with social independence and personal liberty, changes taking place in the structure of the economy threatened to expose this promise as empty for increasing numbers of workers. Around the time of the founding most (nonslave) producers of American goods approximated Jefferson's image of the virtuous and self-reliant farmer or artisan-craftsman. These producers owned their own land or workshops and the tools of their trade; they controlled virtually all aspects of production or worked with journeymen or apprentices in relationships governed by communal traditions or guilds; the work routine was flexible if not leisurely; there was pride in the craft or workmanship needed to make a fine product; and markets were arranged to ensure at least a subsistence living—some mechanics' societies even set aside funds for loans to young mechanics to enable them to become independent producers.[62] So long as people continued to believe that their well-being could be ensured by a harmonious market uncorrupted by the imposition of artificial government burdens or benefits, there was little reason to question the legitimacy of the ethos of the neutral polity. But the advent of the factory system of production, new sources of power to fuel production, and the intensification of competition brought on by an expansion of markets (made possible by steamboats and railroads) fundamentally altered the social experiences of producers.[63] Because new technologies made the ownership and control of production more expensive, those with sufficient capital or access to credit began to organize large-scale production, the result being "the emergence of the merchant-capitalist as employer in place of the master craftsman."[64] Machines made it possible to replace the labor of apprentices or journeymen with cheap repetitive labor—labor power as opposed to labor skill. The relationship between employer and employee was characterized not by the shared experiences of producers working closely together but rather by the more impersonal mechanism of the wage; and because the labor power being purchased by "nonproducers" was readily available, factory workers were more easily subjected to rigorous labor discipline. While the master craftsman along with a handful of journeymen and apprentices continued to hold onto preindustrial traditions by relying on the quality of his products, he found it "difficult to compete when he was undersold by quantity production in a market increasingly oriented toward price."[65]

This transformation from a preindustrial to an industrial society would proceed gradually throughout the century, intensifying in the decades after the Civil War.[66] But around the time of Jackson the first signs of discontent over the maturation of capitalist forms of production began to appear. Throughout the nineteenth century artisans, skilled workers, small farmers, and petty producers kept alive their more democratic, egalitarian, and communal traditions in alternative "producer ideologies" and precapitalist agrarian life-styles.[67] These nonauthoritative visions of republicanism found expression initially in family and community rituals, town meetings, neighborhood taverns, personal journals, and pamphlets. Eventually they began to appear in petition drives, sympathetic union and agrarian newspapers, and occasional third-party platforms. In response to the emergence of capitalists at the helm of production, the deepening division between skilled and unskilled labor, the separation of workers from control of the products they produced, the expansion in the number of wage earners, and the more widespread experience of owners and managers imposing labor discipline, affected groups began to reassert the older customs of the moral economy in popular challenges to the framers' conception of appropriate state-society relations. As Sean Wilentz has noted, for increasing numbers of laborers "the measure of capitalist tyranny . . . was precisely that it obliterated republican independence, equality, and commonwealth, not simply by creating a corrupt hierarchy of wealth and privilege (as some claimed) but by attempting to make one class of citizens [in the words of trade union leader John Commerford] 'the willing tools of other men.' "[68]

Within the context of the changing social patterns brought on by industrialization, the Jacksonians' assertion of political equality "raised inevitably the whole range of problems involved in property and class conflict";[69] a government that chose to remain neutral while one class was becoming dependent on another was a government that in fact served the interests of the dominant class. By the second quarter of the nineteenth century many writers had begun to complain that Jefferson's harmonious marketplace was being transformed into a more European system of class domination and social dependency. A correspondent in the New York *Evening Journal* denounced the invasion of "monopolists and capitalists usurping the rights of mechanics . . . abridging their privileges by opposing them in their business with the advantages of large capital. . . . [M]en who are not mechanics . . . are engaged in mechanical concerns . . . at the expense of the interest of the legitimate mechanics; . . . and in many cases, preventing the industrious, enterprising, but, perhaps indigent mechanic, from following his trade to advantage, or from following it at all." Another writer expressed a pervasive theme of the period: "There are in truth two parties in our country that can be said to have distinct interests. . . . Mechanics, farmers, artisans, and all who labor, whether as bos [*sic*] or journeyman, have a common interest in sustaining each other—the rich men, the professional men, and all who now live . . . without useful labor, depending on the sweat of their neighbor's brow for support, have also a common interest. And their interest is promoted by working us hard, and working us cheap."[70] Even Daniel Webster agreed that the factory hand was "necessarily at the mercy of the capitalist for the support of himself and family."[71] Samuel Clesson Allen, who rejected overtures by the National Republicans to be their nominee for governor of New York, declared in 1830 that "however complicated the economical relations of men may become in an artificial state of society, the great truth cannot be concealed, that he who does not raise his own bread, eats the fruits of another man's labor."[72]

The resistance to new conditions of social dependency was evident in extraparty movements such as the New York Working Men of the late 1820s and early 1830s.[73] However, after some early victories many of these independent movements were derailed either by internal political intrigues (such as those undertaken by Noah Cook and Clarkson Crolius, Jr., who were interested in using the Working Men's movement as a counterpoint to Tammany)[74] or by being incorporated into more mainstream movements such as the Locofocos. Martin Van Buren was one of many who lectured workers on the virtues of market liberty and political equality: "Left to itself, and free from the blighting influence of partial legislation, monopolies, congregated wealth, and interested combinations, the compensation of labor will always [ensure to the laboring classes the full enjoyment of the fruits of their industry]. It is only when the natural order of society is disturbed by one or other of these causes, that the wages of labor become inadequate."[75] Leggett warned workers who responded to the special privileges enjoyed by the merchant elite by requesting their own special privileges that "whenever an exception is made to the general law of the land, founded on the principle of equal rights, it will always be found to be in favor of wealth. . . . Thus it will be seen that the sole reliance of the laboring classes, who constitute a vast majority of every people on the earth, is the great principle of equal rights; that their only safeguard against oppression is a system of legislation which leaves all to the free exercise of their talents and industry within the limits of the general law and which, on no pretense of public good, bestows on any particular class of industry or any particular body of men rights or privileges not equally enjoyed by the great aggregate of the body politic."[76] Frederick Robinson echoed this theme in a speech before the Trades' Union of Boston in 1834, in which he declared, "Equality comprises everything that is good; inequality everything that is evil. Equality is liberty. Liberty without equality is dead. . . . Equality is democracy. Everyone who truly loves the human race will favor such governments, constitutions, laws, and administrations as he believes to be productive of equality."[77] The next year, in a speech before the mechanics of Boston, Theophilus Fisk argued that the principle of equality made it necessary for workers to flock to the ballot box, for "it is quite impossible for the laboring classes to make laws to rob one another; they cannot steal from themselves by partial legislation. What is for the interest of one is for the interest of all. But let the privileged few make the laws and what is the result? . . . We ask no protection; we simply desire *to be let alone*."[78]

Wilentz has argued that by 1836 party leaders "had perfected the essentials of a republican defense of capitalist growth and wage labor" by emphasizing the "supposed harmony of interests between employer and employed, the reciprocity and essential fairness of the wage, the promise of social mobility and an independent competence for all industrious men, a model of private charity and benevolence, a nearly religious devotion to the market as an economic arbiter."[79] In the end, like Jacksonianism in general, the Working Men ended up "struggling against law-created privilege, rather than attacking the business community of which they considered themselves actual or potential members."[80]

In their attempt to preserve the tradition of artisan republicanism some workers turned to self-help by organizing unions and other labor societies; by 1833 more than eight trades in New York had organized into the General Trades' Union, with another twenty trades being added the following year, giving the union about 30 percent of the city's entire white male work force.[81] When another round of inflation hit the city in the mid-1830s and wages rose at only half the rates of prices, there was a crescendo of labor activity; strikes were also called to protect work customs governing the number of apprentices, the length of indenture, and the practice of no work on Sundays.[82] These efforts were explicitly defended with reference to the principle of equality. Ely Moore asked, "[Why] have not journeymen the same right to ask their own price for their own property or services that employers have? or that merchants, physicians, and lawyers have?"[83] But collective action was vulnerable to attack by masters and courts on the grounds that it illegitimately interfered with market liberties by "oppressing" the freedom of employers and nonmembers to the advantage of organized workers.[84] For Frederick Robinson, workers' efforts to unite and regulate the amount of production represented the true democratic alternative to asking the legislature for special favors, because "when the market is but scantily supplied, the producer receives a more adequate return for his labor, and the nonproducer is obliged to part with a larger portion of his funds to command the necessaries, conveniences, and luxuries of life. In such times things tend to equality."[85]

After the Panic of 1837 broke the back of the Trades' Union movement,[86] some in the movement began to look back to the revolutionary period to find clues as to how to prevent the development of what seemed to be a permanent class of dependent wage earners without violating the injunction against special government favors for particular classes. George Henry Evans had been a part of the Working Men's movement since its inception in 1829; his newspaper, *The Working Man's Advocate*, was the movement's mouthpiece, carrying on the masthead the slogan "All children are entitled to equal education; all adults to equal property, and all mankind to equal privileges." He joined the Locofoco fight against "monopoly Democrats" in 1834, but after the defeat of the union movement he considered the status of labor more deeply. His analysis harked back to Franklin and Jefferson's conception of using the freehold as a safety valve to prevent workers from becoming dependent on employers. "Land speculation kept them from taking up vacant land near by or in the West," Evans thought. "If they could only get away and take up land, then they would not need to strike. Labor would become scarce. Employers would advance wages and landlords would reduce rents."[87] As an elder statesman, James Madison continued to argue that an expanded population of freeholders and access to foreign markets sufficient to absorb the surplus production of farmers was America's best hope for delaying the development of a large class of dependent wage earners. (Madison also believed that the United States would eventually see the rapid growth of manufactures; he was less certain about what kinds of policies would be appropriate to mitigate the social consequences of such a development, but he stressed that whatever the response, the government should adopt impartial policies: "the Government should forbear to intermeddle" in industry particularly when "one part of the community would be materially favoured at the expense of another.")[88] A similar analysis was adopted by Orestes Augustus Brownson in 1840 in his discussion of the increasingly serious predicament of wage earners: "The wilderness has receded, and already the new lands are beyond the reach of the mere laborer, and the employer has him at his mercy. . . . There must be no class of our fellow men doomed to toil through life as mere workmen at wages. If wages are tolerated it must be, in the case of the individual operative, only under such conditions that, by the time he is of a proper age to settle in life, he shall have accumulated enough to be an independent laborer on his own capital, on his own farm or in his own shop. Here is our work."[89]

When in the 1850s this analysis of commercial relations in the North combined with the cause of the abolitionists (who "understood slavery not as a class relationship, but as a system of arbitrary and illegitimate power exercised by one individual over another"), the result was the Republican party and its motto Free Soil, Free Labor, Free Men.[90] It was another attempt at a faction-free solution to the problem of social dependency, another political program that fit into the systems' structural and ideological aversion to government interventions in relations among groups competing in the private economy. Eric Foner wrote that

the Republicans accepted the labor leaders' definition of freedom as resting on economic independence rather than, as the abolitionists had insisted, on self-ownership. To Lincoln, the man who worked for wages all his life was indeed almost as unfree as the southern slave. . . . But like the abolitionists, Lincoln and the Republicans located the threat to the independence of the northern workingman outside northern society. It was not the wage system, but the expansion of slavery, which threatened to destroy the independence of the northern worker, his opportunity to escape from the wage-earning class and own a small farm or shop. For if slavery were allowed to expand into the western territories, the safety-valve of free land for the northern worker and farmer would be eliminated, and northern social conditions would soon come to resemble those of Europe.[91]

The cause of free land was won on the battlefields of the Civil War. In the decades following the war America would see whether this bloody victory had put an end to the threat of factional politics by ensuring a plentiful freehold for dependent laborers looking for social independence. What was clear by the mid-nineteenth century, however, was that early agitation against the ethos of market liberty and political equality did not amount to very much; political intrigue, party co-optation, and the diversion of the frontier combined to defuse the first challenge to the framers' aversion to factional politics. Almost one hundred years after the framers institutionalized the ethos of the neutral state in the Constitution, Parke Godwin, an old New York Jacksonian, could write with confidence and conviction in his *Life of William Cullen Bryant* (1883) that "government is the organ and representative of the whole community, not of a class, or of any fraction of that community."[92] As we shall see, many jurists writing around the same time as Godwin shared these Jacksonian sensibilities; they responded to labor's claim for "special legislation" in much the same way that leaders in the age of Jackson responded to the agitation of workingmen. Moreover, they were able to use these principles to evaluate late-nineteenth-century legislation because judges in the age of Jackson had transformed the ethos of market liberty and equal rights into constitutional law.

The Formative Years of Nineteenth-Century Police Powers Jurisprudence

It is not uncommon for legal principles, doctrines, standards, tests, and rules to sound like meaningless generalizations. When *Lochner* era jurists insisted that legislation affecting property rights or market freedom had to be reasonably related to a legitimate interest in public health, safety, or morality, it is understandable how people might conclude that the key words in the formulation—"reasonable" and "legitimate"—essentially allowed judges to decide cases any way they wanted. But it would be wrong to assume that words or phrases that seem indeterminate when abstracted away from their contexts must in fact be nothing more than empty rhetoric. Today, whether a court evaluates legislation alleged to discriminate against women by invoking "strict scrutiny" and requiring a "compelling state interest" or by invoking some "rational relationship" test is an important issue; similarly, whether a court allows legislators to punish speech that has a "bad tendency" to lead to some problem or whether speech can be suppressed only if it poses a "clear and present danger" is considered important. One can certainly imagine how a judge could apply any of these "tests" to achieve any result he or she liked; the words themselves are not inherently more or less likely to lead to particular results in particular cases. Nevertheless, people find it meaningful to argue about these alternative "abstract" legal formulations because, historically, these formulations have been associated with particular patterns of previous judicial decisions. Familiarity and context give these words and phrases whatever force and significance they appear to have. Similarly, in order for the legal doctrines of the *Lochner* era to come to life—in order for them to be seen as more than vague words rationalizing arbitrary preferences—it is necessary to appreciate how those phrases originated and what kinds of decisions, opinions, and assumptions were associated with them as they were formulated and elaborated in history.

The early United States Supreme Court had little opportunity to look specifically at the question of what kinds of laws were, in Hamilton's words, "unjust" or "partial"[93]; before the Civil War the justices had few constitutional avenues through which they could actively scrutinize the behavior of state legislatures (the restrictions of Article I, section 10, and later the commerce clause). Still, in one of the few cases in which the pre-Marshall Court could elaborate on the nature of the legislative authority, Justice Samuel Chase did assert (albeit not without some controversy) that "an act of the legislature (for I cannot call it a law), contrary to the great first principles of the social compact, cannot be considered a rightful exercise of the legislative authority"; for example, an act "that takes property from A. and gives it to B." exceeds legislative power.[94] The first example in American constitutional law of legislation that violated the "great first principles of the social compact" involved a government using its powers not to promote the general welfare but rather to advance the well-being of some individuals at the expense of others.

Chief Justice John Marshall built on these early steps by asserting the power of judicial review, expanding the ability of the national government to direct economic development, and constraining the ability of state legislatures to interfere with that development through the invocation of either "general principles, which are common to our free institutions, or by the particular provisions of the Constitution."[95] These latter goals reflected his interest in embodying Hamiltonian political economy into constitutional ideology. His decision in *Dartmouth College v. Woodward* (1819) to protect established charters of incorporation from legislative interference is just one example of how his conception of the legitimate scope of government power can be traced back to his experiences as a leader of the urban mercantile-financial class in Virginia, where the use of the joint stock corporation as a means of channeling scarce capital into ostensibly beneficial commercial enterprises was favored by the merchant elite but came under increasing attack in the 1810s by farmers and petty merchants, who felt trapped by the "odious monopolies" and special privileges granted to particular interests.[96] (Judge Spencer Roane of the Virginia Supreme Court of Appeals gave voice to this latter group's Jeffersonian sensibilities when he held that if the object of investors seeking corporate privilege was "merely private or selfish; if it is detrimental to, or not promotive of, the public good, they have no adequate claim on the legislature for the privilege." He relied largely on Article IV of the Virginia Declaration of Rights, which stated that "no . . . set of men, are entitled to exclusive or separate emoluments or privileges from the community, but in consideration of publick services."[97]) Similarly, the Marshall Court extended the proper republican protection to the sanctity of the relationship between debtors and creditors.[98]

The Jacksonian conception of classlessness and commercial development was largely a reaction to the assumptions that drove Marshall's jurisprudence. These competing conceptions of constitutional legitimacy are represented in the majority and dissenting opinions in *Charles River Bridge Company v. Warren Bridge Company* (1837). Justice Joseph Story's dissent ("I stand upon the old law") stressed the initially established Marshallian view that corporate expansion would remain a viable tool for community development only if investors were confident that the bargains they struck with legislatures would be jealously safeguarded.

Chief Justice Roger Taney's majority opinion was also supportive of corporate rights—he acknowledged that if an express monopoly was indicated in a corporate charter, then a state would be bound to respect it—but went on to hold that, absent an express grant of monopoly, the general welfare would best be served if special privileges in the market were eradicated and new investment opportunities created. The opinion singled out as particularly important the need to take advantage of opportunities to expand the infrastructure of the market to improve the flow of goods from producers to consumers. According to Taney, if the Court went out of its way to protect these older holdings, "we shall be thrown back to the improvements of the last century, and obliged to stand still, until the claims of the old turnpike corporations shall be satisfied, and they shall consent to permit these States to avail themselves of the lights of modern science, and to partake of the benefit of those improvements which are now adding to the wealth and prosperity, and the convenience and comfort of every other part of the civilized world."[99]

It has been well documented that Taney's opinion represented a more widespread movement in American law which accommodated Jacksonian politics by making the release of market energies (in the form of new capital investments and the promotion of competition) a higher priority than the protection of static holdings (in the form of vested rights of property or corporate privilege)—this was the bourgeois ideal, the principal goal of groups who were interested in breaking down the political and economic barriers to their self-improvement and who believed that the general welfare would be better served by unleashing this new energy.[100] The Supreme Court played a minor role in creating the conditions for a more robust national economy,[101] but when Marshall insulated the states from more expansive federal court review under the Bill of Rights, he ensured that the responsibility of outlining the boundaries of a state's power to promote, manage, and control the release of new entrepreneurial energy rested mostly with state legislatures and state courts.[102]

When the corporate form became the preferred means of accumulating and protecting investment capital (over practices like the limited partnership or the business trust), more entrepreneurs wanted access to it. In response, legislators replaced the practice of granting special charters of incorporation with general incorporation statutes, and courts safeguarded those investments (while still recognizing the ultimate right of the state to reserve power over the enterprise).[103] Property law was shifting away from its feudal preoccupation with safeguarding a person's undisturbed dominion over land to accommodate the more fluid (and abstract) properties of capital and the greater interest in efficient resource development; contract law lost its moorings in older notions of equity and instead began to reflect new assumptions about the "convergence of the wills of the contracting parties" in a market economy; and tort law protected new investment by developing more flexible standards of liability. In general this era saw the eclipse of a heavy-handed conception of vested rights in favor of a greater tolerance for legislative and doctrinal innovations that attempted to promote and regulate the expansion of market opportunities: the removal of special market privileges, assistance in fostering capital-intensive development in the market's infrastructure (the construction of bridges, turnpikes, canals, and railroads), and other changes that would create more favorable conditions for new investors.[104]

But with the barrier of vested rights eroding, it became necessary to find an alternate means of controlling those democratized legislatures that might be tempted to intervene in social conflicts. The alternative that emerged was for courts to use the aversion to factional or class politics as the standard by which exercises of the police power would be tested. Judges would continue to protect vested legal rights against legislative interference,[105] but by mid-century, when it came to elaborating general principles regulating the boundaries of the police powers, it was much more common for judges to emphasize the illegitimacy of so-called unequal, partial, class, or special legislation; that is, legislation which advanced the interests of only a part of the community. An exercise of legislative powers would be considered valid only if it could reasonably be justified as contributing to the general welfare. The adjudicative task was to give meaning to this standard. What emerged over time were principles of constitutional law that had a lasting impact on the Supreme Court's understanding of appropriate state-society relations. Specifically, it came to be determined, first, that laws that singled out specific groups or classes for special treatment would withstand constitutional scrutiny only if they could be justified as really related to the welfare of the community as a whole (like expansions of market opportunities or class-neutral regulations designed to advance traditional concerns involving community health, safety, or morality) and were not seen as corrupt attempts to use the powers of government to advance purely "private" interests (unnecessary class privileges or burdens); and, second, that acts that interfered with an individual's property or market liberty would be considered legitimate so long as they were not designed to advance the interests of just certain groups or classes. While many in this generation worshipped their property and their market liberty, they envisioned that each would be secure so long as legislation was free from the corruption of factional politics.

One of the earliest judicial pronouncements of equal treatment as a constitutional test can be found in an 1815 Massachusetts decision upholding a tax of 0.5 percent on the amount of the original stock of incorporated banks. More than any other power, the legislature's authority to raise taxes raised the specter of class warfare—powerful groups excluding themselves, majorities exploiting vulnerable minority classes to pay the public tab. Not surprisingly, questions about the scope of this power were among the most frequently debated. In this case a 1812 tax act was challenged on the grounds that the legislature did not make provisions for such a tax in the original charter (granted in 1799) and "has not the power to select any individuals or company, or any specific object of property, and demand a tax of them, separate and distinct from such tax as might result from its equal and proportionate share of such taxes as should be required of all individuals, companies, or property, within the Commonwealth." Chief Justice Isaac Parker began by noting that if an act of the legislature is repugnant to the "character and principles" of the Constitution, it "must be declared void and inoperative"; therefore it was the court's duty "to determine whether [the act] militates with the general principles or any positive provision of the Constitution." But in this case "the result of our inquiry is, that it does not." The court was willing to uphold special taxes on businesses that were already distinguished by their special privileges. "[T]here can be no doubt that the legislature might as well exact a fee or tribute from brokers, factors, or commission merchants, for the privilege of transacting their business. . . . It will, undoubtedly, be the policy of a wise legislature, not to multiply the burdens of this sort; but we speak only of their power, presuming that it will never be exercised but for wise or necessary purposes." Still, the legislature does not have a free hand to determine what kinds of special tax burdens or benefits it will distribute: "Taxes of this sort must undoubtedly be equal; that is, they must operate upon all persons who exercise the employment which is so taxed. A tax upon one particular moneyed capital would unquestionably be contrary to the principles of justice, and could not be supported; but a tax upon all banks we think justifiable upon the grounds we have stated."[106]

In the same year that Andrew Jackson was first elected president the Massachusetts Supreme Court decided *Vadine's Case* (1828).[107] Henry Vadine had been prosecuted for violating a Boston bylaw that prohibited any person not duly licensed by the mayor and aldermen from removing "any house-dirt, refuse, offal, filth or animal or vegetable substance from any of the dwellinghouses or other places occupied by the inhabitants." The city claimed that the bylaw was a "reasonable and proper" regulation designed to promote the careful removal of materials that might cause disease or discomfort. In his defense Vadine argued that the bylaw was an unreasonable restraint of trade; while "the city may direct the time and manner of removing filth," it had "no right to say that it shall be removed only by persons having a license." At issue, then, was the question of under what circumstances the state may interfere with market liberty. The court agreed with the parties that the appropriate test was whether the act "reasonably" advanced the general welfare: if a restraint of trade was "unreasonable, it is void; if necessary for the good government of the society, it is good." With this as the controlling standard, it was incumbent on the court to take into account both the object and the necessity of the bylaw. "The great object of the city is to preserve the health of the inhabitants." If Boston did not regulate when people could take away this material, "there would be continual moving nuisances at all times, and in all the streets of the city, breaking up the streets by their weight and poisoning the air with their effluvia." In light of the nature of the problem and the operation of the bylaw the court was "satisfied that the law is reasonable, and not only within the power of the government to prescribe, but well adapted to preserve the health of the city."

To further illustrate the standard the court provided an illuminating example of an act that would *not* be reasonable: "The mayor and commonality of London made a by-law, that no carman within the city should go with his cart, without license from the wardens of such an hospital, under a certain penalty for each offence; and it was held to be a void by-law, because it was in restraint of the liberty of the trade of carman, and it was held to be unreasonable, because it went to the private benefit of the wardens of the hospital, and was in the nature of a monopoly." When we compare the regulation upheld in *Vadine's Case* with the court's example of the illegitimate bylaw, it is clear that the distinction does not rest on the extent to which market freedom is impaired—the impairment is identical in each case—but rather on the consideration of whether the interference legitimately advances the general welfare of the community or illegitimately advances the particular welfare of private interests.[108]

A similar issue arose in the same court a few years later when Simon C. Hewitt, an unlicensed bonesetter and healer of sprains, complained that a statute which permitted only licensed physicians and surgeons to recover a debt for professional services violated the sixth article of the Massachusetts Bill of Rights, which says that "no man nor corporation or association of men, have any other title to obtain advantages of particular and exclusive privileges, distinct from those of the community, than what arises from the consideration of services rendered to the public." In light of this provision, Chief Justice Lemuel Shaw's opinion was centered on the consideration of "whether it was the intent, or one of the leading and substantive purposes of the legislature, to confer an exclusive privilege on any man or class of men." Shaw began by observing that, like attorneys, brokers, carriers, and pilots, physicians and surgeons are members of a profession whose skill "will depend much upon the state of science and the means of education at any particular period." His understanding of the reasoning behind the statute was that the legislature, acting according to the maxim "prevention is better than the cure" and "not content with holding the ignorant, careless and unskilful [sic] responsible in damages, have provided by positive enactment, for giving encouragement to those, who before they engage in the practice shall give evidence of their having enjoyed the means of a good professional education . . . by requiring such persons to obtain the sanction and permission of those who have the best means of judging of their qualifications, the members of the Medical Society, or the customary sanction of a degree from the University." In light of this, "it appears to us that the leading and sole purpose of this act was to guard the public against ignorance, negligence and carelessness in the members of one of the most useful professions, and that the means were intended to be adapted to that object." It is true that "many legislative acts have a direct effect to confer on persons and sections of country very important advantages, such as those establishing roads, bridges, ports, and very many others, which have an immediate effect to enhance the value of real estate, to encourage particular branches of trade, and in various ways to confer valuable privileges. But when this is indirect and incidental, and not one of the purposes of the act, it cannot be considered as a violation of this article of the Bill of Rights."[109] Similarly, Shaw upheld the conviction of a man for selling intoxicating liquors without a license on the grounds that the licensing scheme was not intended "as a benefit or privilege to him [the holder of a license], or with a view to give him an exclusive right; but solely because the peace and security, the morals and good order of the community, will be promoted by it, and the exclusive power therefore is collateral and incidental, and not one of the objects and purposes of the law."[110]

During the first few years of Jackson's presidency three opinions were handed down by his home state's supreme court that would become among the most widely cited in state and federal courts in the waning decades of the nineteenth century. The issues in the first two cases were quite different: in *Vanzant v. Waddel* (1829) the court upheld an act which gave the creditors of two banks additional remedies to enforce the payment of their debts, on the grounds that it was a general law which applied to everyone similarly situated; in *Wally's Heirs v. Kennedy* (1831) the court struck down a law authorizing the state judiciary to dismiss Indian reservation cases if it could be shown that the suit was prosecuted for the benefit of another, on the grounds that there was no legitimate reason to distinguish these types of suits from others. In both cases Judge John Catron took the opportunity to ruminate on the scope of legislative authority, and in almost identical opinions he laid out a standard that became a cornerstone of many subsequent discussions of the police powers:

> [The Tennessee constitution, art. II, sec. 8, declares that no free man shall be deprived of his life, liberty or property,] but by the judgment of his peers, *or the law of the land.* What is "the law of the land?" [It] means a general public law, equally binding upon every member of the community. The rights of every individual must stand or fall by the same rule or *law*, that governs every other member of the body politic, or land, under similar circumstances; and every partial, or private law . . . is unconstitutional and void. Were it otherwise, odious individuals or corporate bodies, would be governed by one law, the mass of the community, and those who made the law, by another; whereas a like general law affecting the whole community equally could not have been passed.[111]

The same year *Wally's Heirs* was decided Catron's statement was adopted by Judge Nathan Green of the Tennessee Supreme Court in *Bank v. Cooper*, which voided an act that had created a special court to handle all lawsuits brought against the Bank of the State of Tennessee. Green clarified the value of Catron's standard in guaranteeing both individual rights and the promise of the neutral state: "Legislation is always exercised by the majority. Majorities have nothing to fear; for the power is in their hands. They need no written constitutions, defining and circumscribing the powers of the government. . . . Does it not seem conclusive then, that this provision [law of the land] was intended to restrain the legislature from enacting any law affecting injuriously the rights of any citizens, *unless at the same time, the rights of all others in similar circumstances were equally affected by it. If the law be general in its operation, affecting all alike, the minority are safe*, because the majority, who make the law, are operated on by it equally with the others. Here is the importance of the provision, and the great security it affords."[112] This same theme was echoed repeatedly in many different state courts across the country over the next few decades.[113] The common assumption was that the rights of nonmajorities would be best protected not by having judges divine a set of "preferred freedoms" and then evaluate whether a state's interest was sufficiently "compelling" (which is the contemporary judicial approach to the protection of individual rights), but rather by simply insisting that laws be generally applicable or serve a real public purpose; that is, whereas contemporary rights jurisprudence focuses on the identification and protection of special pockets of "liberty," constitutional jurisprudence in the nineteenth century tended to be organized around the core value of *equality* under the law—although it was assumed that this emphasis on equality would have as one of its residual benefits the protection of important individual liberties.

Just as modern courts have had to develop a theory of *preferred freedoms* in order to identify which important liberties the government should not touch without a really good reason, nineteenth-century jurists had to develop a jurisprudence of *public purpose* that would be useful in distinguishing general from partial laws and laws that treated people differently for justifiable reasons ("reasonable" laws) from laws that treated people differently for unjustifiable reasons ("unreasonable" laws). Unlike the emphasis on "balancing" which is so much a part of contemporary constitutional jurisprudence, this nineteenth-century approach to legislative power was essentially categorical—laws either promoted the public welfare or were arbitrary and unreasonable.[114] As is evident from the kinds of analysis conducted by Chief Justice Shaw or by the court in *Vadine's Case*, as a starting point judges asked themselves whether a particular law was better understood as an example of unnec-essary government favoritism or hostility or whether it was a sincere effort to achieve some general public good. This standard of decrying unfair favoritism or hostility was useful in advancing traditionally con-servative concerns, such as preventing state interference with debtor-creditor relationships.[115] But in the age of Jackson this standard was directed against all special privileges that did not contribute to the welfare of the community as a whole, particularly those privileges that were likely the product of the corrupt manipulation of legislatures by powerful interests. The requirement that legislatures demonstrate a legit-imate public purpose became a standard limitation on the taxing power and the power of eminent domain,[116] thereby voiding subsidies to pri-vate businesses such as millers, manufacturers, bankers, and (less fre-quently) railroads.[117] But "public purpose" as a limit on the powers of government did not mean "laissez-faire"; it meant, by and large, class-neutral legislation—legislation that did not impose special burdens or benefits on certain market competitors. Judges upheld inspection and public health laws, ordinances restricting dangerous or unhealthful busi-nesses to certain locations, regulations of weights and measures, licens-ing schemes, and prohibition acts; in other words, regulations that were arguably neutral with respect to struggles going on among interests in society.[118] By the time of the Civil War this conception of the legitimate scope of the police powers had not only become a mainstay of constitu-tional jurisprudence but had also been incorporated into the constitution of virtually every state in provisions such as "[N]o men or set of men are entitled to exclusive or separate emoluments or privileges from the community, but in consideration of public services"; "Government [is] instituted for the common benefits, protection, and security of the whole community, and not for the private interest or emolument of any one man, family, or class of men"; and "The general assembly shall not grant to any citizen or class of citizens privileges and immunities which upon the same terms, shall not equally belong to all citizens."[119]

The most familiar, and maybe most misunderstood, exponent of this conception of political legitimacy was a man who had a major influence over late-nineteenth-century constitutional jurisprudence. As a Loco-foco Democrat, Thomas Cooley consistently assailed special favors to banks, railroads, and other privileged monopolies—he was a persistent critic of Marshall's opinion in *Dartmouth College*—and at the center of his republican ideology was the idea of equal treatment before the law.

According to Alan Jones, "When Cooley spoke of the dangers of class legislation in the early 1850s, when he defended equal rights, free trade, free schools, free discussion, and free soil, and when he spoke of liberty and constitutional limitations, he echoed the sentiments of [John] Pierce [a radical leader of the Michigan constitutional convention] and [William] Leggett, who sought constitutional limitations to legislative power because they feared arbitrary and unequal legislation, as well as the identification of legislation with the interests of the privileged and powerful capitalists."[120] When a special act of the Michigan legislature in 1864 authorized the town of Salem to pledge its credit in aid of the Detroit and Howell Railroad, Judge Cooley of the Michigan Supreme Court denied the railroad's application for a writ of mandamus to compel the township to execute and issue its bonds. In *People v. Salem* (1870) he wrote: "[T]he discrimination between different classes or occupations, and the favoring of one at the expense of the rest, whether that one be farming, or banking, or merchandising, or milling, or printing, or railroading is not legitimate legislation, and is a violation of that equality of right which is a maxim of state government. . . . [The business of the state is] to protect the industry of all, and to give all the benefit of equal laws. . . . [W]hen the State once enters upon the business of subsidies, one shall not fail to discover that the strong and powerful interests are those most likely to control legislation, and that the weaker will be taxed to enhance the profits of the stronger."[121] Cooley's opinion in *Salem* differed from the prevailing wisdom about the police power only in his conclusion that grants to railroads did not serve the general welfare; but the principle Cooley applied was well established: "the state could have no favorites."[122]

The prevalence of this standard is also evident in Cooley's *Constitutional Limitations*, first published a few years after the Civil War and written "in full sympathy with all those restraints which the caution of the fathers had imposed upon the exercise of the powers of government, and with faith in the checks and balances of our republican system."[123] In this volume Cooley accumulated many of the constitutional principles that had been developing in state courts during the previous few decades. He wrote that while the specific applications of the phrases "due process of law" and "law of the land" have varied from state to state, "perhaps no definition is more often quoted than that given by Mr. Webster in the Dartmouth College Case: 'By the law of the land is most clearly intended the general law; a law which hears before it condemns; which proceeds upon inquiry, and renders judgment only after trial. The meaning is that every citizen shall hold his life, liberty, property, and immunities, under the protection of the general rules which govern society.' "[124] With respect to rights to property, Cooley made it clear that they have their "reasonable limits and restrictions," limits that "must have some regard to the general welfare and public policy . . . which embrace the welfare of the whole community, and which seek the equal and impartial protection of the interests of all."[125] During his discussion of the police powers he cited Shaw's definition in *Commonwealth v. Alger* that "all property . . . [is] held subject to those general regulations which are necessary to the common good and general welfare." "The dimensions of the government's police power are identical with the dimensions of the government's duty to *protect* and *promote* the public welfare. The measure of police power must square with the measure of public necessity. . . . *Police regulations cannot be purely arbitrary nor purely for the promotion of private interests. It must appear that the general welfare is to be in some degree promoted.*"[126]

While Cooley is best known for his sympathy for market freedoms and his concern about the protection of contract and property rights, these aspects of his jurisprudence have to be understood within the larger context of his background as a Locofoco Democrat and his more general commitment to the neutral state. For Cooley, as for many of his contemporaries, liberty in the private economy and rights to property had to be protected not from any government interference but specifically from *class* interference, attempts by special groups to use public power to advance their private interests. Because this issue was the keystone of constitutional legitimacy, it is not surprising that a good part of Cooley's treatise is devoted to a discussion of laws that extend special privileges or burdens to particular groups. "Under the rulings of the Federal Supreme Court," he wrote somewhat disapprovingly, "the grant of any exclusive privilege by a State, if lawfully made, is a contract, and not subject to be recalled. . . . In former times, such grants were a favorite resort in England, not only to raise money for the personal uses of the monarch, but to reward favorites; and the abuse grew to such enormous magnitude that Parliament in the time of Elizabeth, and again in times of James I, interfered and prohibited them." However, these grants of privilege were particularly unjust because they "were monopolies in the ordinary occupations of life." By contrast, "where the grant is of a franchise which would not otherwise exist, no question can be made of the right of the

State to make it exclusive, unless the constitution of the State forbids it; because, in contemplation of law, no one is wronged when he is only excluded from that to which he never had any right. An exclusive right to build and maintain a toll bridge or to set up a ferry may therefore be granted; and the State may doubtless limit, by the requirement of a license, the number of persons who shall be allowed to engage in employments the entering upon which is not a matter of common right, and which, because of their liability to abuse, may require special and extraordinary police supervision. The business of selling intoxicating drinks and of setting up a lottery are illustrations of such employments." But, he stressed, "the grant of a monopoly in one of the ordinary and necessary occupations of life must be as clearly illegal in this country as in England."[127]

This discussion continued with greater depth under the heading "Unequal and Partial Legislation." Cooley recognized that "an enactment may . . . be the law of the land without being a general law"; for example, laws "confined to particular classes, as minors or married women, bankers or traders, and the like. . . . The legislature may also deem it desirable to prescribe peculiar rules for the several occupations, and to establish distinctions in the rights, obligations, duties, and capacities of citizens." Some businesses, such as banking or common carriers, "may require special statutory regulations for the general benefit." Because of the central importance of separating state power from private interests, however, any such class distinctions in legislation "*must rest upon some reason upon which they can be defended*"; that is, on some reason unrelated to class conflict, "like the want of capacity in infants and insane persons." By contrast, "a statute would not be constitutional which should proscribe a class or a party for opinion's sake, or which would select particular individuals from a class or locality, and subject them to peculiar rules, or impose upon them special obligations or burdens from which others in the same locality or class are exempt." The North Star of American constitutionalism in the mid-nineteenth century was the conviction that "every one has a right to demand that he be governed by general rules, and a special statute which without his consent, singles his case out as one to be regulated by a different law from that which is applied in all similar cases, would not be legitimate legislation, but would be such an arbitrary mandate as is not within the province of free governments." Quoting from *Locke on Civil Government* and citing *Vanzant v. Waddell* and *Wally's Heirs v. Kennedy,*

Cooley's next passage would win the favor of courts and counselors later in the century: "Those who make the laws 'are to govern by promulgated, established laws, not to be varied in particular cases, but to have one rule for rich and poor, for the favorite at court and the countryman at plough.' This is a maxim in constitutional law, and by it we may test the authority and binding force of legislative enactments."[128]

The addition of an equal protection clause to the Constitution was in many respects just a formalization of what Cooley (and the framers) had already considered the singular aim of the law, which was the protection of equality of rights and privileges. Cooley chose to anchor the meaning of the equal protection clause in the larger constitutional tradition instead of in the particular historical context that gave rise to it: simply put, "it is aimed at *undue favor* and individual or class privilege, on the one hand, and at *hostile discrimination* or the oppression of inequality, on the other." In general, "legislation discriminating against some and favoring others, is prohibited, but legislation which, in carrying out a public purpose, is limited in its application, if within the sphere of its operation affects alike all persons similarly situated, is not within the amendment"; this simple summary of the prevailing ideology is followed by twenty solid pages of footnotes listing and describing cases in support of the proposition.[129]

A similar summary can be found in an opinion of the Wisconsin Supreme Court just a few years after Cooley first published his treatise. In *Durkee v. City of Janesville* (1871) the justices had an opportunity to reflect on "that principle of constitutional law which prohibits unequal and partial legislation upon general subjects." "There is," wrote Chief Justice Luther S. Dixon, "no reason to doubt the existence or correctness of the constitutional provision that forbids such legislation. Enactments of the kind have frequently been held unconstitutional and void" (the latter remark prompted a brief tour of twelve state court cases that relied on this principle). All this led the chief justice to the conclusion that the attempt on the part of the state to issue a special exemption to the city of Janesville freeing it from the obligation to pay court costs in a previous case was simply "arbitrary, unjust, and odious. . . . [A]nd in declaring my opinion," he continued with some impatience, "I care very little whether it is placed on those fundamental principles of law and justice which, in our form of government it has been held no legislative body can override, even though not prohibited by the written constitution, or upon the provisions of the constitution itself." Judicial reliance on clear principles of justice had been the practice since the decisions of the U.S. Supreme Court in *Calder v. Bull* and *Fletcher v. Peck* and the numerous restrictions placed on the eminent domain and taxing power of states. For "if the legislature might thus exempt the *city of Janesville* from the operation of the general law, or from burdens cast upon all other corporations and persons, under like circumstances, then why might it not, in like manner, exempt any other corporation or person by name, thus opening the door to the greatest corruption, *partiality and favoritism*."[130]

The same year that *Durkee v. City of Janesville* was decided the House of Representatives of the State of Maine ordered the justices of the supreme judicial court to furnish their opinion as to whether the legislature could "pass laws enabling towns, by gifts of money or loans of bonds, to assist individuals or corporations to establish or carry on manufacturing." The response was familiar: "There is nothing of a public nature any more entitling the manufacturer to public gifts than the sailor, the mechanic, the lumberman, or the farmer. Our government is based on equality of rights. . . . The State cannot rightfully discriminate among occupations, for a discrimination in favor of one branch of industry is a discrimination adverse to all other branches. The State is equally to protect all, giving no undue advantages or special and exclusive preferences to any." The "cardinal principle" is that "the State shall give all alike the benefit of equal laws without favoritism or partiality."[131]

In the years immediately preceding the U.S. Supreme Court's participation in the discussion of the legitimate scope of government power, the cardinal principle defining the legitimate boundaries of public power had been well established.

CHAPTER TWO

The Master Principle of Neutrality

and the Rise of Class Conflict

[The fourteenth amendment was] designed to prevent all discriminating legisla-
tion for the benefit of some to the disparagement of others. . . . [States] can now,
as then, legislate to promote health, good order and peace, to develop their
resources, enlarge their industries, and advance their prosperity. It only inhibits
discriminating and partial enactments, favoring some to the impairment of the
rights of others. The principal, if not the sole, purpose of its prohibitions is to
prevent any arbitrary invasion by State authority of the rights of person and
property, and to secure to every one the right to pursue his happiness unre-
strained, except by just, equal, and impartial laws.—Justice Stephen J. Field
(1883)[1]

Police powers jurisprudence during the *Lochner* era had its origins in the
founders' desire to delegitimize "factional politics," attempts by competing classes to use public power to gain unfair or unnatural advantages
over their market adversaries. The object of this agenda was not to
promote the value of market liberty per se, nor to reduce government
intervention in the market to a bare minimum; rather, the goal was to
prohibit the government from passing laws designed merely to promote
the interests of certain classes at the expense of their competitors, to
impose special burdens and benefits on particular groups without linking these burdens and benefits to the welfare of the community as a
whole. The legitimacy of this vision rested on the assumption that
market relations in the new American Republic (with its vast frontier)
were essentially liberty loving and harmonious and did not pose a threat
to any citizen's republican independence—the condition whereby one

did not depend on another for his well-being. So long as this assumption was in place it could be argued persuasively that there was no legitimate reason in republican ideology for certain classes to receive special government privileges or immunities. This was the authoritative ideology of the new American Republic, and during the period of Jacksonian democracy this founding vision guided the opinions and decisions of state court judges, who in the course of creating police powers jurisprudence struggled to make meaningful the distinction between legitimate "public purpose" legislation and illegitimate "class" legislation.

While *Lochner* had its origins in antebellum traditions and practices, the decision itself, and the controversy surrounding it, were by-products of two postbellum developments as well. First, and most obvious, the U.S. Supreme Court had to adopt the conception of police powers jurisprudence that state court judges had developed. During the first half of the nineteenth century the Court had no real opportunity to develop its own distinctive police powers jurisprudence. Before the war federal courts could only review state legislative activity if a case raised an issue involving the supremacy clause, the particular proscriptions on state power found in Article I, section 10, or the protection of exclusive federal powers (over the regulation of international commerce or the return of fugitive slaves, for example) against state encroachment. This changed, however, after the Civil War, when Republicans added sweeping new federal constitutional restrictions on state behavior, most notably in the fourteenth amendment's due process and equal protection clauses.[2] According to William E. Nelson, Republican leaders insisted that the "effect of the amendment was to prevent the states from discriminating arbitrarily between different classes of citizens"; in the years immediately following passage of the amendment state judges insisted that "its 'fundamental idea and principle' was 'an impartial equality of rights.' Its 'plain and manifest intention was to make all citizens of the United States equal before the law'—to insure that '[s]pecial privileges can be conferred upon none, nor can exceptional burdens or restrictions be put upon any.'"[3] Importantly, the fourteenth amendment enabled federal courts for the first time to scrutinize the kind of day-to-day legislation that state judges had been looking at since the early nineteenth century, and as I intend to show presently, the Supreme Court justices consistently drew on the standards that had been developed by those state judges as they elaborated the boundaries of state legislative power under the fourteenth amendment.[4]

The other significant postbellum development was the maturation of capitalist forms of production and the extent to which the transformation of the economy eroded the assumption about market liberty and republican independence that justified the prohibition against factional or class politics. The hegemony of the Republican party in the national government during the years immediately following the Civil War cleared the way for the promotion of the commercial republic favored by northern industrialists and manufacturers. The war gave this effort a good start: in the mid-1860s the United States was second in the world in manufacturing output; by 1870 two out of three Americans depended for their livelihood upon employment by others; and as the century wound down, the number of nonagricultural wage earners increased more than twice as rapidly as the country's population. By 1869 the *New York Times* was noting how little workshops and small manufacturers were "far less common than they were before the war" because they had been "swallowed up" only to "become workmen on wages in the greater establishments." The unprecedented frequency of depressions dried up the source of wages for millions of people and made commercial competition more cutthroat. By the 1880s the protracted postwar deflationary crisis had resulted in a record rate of business failures and a further consolidation of large-scale enterprise. In all, the last quarter of the nineteenth century witnessed changes that crushed the Lockean state of nature that had inspired many of America's founders and replaced it with a Darwinian social order in which dependence rather than independence was becoming the more common social experience, manifesting most pointedly in a "chronic conflict between employers and workers over the costs of production";[5] that is, in widespread and violent class conflict.

A century after the "critical period" of the 1780s America was experiencing a similar yet more intense era of factional politics. At precisely the same time that the Supreme Court was incorporating the prohibition against class legislation into the fourteenth amendment it was becoming more and more clear to great numbers of people that industrialization had robbed the vision of a neutral polity of much of its attractiveness. For many groups the inescapable coercion of the market led to pleas that public power be used on their behalf to counter private power. To use David Montgomery's phrase, vulnerable classes insisted that the system move "beyond equality" as the sole standard of political legitimacy and instead renew its commitment to actively guarantee personal autonomy and social independence. Montgomery wrote that "equality before the law within a securely unified nation . . . was the political goal toward which Radicals aspired. But beyond equality lay demands of wage earners to which the equalitarian formula provided no meaningful answer, but which rebounded to confound the efforts of equality's ardent advocates. Class conflict, in other words, was the submerged shoal on which Radical dreams foundered."[6]

These two strands of postwar politics—the nationalization of a jurisprudence averse to class legislation and the intensification of class conflict—eventually collided, setting the stage for a crisis of American constitutionalism.

The Supreme Court Considers the Police Powers

Just five years after Cooley's *Constitutional Limitations* was first published, the U.S. Supreme Court had its first chance to discuss and apply the principles governing the nature of the police powers that had been forged by state judges during the preceding decades. Unfortunately, the specific issue raised in the *Slaughterhouse Cases* (1873)[7] exposed the central point of contention in what otherwise was a fairly coherent set of rules and principles: Does a monopoly created ostensibly for purposes of public health and community prosperity fall into the category of a legitimate exercise of the police power, or is it an illegitimate granting of special privilege? In 1869 the Louisiana legislature granted a slaughtering monopoly to the Crescent City Live Stock Landing and Slaughterhouse Company.[8] The legislature was hoping to reconstruct the war-shattered economy of New Orleans by making that city the commercial center through which Texas cattle would be channeled on their way to the nation's markets. In addition, the military governor of New Orleans, General Benjamin Butler, considered the monopoly a necessary feature of his larger effort to keep New Orleans free of yellow fever by putting an end to the small private butchering which had long caused serious sanitation problems on the streets of New Orleans and on the Mississippi River. The new facility was billed in the New Orleans press as a "model" industrial plant which put a premium on cleanliness. But there was another side to the story. The nearly one thousand butchers who lost their livelihood to the seventeen privileged operators protested from the beginning that the monopoly, which they estimated to be worth some $245 million over the course of the twenty-five-year period for which the charter had been conferred, had been procured through bribery by outside investors interested in gaining control of the commercial infrastructure of the South by controlling railway rights and commercial centers. (This corruption charge was later proved to the satisfaction of a Louisiana court.)[9] The dispossessed butchers acknowledged that the legislature had a legitimate interest in promoting public health and had the power to restrict business practices through the passage of legitimate public health regulations—theirs was not a laissez-faire argument. But they did insist that any such efforts could and ought to be carried out in ways consistent with prevailing principles of political legitimacy; that is, without the grant of unnecessary and corrupt special privileges.

The question before the Supreme Court, then, was whether the slaughterhouse should be treated as a legitimate promotion of the interest of the community as a whole or whether it was an illegitimate use of government power to advance the special interests of a privileged elite at the expense of the well-being of many others. The fact that features of both claims were present in the case explains why the justices divided five to four. Justice Samuel F. Miller's majority opinion began by noting that the statute was being challenged not just because it deprived "a large and a meritorious class of citizens . . . of the right to exercise their trade, the business . . . on which they depend for the support of themselves and their families," but also on the grounds that it "creat[ed] a monopoly and conferr[ed] odious and exclusive privileges upon a small number of persons at the expense of the great body of the community of New Orleans." At this early stage a majority of the justices were willing to accept that the public health argument was sufficient to allay any concerns they might have had about the propriety of the New Orleans monopoly. (This conclusion might have been influenced by Randall Hunt's argument before the justices that the dispossessed butchers had a history of arranging secret agreements to keep prices high, and that the new system was no less monopolistic than the old one. The new company did bring down the price of meat from thirty cents a pound to about ten cents, although the displaced butchers called it a short-term trick to win the favor of the people and the courts.)[10] Beyond the question of the appropriate application of the fourteenth amendment's limitations, Miller was clearly tentative about exploiting the Court's newly expanded jurisdiction to impose a federal trump on activities that had previously been the exclusive domain of local government. He wrote that overturning the Louisiana Supreme Court's decision would make the U.S. Supreme Court "a perpetual censor upon all legislation of the States," and this would be too "great a departure from the structure and spirit of our institutions" because it "radically changes the whole theory of the relations of the State and Federal governments to each other."[11]

The dissenters responded that this radical departure was precisely what was intended by the fourteenth amendment, and that given these changes the justices ought to hold the states accountable to fundamental principles of political legitimacy. The dissenters were led by Stephen J. Field, who, like Cooley, had been a Locofoco Democrat; his opinion reflected the Republican party's version of the Jacksonian vision of economic independence and, most importantly, equality before the law.[12] Like the majority, Field cited a passage from Justice Bushrod Washington's opinion in *Corfield v. Coryell* (1823) as a "sound construction" of those "privileges and immunities" that were to be protected by the fourteenth amendment. These included "protection by the government; the enjoyment of life and liberty, with the right to acquire and possess property of every kind, and to pursue and obtain happiness and safety, *subject, nevertheless, to such restraints as the government may justly prescribe for the general good of the whole.*" According to Field, this meant that the fourteenth amendment protected "the right to pursue a lawful employment in a lawful manner, *without other restraint than such as equally affects all persons. . . . This equality of right, with exemption from all disparaging and partial enactments, in the lawful pursuits of life, throughout the whole country, is the distinguishing privilege of citizens of the United States. . . .* The State may prescribe such regulations for every pursuit and calling of life as will promote the public health, secure the good order and advance the general prosperity of society, but when once prescribed, the pursuit or calling must be free to be followed by every citizen who is within the conditions designated, and will conform to the regulation."[13] (James Bradley Thayer told his students at Harvard Law School that this opinion was a sounder construction of the fourteenth amendment than the one offered by the majority.)[14]

Similarly, Justice Joseph P. Bradley, who seventeen years later would earn a reputation as a friend of the police powers by opposing the Court's review of railroad rates,[15] anchored his dissent in the proposition that "citizenship of the United States ought to be, and, according to the Constitution, is, a sure and undoubted title to equal rights in any and every State in this Union, subject to such regulations as the legislature may rightfully prescribe. If a man be denied full equality before the law, he is denied one of the essential rights of citizenship as any citizen of the United States. . . . [F]undamental rights . . . can only be interfered with . . . by lawful regulations necessary or proper for the mutual good of all." As for the monopoly, "it is onerous, unreasonable, arbitrary, and unjust. It has none of the qualities of a police regulation." The same objection did not apply to that "portion of the act which requires all slaughter-houses to be located below the city, and to be subject to inspection," which "is clearly a police regulation." However, "that portion which allows no one but the favored company to build, own, or have slaughter-houses is not a police regulation, and has not the faintest semblance of one. *It is one of those arbitrary and unjust laws made in the interest of a few scheming individuals.* . . . It seems to me strange that it can be viewed in any other light."[16]

For the *Slaughterhouse* dissenters, it was not the interference with market liberty per se that was inconsistent with the constitutional vision; zoning ordinances, health regulations, and inspection schemes were acceptable interferences. While market liberty was clearly understood to be an important value, and judicial decisions at the federal and state level would continue to celebrate that value, the constitutional question raised in these cases involved a consideration of the circumstances under which that liberty could be restricted. Was it being restricted to further the well-being of the community as a whole, or was the restriction an attempt by special interests to use the powers of government to gain an advantage over other social groups? The justices did not always agree on how this standard should be applied; nevertheless, it was this standard that organized virtually all of the late-nineteenth-century constitutional debates over the appropriate scope of police powers. For the *Slaughterhouse* majority the monopoly furthered the well-being of the community as a whole; for the dissenters, it was a corrupt attempt by powerful groups to use the public power to advance their special interests at the expense of others.

It should be recognized that even among the tentative *Slaughterhouse* majority there was agreement that the fourteenth amendment imposed some limitations on state government—Miller noted that the existence of a due process clause in the federal Constitution that applied to the states meant that the "amendment may place the restraining power over the States in this matter in the hands of the Federal government"—and that the police powers were something other than the use of public power to service particular groups or interests.[17] One year after *Slaugh-*

terhouse, when the question of the privileged use of the police power was raised in *Loan Association v. City of Topeka* (1874) without the additional confound of the public health argument, the Court *unanimously* held that an act authorizing towns and municipalities to issue bonds or lend their credit to aid "the enterprises of others which were not of a public character" was a "perversion" of the legislative power, which "does not extend to aid private objects."[18]

This same concern with distinguishing public from private legislation and special interests from the general welfare was evident in the Court's discussion of a similar issue a few years later. The question to be decided in *Munn v. Illinois* (1877) was not whether a legislature had any power to regulate private industries such as grain elevators (for example, by setting standards for their construction or their location); more specifically, the issue was whether the legislature could set rates, a power that, like taxation, raised the specter of class politics. The plaintiffs, citing not only Cooley but also *Wally's Heirs v. Kennedy*, argued in their briefs that the Illinois scheme was in fact "class legislation" because it was passed for the benefit of "one class of citizens" and required a "gratuitous service" to them from another class, in violation of the "maxim in constitutional law" that "those who make the laws 'are to be governed by promulgated, established laws, not to be varied in particular cases, but to have one rule for rich and poor, for the favorite at court and the countryman at plough.'" They warned that this practice would establish the principle that "when capital is in control, the price of labor will be fixed; when labor holds the power, the investment of the capitalists must suffer."[19]

In his opinion upholding the regulation, Chief Justice Morrison R. Waite emphasized the long-standing principle that a person's rights and liberties are subordinate to the general welfare. "When one becomes a member of society, he necessarily parts with some rights and privileges which, as an individual not affected by his relations to others, he might retain." It is, he wrote, "the very essence of government" to regulate "the conduct of its citizens one towards another, and the manner in which each shall use his own property, when such regulation becomes necessary for the general good." It was on the basis of this principle that legislatures established the common practices of regulating, for example, the weight and quality of bread and the rates charged by owners of private wharves, chimney sweeps, innkeepers, hackney carriages, cartmen and wagoners, and auctioneers. Of course, this principle did not

justify *all* interferences with liberty or property; "[u]nder some circumstances" statutes regulating the use of property may violate due process,
"but not under all." (Waite did make it clear that on the question of "the
propriety of legislative interference *within the scope of legislative power*,
the legislature is the exclusive judge.") The standard that distinguished
legitimate from illegitimate regulations was found in the common-law
doctrine that "when private property is 'affected with a public interest, it
ceases to be *juris privati* only' "; this occurs when property is "used in a
manner to make it of public consequence, and affect the community at
large." Tying the legitimacy of rate regulation (price-fixing) to this standard would preempt the unleashing of the kind of factional free-for-all
about which the petitioners warned, where businesses, workers, and
consumers would vie to use this legislative power to gain "unnatural"
advantages over their competitors. Given this standard, the question
before the Court was "whether the warehouse of these plaintiffs in
error . . . are within the operation of the principle," and to this Waite
responded, "It is difficult to see why, if the common carrier, or the miller,
or the baker, or the cartman, or the hackney-coachman" fall within its
operation, "these plaintiffs in error do not." In his dissent, Justice Field
did not challenge the principle that state power could be used to regulate
the prices set by owners of businesses that affected the public interest. He
merely disagreed with the Court's judgment that the defendants' business was clothed with a public interest and expressed his concern that if
this principle were not limited in its application it might invite interference with a person's liberty "to act in such manner, not inconsistent
with the equal rights of others, as his judgment may dictate for the
promotion of his happiness," including the freedom "to pursue such
callings and avocations as may be most suitable to develop his capacities,
and give to them their highest enjoyment."[20]

The constitutional mandate separating public power from private or
class benefit was made even more explicit in the 1880s. In the *Civil Rights
Cases* (1883), Bradley went out of his way to make the point that "many
wrongs may be obnoxious to the prohibitions of the Fourteenth Amendment which are not, in any just sense, incidents or elements of slavery";
for example, "what is called class legislation . . . would be obnoxious to
the prohibitions of the Fourteenth Amendment, . . . [which] extends its
protections to races and classes, and prohibits any State legislation which
has the effect of denying to any race or class, or to any individual, the
equal protection of the laws."[21] When Louisiana moved to a system of

general incorporation and thus eradicated the special privilege represented in *Slaughterhouse*, the justices in *Butchers' Union v. Crescent City* (1883) rejected a challenge based on the protections of the federal Constitution, just as Taney had done almost half a century earlier when he permitted the legislature to remove the corporate privilege in *Charles River Bridge*. In a separate concurring opinion, Field reasserted his belief that the earlier monopoly was not a legitimate exercise of the police powers and that "[the fourteenth amendment was] designed to prevent all discriminating legislation for the benefit of some to the disparagement of others. . . . [States] can now, as then, legislate to promote health, good order and peace, to develop their resources, enlarge their industries, and advance their prosperity. It only inhibits discriminating and partial enactments, favoring some to the impairment of the rights of others. The principal, if not the sole, purpose of its prohibitions is to prevent any arbitrary invasion by State authority of the rights of person and property, and to secure to every one the right to pursue his happiness unrestrained, except by just, equal, and impartial laws."[22] In a separate concurring opinion joined by Justices John M. Harlan and William B. Woods—both appointed in the interim after *Slaughterhouse*—Bradley also looked back to the earlier decision to reassert his belief that while the provision in the old act prescribing the location of slaughterhouses "was a police regulation, proper and necessary," the "exclusive right given to the company had nothing of a police regulation about it whatever. It was the creation of a mere monopoly, and nothing else."[23]

The following year, in *Barbier v. Connolly* (1884), a unanimous Court led by Field upheld a San Francisco municipal ordinance which prohibited washing and ironing in public laundries between ten o'clock at night and six in the morning. In a fairly brief opinion, the Court noted that the equal protection clause "undoubtedly intended not only that there should be no arbitrary deprivation of life or liberty, or arbitrary spoliation of property, but that equal protection and security should be given to all under like circumstances in the enjoyment of their personal and civil rights." However, in this case, even though the legislature was interfering with entrepreneurial liberty, "all persons engaged in the same business within it are treated alike; are subject to the same restrictions and are entitled to the same privileges under similar conditions." This was significant because it made it unlikely that the law was designed to extend special advantages to some businesses or operators by disadvantaging others. The justices did make it clear, however, that while "special burdens are often necessary for general benefits" involving legitimate health and safety measures (like fire prevention), "class legislation, discriminating against some and favoring others, is prohibited" by the fourteenth amendment.[24]

This admonition took center stage in a similar case two years later; the Court's treatment of the case is instructive in helping us understand the distinctions being drawn being legitimate and illegitimate exercises of the police powers. *Yick Wo v. Hopkins* (1886) involved a challenge to a San Francisco ordinance that required all persons who wanted to operate a laundry in a building not constructed of brick or stone to first obtain the consent of the board of supervisors. Because it had been demonstrated that the board of supervisors refused to grant permission to Chinese applicants and that the penalties associated with operating without a license were levied only against Chinese operators, the case is usually treated as a discussion of how a law that is neutral on its face may still violate the equal protection clause if it is applied in a discriminatory fashion. But Justice Stanley Matthews's opinion actually focused on a problem with the ordinance itself, which set up no general standards to determine who would or would not receive permission and therefore gave the board of supervisors complete discretion as to whom they would reward or punish. "There is nothing in the ordinances which points to such a regulation of the business of keeping and conducting laundries. They seem intended to confer, and actually do confer, not a discretion to be exercised upon a consideration of the circumstances of each case, but a naked and arbitrary power to give or withhold consent, not only as to places, but as to persons." Unlike the situation in *Barbier*, the ordinance in *Yick Wo* did not "prescribe a rule and conditions for the regulation of the use of property for laundry purposes, to which all similarly situated may conform"; instead it arbitrarily divided those who operated laundries in wood buildings "into two classes," distinguished not by some talent or characteristic related to public health and safety but rather by the consequence that one class was "permitted to pursue their industry by the mere will and consent of the supervisors" and the other was not.[25] The governing standard being used by the Court in this case was summarized by Richard S. Kay: "It is not the presence of race but the absence of justification which is paramount. . . . This is one application of the general proposition that the mere preference of one group over another, that is, legislation based only on favoritism or on spite, is outside the scope of proper governmental activity."[26]

In cases involving legislation that singled out certain classes or groups for special treatment, the justices attempted to maintain a distinction between those "special burdens that were necessary for general benefits" and "class legislation that discriminated against some and favored others." This distinction could be meaningful only if the justices were able to consider whether the general benefit being asserted was promoted by the classification scheme adopted; or, to put it another way, the justices needed to be able to consider whether the imposition of a special burden (or benefit) could be better explained as an example of illegitimate factional politics or as a necessary special burden. The judicial exercise in *Yick Wo* is a good example of the kind of scrutiny necessitated by the constitutional prohibition against partial or unequal legislation. The government asserted an interest in making sure that laundries operated in a way that did not endanger the community as a whole (by burning down the city, for example)—clearly, this was considered a valid, or "reasonable," police power concern. At the same time, constitutional ideology directed judges to be on guard against the possibility that factions might attempt to use the powers of government to advance their "arbitrary" private interests at the expense of others (such as an interest in getting rid of unwanted competition in the laundry business). How was a judge to differentiate between these two cases? One way might be to look more carefully at the legislative scheme being used and to ask whether that scheme was more consistent with acceptable concerns or more consistent with the unacceptable explanations. For example, a regulation that prohibited laundries from operating in wood buildings or that zoned laundries into isolated areas of a city would make sense in light of the community's general interest in not burning down. But a regulation that permitted only whites to run laundries or that required only some laundry operators to abide by burdensome safety regulations would seem more consistent with explanations rooted in factional politics. In *Yick Wo*, the judges concluded with good reason that the particular scheme set up by the supervisors made more sense as an attempt to exercise "arbitrary" power—that is, power based simply on favoritism or spite, and not on any "good reason" related to the advancement of the community's general interest in promoting concerns shared by all, such as health, safety, or morality; the scheme was not "reasonably" related to the advancement of the asserted community interest.[27]

In the language of late-nineteenth-century constitutional law, *arbitrary* was quite often the word of choice used to characterize factional politics; *reasonableness* was the concept that embodied the system's tolerance of class-neutral policies that advanced a public purpose. As Harlan explained in *Mugler v. Kansas* (1887), "There are, of necessity, limits beyond which legislation cannot rightfully go. . . . The courts are not bound by mere forms, nor are they to be misled by mere pretences. They are at liberty—indeed, are under a solemn duty—to look at the substance of things, whenever they enter upon the inquiry whether the legislature has transcended the limits of its authority. If, therefore, a statute purporting to have been enacted to protect the public health, the public morals, or the public safety, has no real or substantial relation to those objects, or is a palpable invasion of rights secured by the fundamental law, it is the duty of the courts to so adjudge, and thereby give effect to the Constitution." As for how to best protect the people's fundamental rights: "Those rights are best secured, in our government, by the observance, upon the part of all, of such regulations as are established by competent authority to promote the common good."[28] Harlan's statement is not a departure from previous holdings; it is, rather, a reassertion of the adjudicative task undertaken by the Supreme Court since *Slaughterhouse*, and by many state courts well before that.

One year later the justices had an opportunity to examine another act designed ostensibly to promote public health. In 1885 the Pennsylvania legislature passed a law that prohibited the manufacture and sale of oleomargarine—an artificial substitute for butter, derived from animal or vegetable fats, that had been invented in 1869 and had gone into production in the United States in 1874. (A version of the law passed two years earlier was entitled "an act for the protection of dairymen," but in 1885 that was changed to "an act for the protection of the public health and to prevent adulteration of dairy products and fraud in the sale thereof.") Pennsylvania was just one of twenty-two states that by the mid-1880s had assaulted this inexpensive, spoilage-resistant substitute for butter through prohibitions, discriminatory taxes, or unattractive coloring or labeling requirements. In 1886 a federal law would subject the product to a high licensing and manufacturing tax.[29] Proponents of these oleomargarine laws often used the argument that they were necessary to protect the public health. When it became increasingly clear that there was nothing unhealthy about oleomargarine (which simply had less butterine and more milk and cream than butter), an alternative justification was offered: the prohibitions were necessary to protect consumers from being defrauded by those who would try to sell oleo-margarine as real butter. However, opponents of the legislation argued that these laws were intended only to protect dairy interests from effective competition. They charged that the laws were protectionism pure and simple, enacted only because of the political influence of large dairy interests. The *Nation* wrote that "the oleomargarine law in this State had its origin in the desire of the 'honest farmer' for protection against the 'poor man's butter.'"[30] The plaintiff in error argued in the brief presented to the justices that "stripped of its pretenses and shown in its nakedness, this Act, then, is an Act favoring dairy butter and those engaged in its production and sale, at the expense of Oleomargarine butter and those engaged in its manufacturing and sale. . . . Is not this as decidedly class legislation as Yick Woo's case [*sic*]. Does not the State of Pennsylvania deny to dealers in oleomargarine butter the right it secures to the dealer in dairy butter?"[31] The state responded that the law was a general law applicable to all persons in the state and did not violate the scope of the police powers for "it does not attempt to take from one individual what is his own and give it to another."[32]

Harlan's majority opinion in *Powell v. Pennsylvania* (1888) announced that the case was "governed by the principles announced in *Mugler v. Kansas*" and upheld the prohibition on the grounds that it was a good-faith effort "to protect the public health and to prevent the adulteration of dairy products." The statute also placed "under the same restrictions, and subjects to like penalties and burdens, all who manufacture, or sell, or offer for sale, or keep in possession to sell, the articles embraced by its prohibitions; thus recognizing and preserving the principle of equality among those engaged in the same business."[33] Harlan's opinion, then, reflected the unwillingness of a Court majority to challenge general enactments that were justified on the basis of public health concerns. But Field, the old Locofoco Democrat, was not as passive as his brethren when faced with a claim of factional politics, and his lone dissent in *Powell* is instructive as to the kinds of concerns that were embedded in his constitutional ideology. Field's complaint was not that the legislature had interfered in the free market per se; rather, his opinion focused on the judicial responsibility to check the evils of class politics, of interferences in the market that were inspired more by factional hostility than by a transcendent community interest. His dissent was anchored in the same sensibilities that had led the New York Court of Appeals to strike down an oleomargarine law a few years earlier. Field quoted approvingly from the decision in *People v. Marx*:[34]

Who will have the temerity to say that these constitutional principles are not violated by an enactment which absolutely prohibits an important branch of industry for the sole reason that it competes with another, and may reduce the price of an article of food for the human race? Measures of this kind are dangerous even to their promoters. If the argument of the respondent in support of the absolute power of the legislature to prohibit one branch of industry for the purpose of protecting another, with which it competes, can be sustained, why could not the oleomargarine manufacturers, should they obtain sufficient power to influence or control the legislative councils, prohibit the manufacture or sale of dairy products?[35]

To prevent this imagined horror, Field argued that courts needed to exercise greater care to ensure that acts ostensibly related to the health, safety, or morality of the community in fact advanced these goals. And while he alone held this position on the Court, he did find support from other commentators. The *Albany Law Journal* wrote that the Supreme Court's decision "denies to the citizen the privilege of a cheap substitute for butter, although honestly and openly sold. . . . We see no reason why the consumer should be compelled to pay a farmer forty cents for butter when he can get a satisfactory substitute for twenty. . . . [We] will not tamely submit to such petty and tyrannical interference, under the pretense of paternal tenderness, for the emolument of a class of producers."[36] Around the same time that *Powell* was handed down, an article in *Political Science Quarterly* discussed the recent passage of a federal oleomargarine law, which the author described as "protection run mad." He based this conclusion on his review of the congressional debates, which were filled with statements like "We propose, if you please, to give incidental protection to the agricultural industries of the country"; and "The manufacture of oleomargarine and butterine has not only threatened damage to the butter and dairy interests of Iowa and all Western states, but has already resulted in serious loss"; and "I, sir, am in favor of protecting the dairy interests of America from competition with the manufacture of oleomargarine."[37] The availability of oleomargarine as an alternative to more expensive butter was also one of the issues that labor unions used in determining which legislative candidates they would support.[38] On this issue, at least, Field's jurisprudence seemed quite consistent with the interests of American workers.

But the same could not be said about labor's more common experiences with the ideology of political neutrality.

Industrialization, Class Conflict, and the Neutral State

Despite the conspicuous presence of some labor reformers in the Republican party coalition, the debates among party leaders over postwar political economy excluded labor's growing reservations about the neutral state.[39] In the late 1860s and early 1870s Republicans and Democrats argued over the size of the tariff and the pace governing the contraction of the currency, not over the use of public power to intervene in social conflicts produced by market relations.[40] Gradually, the growing power of capital validated the fears of men like Ignatius Donnelly, who had "interpreted the war as the final fulfillment of a classless democracy of free and equal producers" and was "horrified as he watched his Republican Party, the instrument which had purged feudal aristocracy from the land, become the vehicle for the expansion of what he saw as a new corporate feudal aristocracy" organized around the "great serpent" of "finance capitalism."[41]

This serpent, hatched in war,[42] became enormously powerful very quickly. Within a few decades industrial and agricultural productivity in the United States grew by roughly fourfold. This social and economic revolution was made possible by innovations introduced by a new generation of industrial leaders—men such as Andrew Carnegie, John D. Rockefeller, J. P. Morgan, Thomas A. Scott, Gustavus Swift, and Franklin P. Gowen—and involving new forms of production (e.g., more specialized divisions of labor, assembly lines, piecework, "scientific management" of labor discipline), sources of power (steam, electricity), marketing structures (like I. M. Singer and Company's distribution network, which handled everything from consumer credit to repairs), networks of transportation and distribution (e.g., the proliferation of railroad routes in general, railroad refrigeration for the meat business in particular), and strategies of financing costly new technology (such as the trust and other practices involving holdings and mergings). The indexes of industrialization indicated an increased output of iron and steel, an accelerated exploitation of natural resources, a multiplication of capital investments in industry, and the steady movement of foreign immigrants, southern blacks, and farmers into the cities and manufacturing centers.[43]

Industrialization imposed brutalizing burdens on masses of people at the same time it showered unprecedented splendors on a select few.[44] Speculative panics, business failures, and substantial unemployment occurred with unprecedented frequency, most notably from 1873 to 1878, 1882 to 1885, and 1893 to 1897. The hard, deflationary ("constitutional") currency fought for by conservatives after the war—represented in the passage of the Resumption Act of 1875, which authorized gold payments on greenbacks and other paper notes in 1879—gradually, and on occasion violently, pushed down wages and agricultural prices and ensured that investment capital would be available only to the select few who could extract new wealth most "efficiently." This resulted in intensified battles between wage earners seeking a greater share of the wealth being produced and owners seeking lower labor costs per unit of production. The latter achieved their goal not only through the innovations in production alluded to above but also through the importation of cheap immigrant labor, the use of convicts and child labor, and routine acts of violence against workers who tried to empower themselves through collective action. The success of financial and industrial elites is evident when one notes the enormous disparities in the distribution of wealth that arose during the Gilded Age. According to the 1890 census, 9 percent of the nation's families controlled 81 percent of the nation's wealth. The 1900 report of the U.S. Industrial Commission concluded that between 60 and 88 percent of the American people could be classified as poor or very poor.[45] New forms of production and labor-saving technological innovations disenfranchised and impoverished traditionally autonomous producers; they also imposed a physical burden on the growing class of unskilled wage earners. It was not uncommon for the fiery furnaces of the steel mills to claim two hundred deaths a year in a single factory. By the 1890s, railroads alone were killing 6,000 to 7,000 and injuring 30,000 to 45,000 people a year; a third of those killed and three quarters of those injured were employees.[46]

The prewar Republican party's plan for the prevention of the establishment of these "European" conditions in the United States was not the abandonment of the ethos of "equality before the law" but rather "free soil," the increased availability of the freehold for those who sought escape from environments of urban or commercial dependency. Obviously, this Jeffersonian safety valve failed. In 1866, 8 million acres of Illinois land and 12 million acres of Iowa land were held by speculators. Only 3.5 percent of the territory west of the Mississippi was settled under the Homestead Act; 84 percent of new farms in the late nineteenth century came not from homesteading but from the subdivision of older private holdings or by purchase from railroads and speculators—the western railroads received over 180 million acres from federal and state governments, more than twice the number of Homestead Act grants. Between 1870 and 1880 the number of farms increased by 1,348,922; but for every farm owned by an independent homesteader there were 5 controlled by capitalists and speculators.[47] The corruption embedded in these transactions came to be represented in the Credit Mobilier scandal and the reputation acquired by the General Land Office.[48] By the 1880s Josiah Strong warned that "when the supply [of western land] is exhausted . . . we shall enter upon a new era, and shall more rapidly approximate European conditions of life." It would not be long before Frederick Jackson Turner would be writing about the significance of the frontier in American history and how the closing of the frontier marked the end of a long tradition in liberal-republican ideology that promised Americans personal autonomy and social independence.[49]

In 1883 Henry George told a Senate committee investigating the relations between labor and capital that "the inventions and improvements of all kinds that have done so much to change all the aspects of production, and which are still going on, tend to require a greater and greater division of labor, the employment of more and more capital, and to make it more and more difficult for a man who has nothing but his labor to become his own employer, or to rise to a position of independence in his craft or occupation." He noted that "the old-fashioned shoemaker, having learned his trade and purchased his kit of tools, was his own master. . . . But now the shoemaker must find a great factory, and an employer with a large amount of capital. Without such an employer he is utterly helpless: He cannot make a shoe." (George also argued that the monopolization of productive land allowed capital to keep wages low. He told the Blair committee, "Where there is free access to the soil, wages in any employment cannot sink lower than that which, upon an average, a man can make by applying himself to the soil. . . . When the soil is monopolized . . . then wages may be driven to the lowest point on which the laborer can live.")[50]

The point, as summarized by Eric Foner, is that industrialization "raised troubling questions about the continued validity of free-labor axioms: that liberty rested on ownership of productive property, and that working for wages was merely a temporary resting place on the road to economic autonomy."[51] As early as 1867 the editor of the *Nation*, Edwin L. Godkin, was warning that "larger and larger masses of the population" were each year being "reduced to the condition of hired laborers, . . . subjected to factory discipline, . . . legally free while socially bound."[52] According to William Forbath, "Just as the capitalist strove to grind down wages, so he abused the 'advances of civilization,' new technologies and 'labor-saving devices,' dissolving skilled occupations into unskilled machine-tending tasks only in order to 'cheapen' labor further, tearing workers' children from school and demanding longer and longer hours of 'mindless toil' that deprived workingmen of the time to educate themselves and participate in public affairs. . . . Progress [under capitalism] seemed to have the ironic consequence of producing its opposite, more 'dependence,' more 'ignorance,' and more 'grinding poverty' among each succeeding generation of workers."[53]

The response to the conditions created by industrialization took many forms. Books such as Henry George's *Progress and Poverty* (1879), Laurence Gronlund's *Cooperative Commonwealth* (1884), Edward Bellamy's *Looking Backward* (1888), and Henry Demarest Lloyd's *Wealth against Commonwealth* (1894) all decried exploitation of the vulnerable by the powerful and explored ways to recover a harmonious social order from the ashes of class conflict. But the most visible manifestation of the response to these conditions was a proliferation of collective action— that is, factional or class politics—on the part of vulnerable groups seeking protection in numbers. Samuel P. Hays referred to it as an "organizational revolution" that "revealed the degree to which industrialism had shifted the context of economic decisions from personal relationships among individuals to a struggle for power among well-organized groups"; another historian of the period, John A. Garraty, emphasized the "greatly expanded reliance by individuals upon group activities."[54]

A significant part of this organizational revolution was the surge of trade union activity. Drawing on the tradition of artisan independence,[55] the purpose of trade unions was to establish and protect traditional work rules and standard wages. As early as 1866 the National Labor Union (NLU) was established to integrate the profusion of workingmen's societies that had sprung up across the country; its principal political goal was the passage of eight-hour laws.[56] By 1872 the eight-hours movement was in full swing, attracting sixty thousand New York City workingmen at one rally. However, given the historical definition of general welfare since the creation of the American Republic, it was exceedingly difficult for labor reformers to come up with an authoritative defense of an eight-hour law which protected it from the charge that it was corrupt class legislation. Ira Steward tried to expose the sham of equal liberty in the marketplace and win support for an eight-hour law on the grounds that it would not only increase wages but would also reduce unemployment, enhance consumer demand, stimulate economic growth, and make workers more informed and effective citizens. But they were up against the resistance of contemporary writers such as Karl Heinzen, who argued that working-class movements were "inherently reactionary" since they "revived the spirit of special interest." His advice was for workers to "abandon their pressure for wage increases and turn instead to the Radical's pursuit of equality before the law."[57] When union organizers and strikers argued that workers had to defend themselves against the power of big business, they were told that "if capital has gained an advantage by special legislation, this is to be counterbalanced, not by special legislation to favor the other side . . . but by earnest united protests against all special legislation."[58]

In light of this ideological barrier to the use of state power, workers' resistance to the emergence of a Darwinian social order quickly took the form of a return to the traditions of artisan republicanism; that is, self-help movements organized around a sense of craft pride, a shared faith in the virtues of producer classes, and a commitment to the moral economy so as to protect the personal development and social independence of their members. This was the vision that inspired the Noble Order of the Knights of Labor, an organization whose members "cast themselves as the last, best defenders of a true republic of individual liberties."[59] The Noble Order was founded in 1869 by Uriah S. Stephens, a tailor who favored a cooperative, craft-based approach to labor's problems. (Only gamblers, liquor dealers, lawyers, and bankers were excluded from membership.) The union's aims were "to make industrial and moral worth, not wealth, the true standard of individual and national greatness. . . . To secure to the toilers a proper share of the wealth they create; more of the leisure that rightfully belongs to them; more of the rights and privileges and emoluments of the world." The order's legislative program included "recognition of worker organizations, improved health and safety standards, access to public lands, mandatory arbitration of labor disputes, protective lien laws, elimination of convict and child labor, collection of labor statistics, imposition of a graduated income tax, implementation of postal savings exchanges, and the nationalization of transport and communications." Ultimately "it hoped to replace the wage system with a 'cooperative industrial system' through the creation of producers' and consumers' cooperatives."[60]

The movement grew steadily during the depression of the 1870s, and when Terence Powderly took over as grand master in 1878 the Knights had a membership of 50,000. Powderly shaped the group into a political force; under his leadership the Noble Order helped secure passage of the Chinese Exclusion Act of 1882 and later the Interstate Commerce Act and the Sherman Anti-Trust Act. In 1882 Powderly explained that his association desired "the abrogation of all laws that do not bear equally upon capital and labor; the substitution of arbitration for strikes; the prohibition of child labor; to secure for both sexes equal pay for equal work; the reduction of the hours of labor to eight per day . . . ; to prevail upon governments to establish a purely national circulating medium, issued directly to the people, without the intervention of any system of banking corporations . . . ; the establishment of cooperative institutions, productive and distributive; the reserving of the public lands—the heritage of the people—for the actual settler. NOT ANOTHER ACRE FOR RAILROADS OR CORPORATIONS." Powderly ended this article by noting that "in order to compel politicians to perform their duty faithfully, the people must be educated up to a standard high enough to enable them to judge for themselves whether a law be passed in the interests of a class or for the public good. *Labor, all its rights—capital, all its rights—no special laws or privileges for either, but 'equal and exact justice for all.'* "[61]

The Knights became particularly popular among American workers "when in 1885 shopworkers on southwestern railroads won a strike against Jay Gould, one of the most notorious railroad capitalists in the country." The year after Gould sat down with the shopworkers' representatives (in a move that was more of a tactical retreat than a defeat) union membership jumped from 104,000 to 702,000 members.[62] But the momentum did not last long. Soon thereafter Gould precipitated the "Great Southwest Strike" by firing a union spokesman for missing work while attending a union meeting which he had been given permission to attend; the striking workers were crushed. In 1886 the Noble Order was caught up in the hysteria over the Haymarket tragedy;[63] by 1890 the order had declined to 100,000 members and continued to decline steadily after that. The institutional heir of the national labor movement was the American Federation of Labor (AFL),organized in December 1886 as an outgrowth of Samuel Gompers's Federation of Organized Trades and Labor Unions, which had been formed in 1881. Gompers's group "disengaged [workers] from the tradition of labor republicanism . . . [and] detached labor's agenda from any vision of change for the nation as a whole. . . . [They] constructed the first serious defense of American trade unionism based on the acceptance of individualist and market-oriented assumptions."[64] (The AFL entered the twentieth century with half a million members and was instrumental in achieving the eight-hour day, the five- and six-day week, factory inspection, workmen's compensation, compulsory education, and an outlawing of the injunction. Its legacy was embodied in President Woodrow Wilson's National War Labor Board, which promised federal protection for the right to organize and national standards of wages and hours; and in the Wagner Act, which reduced the interests of labor to "the right to organize and bargain collectively," thus effectively ending the vision for "a universal eight-hour day, nationalization of the railroads, cooperative forms of production, in short, for a redistribution of power within the Republic.")[65]

The cooperative vision of the Knights of Labor was shared by farmers struggling to break free from a national credit system that did not service their seasonal needs and a "crop-lien" system that made them dependent on the local "furnishing merchants" (who had first claim on the fruits of a year's toil or, when prices plummeted and accounts could not be squared on "settlin' day," first claim on the land). Cooperative "alliances" sprang up in the South and West during the late 1870s and 1880s: farmers created "trade store systems" so that alliance members could contract exclusively with one merchant and practiced "bulking," or the large-scale sale of cotton with previously contacted buyers, in order to circumvent the furnishing merchant. In 1886 the alliancemen advanced a plan at their state convention in Cleburne, Texas, that among other things called for a federally administered national banking system that would support a more "democratic" flexible currency. But the "Cleburne Demands" were denounced as fostering "the spirit of class legislation, class aggrandizement, class exclusiveness, and class proscription. The discontented classes are told," wrote the Dallas *News*, "and are only too ready for the most part to believe, that the remedy is more class legislation, more government, more paternalism, more State socialism." The next year Charles W. Macune called for the creation of a central statewide Farmers' Alliance Exchange as a giant cooperative to oversee the marketing of crops and serve as the central purchasing medium for Texas farmers. Later he would work for the creation of a system of federal warehouses and would propose his "sub-treasury system," which requested that the federal government underwrite farmers' cooperatives by issuing greenbacks; but this was also denounced as "class legislation."

These efforts all represented attempts to circumvent patterns of social dependency established by the market power of furnishing merchants, wholesale houses, cotton buyers, bankers, grain elevator companies, railroads, land companies, and livestock commission agencies. But, as Lawrence Goodwyn has told us in compelling detail, against the coercive power of the state and the cultural hegemony of dominant classes, the determination of small farmers, stump speakers, and some sympathetic newspaper editors to transform existing social relations was simply insufficient.[66]

One can appreciate the unprecedented level of collective action in the final quarter of the century by cataloging the institutional histories of organizations like the NLU, the Knights, the Grangers, the Farm and Labor parties, and the Populists.[67] But these groups represented only the most formal expression of the social significance of industrialization. The generation of the Gilded Age also bore witness to the "Great Up-heaval"—the often spontaneous and inordinately violent clashes that erupted between labor and capital. In order to appreciate the social context of late-nineteenth-century constitutionalism it is important to be reminded of the frequency and intensity of these unprecedented conflicts. This background is particularly important if we are to understand why state and federal judges and legal commentators almost universally chose to treat labor legislation as illegitimate "class" politics—particularly when it appeared to respond to the demands of strong unions, like those in the mining or bakery industries—and not as reasonably related to the general welfare.

Some of the class warfare of the period was precipitated by labor. For example, the miners' group known as the Molly Maguires, born in the unsafe and unsanitary conditions of the anthracite mines of Pennsylvania, were inspired by the brutality of the secret and sinister Irish terrorist organization from which they took their name; their tactics included the use of murder and intimidation against workers, contractors, bosses, and strikebreakers. (The Mollies were finally exposed after a coal boss hired a Pinkerton detective to infiltrate their inner circle; it resulted in ten members being hanged on June 21, 1877.) But quite apart from the violence of the Molly Maguires, "the major political reality in these years was the extraordinary repression visited upon organized workers by employers' associations, with the cooperation of the courts, state legislatures, and, increasingly, the federal government."[68]

The pattern was first evident during two weeks in July 1877, just months after the major parties had averted a civil war over the disputed election of 1876 with the Compromise of 1877, giving the Republicans the presidency and southern support for their policy of rapid industrialization in exchange for southern internal improvements and an end to the federal commitment to the protection of black civil rights in the South.[69] Not long after President Rutherford P. Hayes ordered federal troops out of the South a group of workers walked out on the Baltimore and Ohio Railroad. Their union demanded better working conditions and protested recent 10 percent cuts in pay, the second round of wage cuts since the depression began. The strike quickly spread to other railroads from New England to the Mississippi and from the Atlantic to the Pacific; more impressively, a new phenomenon, sympathy strikes, engulfed industry across the country.[70] In response to these events, federal and state governments demonstrated little subtlety. Two days after the Baltimore and Ohio Railroad workers went on strike, on July 16, 1877, President Hayes had his secretary of war send federal troops to break up a strike on the B & O railroad at Martinsburg, West Virginia. On July 20, nine strikers were killed in Baltimore when the state militia fired point blank at a crowd moving toward the railway station, which was in the hands of angry strikers; in the four days of rioting that followed, fifty more people were killed. A railroad sustained $10 million in damages after a riot broke out on July 21 in Pittsburgh (where railway property was concentrated) when the Pennsylvania militia attempted to clear a street of strikers and sympathetic supporters. On July 26, 1877, a Chicago strike turned into a massacre when an unorganized gathering was attacked by police aided by cavalry; nineteen people were killed.[71]

This pattern intensified during the 1880s and 1890s. There were 477 work stoppages in 1881; that number increased to 1,897 by 1890. Omaha labor disturbances in 1881 brought out four companies of infantry. Illinois quarrymen in 1886 were fired upon by sheriffs' forces as they tried to drive away scab replacements.[72] On May 1, 1886, about fifty thousand workers representing the Knights of Labor, the Black International anarchists, the Socialist Union, and the trade unions joined in strikes and demonstrations for an eight-hour day. On May 3, 1886, an attack by a crowd on strikebreakers at the McCormick Reaper Manufacturing Company (which had been on strike since February) drew police fire; six people were killed and at least a dozen were wounded. Anarchist August Spies took advantage of the crowd's feelings and called a meeting at Chicago's Haymarket Square to protest the police action.

Leaflets passed out in advance of the meeting were headlined "Revenge! Workingmen! To Arms!" About fourteen hundred people gathered at Haymarket on May 4. As policemen began to break up the crowd a bomb was thrown in their midst, killing seven officers and severely wounding fifty. The sense of forboding that gripped the dominant culture (and the popular imagination) in the aftermath of the Haymarket tragedy seemed so reasonable to so many people precisely because recent history had prepared them for the specter of class warfare.

By the early 1890s employers had become more expert at battling labor, particularly in their use of sympathetic lockouts and the injunction to counter sympathy strikes and boycotts. In 1889 and 1890 the percentage of strikes lost was about 40 percent; in 1891 and 1892 this percentage rose to about 54 percent.[73] But the battles continued. In January 1890 workers from the weakening Knights of Labor and from the burgeoning American Federation of Labor formed the United Mine Workers to battle the scandalous working conditions in the mines. It was not easy. In July 1891, in Briceville, Tennessee, two hundred convicts were used to break a miners' strike; in April 1892 miners in the Coeur D'Alene silver mines in Idaho started a three-month strike that amounted to a mini guerilla war. A few months later strikes again broke out across the country. The most significant was called against Carnegie's Homestead Mill in Pennsylvania, which had cut wages and refused to recognize the Amalgamated Association of Iron and Steel Workers. On July 6 some five thousand Homestead Steel workers battled three hundred Pinkertons brought in to break the strike; twenty people were killed and hundreds were wounded. On July 9 Governor Robert Pattison ordered seven thousand state troopers to the mill, causing President Grover Cleveland ironically to note the "tender mercy the workingman receives from those made selfish and sordid by unjust government favoritism."[74] By July 15 the mill was back in operation with strikebreakers under military guard. The strike lasted five months and the workers gained nothing.

The depression brought on by the stock market crash in June 1893 was the most severe in history and predictably was followed by some of the most serious labor-capital conflicts to date. On April 5, 1894, fierce riots broke out among miners striking in Connellsville, Pennsylvania. Eleven men were killed. On April 20, 1894, 136,000 desperate coal miners struck at Columbus, Ohio. On April 24, another in a series of mine accidents at Franklin, Washington, killed thirty-seven men. On

April 30, 1894, Jacob Sechler Coxey led four hundred people from Ohio to Washington, D.C., on a march to protest unemployment. When "Coxey's Army" arrived, Coxey and his lieutenants were arrested for trespassing on the grass, and the army disbanded. On May 11, 1894, workers at the Pullman Palace Car Company called a strike in response to the company's decision to reduce wages without reducing rents in its model workers' homes or prices in its company stores. The Railway Managers' Association refused to negotiate; instead, they hired 3,600 deputy marshals to break the strike. On July 6, two men were killed and several were injured as strikers were fired upon by troops in Kensington near Chicago; strikers and sympathetic unemployed workers responded by rioting and causing some $3 million in damage to railway property. In September 1894, twelve thousand tailors went on strike in New York City to protest sweating and piecework. Pennsylvania had fifty-two major strikes in 1894, twice as many as in 1892, none of which was successful. By the end of 1894, three quarters of a million workers had been on strike, more than 8 percent of the employed wage earners in the country; two million persons were unemployed in a total nonagricultural labor force of fifteen million.[75]

Political and industry leaders responded in other ways besides violence and the force of law to try to contain or put an end to class conflict and factional politics. Some bones were thrown to workers—Congress created a Bureau of Labor Statistics and later a non-cabinet level Department of Labor; it also established Labor Day. Party leaders attempted to contain these movements by channeling their political aspirations into the party systems; in combination with other electoral reforms (like those making registration more difficult), these efforts transformed the American political system from perhaps the most democratic in the world to one much less fettered by the participation of underclasses.[76] But in spite of these responses, labor did occasionally convince sympathetic or frightened legislatures to offer them protection against powerful employers who disregarded their well-being. When that happened, labor experienced the power of constitutional ideology.

State Courts Respond to the Challenge of Class Conflict

As the nation painfully adjusted to the experience of industrial revolution, state courts were busily upholding the standard of equal treatment before the law. While some judges occasionally found it convenient to cite the works of true laissez-faire constitutionalists such as Christopher Tiedeman,[77] the arguments that dominated their opinions and decisions expressed a specific aversion to class politics rather than a general hostility to what a conservative might have considered unnecessary government interference in market relations. State judges consistently upheld "health regulations; building laws; regulation of noxious trades; Sunday laws; street and highway rules; wharf, levee and drainage laws; limits on charges by persons or corporations 'affected with a public interest' or that enjoyed special privileges or monopolies; factory regulations"; and many other exercises of the police power.[78] But when the subject was labor legislation their deference was much less apparent because arguably, by its very nature, it was assaultive of the dominant conception of political legitimacy shared by political elites—much like laws that use racial classifications would be today. While judges occasionally disagreed over whether some police power measures (such as slaughterhouse monopolies or prohibitions on oleomargarine) illegitimately extended special burdens and benefits, there was a much greater degree of consensus about how to treat laws designed to improve the status of labor vis-à-vis employers, especially laws that seemed to have their roots in the collective action of particularly influential unions.

State courts began scrutinizing the political reaction to labor agitation within a few years after the first wave of serious strife. When in 1880 the California legislature made it a misdemeanor for bakers to compel their employees to work between 6:00 P.M. on Saturday and 6:00 P.M. on Sunday, the justices on the state supreme court unanimously voided the law. Justice Milton H. Myrick explained in *Ex parte Westerfield* that this law was "special legislation." A "certain class" had been selected for special benefits or burdens. "As well might it have said, if master carpenters or blacksmiths, or if attorneys having clerks, shall labor or permit employes to labor, they shall be deemed guilty of a misdemeanor and be punished; carpenters or blacksmiths, not master workmen, or attorneys without clerks, may labor at their will. . . . [I]f there be authority to restrain the labor on some one day, it must be, if at all under a general law restraining labor on that day." Justice Elisha W. McKinstry concurred, noting that it was not sufficient to respond that the law applies equally to all bakers, for "to say that every law is 'general' within the meaning of the Constitution, which bears equally upon all to whom it is applicable, is to say that there can be no special laws." Given his understanding of the intent of the law, there was, and could be, "no reason, why bakers should be forced to rest from their labors periodically, which is not applicable to many other classes of artisans and workmen."[79]

By the mid-1880s, in the wake of the second depression since the end of the Civil War, the opportunities for state judges to scrutinize labor legislation had become more common. At issue in *In re Jacobs* (1885) was a New York act which attempted to remedy the deplorable conditions under which cigar makers labored in tenement houses by prohibiting the manufacture of cigars in those dwellings. Opponents called the act "glaringly indefensible," an example of "the power of a few trade monopolists,"[80] and the justices in the New York Court of Appeals unanimously agreed. Judge Robert Earl's opinion centered on the arbitrary nature of the prohibition; in his judgment it was unconnected to any valid police power interest in health or safety. "What does this act attempt to do? In form, it makes it a crime for a cigarmaker in New York and Brooklyn, the only cities in the State having a population exceeding 500,000, to carry on a perfectly lawful trade in his own home. . . . [H]e will become a criminal for doing that which is perfectly lawful outside of the two cities named—everywhere else, so far as we are able to learn, in the whole world." The court agreed that "it is for the legislature to determine what laws and regulations are needed to protect the public health and secure the public comfort and safety," but added that those laws and regulations "must have some relation to these ends. . . . Although the legislature may declare it to be public, that does not necessarily determine its character; it must in fact be public, and if it be not, no legislative fiat can make it so, and *any owner of property attempted to be taken for a use really private can invoke the aid of the courts* to protect his property rights against invasion." The court was suggesting—as it did this same year when it struck down the oleomargarine law in *People v. Marx*—that the real intent of this act was to give an advantage to cigar makers elsewhere by imposing special burdens on New York and Brooklyn cigar makers. The court reasoned that if the legislature had really intended to advance the public health and safety it would have imposed general standards governing the working conditions within which all cigar makers had to operate or standards governing conditions in tenement houses. The law under consideration "does not deal with tenement-houses as such; it does not regulate the number of persons who may live in any one of them, or be crowded into one room, nor does it deal with the mode of their construction for the purpose of securing the health and safety of their occupants or of the public generally. . . . This law was not intended to protect the health of those engaged in cigarmaking, as they are allowed to manufacture cigars everywhere except in the forbidden tenement-houses." Consequently, "It is plain that this is not a health law, and that it has no relation to the public health." The real purpose of the act was simply to "disturb the normal adjustments of the social fabric."[81] As the same court reiterated a few years later, the issue in *Jacobs*, like the issue in *Marx* and *Slaughterhouse*, involved a kind of legislation "meant to protect some class in the community against the fair, free and full competition of some other class, the members of the former class thinking it impossible to hold their own against such competition, and therefore flying to the legislature to secure some enactment which shall operate favorably to them or unfavorably to their competitors in the commercial, agricultural, manufacturing or producing fields."[82]

A year after *Jacobs*, the Illinois Supreme Court, in *Millett v. People* (1886), considered the issue of whether the legislature could set regulations for the manner of payment in the mining industry. Specifically, the law required mine operators who tied wages to the amount of coal extracted to keep a scale at the mines so that coal could be weighed as it was extracted rather than after managers had had a chance to separate unusable material. The counsel for the appellant protested that a "regulation made for any one class of citizens or property owners, as this, is entirely arbitrary in its character." In response, the state attorney general (in an argument that would become more prominent in the legal community the following decade) attempted to redefine the scope of the police powers by arguing that it was legitimate for the government to assist vulnerable classes: the "operation of coal mines usually involves large amounts of capital and powerful individual combinations, against which the individual miner is powerless if left to the ordinary remedies which apply to business transactions generally. The General Assembly, recognizing these necessities for special protection, has placed upon the statutes the law in question, for the purpose of affording proper protection to an otherwise helpless class."

In an age of increasingly large combinations of capital, acceptance of the argument that workers working in large industries were "helpless" and in need of "special protection" would have signaled the collapse of the long-standing distinction between legitimate public-purpose legislation and illegitimate class politics, at least as applied to most labor legislation. Not surprisingly, at this time the Illinois Supreme Court was not willing to abandon the traditional standard governing the legitimate exercise of state power and in a unanimous decision struck down the law. Citing Cooley's discussion of "the law of the land" and the Jacksonian era standard-bearers *Wally's Heirs v. Kennedy* and *Vanzant v. Waddel,* Justice John Scholfield wrote that due process requires that laws must be general and "binding upon all members of the community, under all circumstances, and not partial or private laws, affecting the rights of private individuals or classes of individuals." While lawmakers might occasionally have to recognize distinctions among groups as they legislate in the general welfare, there is always a lingering doubt as to whether "a regulation made for any one class of citizens . . . could be sustained. Distinctions in these respects should be based upon some reason which renders them important—like the want of capacity in infants and insane persons."[83] The court recognized that some aspects of the mining industry might invite special legislation—such as laws requiring mine shafts to be reinforced or other regulations addressing the unique health and safety concerns of miners—but these special conditions did not justify every attempt at regulating this industry, and in particular could not justify government interference with the setting of the price of labor, which is an archetypical example of government abandoning the pledge of neutrality and taking sides in a dispute between competing social classes.

A similar attempt to regulate the manner of employee payment met the same fate in a West Virginia court. In *State v. Goodwill* (1889) the justices struck down a so-called truck store act which prohibited the payment of wages in anything other than lawful money. The legislature was interested in putting an end to the practice of issuing payment in company scrip redeemable only at company stores. The court's opinion focused not on the question of whether the act interfered with the free operation of the market but rather on whether the law advanced the general welfare of the community as a whole (in which case it would be constitutional since individual liberty is always subject "to such restraints as are necessary for the common welfare") or whether it was special or class legislation. In striking down the act the justices cited and relied on the authority of *Wally's Heirs v. Kennedy,* the *Civil Rights Cases, Yick Wo v. Hopkins,* the *Slaughterhouse Cases, Butchers' Union v. Crescent City, In re Jacobs, People v. Marx, Ex parte Westerfield,* and *Millett v. People,* cases which had as their common denominator a consideration of the issue of personal liberty constrained by a regime of legal equality and state neutrality. "The rights of every individual must stand or fall by the same rule of law that governs every other member of the body politic under similar circumstances; and every partial or private law which directly proposes to destroy or affect individual rights, or does the same thing by restricting the privileges of certain classes of citizens and not others, when there is no public necessity for such discrimination, is unconstitutional and void. Were it otherwise, odious individuals or corporate bodies would be governed by one law, and the mass of the community, and those who make the law, by another; whereas, a like general law, affecting the whole community equally, could not have been enacted. . . . In view of what the courts have uniformly held in respect to this class of legislation, it is needless to prolong this discussion."[84]

It was the same story when the Illinois Supreme Court struck down a truck store act in 1892. "We must take judicial notice that employes in mines and manufactories include but a part of those who are employed by others and who depend upon their daily labor for subsistence," wrote Justice Scholfield. Those who employed builders, transportation workers, quarrymen, salesmen, or domestic servants could still engage "in truck stores or shops or schemes for the furnishing of supplies, tools, clothing, provisions and groceries to their employes." (Scholfield acknowledged that some employees are more dependent on their employer than are others; but because "there are instances of entire destitution, and consequently, of the dependence presumed to result therefrom, in all branches of industry," he concluded that this did not constitute sufficient justification to single out mines and manufacturing for special treatment. While it is not said, the suggestion is that these industries were singled out not because their workers suffered under some unique conditions of dependency but rather because of the political power of their unions.) "[U]nder what is denominated the 'police power,' laws may be constitutionally enacted imposing new burdens on persons and property, and restricting personal rights of enjoyment of property, where, in the opinion of the General Assembly, the public welfare demands it—under which may be instanced license laws, laws or ordinances fixing fire limits, quarantine laws, laws imposing liability upon masters on account of death or injury of servants, laws requiring dangerous machinery to be so guarded and used as to avoid injuries to others, laws to prevent monopolies." However, "it is impossible that, under that power, what is lawful if done by A, if done by B can be a misdemeanor, the circumstances and conditions being the same. *Theo-*

retically there is among our citizens no inferior class, other than that of those degraded by crime or other vicious indulgences of the passions. *Those who are entitled to exercise the elective franchise are deemed equals before the law,* and it is not admissible to arbitrarily brand, by statute, one class of them, without reference to and wholly irrespective of their actual good or bad behavior, as too unscrupulous, and the other class as too imbecile or timid and weak, to exercise that freedom in contracting which is allowed to all others."[85] Another court expressed the relevance of the founding ideology more clearly in an identical case: "If [these laws] can stand, it is difficult to see an end to such legislation, and the government becomes one of special privileges, instead of a compact 'to promote the general welfare of the people.' "[86]

(In something of a mixed blessing for the cause of equal rights for women, the Illinois court was one of the few state courts to hold that women workers deserved better than to be treated as weak, timid, and imbecilic. In *Ritchie v. People* (1895) the judges struck down a maximum hours law for women in the garment industry. Justice Benjamin Magruder's opinion opened with the usual litany, that the "law of the land" is the opposite of "arbitrary, unequal and partial legislation," and the "legislature has no right to deprive one class of persons of privileges allowed to other persons under like conditions." He acknowledged "that the right to contract may be subject to limitations growing out of the duties which the individual owes to society, to the public or to the government. These limitations are sometimes imposed by the obligation to so use one's own as not to injure another, by the character of property as affected with a public interest or devoted to a public use, by the demands of public policy or the necessity of protecting the public from fraud or injury, by the want of capacity, by the needs of the necessitous borrower as against the demands of the extortionate lender. But the power of the legislature to thus limit the right to contract must rest upon some reasonable basis, and cannot be arbitrarily exercised." In this case the court considered the act "partial" in part because it "discriminates against one class of employers and employees and in favor of all others" and more generally because it "is not the nature of the things done, but the sex of the persons doing them, which is made the basis of the claim that the Act is a measure for the promotion of the public health," a claim that neglects the fact that "woman is entitled to the same rights, under the constitution, to make contracts with reference to her labor as are secured thereby to men.")[87]

The federal and state judiciary's struggle to distinguish laws passed in the common good or for the general welfare from illegitimate class legislation was noted by contemporary legal commentators. As one anonymous commentator explained, the "common good" mentioned in cases like *Mugler, Powell, Yick Wo,* and *Jacobs* refers to "the material good the whole body of the people associated in communities. Statutes . . . which reasonably tend to secure this good are police measures, *and to them private right is subordinated.* A familiar instance of this legislation for the good of the people generally is a health or quarantine law." This kind of law "is general in its operation and is enacted professedly for the common good" in that it "reasonably tend[s] to secure, the public health, the public safety, the public morals or the public welfare." However, there are also "classes or orders, various trades and businesses among the people. *The Legislature cannot legislate for the good of one of these at the expense of the others. Such is class legislation.*" On the other hand, "where such distinctions exist, and they demand special legislation and are themselves the basis of the statute professedly enacted for the public good, the statute is not class legislation. . . . [When] a statute is enacted applying only to a particular class, it must appear that the public welfare demands such legislation by reason of the distinguishing characteristic of the class." The example offered to illustrate some of these propositions involves an act which would forbid employers from docking the wages of workers who leave work on election days in order to vote. Such an act "takes the property of the master and transfers it to the pocket of the servant as a reward to the servant for the performance of a public duty." This would be illegitimate factional politics; it would be no different than if the legislature required "the master to pay full wages for a half day's work, basing its power upon the elevating and refining influence of leisure and opportunity to improve themselves upon a class that needed elevation and refining," which would "scarcely be contended" as a constitutional exercise of authority. On the other hand, the legislature could promote the same interest in a way that did not favor a particular class; for example, it could enact a statute that closed down all commercial activity on election day or that protected workers from discharge in the event that they left work to vote. The difference between the illegitimate and legitimate approaches to promoting the general interest in voting does not involve the degree of interference in market liberties—there are few government acts more assaultive of laissez-faire than closing down all commercial activity; it involves the extent to which the exercise of public power places special burdens and benefits on particular classes.[88]

Other examples of legitimate and illegitimate labor regulations were reviewed and discussed by F. J. Stimson in his *Handbook to the Labor Law of the United States*. Among the laws characterized as illegitimate class legislation were "statutes limiting the hours of labor for adults ... ; *truck-acts*, or laws providing that employees shall be paid in money only, not in goods or orders; laws forbidding dealers to give or offer prizes with goods sold; laws forbidding employers to measure wages by screened coal; or to withhold wages for imperfect work, or damage to material; laws providing that employees must be paid at stated intervals and forbidding contracts for a longer time; laws limiting the right of a person to contract with whom he will, as for instance, with non-union employees; laws forbidding the citizens of a state to engage in any specified business." However, other laws designed to protect labor fell within that category of legislation that was "clearly necessary to the safety, comfort, or well-being of society," including

statutes providing for the preservation of the health of employees in factories by the removal of excessive dust, or for securing pure air, or requiring fans or other special devices to remove noxious dust or vapors peculiar to the trade; statutes requiring guards to be placed about dangerous machinery, belting, elevators, wells, air-shafts, etc.; statutes providing for fire-escapes, adequate staircases with rails, rubber treads, etc.; doors opening outward, etc.; statutes providing against injury to the operatives by the machinery used, such as laws prohibiting the machinery to be cleaned while in motion, or from being cleaned by any woman or minor; laws requiring mechanical belt shifters, etc., or connection by bells, tubes, etc., between any room where machinery is used and the engine-room; laws aimed at overcrowding in factories, and at the general comfort of the operatives; and many special laws in railways, mines, and other special occupations, such as the laws requiring warning guards to be placed before bridges upon railroads, requiring the frogs and switches or other appliances of the track to be in good condition and properly protected by timber or otherwise, providing automatic couplings to both freight and passenger trains, and, in building trades, providing for railings upon scaffolds and for suitable scaffolds generally.[89]

Similarly, in their 1892 survey, *The Law of Public Health and Safety, and the Powers and Duties of Boards of Health*, Leroy Parker and

Robert H. Worthington advised that for a statute to be considered a legitimate exercise of the police power it must bear some relationship to public health, safety, or morality, and added, "It is the duty of the court to inquire whether there is a real and substantial relation between its avowed objects and the means devised for obtaining those objects." They cited *In re Jacobs* as an example of an act "purporting to be an act to improve the public health, by prohibiting the manufacture of cigars and preparation of tobacco in any form in tenement-houses, but which, in its provisions, manifestly did not relate to and was inappropriate for the ostensible and declared purpose." They noted that it was "the settled doctrine" of the U.S. Supreme Court that the fourteenth amendment permitted states "to promote health, good order and peace, to develop their resources, enlarge their industries, and advance their prosperity" but prohibited them from passing "discriminating and partial enactments, favoring some to the impairment of the rights of others. The principal, if not the sole purpose of its prohibitions, is to prevent any arbitrary invasion by State authority of the rights of persons and property, and to secure to every one the right to pursue his happiness unrestrained, except by just, equal and impartial laws."[90]

Around this same time the *American Law Register* published perhaps the most comprehensive treatment of the subject of special versus general legislation, a series of six articles (totaling 160 pages) entitled "Restrictions upon Local and Special Legislation in the United States." The author, Charles Chauncey Binney, explained that the editors believed that the "considerable space" devoted to the issue was due to the subject's "importance and "the entire absence from legal literature of all intelligent treatment of it." He described how during the Jacksonian period there "was a growth of a very general feeling of hostility to all local and special legislation," those "private schemes" that "were often pushed through the legislatures by unscrupulous men, to the sacrifice of the public interest." The result was that "one State after another . . . [changed] its Constitution, to check the excesses into which its legislature had fallen in this respect, and the influence of the example so set can be seen in the Constitutions of all the more recently organized States." These changes reflected a renewed commitment to general laws, "designed neither for one or more particular persons, nor to operate exclusively in any particular part or parts of the State." This was not to say that all laws had to "operate upon all persons or all things"; legislatures could single out some groups or classes for special treatment (such as "laws in regard to married women, minors, corporations, contracts, real estate") provided "that they regulated these various classes of persons and things in matters peculiar to each class." To put it another way, "all classifications must be based upon substantial distinctions, which make one class really different from another," and the "classification adopted in any law must be germane to the purpose of the law." For example, an act that makes railroads liable for double damages for stock killed is a general act because it applies to all railroads and because no other carriers are in the same position to kill stock. On the other hand, an act requiring railroad companies to pay their employees within fifteen days of a demand for wages, under penalty of an additional payment of 20 percent, is a special law because railroad companies' relation to their employees is the same as that of all other employers. In other words, "to make such a law general there must be some distinguishing *necessity* for the law as to the designated class. A mere classification for the purpose of legislation, without regard to such *necessity*, is simply special legislation of the most pernicious character." Some acts may affect only a limited number of people—acts promoting the preservation of fish, regulating the pilotage in harbors, regulating the putting of pine timber into rivers, authorizing lands to be sold, authorizing elections, or incorporating banks—but they are nevertheless general and public because "the under-lying principle in all these cases is the same, viz., that though the law might operate within a restricted territory, it affected a large number of people, treating them simply as members of the community and without any distinctions among them as individuals; or, in other words, that the law was for the public benefit, not for that of particular individuals."[91]

By the mid-1890s this standard would finally be applied to one of the principal goals of the labor movement, the eight-hour law.[92] It took awhile—it was not until April 1891 that labor was able to get a solid eight-hour-day law passed in a state, in this case Nebraska.[93] In *Low v. Rees Printing Company* (1894) the Nebraska Supreme Court considered the act, which provided "that for all classes of mechanics, servants, and laborers, excepting those engaged in farm or domestic labor, a day's work should not exceed eight hours" unless accompanied by extra com-pensation. "Until a comparatively recent period," wrote the court, "it would have been quite difficult to find adjudications pertinent to the legal propositions involved." But recent popular sentiment has been in favor of "legislation for the regulation of the media of payment; the manner in which products shall be measured or weighed when compen-sation depends upon measure or weight; the hours of labor, and other kindred subjects." Unfortunately for these efforts, "the decided weight" of judicial authority was against the constitutionality of these acts. In this case, "the argument made in favor of the necessity that each day the excess over eight hours should be devoted to rest, recreation, and mental improvement loses much of its force when these very desirable benefits are by the statute itself restricted to certain defined classes of laborers, no one of which, independently of the statute, devotes so many hours to labor as do the classes denied the protection of the statute. Legislation of this kind is always fraught with danger, hence arose the prohibition of special legislation." The opinion cites dozens of cases, all of which provide authority for the central point that "there can be no liberty protected by government that is not regulated by such laws as will preserve the right of each citizen to pursue his own advancement and happiness in his own way, subject only to the restraints necessary to secure the same right to all others. The fundamental principle upon which such liberty is based, in free and enlightened government, is equality under the law of the land."[94]

When the Indiana Supreme Court struck down a "weekly wage" law in 1902, the justices summarized police powers jurisprudence this way: "[A]ll authorities seem to agree that [the police powers] may be exerted only on behalf of some general, public interest, as distinguished from individuals or classes; that is to say, to protect the public health, safety, morals, prevent fraud and oppression, and promote the general welfare. It is not to be invoked to protect one class of citizens against another class unless such interference is for the real protection of society in general."[95]

Equality, state neutrality, and a demonstrable relationship to the general welfare were the central preoccupations of late-nineteenth-century constitutionalism, not liberty or laissez-faire specifically. In the course of his *Lectures on the Fourteenth Amendment* (1898), William D. Guthrie explained that the central judicial inquiry of police powers jurisprudence was "whether the regulation or classification has been designed to subserve some reasonable public purpose, or is a mere device or excuse for an unjust discrimination, or for the oppression or spoilation of a particular class. . . . The distinctive and characteristic feature of the American system is equality before the law. The first declaration of the American people, upon asserting their independence as a nation, was 'that all men are created equal'; and the purpose of the founders of the Union was to establish a government of equality before the law in which privileged classes should not exist—a government of equality of rights, equality of duties and equality of burdens."[96] One observer recognized that this master principle represented a serious barrier to attempts by state legislatures to regulate employment contracts, a barrier that could be "cleared away" only with a constitutional amendment. He advised against such a course of action because he feared it would result in "that venerable instrument [being] dragged further into the vortex of the conflict between capital and labor than it has ever been yet, and will probably emerge from the struggle bereft of its true and only fitting character as the bulwark of the fundamental, elementary rights of the citizen, and bearing a deep and ineradicable impress of class jealousies and class prejudice."[97]

In light of these highly Federalist-Jacksonian sensibilities, the use of public power to intervene in routine relations between employer and employee was by and large not permitted. But as the courts played their role as guardians of first principles, others despaired at what seemed to be a growing disparity between a long-standing tradition of political legitimacy and the well-being of millions of Americans. Among those discouraged by the changes in American life—the labor violence and employers' disregard for the well-being of their employees—was Thomas M. Cooley. In the mid-1880s he warned that "the demand for [class legislation] in the immediate future is likely to be more frequent and more persistent than ever. It is also likely to be directed against classes that may easily be made the objects of popular prejudice; against those who carry on particular employments, or perhaps against the managers of many kinds of employment." He also prophesied that "as the benefit of [the protection of property] is reaped by those who have possessions, the Constitution itself may come to be regarded by considerable classes as an instrument whose office is to protect the rich in the advantages they have secured over the poor. . . . Mr. Gladstone, with the power of Parliament behind him, when landholdings are oppressive, forces better terms from the landlords; and it is not difficult to make classes that conceive themselves oppressed believe that a government that is powerless to give such relief is unworthy of their support." Cooley bemoaned the fact that labor and capital were organizing against one another, "behind walls of defense" that "invite[d] attack." He observed that strikes and lockouts made the employer "bitter in proportion as he sees his anticipated profits becoming impossible" and the laborer "bitter in proportion as he feels himself at a disadvantage." In this kind of environment the "legislation of the state comes to be suspected; one party believing that laws that may or may not be proper in themselves are adopted to win the favor of a rabble, and the other suspecting that corruption controls." But for Cooley the "remedy for such a state of things is not so manifest as the evils"; the best he could offer was the suggestion that "employers recognize how intimately they are concerned with the welfare of those whose labor they employ, and how important it is that their relations should be on a basis satisfactory to both."[98] As Alan Jones remarked more than twenty years ago, Cooley's "older equalitarian and individualist values were ever more difficult of reconciliation in the rapidly changing society of post-1865 America." His "predicament in maintaining them lent a special tension to his thought and a tone of anxiety and strain to his life."[99]

It was a predicament shared by all who at one time or another felt inspired by the vision of a government that did not play favorites. Different people handled this predicament differently. For some, America's social revolution necessitated a concurrent revolution in political thought and practice. Many had become convinced that in the context of the coercion embedded in industrial markets a continuing insistence on state neutrality in fact biased the system in favor of the powerful classes. But others felt no need to capitulate to the agitation for class politics. In fact, in the minds of these traditionalists—particularly those (like judges) who were institutionally obligated to preserve the dominant vision—it was precisely at times like these that the commitment to first principles was most important; this was why judges had been given independence from electoral politics. This was the tone most evident in a speech given by Field at the Court's centennial celebration in 1890: "As population and wealth increases—as the inequalities in the conditions of men become more and more marked and disturbing—as the enormous aggregation of wealth possessed by some corporations excites uneasiness lest their power should become dominating in the legislatures of the country, and thus encroach upon the rights or crush out the business of individuals of small means—as population in some quarters presses upon the means of subsistence, and angry menaces against order find vent in loud denunciations—it becomes more and more the imperative duty of the court to enforce with a firm hand every guarantee of the Constitution."[100]

As the justices continued to give meaning to the founding vision of the American Republic, they increasingly discovered that they were becoming the guardians of a Constitution besieged.

The Old Constitution

and the New Realism

Classes interested in policies, ostensibly for the promotion of the welfare of society but really for their own benefit, zealously advocate the absolute sovereignty of government, and artfully maintain public opinion in an unsettled and confused condition. . . . It is peculiarly the province of jurisprudence, as a passionless and impartial factor, to guide the conscience of the people, and to restore the disinterestedness of law, that it may serve to shelter the freedom of man in his pursuit of the highest ethical aims of civilization.—H. Teichmueller (1895)[1]

The late-nineteenth-century admonition against class legislation can be found in the most unexpected places. In an article for the *Albany Law Journal* entitled "Should Women Be Executed?" Clara Foltz rested her affirmative answer firmly on the concurrent propositions that murder victims are equally dead "whether by a man's pistol or a woman's poison," and that men and women "are possessed of the same moral perceptions, the same reason, the same passions, the same volition and the same self control. . . . To vary the punishment for different classes is to excuse one class in the exact degree of the variation. . . . Equality before the law is the spirit of our Constitution," she emphasized. "The old system of exempting lords from the law and preachers from punishment worked untold evil, and is dead, as all unequal laws ought to be. . . . [E]very consideration of good government, good morals, exact justice and harmony with the strict spirit of the time is against class legislation and in favor of an exact and equal distribution of the benefits and an impartial imposition of the penalties of the law."[2] Similarly, Charles T.

Saxton, former lieutenant governor of New York, expressed concern over reports that a broker who was sent to jail for refusing to answer questions relating to the operation of the Sugar Trust was "living in a Washington jail as comfortably as he might at a good hotel. There must be no class distinction in this country, and there certainly ought not to be inequalities of conditions among convicted criminals. One of the gravest dangers to our institutions is the growing belief that citizens are not all equal before the law; that there is one kind of justice for the rich, and another for the poor."[3]

More often, however, this sensibility found expression in discussions of constitutional ideology that addressed the "new and very disturbing element" of "class prejudice and animosity," a tension between labor and capital which had intensified because of "the increase of capital and the invention of labor-saving machinery, large numbers of workmen collected together in factories under the eye of the master, working not by the piece, but by the day"; and the "modern aristocracy of wealth," in which "the standard of living of the master rose far above that of his laborers, and his communication with them was usually made through agents and superintendents."[4] For many of this generation, the particular challenge of industrialization was that it seemed to make more widespread and routine the attempts by groups and classes to promote their own special interests in legislation, efforts that were assaultive of the traditional understanding of the legitimate scope of police powers. As Justice Henry B. Brown noted in an address before the American Bar Association in 1893, "Underlying all these conflicts between the different classes of society, whatever shape they take, is the desire of one class to better itself at the expense of the other."[5] He told a group of graduates in a commencement address at the Yale Law School two years later that "the reconciliation of this strife between capital and labor . . . is the great social problem which will confront you as you enter upon the stage of professional life."[6]

In the last decade of the nineteenth century greater numbers of political and social elites were expressing their concern that the "stress of competition in business, the prevailing social unrest, the distinct trend of a certain class of social agitators in direction of State socialism, the superstition that legislation is a sovereign cure-all for social ills, and . . . the competition of reckless politicians for the unthinking vote, all have been . . . potent factors . . . in inducing legislation, which is forcing upon the attention of our profession and the courts *a new class of constitu-*

tional questions, and signs are not wanting that these are to be the weighty questions of the future in jurisprudence, as well as in social economy."[7] For many, the most natural response to these developments was for courts simply to use the well-defined conception of political legitimacy embodied in legal ideology as the standard with which to distinguish appropriate and inappropriate state action. Frederick N. Judson was not the only commentator to remind his audience that "it is a notable fact that in the course of English history, while parliament was enacting class legislation, such as the statutes of Laborers, and of Apprentices, the judges, in their construction of these statutes, favored liberty of trade, as the common right of English secured by the great charter."[8]

The responsibility of courts in an era of class conflict was put even more forcefully by John F. Dillon: "The State is a commonweal. It exists for the general good, for rich and poor alike. It knows or ought to know no classes. . . . The blessings and benefits of the State are intended to diffuse themselves over all. . . . The one thing to be feared in our democratic republic, and therefore to be guarded against with sleepless vigilance, is class power and class legislation. Discriminating legislation for the benefit of the rich against the poor, or in favor of the poor against the rich, is equally wrong and dangerous. Class legislation of all and every kind is anti-republican and must be repressed." In what could have been a page lifted out of Andrew Jackson's Bank Veto message, Dillon continued by making the point that "all who compose the State, the rich and poor, the plutocrat and the proletariat, all who share in the associated life, are each and equally entitled to the protection, support and care of the State, whose blessings, like the air, the dew, the rain and the sunlight, should fall upon all without discrimination or preference."[9]

The Supreme Court had prepared itself for the task of repressing class legislation. In the twenty years since they had acquired the responsibility of actively scrutinizing the behavior of state legislatures, the justices had made the Jacksonian conception of equal rights and hostility to special government privileges the central feature of police powers jurisprudence; that is to say, by the late nineteenth century the Supreme Court expected the nation's legislation to be free from the injustice of special burdens or benefits imposed on favored or despised classes. As I intend to show, at the turn of the century the Court used this standard consistently to evaluate legislation affecting both business and labor. At the same time, a small number of people in the legal community began seriously to question the continued virtue and efficacy of faction-free legislation, particularly in light of what they considered to be the responsibility of government to protect the well-being of wage earners, who in their eyes were in no position to contract for their own protection against an increasingly hazardous and cutthroat work environment.

Still, this burgeoning internal assault against traditional police powers jurisprudence did not deter eight of the nine justices on the Court from using the principles associated with this tradition to evaluate the constitutionality of a maximum hours law for bakers in *Lochner v. New York*. Moreover, in the months and years following *Lochner*, most of the criticisms of the decision from legal elites took the form not of a rebuke of the constitutional tradition but of an admonition that the justices simply must be more "realistic" or scientific, and less "intuitive," about evaluating the relationship between legislation and traditionally accepted public purposes. From the point of view of legal reformers the "new realism" of sociological jurisprudence achieved some successes, particularly with respect to the Court's attitude toward the health benefits of maximum hours laws; but this movement did little to erase the distinction between illegitimate class legislation and legitimate general welfare legislation. If anything, in the decade following *Lochner*, the new realism helped reinforce a constitutional tradition that authorized judges to evaluate legislation on the basis of whether it was reasonably related to public health, safety, or morality. It would take more time before a more fundamental challenge to this tradition would develop within the legal community.

The Tradition of the Neutral Polity and the Regulation of Business

By the late 1880s and early 1890s, the Supreme Court had clarified the test used to determine whether legislatures were acting within their proper authority, as summarized in *Lawton v. Steele* (1893): "To justify the State in thus interposing its authority in behalf of the public," explained Justice Brown, "it must appear, first, that the interests of the public generally, as distinguished from those of a particular class, require such interference, and second, that the means are reasonably necessary for the accomplishment of the purpose."[10] So, for example, it had been decided that government could regulate the laundry business in order to safeguard the public's interest in fire prevention but could not pass laws that helped one class of laundry owners remove another class from competition. It was not always easy to distinguish valid exercises of the police power from class politics because sometimes the imposition of special burdens was necessary to accomplish general benefits; for example, it was all right to prohibit *all* laundry operators from setting up establishments in wood buildings. But because the elimination of class politics was considered important—fundamental, actually—the justices were determined not to be "bound by mere forms" or "misled by mere pretences" as they investigated whether "a statute purporting to have been enacted to protect the public health, the public morality, or the public safety, has no real or substantial relation to those objects," since that kind of careful scrutiny was the only way they could fulfill their constitutional role and filter out the impurities of factionalism from America's legislatures.[11]

Just one year after Harlan issued the admonition just cited calling for careful judicial scrutiny of legislation the Court considered one of the first in a series of cases concerning state regulation of railroads. At issue in *Minneapolis and St. Louis Railway v. Beckwith* (1888) was an Iowa law which authorized the recovery of double the value of stock killed or damages caused by a railroad if the injury took place at a point where the railroad had an obligation to build a fence and had failed to do so. Citing among other cases *Wally's Heirs v. Kennedy*, the railroad challenged the act on the grounds that it subjected them "to a different rule of law . . . from any other person in the State," not because it was necessitated by the public good but rather "for the benefit of the owner of stock killed or injured."[12]

The justices, however, disagreed with the railroad's characterization of the purpose of the law and unanimously upheld the legislation. In his opinion for the Court, Field followed the distinction he had made in *Barbier* between class legislation which "discriminat[ed] against some and favor[ed] others" and public-purpose legislation which was "limited in its application." He wrote that while the fourteenth amendment "does undoubtedly prohibit discriminating and partial legislation by any State in favor of particular persons as against others in like condition," it also recognizes that sometimes an exercise of the police powers requires special legislation. For example, "if one is engaged in the manufacture or sale of explosive or inflammable articles, or in the preparation or sale of medicinal drugs, legislation, for the security of the society, may prescribe the terms on which he will be permitted to carry on the business, and the liabilities he will incur from neglect of them." In this case the Court concluded that the state had an interest that went beyond the particular benefits that might be enjoyed by cattle owners, an interest in providing "against accidents to life and property" resulting from derailments caused by collisions with livestock.[13] Similarly, in another case the Court upheld a Kansas statute which provided that railroad companies operating in the state were "liable for all damages done to any employe of such company in consequence of any negligence of its agents, or by any mismanagement of its engineers or other employes," on the grounds that "the hazardous character of the business of operating a railway called for special legislation . . . which was not required by the business of other corporations."[14]

However, in light of the hostility railroads generated in many communities, the justices were careful to make it clear that not all railroad regulation would be tolerated. In Bell's Gap Railroad v. Pennsylvania (1890), while upholding a taxation scheme which assessed corporate bonds at their nominal or par value while other obligations were assessed at their actual value (on the grounds that states traditionally taxed different kinds of property differently), the justices issued a warning that "clear and hostile discriminations against particular persons and classes" were prohibited.[15] Still, as had been the case in the past with the problem of slaughterhouse monopolies and prohibitions on oleomargarine, the justices did not always find themselves in agreement as to whether a particular act should be seen as public-purpose legislation of limited application or discriminatory class legislation. A few years after Bell's Gap the Court considered a Texas law which made losing railroad defendants liable for attorneys' fees in actions involving fifty dollars or less. The plaintiffs in the case of Gulf, Colorado and Santa Fe Railway Company v. Ellis (1896) took the position that while the legislature clearly had the power to fix the measure of damages, it was "a different question" whether "under the guise of determining the measure of damages it can prescribe discriminatory regulations against one class of citizens founded on no reason peculiar to that class." In attempting to establish this point, the attorneys for the railroad filed an eighty-four-page brief which contained a sweeping and comprehensive review of nineteenth-century state and federal case law on restrictions against unequal, partial, or class legislation, starting back in the early part of the century with reference to Webster's conception of "the law of the land" as being a "general law" and continuing with the 1829 decision of the Tennessee Supreme Court in Vanzant v. Waddel, declaring that any partial law which tended to deprive a person of "the equal benefits of the general and public laws of the land" was unconstitutional and void; the same court's position in *Wally's Heirs v. Kennedy* and *Bank v. Cooper* that the "law of the land . . . meant a general and public law, operating equally on every individual in the community"; the principle articulated by the Texas Supreme Court in *Janes v. Reynolds* that the law of the land refers to "general public laws, binding all the members of the community under similar circumstances, and not partial or private laws, affecting the rights of private individuals or classes of individuals"; the declaration of the Massachusetts court in *Holden v. James* that "it is manifestly contrary to the first principles of civil liberty and natural justice, and to the spirit of our constitution and laws, that any one citizen should enjoy privileges and advantages which are denied to all others under like circumstances, or that any one should be subject to losses, damages, suits or actions, from which all others under like circumstances are exempted"; the principle announced in *Durkee v. Janesville* that the legislature does not have the power to "discriminate and do gross and palpable injustice between man and man by the passage of unequal and partial laws"; Cooley's more recent statement of the proposition that people had a right to be governed by general rules that applied to rich and poor alike, and not by regulations "made for any one class of citizens, entirely arbitrary in its character"; and identical statements found in *Baggs' Appeal, Millett v. People, Sears v. Cottrell, City of Jacksonville v. Carpenter, Ex parte Westerfield, State v. Goodwill, State v. Fire Creek Coal and Coke Company, State v. Loomis, Barbier v. Connolly,* and dozens of other long-standing and contemporaneous discussions of the police power.

The railroad's claim was that this law was simply another attempt on the part of legislative factions to use the police powers as a pretext to pass discriminatory legislation, a practice the Court had claimed it would be on guard against. The plaintiffs reminded the justices that while legislatures undoubtedly have the power to tax, this does not empower them to "establish a rule of taxation in regard to a particular class of people, which is not applicable to other classes under exactly the same circumstances." While "Sunday laws are generally held constitutional," the legislature "may not make a Sunday law applying to bakers or barbers only." While the "legislature may regulate the use of buildings in cities for laundries," it cannot "distinguish between that class who can obtain permits from the city authorities and that class which can not." While the "legislature may undoubtedly regulate the occupation of a farmer, . . . we do not think that a statute directing that in any suit on a mortgage against any farmer or stock raiser an attorney's fee shall be allowed, without permitting such a fee in suits on mortgages generally, would be a constitutional exercise of the legislative power." The principle captured by these examples is not simply that the government must pass laws that "embrace all who come under the sphere of its operation"; the government has to advance a reason justifying a legislative classification which imposes special burdens or benefits, and that reason cannot be based on favoritism or spite toward certain groups or classes. Deviating from their references to settled law, the attorneys suggested a hypothetical case to illustrate their point: "Suppose the legislature should partially revive the Curfew by enacting that all doctors, lawyers and bakers caught out between 8 P.M. and 5 A.M. shall be fined $25.00 a head. . . . [It] would in one sense embrace all who came under the sphere of its operation. . . . [I]f our suggested Curfew law would be constitutional, then we admit that here we have no case; but if the court would hold our Curfew law . . . invalid then, we think, the court should hold this act invalid." The question that the justices had to consider was "what is there in the collection of debts and damages from railway companies which distinguishes them in that respect from all others and justifies special legislation, not extending to all others under similar circumstances?"[16]

In *Ellis* the justices split six to three in their response to that question. From the point of view of the majority, no satisfactory justification was linked to the advancement of a general societal interest for singling out railroad corporations for this burden; they therefore voided the act as a case of unjust discrimination (an example of what Federal Judge William Howard Taft had referred to the year before as the tendency of a "corporation-hating community" to pass "legislation hostile to corporations").[17] Justice David J. Brewer wrote that "the act singles out a certain class of debtors and punishes them when for like delinquencies it punishes no others. They are not treated as other debtors, or equally with other debtors. . . . They do not stand equal before the law." Citing (among other cases) *Vanzant v. Waddel, Millett v. People, Frorer v. People, State v. Goodwill,* and *State v. Fire Creek Coal and Coke Company,* Brewer noted that "while good faith and a knowledge of existing conditions on the part of a legislature is to be presumed, [to] carry that presumption to the extent of always holding that there must be some undisclosed and unknown reason for subjecting certain individuals or corporations to hostile and discriminating legislation is to make the protecting clauses of the Fourteenth Amendment a mere rope of sand, in no manner restraining state action." The majority considered the act before them constitutionally deficient for the same reason and voided it just as they would have voided legislation mandating "that all white men shall be subjected to the payment of the attorney's fees of parties successfully suing them and all black men not. . . . These are distinctions which do not furnish any proper basis for the attempted classification." Unlike the legislation upheld in *Beckwith*, which proceeded on "the theory of a special duty resting upon railroad corporations by reason of the business in which they are engaged," the statute in *Ellis* suffered from a lack of congruence between the classification and the alleged public purpose, since the "hazardous business of railroading carries with it no special necessity for the prompt payment of debts. That is a duty resting upon all debtors." Therefore, the special treatment afforded railroad corporations was arbitrary and unconstitutional.[18]

The three dissenters, Chief Justice Melville W. Fuller and Justices Horace Gray and Edward D. White, disagreed that no general public purpose was served by the special treatment. They argued that the legislature might have discovered "that railroad corporations within the State were accustomed, beyond other corporations and persons, to unconscionably resist the payment of such petty claims, with the object of exhausting the patience and the means of the claimants, by prolonged litigation and perhaps repeated appeals." In support of this legislative conclusion the dissenters ended their fairly short dissent by taking note of the fact that only the railroad was represented before the Supreme Court. They expressed regret "that so important a precedent, as this case may afford, for interference by the national judiciary with the legislation of the several States on little questions of costs, should be established upon argument *ex parte* on behalf of the railroad corporation, without any argument for the original plaintiff. But it is hardly surprising that the owner of a claim for fifty dollars only, having been compelled to follow up, through all the courts of the State, the contest over this ten dollar fee, should at last have become discouraged, and unwilling to undergo the expense of employing counsel to maintain his rights before this court."[19] Within a decade this willingness to go beyond the "common understanding" of the kinds of ways a particular industry might threaten the general welfare (railroads and not other businesses kill cattle and start fires) and accept legislative findings relating to other harmful practices (railroads and not other businesses prevent worthy claimants from successfully pushing their claims) would be encouraged by those advocating a new realism on the judiciary. However, as we shall see, the *Ellis* dissenters advanced no suggestion that this new realism necessitated an abandonment of the ethos of the neutral state or of traditional distinctions between legitimate health and safety legislation and illegitimate class legislation. The justices agreed that the central constitutional question in police powers jurisprudence was whether legislation was motivated by unreasonable hostility or favoritism toward certain businesses or classes or by a reasonable concern for the general welfare; they simply disagreed in the application of that standard, just as the *Slaughterhouse* justices had done some two decades earlier.

A few years later the Court found itself even more deeply split when it faced a similar issue in *Atchison, Topeka and Santa Fe Railroad Company v. Matthews* (1898). This case involved a railroad's challenge to a statute which imposed attorney's fees on unsuccessful railroad defendants in actions for damages from fires caused by railroad operations. Among the attorneys representing the railroad company was one who had helped prepare the mammoth brief in *Ellis*. No doubt because of his prior experience he was able to better his previous effort and contribute to a new brief that spanned 109 pages. In addition to the comprehensive case review offered in the *Ellis* brief, the *Matthews* brief included references to histories which indicated that "the outrageous, partial and unjust legislation in the new states" in the 1780s "was one of the causes which aided . . . the adoption of the Federal constitution." References to the Federalist Papers established that the founders believed that the "public good" should not be "disregarded in the conflict of rival parties" and that "it is of great importance in a republic not only to guard the society against the oppression of its rulers, but to guard one part of the society against the injustice of the other part." Counsel accounted for the postwar changes in the Constitution by arguing that the provisions of the original Constitution "were but a partial protection in respect to a few specified subjects" and did not prevent states from passing "discriminating, unjust and partial legislation"; hence, the fourteenth amendment was added to embody "in the Federal Constitution a universal principle of right and justice, forbidding the political power in each of the states to touch the life, liberty or property of the most abject and powerless person, except in pursuance of the same laws which equally affected the majority who promulgated them."

Counsel for the railroad acknowledged that the legislature could act to promote the public health and safety by regulating activity that might lead to fires, but argued nevertheless that it was not legitimate to single out railroads for special treatment as the state had done in this case, both because railroads were not uniquely predisposed to cause fires (farmers posed a similar threat when they used steam threshers) and more generally because the legislative scheme seemed far removed from the community's legitimate interest in fire prevention. In fact, from the point of view of the railroad company, the major effect of the statute at issue was simply to make railroads uniquely vulnerable to "any lawyer hungry for a fee."[20]

In spite of this impressive effort, a bare majority of the justices in *Matthews* was not persuaded by the railroad's claim that it was the victim of invidious discrimination. Brewer, who had also authored the decision in *Ellis*, led the majority in upholding the law on the grounds that the public might be served to the extent that the act might encourage railroads to be more cautious about avoiding fires. "The purpose of this statute is not to compel the payment of debts, but to secure the utmost care on the part of railroad companies to prevent the escape of fire from their moving trains. This is obvious from the fact that liability for damages by fire is not cast upon such corporations in all cases, but only in those in which the fire is 'caused by the operating' of the road. . . . [The legislature's] admonition to the railroads is not, pay your debts without suit or you will, in addition, have to pay attorney's fees; but rather, see to it that no fire escapes from your locomotives, for if it does you will be liable, not merely for the damage it causes, but also for the reasonable attorney's fees of the owner of the property injured or destroyed."[21] Apparently, however, this public purpose was not so obvious to the four dissenters. Harlan's opinion, joined by Justices Brown, Peckham, and Joseph McKenna, relied on *Ellis* and emphasized that the act "imposes upon the defendant railroad corporation, if unsuccessful in its defence, a burden not imposed upon any other unsuccessful defendant sued upon a like or upon a different cause of action." The dissenters suggested that the law before them was in principle no different from an act that would "give the railroad corporation a special attorney's fee if successful in its defence, but did not allow such a fee to an individual plaintiff when successful."[22]

Brewer was keenly aware that some fairly fine distinctions were being derived from the central principle of state neutrality. After *Matthews*, the position of a majority of the Court was that a state, on the one hand, may not force railroads that have been successfully sued to pay lawyers' fees in actions involving fifty dollars or less, and, on the other hand, may require railroads that have been successfully sued for damages caused by fires to pay lawyers' fees. In his majority opinion in *Matthews*, Brewer addressed this controversy head-on:

> Many cases have been before this court, involving the power of state legislatures to impose special duties or liabilities upon individuals and corporations, or classes of them, and while the principles of separation between those cases which have been adjudged to be within the power of the legislature and those beyond its power, are not difficult of comprehension or statement, yet their application often becomes very troublesome, especially when the case is near to the dividing line. It is easy to distinguish between the full light of day and the darkness of midnight, but often very difficult to determine whether a given moment in the twilight hour is before or after that in which the light predominates over the darkness. . . .
>
> . . . Class legislation, discriminating against some and favoring others, is prohibited, but legislation which, in carrying out a public purpose, is limited in its application, if within the sphere of its operation it affects alike all persons similarly situated, is not within the [fourteenth] amendment. . . . It is not at all to be wondered at that as these doubtful cases come before this court the justices have often divided in opinion. . . . [B]ut the division in all of them was, not upon the principle or rule of separation, but upon the location of the particular case one side or the other of the dividing line.[23]

Of course, it was not always difficult for the justices to tell night from day. In *Cotting v. Kansas City Stock Yards Company and the State of Kansas* (1901) Brewer again wrote the opinion, this time for a unanimous Court. He cited (among other cases) *Vanzant* ("every partial or private law . . . is unconstitutional and void"), *Barbier* ("no greater burdens should be laid upon one than are laid upon others in the same calling and condition"), *Ellis* ("arbitrary selection can never be justified by calling it classification"), and Cooley's *Constitutional Limitations* (those who make the law are "to have one rule for rich and poor, for the favorite at court and the countryman at plough") to support the judgment that a set of Kansas stockyard regulations which applied only to one company and not to other similar companies was a violation of the fourteenth amendment.[24] And in *Connolly v. Union Sewer Pipe Company* (1901) the justices voided an Illinois antitrust statute that exempted farmers and cattlemen. Harlan acknowledged that "what may be regarded as a denial of the equal protection of the laws is a question not always easily determined, as the decisions of this court and of the highest courts of the States will show." But he had little difficulty concluding that "to declare that some of the class engaged in domestic trade or commerce shall be deemed criminals if they violate the regulations prescribed by the State for the purpose of protecting the public against illegal combinations formed to destroy competition and to control prices, and that others of the same class shall not be bound to regard those regulations, but may combine their capital, skill or acts to destroy competition and to control prices for their special benefit, is so manifestly a denial of the equal protection of the laws that further or extended argument to establish that position would seem to be unnecessary."[25]

The editors of the *American Law Review* agreed. Laws such as these "have in them this element of demagoguery and injustice: that they condemn every other trust except the trust which the dominant party in the legislature is interested in upholding. In those States where the so-called 'farmer element' predominates in the legislature, anti-trust laws are so framed as to defeat and suppress commercial trusts, while suffering and upholding agricultural trusts. In those legislative bodies whose members rest under a constant fear of the effect of the so-called 'labor vote' on their future political careers, it will be found that some of the Anti-Trust acts contain an exception favor of labor combinations." With this decision, "the court has earned the public thanks and has given new proof of its right to the public confidence."[26]

Even in light of the occasional difficulties the justices experienced in applying the limits of the neutral state on police power regulations of business, there was no discernible hue and cry in the legal community with respect to the Court's basic approach to this issue. Most, like the *American Law Review*, applauded the judiciary's stand against the illegitimacy of factional politics and attempts to politicize market competition by exploiting state power. The only apparent criticism was the occasional complaint that the justices were not going far enough, as was the case previously with the reaction to the decision upholding a ban on oleomargarine. Yet, while the judiciary's use of the standard of state neutrality in cases dealing with business regulation generated little comment, the same cannot be said of the way that same police power standard was used in passing judgment on the constitutional legitimacy of labor legislation.

Labor Legislation, the Neutral Polity, and the Bumpy Road to Lochner

The foundation upon which the vision of the neutral state was originally erected and subsequently reproduced was the argument that the market could provide for and protect personal autonomy and social independence. It was because of that claim that the founders could insist on removing state power from the struggles that shaped the relationships between groups or classes in the market, be they debtors and creditors, employees and employers, or producers and consumers. The assumption underlying the constitutional structure and its supporting ideology was that the most serious threat to liberty and the most serious violation of the principle of equality was the injustice of factional politics, as represented by the allegedly unsavory behavior of state legislatures in the 1780s. The market freedom repeatedly and forcefully celebrated in party platforms and court opinions was not freedom from all restraint; it was freedom from the corrupt use of public power by competing social groups. Market freedom, or "liberty of contract," was linked inextricably with the commitment to faction-free legislation.[27]

The resistance to this vision had always rested on the argument that individual social independence was not guaranteed by state neutrality or even by a public commitment to increase opportunities in the market (through trade or land policies). This was the position of the "producers' ideologies" that were delegitimized at the time of the founding; it had also been the position of the representatives of the early labor movement in the days of Jackson (before many were lured away by appeals to equal rights and the promise of free soil) and the postbellum labor and agrarian reformers (whose movements were met both by ideological defenses and by less subtle state responses). This alternative conception of republicanism, so fundamentally at odds with the dominant vision, never gained much currency among political and social elites. But by the final decade of the nineteenth century, in light of the obvious failure of the industrialized economy to order social relations harmoniously and without coercion and to guarantee opportunity and self-sufficiency for all, the position began to be advanced by some commentators in legal scholarship that the long-standing aversion to special burdens and benefits had become anachronistic, and that consequently the judiciary's conception of the scope of the police powers had to adjust to a new social order, one that was unknown to both Jefferson and Hamilton.

Among the first in the legal community to advance this position was the editor of the *American Law Review*, Seymour D. Thompson. In 1890, as part of a discussion of so-called truck store or store-order legislation, which prohibited employers from paying employees in company scrip redeemable only in company stores, Thompson argued that one of "the true functions of government" is to act as "an arbitrator between the strong and the weak, the rich and poor." Not wanting to be labeled a socialist or anarchist for his beliefs, Thompson was careful to make it clear that "we are opposed to much of the legislation which is defacing the statute books, enacted in the pretended interest of labor, much of which is the lowest species of demagoguery, not devised from any honest desire to promote the rights of the laboring classes, but contrived for the mere purpose of catching their votes. But," he added, "we renew an expression of opinion that it is the true office of government to arbitrate between those who must work for their daily bread and those who have the power to oppress them."[28]

The assumptions about social dependency underlying this conception were elaborated by Thompson in an address before the Kansas Bar Association in 1892. Most of his remarks focused on the enormous powers that corporations had attained over the previous few years, how the "barons of corporate power, outrivaling in wealth and splendor the merchant kings of Venice," had "purchased, by bribery and corruption, exclusive privileges from the temporary tenants of legislative power" and how they had "found means to combine all the corporations engaged in producing particular commodities so as to engross those commodities, suppress all competition therein, crush out and destroy all rival producers; and, aided by the Chinese Wall of a protective tariff excluding the world's competition." But toward the end of his discussion Thompson addressed the topic of the state judiciary's approach to labor legislation, which led him to exclaim: "What mockery to talk about the freedom of contract where only *one* of the contracting parties is free!" He observed that economists proceed on the assumption that "labor, like any other commodity, is subject merely to the law of supply and demand. I grant that such is the general and often the inexorable law; but I protest that it is within the power of human institutions to mitigate its rigor." He argued that this public responsibility was especially important when dealing with the condition of wage earners in capitalist forms of production. "The owner of a horse has an interest that it shall be well fed, warmly housed and kept in good condition. The late slave-owner had the same motive in respect of his human chattel, and this motive operated as a protection to his chattel. But the corporate manager has no such motive. . . . [T]he worn out wage-worker of the corporation [who] falls by the wayside finds his place immediately filled in by the 'hungry pauper that crowds forward from some human breeding ground.'" Thompson cited a recent encyclical from the pope insisting that the remuneration offered a workman by an employer "must be enough to support the wage earner in reasonable and frugal comfort." Thompson added: "Surely the State can find some way, without too much repressing human liberty, to see to it that every man who is able and willing to work shall get enough to support a family and a home in frugal economy."[29]

This position was shared by other contributors to the *American Law Review*. One offered a suggestion (relied on more and more in the years to come) as to how the state may claim a general community interest in the bargaining relationship between employers and employees; it emphasized the recent breaches of the peace that had been caused by industrial conflict. "No well-wisher of his country's peace and prosperity can view the present relations of capital and labor, or more correctly, of employer and employed, without serious alarm," wrote Conrad Reno in 1892. "Scarcely a week passes that some widespread strike or lockout does not endanger the public peace and order. Both sides are well organized, armed and determined to succeed. . . . The spectacle is then presented to the world of two private armed forces holding a bloody carnage, in the midst of a great nation, calling itself civilized, but which has not devised any peaceful means of settling such labor disputes." In light of these events, Reno argued that the state had a neutral interest in regulating and harmonizing relations between employers and employees: "The constant and wide-spread strikes and lockouts which occur under the present plan of non-intervention by the State are highly detrimental to the public interests." While he tried to avoid the charge that he was advocating having the government play favorites in these disputes— he stressed that the state's interest was only in protecting the public peace—he nevertheless argued that breaches of the peace were largely a by-product of poor wages and intolerable working hours. He suggested the creation of a "disinterested" tribunal to decide wage and hours disputes between workers and management in those employments in which there was an oversupply of labor. "In determining the minimum wage the labor court should not be controlled by the rate of wages now prevailing under the 'iron law of wages' of supply and demand, and the system of alleged freedom of contract, but should be controlled by what may be called the *golden rule of wages*, by which labor is entitled to receive a fair and just proportion of the wealth which it creates, irrespective of supply and demand."[30]

The same argument for government arbitration of labor disputes was advanced by U. M. Rose, who opened his discussion with the observation that there was nothing new about strikes and labor disputes (he recounted one of the first recorded "strikes," a walkout by flute players some three hundred years before Christ) but went on to point out that industrial strikes "are more destructive than formerly, not only because of the great expansion of the agencies of production, and the grouping of vast numbers of laborers together, but because, owing to the minute subdivision of labor that exists in modern times, there is a more complex interdependence between different classes of laborers." For example, "the strike among cotton spinners of Preston, England, in 1839, including only 660 operatives, had the effect to throw out of employment 7,840 weavers and others who had nothing to do with the subject matter of the quarrel." For this reason the state had an interest in resolving these conflicts. This required the state to address their root cause, which had to do with labor's "many disadvantages" in selling its unique "commodity." "He [labor] is single, while capital, which is the result of the toil of many laborers, may be said in its force to be collective. Usually the laborer's case will brook no delay—he must have work or he and his family must starve. Capital, however, can wait until approaching famine compels a surrender. The sale of the laborer is a forced sale; and at forced sales commodities usually bring only ruinous prices." It was because of labor's dependency on capital "that in England and in this country many laws have been passed during the present century to protect laborers against the oppression of employers, and it is partly to remedy this inequality that trades unions are formed, the chief object being to withhold labor from the market in times of urgent pressure until remunerative prices are offered," which helps workers "overcome in a measure the inequality that otherwise would exist between them and their employers."[31]

The kinds of changes in constitutional theory necessitated by these discussions was addressed directly by another commentator, who noted that recent legislation designed "to regulate and adjust the relations of employer to employee"—such as antitruck statutes, regulations on employer fines for imperfections in work, laws governing the time and payment of wages and the hours of labor, and statutes forbidding yellow-dog contracts—had been declared unconstitutional in most state courts on the grounds that it was "aimed at a particular class." But, he argued, given changes in class relations brought on by industrialization, it ought to be the case that a "State legislature may, in the exercise of its police power, place any limitation upon freedom of contract, which it may deem necessary for the protection of one class of persons against the oppression of another class." He explained that "it is apparent to every observer of current affairs that many employes are practically *compelled* to accept the terms offered by their employers." Legislative efforts like antitruck laws "are not insulting attempts to degrade the virtue and manhood of the American laborer," as one court had remarked, "nor do they assume that he is an imbecile." Rather, "they are designed to protect the workingman from just such insulting attempts on the part of his employer; to place these two great classes on an equal basis, so that they may deal with each other not only at arm's length, but with an equal length of arm. In short, the purpose of the statutes is to protect one great class of persons against the over-reaching and duress of another class, which by reason of its stronger position, has acquired an undue advantage."[32]

The *American Law Review* responded to one state court decision holding that store order legislation violated the provision in the state constitution which held that "all constitutional government is intended to promote the general welfare of the people" with the (somewhat ahistorical) retort that "it would require a stronger magnifying lens than that possessed by most judges to discover anything in this merely theoretical declaration which lays an inhibition upon the legislature of the State against passing a regulation as wholesome and as necessary to the rights of the honest poor as the statute under consideration."[33] It is a "miserable jurisprudence" that would "set aside as invalid a statute having for its object the protection of the poorest and most helpless class of the community, against grasping wealth, monopoly and power," while at the same time sustaining regulations of fire insurance, "which is the most competitive business that can be named, and in respect of which the two contracting parties stand absolutely in a position of freedom, and on an equal footing."[34] After the Illinois Supreme Court struck down that state's "store order" act, the *American Law Review* reproduced a piece from the *Times-Herald* (Chicago) entitled "The Ghastly Irony of Protecting Lazarus at the Expense of the Dives," which commented, "It is questionable whether, under the same construction of the law, a man would not be upheld by the Supreme Court of the State of Illinois in selling himself into absolute slavery for the period of his life." It was a "ghastly irony" that the court attempted to "excuse its decision upon the plea that it is protecting the rights of weak individuals with labor to sell. Of course, a judicial tribunal cannot be expected to take cognizance of the fact that working people, in so far as they are represented by labor organizations and earnest but unofficial friends of the laboring classes, urged the enactment of the law, and that millionaire firms attacked its constitutionality." But these things "can and shall be presented to the people. What a mockery it is to read that the Supreme Court has demolished this humane, this civilizing law, on the plea that it robs the poor of their right to sell their labor as they will. Dives demands protection. The court accedes to his demand, but pleads that it acts in the interest of Lazarus."[35]

Not too surprisingly, aside from the frequent contributions to the *American Law Review* and the odd passing remark in other law reviews, there was not much discussion in the legal community critical of the judiciary's conception of the scope of the police powers prior to *Lochner*. Most of the commentary of the 1890s echoed traditional sensibilities: "Classes interested in policies, ostensibly for the promotion of the welfare of society but really for their own benefit, zealously advocate the absolute sovereignty of government"; it is "peculiarly the province of jurisprudence, as a passionless and impartial factor, to guide the conscience of the people, and to restore the disinterestedness of law"; "[e]quality before the law is the spirit of our Constitution"; "[t]here must be no class distinction in this country"; "[u]nderlying all these conflicts between the different classes of society, whatever shape they take, is the desire of one class to better itself at the expense of the other"; "the prevailing social unrest . . . is forcing upon the attention of our profession and the courts a new class of constitutional questions"; "[t]he one thing to be feared in our democratic republic, and therefore to be guarded against with sleepless vigilance, is class power and class legislation."[36] At the same time the *American Law Review* was decrying the judiciary's treatment of labor legislation, the *Albany Law Journal* lashed out at the Pennsylvania legislature's passage of a "new and radical labor law, the object of which is to protect employes of corporations in their right to join or continue their membership in labor organizations," a law that "was successfully urged by the great labor organizations of the State." The journal applauded the decision of the Federal Circuit Court to strike it down on the grounds that it "divides labor into classes, and grants privileges to one class" that are denied to others (that is, to workers who work for corporations and not those who work for other kinds of employers).[37] The journal also noted with favor the decision of a judge in the Criminal Court of Cook County, Illinois, to void an identical law as "class legislation" due to the special privileges it afforded men who joined labor associations and not those who were members of a "Don't Worry Club" or a "Fat Man's Club." "As the Chicago Law Journal remarks, 'If it be an offense punishable under the law to discharge a man because of his affiliation with labor societies, with equal reason it would be an offense to discharge him because he is a Democrat, a Republican, a Populist, or on account of his nationality.' "[38]

Those adhering to the established wisdom were unwilling to treat labor unions as privileged forms of association because that would imply that individuals in the market were vulnerable to exploitation by powerful employers, an admission that would undermine the ethos of the neutral state. Similarly, they could not accept the argument that labor unrest had created a general government interest in regulating contractual relations between employers and employees; that would imply that any social group interested in special government protection simply needed to cause a disturbance of the public peace. The existence of social unrest did not lead those who believed in the value (or utility) of faction-free legislation to abandon that belief; for them, social unrest was reason to reassert society's commitment to the principles of the founders' Constitution, principles that had themselves been forged during an era plagued by unrest.

It was not until 1898, in the case of *Holden v. Hardy*, that the Supreme Court had the opportunity to review a state labor law and join these debates.[39] In 1896 the Utah legislature enacted an eight-hour law for miners. It was immediately challenged on grounds that by now should sound familiar: "It is class legislation, and not equal or uniform in its provisions." Relying in particular on the authorities of *Wally's Heirs v. Kennedy, Godcharles v. Wigeman, Butchers' Union v. Crescent City, State v. Goodwill, Commonwealth v. Perry, In re Jacobs, People v. Marx, Millett v. People, Low v. Rees Printing,* and *Frorer v. People,* counsel for plaintiff in error reminded the Court that well-established principles governing the exercise of the police power made it clear that "to be valid, legislation enacted for the purpose of promoting the public health, morals or welfare must be of such a character that it will affect and be for the benefit of the whole community . . . and not of an individual or segregated class of individuals." This law singled out "a comparatively small class of people" who were made to bear (in the opinion of counsel) "this unjustifiable and unequal burden"; consequently it infringed on the "distinguishing privilege of citizens of the United States" to engage "in any calling that is permitted under the law . . . without let or hindrance, except that which is applied to all [other] persons." Moreover, counsel continued, "we have nowhere found a decision of any court upholding such a law as the one here involved" except in cases involving "public employes," "employments affected with a public interest," and statutes "enacted for the protection of the health and safety of women, children, insane persons, and the like."[40]

In this first test of labor legislation under the fourteenth amendment, a majority of the justices voted to uphold the law in *Holden v. Hardy* (1898). There is a self-consciousness about Brown's opinion which suggests that he understood the need to place the discussion of labor legislation in the context of the Court's previous pronouncements on the police power. He began by observing that the "Fourteenth Amendment . . . largely expanded the power of the Federal courts and Congress, and for the first time authorized the former to declare invalid all laws and judicial decisions of the State abridging the rights of citizens." Over the previous few decades two kinds of cases had arisen under the fourteenth amendment: "first, where a state legislature, or a state court, is alleged to have unjustly discriminated in favor of or against a particular individual or class of individuals, as distinguished from the rest of the community, or denied them the benefit of due process of law," and, second, where state criminal procedure was involved. With respect to the first, it had been decided that states could not take one man's property "for the benefit of another" or "deprive any class of persons of the general power to acquire property" or (citing *Allgeyer v. Louisiana*, decided the previous year by a unanimous Court)[41] enter "into contracts with respect to property." However, as is the case with all rights, this "right of contract" is "subject to certain limitations which the State may lawfully impose in the exercise of its police powers. . . . While this court has held . . . that the police power cannot be put forward as an excuse for oppressive and unjust legislation, it may be lawfully resorted to for the purpose of preserving the public health, safety or morals, or the abatement of public nuisances," so long as the regulations are "general" and "necessary to the common good and general welfare."

By the 1890s there were two possible rationales upon which the Court might have justified special treatment for particular classes: under the conception of the police power developed by the justices over the previous twenty years the Court could have emphasized something about the nature of the industry or occupation that involved *traditional* police power concerns of health and safety, as had been the case previously with laundries, railroads, or slaughterhouses; alternatively, under the more recent critiques of this tradition, it had been suggested that market inequalities per se justified a general government interest in interfering with contractual relations regardless of whether the circumstances directly involved traditional concerns of health and safety. Brown's opinion made it clear that the Court would treat labor legislation in precisely the same way that it had been approaching all exercises of the police powers. He noted that the use of the police powers "has doubtless been greatly expanded in its application during the past century," not because of the general social effect of capitalist forms of production on the employer-employee relationship but rather "owing to an enormous increase in the number of occupations which are dangerous, or so far detrimental to the health of employes as to demand special precautions for their well-being and protection." These protections were in the form of regulations requiring fire escapes in large buildings and inspections of boilers and other dangerous machinery. In the particular case of the mining industry statutes were passed requiring the shoring up of dangerous walls, the existence of ventilation and escape shafts, adequate means of signaling the surface, and safe procedures for hoisting and lowering cages. Upon this principle "we think the act in question," which limits the hours of those "employed in underground mines, or in the smelting, reduction or refining of ores or metals," employments which "when too long pursued" have been "judged to be detrimental to the health of the employes," may be "sustained as a valid exercise of the police power of the State."

Interestingly, Brown did use a half page of his nineteen-page opinion to recognize the existence of inequalities in the contractual relation between employers and employees. He noted that legislators in many states had concluded that the owners of mines and their workers did not stand in equal relation to one another, the result being that employees "are often induced by the fear of discharge to conform to regulations which their judgment, fairly exercised, would pronounce to be detrimental to their health or strength. . . . In such cases self-interest is often an unsafe guide, and the legislature may properly interpose its authority. . . . [T]he fact that both parties are of full age and competent to contract does not necessarily deprive the State of the power to interfere where the parties do not stand upon an equality, or where the public health demands that one party to the contract shall be protected against himself." But it should be pointed out that the opinion makes sense only if the word *or* in this last sentence is read as *and*, since Brown's concern was with establishing the proposition that the state may legitimately act when unequal bargaining power leads to the neglect of an individual's health and safety—health and safety provides the justification for state intervention, not the presence of unequal bargaining power per se.[42] In other words, the discussion of unequal bargaining power was intended as an explanation for why these issues were not resolved by the workers themselves, and not as a departure from previous discussions that had distinguished legitimate police power goals (promoting health, safety, and morality) from illegitimate goals (promoting the particular interests of some classes at the expense of others). Brown stressed at the end of the opinion that "the question in each case is whether the legislature had adopted the statute in exercise of a reasonable discretion, or whether its action be a mere excuse for an unjust discrimination, or the oppression, or spoilation of a particular class. The distinction between these two different classes of enactments cannot be better stated than by a comparison of the views of this court found in the opinions in *Barbier v. Connolly* . . . with those later expressed in *Yick Wo v. Hopkins*."[43] Brown thereby ended his opinion with reference to those authorities that had been organizing virtually all of the Court's police power discussions requiring the justices to make a distinction between general welfare legislation with a partial application and class legislation.

Brewer and Peckham dissented without comment in *Holden*. It is reasonable to assume that they were concerned about the implications of expanding the doctrine that states can regulate when certain enterprises pose dangers to the public generally (slaughterhouses, liquor, maybe even spark-producing, cattle-killing railroads), or when certain standards and practices are necessary to ensure that enterprises are operated safely (inspection of boilers, shoring up dangerous walls), to include interferences predicated on a desire to promote the health and safety of a particular class. While regulating the hours of labor had previously been upheld in *Barbier* (involving a law that prohibited washing and ironing in public laundries from ten o'clock at night to six in the morning), the justification was that it was necessary to promote the well-being of the community as a whole. Expanding the police powers to justify legislation that advanced the physical well-being of only certain workers threatened to explode the prevailing distinction between legitimate and illegitimate uses of the police power: if interfering in employer-employee relations to the advantage of employees could be considered general welfare legislation, then it would be difficult to imagine what counted as class legislation. The dissenters' position, like the position of some state court judges, was that traditional police powers jurisprudence required the Court to draw a sharp distinction between laws designed to promote the community's well-being and laws designed to promote the well-being of a particular class. As the justices of the Colorado Supreme Court explained when they invalidated a similar law, "It would be absurd to argue that . . . limiting the hours of those laboring in a smelter in any wise [*sic*] conduces to preserve the health of any portion of the public. That is to say, three shifts of laborers, working eight hours each, would affect the public health to the same extent, if at all, as would two shifts at twelve hours each. . . . Indeed, the only object that can rationally be claimed for it, is the preservation of the health of those working in smelters. . . . How can an alleged law that purports to be the result of the exercise of the police power, be such in reality, when it has for its only object not the preservation of the health of others or of the public health, safety or morals or general welfare, but the welfare of him whose act is prohibited when if committed, it will injure him who committs [*sic*] it, and him only?"[44]

The *Holden* majority's response to this concern was to reemphasize that class legislation was still considered illegitimate and that laws which imposed special burdens or benefits on particular groups or classes had to be closely scrutinized to make sure they really advanced health and safety concerns and were not designed merely to make one class better off at the expense of another. From the majority's point of view, if the harm-causing characteristics of certain industries could justify state interference in conflicts between competing claimants under some circumstances (e.g., when litigation against railroads involved damage caused by fire but not when it involved harms unrelated to the distinctive characteristics of railroads), then the harm-causing characteristics of certain industries could also justify state interference in employer-employee relations—if, that is, there was a reasonable relationship between the regulation and a concern about health or safety.

Holden stood for the proposition that the police powers could be used not only to promote the general well-being of the community but also the specific physical well-being of a class of workers who were not in a position to make contracts favorable to their health and safety.[45] In the mind of the majority, this development was consistent with traditional police powers jurisprudence to the extent that the Court was willing to distinguish legislation motivated by a concern with worker health and safety from legislation intended simply to intervene in the competition among social groups on behalf of favored classes. The master principle of nineteenth-century American constitutionalism was that it was il-legitimate for government to single out for special treatment and atten-tion certain groups or classes simply to improve their position in relation to competing classes; government could impose special burdens and benefits only if it could be demonstrated that the special treatment would advance public health, safety, or morality. It was this principle that organized and informed the justices' debates on the regulation of slaugh-terhouses, laundries, railroads, grain elevators, liquor, and oleomar-garine. Previously, the principle had enabled Federalists to protect cor-porate charters and had led Jeffersonians to attack them; it had led Jacksonians to tie special burdens (like eminent domain) and benefits (like public subsidies and monopolies) to an explicit "public purpose" and to tolerate the regulation of property (whether it took the form of prohibition statutes or ordinances specifying the location of potentially hazardous businesses). And it was the late-nineteenth-century Court's heightened sense of class conflict and careful scrutiny of exercises of the police powers that led a majority of the Court to strike down a max-imum hours law for bakers in *Lochner v. New York* (1905).

A decision by the Supreme Court on the general question of eight-hour laws had been anticipated for some time. "It is doubtful if any doctrine advanced by courts in recent years has met with more general difference of opinion than that class of cases in which the legislature has attempted to exercise its police power in favor of some special class of people or of the supposed betterment of social conditions,"[46] wrote the editors of the *Yale Law Journal* around the turn of the century. The journal remarked in 1903 that the "present rivalry between capital and labor" made the issue of the constitutionality of laws regulating hours of employment "of great interest and importance." While some courts had upheld maximum hours laws, most of the existing authorities were against the validity of these enactments. "[I]t is patent from all authorities, that police regulations can only be valid on one of the three well-known grounds of public health, public safety or public morals," and that maximum hours laws are valid only if "the employment sought to be regulated [is] such an one [sic] that its exercise affects the public at large to a degree where the interference may be justified under the police power."[47] The settled wisdom as of 1904 was that "the general tendency of the courts is to uphold the power of the legislature to regulate the hours of adult male labor in private employments whenever the employment involved may fairly be deemed inimical to the health of employes and the resulting welfare of the State. . . . From these decisions, however, the inference by no means follows that the power of the legislature to enact laws of a penal character limiting the hours of daily labor in all private employment must be conceded." In a minor display of clairvoyance, the journal concluded its discussion of maximum hours laws with the remark that "further development of this subject in the near future may fairly be anticipated."[48]

That anticipated future arrived in less than a year. Joseph Lochner, a bakery owner, was convicted of violating a New York statute requiring that employees of bakeries not work more than ten hours per day or sixty hours a week.[49] One of his lawyers was Henry Weismann, who in the 1890s had been head of the Journeymen Bakers' and Confectioners' International Union of America and editor of the Bakers' Journal, and had worked for the passage of the Bakeshop Act that he was now asking the Court to strike down.[50] In the brief presented to the Court on behalf of Lochner by Weismann and Frank Harvey Field, the emphasis was not on liberty of contract—Allgeyer v. Louisiana (1896) was not even mentioned. Counsel instead cited Ernst Freund on the police power to make the point that "equality is for the purpose of controlling the validity of legislation, a more definitive conception than liberty, for it has the advantage of being measurable. . . . It is an elementary principle of equal justice, that where the public welfare requires something to be given, or done the burden be imposed or distributed upon some rational basis, and that no individual be singled out to make a sacrifice for the community. . . . To prevent an abuse of the police power, for the alleged protection of the health or safety . . . , the Court must be allowed to judge whether protective measures have really these ends in view."[51] The principal authorities used to support this argument were *Butchers' Union v. Crescent City*; *Barbier v. Connolly*; *Gulf, Colorado and Santa Fe Railway Company v. Ellis*; *Atchison, Topeka and Santa Fe Railroad Company v. Matthews*; *Cotting v. Kansas City Stock Yard Company*; and *Connolly v. Union Sewer Pipe Company*. These cases demonstrate that the focus of the discussion in the brief centered not on liberty of contract (which barely figures in these cases) but rather on the issue of impartial treatment and, especially, whether the special classification used in the statute could be rationalized in terms of a legitimate police power interest. Counsel began by noting that many people engaged in the baking trade were not included in the terms of the statute, like employees of pie bakeries, hotels, restaurants, clubs, and boardinghouses. ("Then there is the American housewife. Here is the real artist in biscuits, cake and bread, not to mention the American pie.") They then moved to a discussion of whether the regulation in fact promoted the public health ("if indeed, the Legislature ever intended this to be a health regulation"), asking specifically whether an hours limitation contributed anything more to the reduction of the amount of flour dust in the air than other provisions that regulated cleanliness and ventilation.

All of this, of course, was to get to the crux of the matter, which was that "the statute in question was never intended as a health provision but was purely a labor law," thus distinguishing it from the Court's holding in *Holden*. Saying it was "purely a labor law" suggested that the act was promoting a class interest unrelated to traditional police power concerns, an interest in singling out for special treatment and attention certain competitors in the market. If this could reasonably be established, then the relevant precedents followed naturally. From *Calder v. Bull*: "[A] law that takes property from A. and gives it to B. . . . is against all reason and justice." From *In re Jacobs*: "Such legislation may invade one class of rights today and another tomorrow. . . . Such governmental interferences disturb the normal adjustments of the social fabric." From *Barbier*: "[N]o impediment should be interposed to the pursuits of any one *except as applied to the same pursuits by others under like circumstances*" (emphasis in the brief). From Peckham's opinion in *People v. Gillson*: "[This legislation] is evidently of that kind which has been so frequent of late, a kind which is meant to protect some class in the community against the fair, free and full competition of some other class, the members of the former class thinking it impossible to hold their own against such competition, and therefore flying to the Legislatures to secure some enactment which shall operate favorably to them or unfavorably to their competitors." From *Ex parte Westerfield* (1880): "This is special legislation. A certain class is selected. . . . There is no reason, and can be no reason, why *bakers* should be forced to rest from their labors periodically, which is not applicable to many other classes of artisans and workmen. To say that every law is 'general' within the meaning of the Constitution, which bears equally upon all to whom it is applicable, is to say that there can be no special laws."[52]

As one New York Court of Appeals judge put it, the "struggle" in the *Lochner* case "was to make what some of us thought was a labor law a health law and so within the police power."[53] (It did not help that the law was inserted into New York's Labor Code and not into its Public Health Regulations.) This was the struggle that was lost when a bare majority of the Supreme Court remained unconvinced that the hours limitation was consistent with a neutral state interest in promoting public health.

Unlike the emphasis in Lochner's brief and in virtually all of the previous discussions in state cases, Peckham's majority opinion (which was joined by two of the justices in the *Holden* majority)[54] does not explicitly rely on the language of unequal, partial, or class legislation in striking down the New York act. However, the authorities and interpretive elements that had become a part of that jurisprudence are in evidence. Peckham began his bare majority opinion with the observation that "the statute necessarily interferes with the right of contract between the employer and employes, concerning the number of hours in which the latter may labor in the bakery of the employer." Yet immediately following a passing reference to *Allgeyer*, he went on to note that "both property and liberty are held on such reasonable conditions as may be imposed by the governing power of the State in the exercise of [the police] powers, and with such conditions the Fourteenth Amendment was not designed to interfere. . . . The State, therefore, has power to prevent the individual from making certain kinds of contracts, and in regard to them the Federal Constitution offers no protection." In fact, Peckham pointed out that the Court had upheld many interferences with rights to contract (even "cases which might fairly be considered as border ones"), including hours legislation for men working in underground mines and smelters, compulsory vaccination laws, and in general "legislation that was enacted to conserve the morals, the health or the safety of the people." The central question to be decided, then, in "every case that comes before this court . . . where legislation of this character is concerned" is whether the act is "a fair, reasonable and appropriate exercise of the police power of the State, or . . . an unreasonable, unnecessary and arbitrary interference" with a person's liberty.

"Viewed in the light of a purely labor law," continued Peckham, "with no reference whatever to the question of health, we think that a law like the one before us involves neither the safety, the morals nor the welfare of the public, and that the interest of the public is not in the slightest degree affected by such an act." If the law is to be upheld at all it must be shown that it reasonably addresses "the health of the individual engaged in the occupation of a baker." But, in the opinion of the majority, unlike that part of the law requiring the inspection of plumbing, ceilings, and floors and the installation of proper washrooms, which were considered valid police power measures, there was "no reasonable foundation for holding this to be necessary or appropriate as a health law to safeguard the public health or the health of the individuals who are following the trade of a baker." While Peckham acknowledged that one could assert some distant and uncertain relationship between the number of hours worked in any job ("[a] printer, a tinsmith, a locksmith, a carpenter, a cabinetmaker, a dry good's clerk, a bank's, a lawyer's or a physician's clerk") and a person's health, he was mostly concerned about the possibility that legislatures might begin to use this pretext as an open-ended excuse to pass class legislation. Thus his remark that "there must be more than the mere fact of the possible existence of some small amount of unhealthiness to warrant legislative interference" with the employer-employee relationship. As he noted at the end of the opinion, "It is impossible for us to shut our eyes to the fact that many of the laws of this character, while passed under what is claimed to be the police power for the purpose of protecting the public health or welfare, are, in reality, passed from other motives. . . . It seems to us that the real object and purpose were simply to regulate the hours of labor between the master and his employes," and this amounts to the use of government power to favor certain groups at the expense of others.[55]

The major block of dissenters, led by Harlan, had a different opinion about whether the state had successfully asserted a neutral interest in this contractual relationship. "While this court has held . . . that the police power cannot be put forward as an excuse for oppressive and unjust legislation, it may be lawfully resorted to for the purpose of preserving the public health, safety or morals, or the abatement of public nuisances." For these three justices, it was "plain that this statute was enacted in order to protect the physical well-being of those who work in bakery and confectionary establishments." They were aware of the charge that the motive behind the enactment was merely to interfere in market relations between two classes, but they argued that it was possible to justify the interference on faction-free grounds: "It may be that the statute had its origin, in part, in the belief that employers and employes in such establishments were not upon equal footing, and that the necessities of the latter often compelled them to submit to such exactions as unduly taxed their strength," wrote Harlan with some defensiveness. But it is wrong "to presume that the State of New York has acted in bad faith. Nor can we assume, that its legislature acted without due deliberation, or that it did not determine this question upon the fullest attainable information, and for the common good." The statute must be taken "as expressing the belief of the people of New York that, as a general rule, and in the case of the average man, labor in excess of sixty hours during a week in such establishments may endanger the health of those who thus labor," either specifically because the inhalation of flour dust in bakeries might cause inflammation of the lungs or bronchial tubes or on the more general grounds that "[s]horter hours of work, by allowing higher standards of comfort and purer family life, promise to enhance the industrial efficiency of the wage-working class—improved health, longer life, more content and greater intelligence and inventiveness."[56]

As Ira Steward had done decades earlier, the dissenters were suggesting a faction-free rationale in support of maximum hours laws. But it should come as little surprise that just as Steward's position was dismissed as "class legislation," so too did a majority of the justices, operating in a social environment of heightened class consciousness and on guard to the possibility that labor interests were attempting to gain control of public power to advance their special interests at the expense of employers, decide that the New York bakery law was a corruption of public power. From the point of view of the majority, the dissenters' suggestion that the majority's refusal to accept this law as a valid contribution to public health was based not on principle but rather on questions of public policy "about which there is room for debate and for an honest difference of opinion" must have seemed unfair; one might doubt whether Harlan would have accepted that same response to his decision in *Connolly v. Union Sewer Pipe* or his position in *Matthews* and *Ellis* rejecting the legislatures' claims that there were good reasons to impose special burdens on railroads (not to mention, as we shall see, his later decision in *Adair*). In essence, by drawing a distinction between hours legislation in the mining industry and in the baking industry, the majority was doing nothing different in kind than what had been done earlier when the Court drew distinctions between different kinds of railroad legislation; in each instance a particular business was identified for special treatment and the question to be decided was whether a sufficient connection was demonstrated between the special treatment and a valid police power concern.

The discussion that has received the most scholarly attention is Holmes's refreshingly short and pointed lone dissent. Unfortunately, in terms of the constitutional tradition within which he was operating, the dissent was, to a large extent, somewhat beside the point, and it should come as no surprise that his remarks were joined by none of his brethren. Holmes's criticism was that "this case is decided upon an economic theory which a large part of the country does not entertain," that is, laissez-faire, and "a constitution is not intended to embody a particular economic theory." He then noted that the "liberty of the citizen to do as he likes so long as he does not interfere with the liberty of others to do the same . . . is interfered with by schools laws, by the Post Office, by every state and municipal institution which takes his money for purposes thought desirable, whether he likes it or not. The Fourteenth Amendment does not enact Mr. Herbert Spencer's Social Statics." However, the majority acknowledged that people's rights and liberties were subject to legitimate police power regulation. And while the Constitution was not intended to embody a particular economic program, it most certainly rested on clearly articulated assumptions about the proper relationship between state and society, and it was on that basis that the majority struck down the act. Holmes's unprecedented admonition that judges ought to respect the "right of a majority to embody their opinions in law" and let the "natural outcome of a dominant opinion" prevail amounted to an abdication of judicial responsibility that was as unacceptable to his peers as it would be today if the same was said about the Court's approach to racial classifications. In order to join the debate, Holmes would have had to show either why the Court was mistaken when it concluded that this measure did not promote public health, safety, or morality—which was the position of the other three dissenters—or, more sweepingly, why the Court's traditional understanding of the police powers should no longer be controlling.[57]

Lochner *and the New Realism*

The Court's decision in *Lochner* provoked a variety of responses. Many commentators joined in a vigorous reexamination of the question of whether judicial review was a legitimate institution in a constitutional democracy. They also debated the extent to which the Court had previously interfered with the exercise of the police power.[58] In addition, there was an upsurge in the number of laws limiting the hours of labor in industries conventionally considered dangerous to employees (or certain classes of employees) or where worker exhaustion posed a potential threat to public safety, such as in railroads, mining, and the drug industry.[59] But the combined efforts of state and federal courts deterred legislatures from extending these same protections more generally to the work force.[60]

Lochner also provoked a more intense debate over the substantive question of what the proper limits on the police powers should be. In general, these substantive discussions of the jurisprudence of *Lochner* paralleled the division on the Court: many commentators supported and elaborated on the Court's decision; others supported the Court's conception of the scope of the police powers but questioned the application of the concept in the particular case; and a few felt that the Court's conception of the police powers had become anachronistic in postindustrial America.

To one extent or another, the *Lochner* defenders shared a common belief that the principal constitutional value was to combat "[c]lass legislation, the most pernicious and most dangerous of all legislation," by ensuring that the "rules of government must not in their operation, impose duties and hardships on one class which, in justice, ought to be imposed upon all classes of like situation; and that there should be no classification with respect to occupations, pursuits, business, professions or property, when a general law can be made applicable to all classes."[61] Or, as another commentator put it, "The American idea of equality, is equality before the law, and must be for all alike; that legislation in favor of a class is as obnoxious as legislation against a class, and that all classes and all persons shall stand alike before the law, and there must be no special law for a particular person or a particular class."[62] These writers agreed with the prevailing constitutional wisdom that the best way to ensure that public power would not be used by particular persons or classes to promote their special interests was to limit its exercise to objectives shared by all members of the community, like personal health and safety. A note in the *Harvard Law Review* summarized the position: "As regards limiting the hours of work, . . . the prevailing doctrine has come to be that reasonable restrictions may be placed upon the length of daily employment of all women and children and of men engaged in particularly dangerous and unhealthful occupations. . . . [The legislature] may constitutionally restrict the bargaining of employer and employee only to an extent determined by the harmful effects of the occupation upon the class of workers in question"; that is, in order to prevent "the employer from using his superior economic position to injure the health of his employees."[63]

Just one year after *Lochner*, S. Whitney Dunscomb, Jr., argued in the *Columbia Law Review* that Peckham's majority opinion safeguarded the constitutional value of equality by correctly recognizing and enforcing the important distinction (noted by Freund) between laws that legitimately promoted public health and safety and laws that illegitimately promoted the special interests of certain economic classes. "There is a sphere of interests embracing safety, health, and morals, in which the exercise of the police power is conceded, and the only question that arises is the extent to which the legislature may *reasonably* and *appropriately* go." On the other hand, "there is another sphere of economic interests, the production and distribution of wealth, in which the exercise of the police power is by no means universally conceded. Legislation in this domain is in the experimental stage, and much that has been attempted is class legislation or unwarranted and oppressive interference with individual rights which cannot be justified as being of equal benefit." Peckham recognized in his opinion that "the point at issue in the Lochner Case is not whether bakers as well as laborers in other occupations would not be benefited by shorter hours of labor, that they might have more leisure for rest, self-improvement and the up-building of their homes." Those interested in more leisure would benefit; those who wanted the freedom to earn more would not. The point according to Dunscomb is that it was dangerous and potentially oppressive for the state to begin taking sides in these economic disputes between classes. Regulations governing the hours of labor should therefore be limited to occupations "especially dangerous or unsanitary, or in which the safety or the public is especially concerned." Dunscomb sided with the *Lochner* majority that this condition was not present in the business of baking.[64]

Another commentator, Frederick Green, explained that "in the Bakeshop case . . . a majority of the Supreme Court, were clear that the law was a pure and simple regulation of the hours of labor in a·particular industry, and rested their decision against it on the principle that to limit the hours that a man may work for reasons unconnected with physical or moral well being is an interference with individual freedom that exceeds the due limits of governmental power." In other words, "limitations of working hours for social or economic, as distinguished from moral or sanitary reasons, . . . is among the things which the people of the United States have forbidden to the people of the States." While it is true that the judges who passed on the case on appeal in the state and federal courts "were divided eleven to ten on the question of fact" as to whether the act did contribute to public health, "only two out of twenty-one dissented from the legal doctrine as to what the legislature had power to do"; it was "therefore untrue" that the Supreme Court had decided that states could not alleviate "unhygienic conditions." It was also a "confusion of thought" to say that "the decision violates the often declared rule that a statute will not be held unconstitutional unless it is evidently so" simply because some justices believed the statute reasonable. "A jury in a criminal case is told to acquit unless guilt is proved beyond a reasonable doubt. That does not mean that if one or more jurors think the prisoner innocent, all should [vote to] acquit because the difference of opinion shows reasonable doubt. It means that each juror should be clear in his own mind" as to whether he believes the standard has been met. Similarly, it would be a "rank absurdity" to suggest that "a judge ought to acquiesce in what he believes to be a violation of constitutional right and a denial of justice to the parties before him, because some of his colleagues think differently."[65]

Some commentators were more circumspect about what they considered the "factual" issue of whether the bakery law contributed to health and safety, but nevertheless argued that that was the central question. "We have in recent years passed into a new stage of industrial and social being," wrote Andrew C. McLaughlin. "[W]e have outgrown in business activity and in social sentiment the conditions of individualism that were dominant in the early days of the Republic and for decades thereafter; we are face to face with the fact that society has duties and responsibilities and that any principles which set up isolated individual right as over against community interest are at least fraught with danger, if they are not pure anachronism. . . . In this changing order the courts have been tested to the utmost; the ingenuity of judges has been strained in efforts to accommodate the law, and inherited principles of individual right under the law, to the demands for the recognition of social justice." But, he argued, this relatively recent concern with "social justice" had led some well-intentioned reformers to dismiss much too casually certain established principles of constitutional limitations that still had validity. "Those who work in the slums of the large cities and give their lives to elevating and comforting their fellow-men, who see the horrors of the tenement and sweat shop, who come face to face with what misery can be wrought by the unbridled energy of avarice and selfish greed, demand now and again, with an energy that comes from conscientious conviction and wholehearted devotion to right, restraints upon individual privilege of contract, and in reality demand a total surrender of the old-fashioned notion that one can do what one will with one's own. That such demands go too far many may believe." Thus "there has arisen constant necessity for watching narrowly this power of the state, for it is often invoked not for the common good, but for the supposed advantage of classes and cliques." In addressing *Lochner*, McLaughlin took advantage of the opportunity for ambivalence or ambiguity afforded academics when they discuss constitutional law and commented, "If a law to limit the hours of work in bakeries, like that of New York recently passed on by the courts, has for its purpose, not the uplifting and protection of the health and well-being of the community, but the giving of advantage to a certain class of workmen without regard to rights and desires of the rest, or if it is merely an attack on an employer's right of contract, it can hardly be rightly supported as an exercise of the police power, which has in recent years made such inroads upon the notion of unrestrained individual struggle."[66]

Other commentators were less tentative about siding with Harlan's block of dissenters and declaring the New York bakers' law a valid promotion of public health. They argued that the majority was not sufficiently attentive to evidence that demonstrated the link between working hours and worker health. In an article published two months after the decision in *Lochner* was handed down, Ernst Freund argued that the available facts indicated that the New York law advanced legitimate police power concerns. His review of previous federal and state indicated that while "the constitutional right of liberty was in all of them emphasized," the "argument of the equal protection of the laws had considerable, if not controlling weight with the courts." In these previous cases it had been established that the legislature could regulate hours only "where long continued work might be reasonably believed to be detrimental to the health of the employees." Moreover, "the power of a court of last resort to form an independent judgment upon the validity of legislation is not to be drawn in question; its exercise is, on the contrary, claimed to be a solemn duty." To this he added that "the mere fact that a measure claims to subserve the public welfare does not ensure its validity" and "the fact that a measure tends remotely to promote health and safety is likewise not conclusive of its validity, since such effect in a very slight degree might be predicted of the most unwarrantable and oppressive interferences with private liberty and property." More specifically, Freund indicated that if the act at issue in *Lochner* was "claimed to be a measure for the social or economic advancement of bakers' employees . . . it would doubtless have been open to the objection of being partial or class legislation." Having laid out the prevailing constitutional principles, he then suggested that, in terms of worker health, the baking and mining industries were more alike than the *Lochner* majority was willing to accept: "Smelting and bakery establishments have this in common, that they vitiate the air, the former by noxious gases and minute particles of metal, the latter by the dust and flour and excessive heat; in either case it is conceded that the respiratory organs are unfavorably affected." The majority's unwillingness to recognize these points could be attributed to the decision to evaluate "the reality of the danger to the public health and safety" on the basis of "common knowledge or understanding" rather than on scientific evidence. "Has not the progress of sanitary science shown that common understanding is often equivalent to popular ignorance and fallacy?" Freund expressed hope that "a future court will allow itself to be convinced that the conditions in the bakers' trade are sufficiently unsanitary to justify a restriction of hours of employment."[67]

When Felix Frankfurter referred to the need for "realism" in the judiciary, and when Roscoe Pound argued in favor of "sociological jurisprudence" and against "mechanical jurisprudence,"[68] they were suggesting that the justices should rely less on their "common understanding" of the health and safety issues surrounding particular occupations and more on an investigation into actual working conditions.[69] In his essay on liberty of contract Pound began by asking why it was that courts persist in reiterating the "utterly hollow" fallacy that employer and employee have "equality of right" in the buying and selling of labor, and why so many judges "force upon legislation an academic theory of

equality in the face of practical conditions of inequality." He dismissed
the simple answer to that question—that "judges project their personal,
social and economic views into the law"—with the remark that "when a
doctrine is announced with equal vigor and held with equal tenacity by
courts of Pennsylvania and of Arkansas, of New York and California, of
Illinois and of West Virginia, of Massachusetts and of Missouri, we may
not dispose of it [the question] so readily." Pound attributed the judiciary's approach to labor legislation to a variety of factors, including an
"individualist conception of justice" which "exaggerates private right at
the expense of public right," the reliance on a "mechanical jurisprudence . . . in which conceptions are developed logically at the expense of
practical results," the training of judges in eighteenth-century natural
rights philosophy, and "the sharp line between law and fact in our legal
system." The cumulative result of these influences has been to imbue in
judges "a narrow view of what constitutes special or class legislation"
and to inhibit them from permitting legislatures to recognize individual
market "incapacities not known to the common law."

Still, Pound balked at the opportunity to expand this analysis of the
social foundations of worker vulnerability into the more general proposition that the state ought to be able to interfere in market relations
simply to secure and protect the social independence of laboring classes;
that is, simply to promote the well-being of labor irrespective of whether
state action also contributed directly to worker health or public safety.
Instead, he maintained that state interference with employer-employee
relations was justified precisely on this traditional basis. A study of the
facts in *Lochner* "has shown that the legislature was right and the court
was wrong. Actual investigation has shown that the output of shops in
which the only kind of men who can be had to work for unreasonable
hours under unsanitary conditions are employed, is not at all what the
public ought to eat, and that long hours in shops of the sort are distinctly
injurious to health."[70]

At the forefront of those who worked to make the justices more
conscientious about the way they applied prevailing police powers jurisprudence was Louis Brandeis, who knew well the Court's expectation
that the public purpose behind legislation must be conclusively demonstrated. It guided his approach in defending Oregon's maximum hours
law for women in *Muller v. Oregon* (1908), in which he devoted virtually his entire brief to the factual question of whether a maximum
hours law promoted the health of women.[71] In response, a unanimous

Court, in an opinion by Justice Brewer (who opposed the legislation at issue in both *Holden* and *Lochner*), permitted this protection of working women on the grounds that "woman's physical structure and the performance of maternal functions place her at a disadvantage in the struggle for subsistence," a struggle in which "she is not an equal competitor with her brother," on whom she still depends. Moreover, the "abundant testimony of the medical fraternity" supports the legislature's conclusion that "continuance for a long time on her feet at work, repeating this from day to day, tends to injurious effects upon the body, and as healthy mothers are essential to vigorous offspring, the physical well-being of woman becomes an object of public interest and care in order to preserve the strength and vigor of the race." Not only, then, was there medical evidence which suggested that working long hours injured women as a class, but it was also suggested that the community as a whole could be injured if this protection was not extended to this class—and this kind of concern, if based on reasonable evidence, certainly fell within the traditional boundaries of the police powers. "The limitations which this statute places upon her contractual powers, upon her right to agree with her employer as to the time she shall labor, are not imposed solely for her benefit, but also largely for the benefit of all."[72]

In *Muller* the traditional police power concern involved maternal health and safety; in another case handed down that same year, *McLean v. Arkansas* (1908), the legislature's asserted interest was in preventing fraud in the workplace. In *McLean*, a seven-man majority upheld a state law requiring coal operators to pay their workers on the basis of the amount of coal mined before it was screened. Justice William R. Day's opinion began by noting that "if there existed a condition of affairs concerning which the legislature of the State, exercising its conceded right to enact laws for the protection of the health, safety or welfare of the people, might pass the law, it must be sustained; if such action was arbitrary interference with the right to contract or carry on business, and having no just relation to the protection of the public within the scope of legislative power, the act must fail." He then noted that Congress in 1898 had ordered an industrial commission to investigate the subject of capital and labor employed in the mining industry; the resulting report indicated that the use of screens "led to frequent and sometimes heated controversies between the operators and the miners." In light of this report the majority was "unable to say . . . that this law had no reasonable relation to the protection of a large class of laborers in the receipt of their just dues." Consequently, this law was analogous to statutes designed "to prevent fraud and to require honest weights and measures in the transaction of business," which were goals that had always been understood to be within the legitimate scope of the police power.[73]

The same could not be said for laws prohibiting the use of so-called yellow-dog contracts, through which employers extracted agreements from workers that they were subject to discharge if they joined a union. The Court first struck down this prohibition in *Adair v. United States* (1908), the same year that *Muller* and *McLean* were handed down, in an opinion written by Harlan, the lead *Lochner* dissenter. In *Adair* Harlan acknowledged that "the rights of liberty and property guaranteed by the Constitution against deprivation without due process of law, is subject to such reasonable restraints as the common good or the general welfare may require," but went on to hold that public health and safety were not served when government sought "to compel any person in the course of his business and against his will to accept or retain the personal services of another, or to compel any person, against his will, to perform personal services for another." He maintained that "the right of a person to sell his labor upon such terms as he deems proper is, in its essence, the same as the right of the purchaser of labor to prescribe the conditions upon which he will accept such labor from the person offering to sell it. . . . In all such particulars the employer and the employee have equality of right, and any legislation that disturbs that equality is an arbitrary interference with the liberty of contract which no government can legally justify in a free land."[74] The justices reasserted this position six years later in *Coppage v. Kansas* (1914). Writing for the Court, Mahlon Pitney—who had been appointed two years earlier to replace Harlan— asked, "[W]hat possible relation has . . . the Act to the public health, safety, morals or general welfare? . . . None is suggested, and we are unable to conceive of any. The Act . . . is intended to deprive employers of a part of their liberty of contract, to the corresponding advantage of the employed and the upbuilding of labor organizations." The legislative interest was simply in removing those "inequalities of fortune" that "are but the normal and inevitable result of" the right of private property by helping some groups at the expense of others—just like the debtor-relief legislation, the paper money schemes, and the calls for wage and price controls that haunted the Federalists and gave rise to the constitutional structure and its supporting ideology, and just like the corporate charters that helped mobilize Jacksonian democracy and gave rise to a more explicit judicial reliance on the founding ideology as the final filter through which exercises of political power had to pass in order to ensure the republican purity of American politics.[75]

Still, despite the outcome in *Adair*, it was assumed by many after 1908 that the justices had started to warm up to the "new realism." Frankfurter expressed hope that *Muller v. Oregon* would signal a turning point away from a time when there was "an unmistakable dread of the class of legislation under consideration" toward a willingness to examine the issues "on the basis of authoritative data." Still, Frankfurter was wrong to suggest that *Muller* implied that *Lochner* is "surely no longer 'controlling.'"[76] The kind of analysis used by the Court in *Muller* indicated strongly that the central tenets of nineteenth-century police powers jurisprudence had not changed. In his discussion of labor legislation in 1910 Ernst Freund noted that virtually all legislation having an immediate bearing on safety and health considerations had been sustained by courts, and that while there was slightly more division on which side of the police powers line maximum hours laws fell, "contrary to the impression produced by the variety of rulings, these cases have given rise to no serious conflict of principle. The courts seem unanimous in the view that the right of the workman to utilize his capacity for work is a valuable constitutional right which will yield to statutory restraints where excessive labor involves some appreciable danger to the particular class of employees or to the community, but not where it is only a question of realizing those aims and ideals which are involved in the eight-hour day. The conflict of decisions seems to be entirely due to the manner in which this principle is applied." Because "it requires some tangible element of danger to compel a reduction in the hours of labor, the existence or non-existence of this danger is a question of fact." Although some had suggested that the courts should defer to the legislature's judgment as to whether the facts warranted legislation, the "faithful application of this theory would in many cases amount to a total surrender of judicial control." The principle ought to be that courts request of the state "evidence of facts within the reach of the legislature sufficient to support its judgement," as illustrated by Brandeis's brief.[77] In 1910, two years after *Muller* and *Adair* were handed down, the assistant secretary for the American Association for Labor Legislation noted that "the courts maintain an unfavorable attitude toward general restrictive legislation, and unless facts of sufficient strength concerning conditions of safety and health can be obtained and clearly set forth, such legislation is likely to be declared unconstitutional." She argued that a willingness on the part of advocates to accept "the principle that some industries are more injurious than others forms the starting point for a scientific grading of all industries according to the degree of the injury inflicted upon the workers employed,"[78] and thus the beginning of the end of the practice of requiring a worker "to sell his life or his health in addition to his labor."[79]

Despite significant changes in the Court's personnel, police powers jurisprudence changed very little in the 1910s.[80] Twelve years after *Lochner* and nine years after *Muller*, the Court, in *Bunting v. Oregon* (1917), upheld an Oregon law that set ten hours a day as the maximum workday for industrial workers but allowed employees to work an additional three hours provided they were paid time and one-half of the regular wage. Attorneys for the plaintiff in error argued that maximum hours laws could be upheld only if the work "directly affected the welfare, health or safety of the public," or if it involved employment that presented "unusual danger to the health of the employee," or if it applied to "the State or one of its subdivisions." They claimed that it was "hardly conceivable that a law with the broad scope of the Oregon act can be held to be necessary for the preservation of the health of employees in mills, factories and manufacturing establishments," which are "ordinary" occupations that "involve only the ordinary dangers to health that accompany manual labor." They contended that the real purpose of the law was not to promote health and safety but merely to extend special economic benefits to workers at the expense of employers, benefits they would not receive but for the state's inappropriate intervention. According to the attorneys, this inappropriate legislative goal was evident in the wage provisions of the act: "The law is not a ten-hour law; it is a thirteen-hour law designed solely for the purpose of compelling the employer of labor . . . to pay more for labor than the actual market value thereof. It is based upon economic grounds exclusively. The provision for overtime at time and one-half the regular wage robs the law of any argument that might be made to bring it within those grounds that justify an exercise of the police power."[81]

Representing Oregon were the state attorney general, the assistant attorney general, and Felix Frankfurter, who in this case took Brandeis's place as the footsoldier of the new realism. Frankfurter insisted that the law was "an hours law, not a wage law; the provision for overtime work and extra pay being merely to allow a limited and reasonable flexibility in time of unusual business pressure." More important, though, he argued that the boundary between the police powers and individual liberty must be drawn "not by resort to theory and assumption, but in the light of experience, granting to the legislature the function of discerning, detecting and remedying the evils which may be obstacles to the 'greater public welfare' . . . and upholding its judgment if in the light of experience the judgment seems not arbitrary or wanton." He noted that the decision in *Lochner* "was based upon a view of the nature of the baker's employment beyond ten hours as known 'to the common understanding,'" and added, "It is now clear that 'common understanding' is a treacherous criterion," particularly in light of the fact that "in the last decade science has been giving us the basis for judgment by experience to which, when furnished, judgment by speculation must yield." What in *Holden* looked like "a specific, and apparently, exceptional instance— the poisoning of the human system through long hours of labor in mines, and the implications of this evil to the general welfare—is now disclosed to be of far wider and deeper application. It is now demonstrable that the considerations that were patent as to miners in 1898 are to-day operative, to a greater or less degree, throughout the industrial system." The Court, Frankfurter insisted, must look at the kind of "data that, partly, was not presented in cases like *Lochner*." He then proceeded to offer to the Court "an extensive systematic review of facts and statistics dealing with the effects of overtime upon the physical and moral health of the worker and so upon the vitality, efficiency and prosperity of the nation," and a discussion of the "good effects following regulation."[82]

The opinion of the Court was written by McKenna, who twelve years earlier voted with the majority in *Lochner* to strike down a ten-hour law for bakers. Most of his opinion was geared toward supporting the holding that the statute was an hours law and not a wage law; the majority noted that the state had made no attempt to fix the standard of wages and that the requirement that time and a half be paid was more properly considered a method of enforcing the hours regulation which provided more flexibility than would be possible with a blanket prohibition. Once that issue was settled, McKenna was satisfied to rely on the evidence presented by the state outlining how the regulation promoted the health and safety of industrial workers; by contrast, the plaintiffs in error provided "no facts to support the contention" that the legislation did not promote health and safety.[83] Not all the justices, however, were as deferential to the Frankfurter brief and the new realism it represented:

Willis Van Devanter and James C. McReynolds were appointed after *Muller* and *Lochner* had been handed down, and in this case continued in Peckham's and Brewer's tradition of dissenting without comment; they were joined by Chief Justice White, a *Lochner* dissenter. It seems reasonable to assume that they were more convinced by the argument of plaintiffs in error that it was "hardly conceivable that a law with the broad scope of the Oregon act can be held to be necessary for the preservation of the health of employees in mills, factories and manufacturing establishments," which "involve only the ordinary dangers to health that accompany manual labor."

By upholding the legislation in *Bunting*, the majority had tacitly overruled the conclusion in *Lochner* that a maximum hours law for bakers was unconstitutional; after all, the Oregon law covered employees in mills, factories, and manufacturing establishments, and this almost certainly included bakers. Frankfurter's plea that the justices disregard their "common understanding" in favor of "data that, partly, was not presented in cases like *Lochner*" apparently paid off. However, while this victory for the new realism was important, the Court was not signaling its willingness to abdicate to well-intentioned social researchers the Court's responsibility to make sure that police powers legislation remained within traditional categories. That same year a bare majority struck down a Washington State law prohibiting employment agents from charging workers for whom they found jobs or job interviews. "We think it plain," wrote McReynolds for the majority, "that there is nothing inherently immoral or dangerous to public welfare in acting as paid representative of another to find a position in which he can earn an honest living. On the contrary, such service is useful, commendable, and in great demand." Taking advantage of the distinction drawn between cases like *Muller* and *Bunting*, on the one hand, and *Adair* and *Coppage*, on the other, McReynolds concluded that rather than promoting legitimate health and safety, the state was interested simply in providing special benefits (free job placement) to certain classes (the unemployed) at the expense of competing classes (employment agents for hire). He observed that the state's argument that this kind of vocation " 'may be beneficial to some particular individuals [but] compels the needy and unfortunate to pay for that which they are entitled to without fee or price, that is, the right to work,' while possibly indicative of the purpose held by those who originated the legislation, in reason, gives it no support." The majority recognized that practitioners of this profession may engage in some abuses and that this "is adequate reason for hedging it about by proper regulation," but this fact alone "is not enough to justify destruction of one's right to follow a distinctly useful calling in an upright way."[84]

For the dissenters—Brandeis, Holmes, John H. Clarke, and McKenna—it was not enough that the majority thought it plain that there was no legitimate public welfare justification for the act. Led by Brandeis, who was writing only the second dissenting opinion of his career, they attempted to demonstrate how the prohibition promoted health, safety, or morals and prevented "fraud" and "general demoralization." They reviewed government reports and public testimony which indicated that these agencies often took advantage of their destitute clients by charging fees without looking for positions, sending applicants to distant places where no work existed, working with employers who hired and fired clients and then split the fee, sending women to houses of prostitution, and misrepresenting terms of employment. They pointed out that the U.S. Commission on Industrial Relations concluded in 1914 that honest employment agents "are the exception rather than the rule" and that the "business as a whole reeks with fraud, extortion, and flagrant abuses of every kind." These agents frequently exacerbated the social problems associated with unemployment by "bringing workers to an already overcrowded city" and by ignoring the most needy of the unemployed, who could not afford their services. The dissenters noted that many states attempted to regulate these agencies, but these efforts were unsatisfactory and "[t]here gradually developed a conviction that the evils of private agencies were inherent and ineradicable, so long as they were permitted to charge fees to the workers seeking employment." The U.S. Department of Labor concluded that workers in Washington were particularly vulnerable to "exploitation by unscrupulous private employment agencies. . . . The most striking evidence of this is that in the State of Washington private agencies made themselves so generally distrusted that in 1915 their complete abolition was ordered by popular vote." After nineteen pages of statistics and reports, Brandeis suggested that the state had ample reason to believe that the general welfare would be served by banning this vocation. "And weight should be given to the fact that the statute has been held constitutional by the Supreme Court of Washington and by the Federal District Court (three judges sitting)— courts presumably familiar with the local conditions and needs."[85]

The new realism and sociological jurisprudence did not fundamentally

alter the turn-of-the-century judiciary's treatment of police powers questions. If anything, these movements nurtured, reinforced, and refined the
kind of analysis courts had been using for some time to differentiate
illegitimate class legislation from legitimate promotion of the general
welfare. In 1908 and 1917 the justices distinguished between acceptable
and unacceptable labor laws in the same way that the Court in the 1890s
had distinguished between acceptable and unacceptable railroad legislation and in the 1880s between acceptable and unacceptable regulations
governing the laundry business. The new realism took for granted the
traditional assumption that for an exercise of police powers to be valid it
had to be demonstrated that the legislation would contribute to the
advancement of health and safety (or the preventing of fraud). Some
social legislation benefited when judges began to set aside their common
understanding of working conditions and business practices and relied
instead on careful research. By the 1910s judges in states such as Illinois
and New York, who had previously treated almost all labor laws as class
legislation, began to uphold hours laws, noting in the process that "there
is no reason why we should be reluctant to give effect to new and
additional knowledge upon such a subject as this, even if it did lead us to
take a different view of such a vastly important question as that of public
health or disease than formerly prevailed," and that "we should give
serious attention and great weight to the fact that the present legislation
is based upon and sustained by an investigation by the legislature deliberately and carefully made through an agency of its own creation, the
present factory investigating commission."[86] Still, it was up to courts to
decide whether the connection between legislation and legitimate government ends had been sufficiently established.

While many continued to treat the debate over *Lochner v. New York*
as a matter that could be resolved by a more expert understanding of the
health risks posed by working long hours in bakeries, others began to
revive the sort of challenges offered by Seymour D. Thompson and
others in the 1890s, challenges directed at the assumptions about social
autonomy in a commercial republic that supported the constitutional
aversion to class legislation. For these critics, the problem was not that
judges didn't read their social science carefully enough; rather, it was
that in attempting to maintain the distinction between general welfare
and class legislation the judiciary was preventing legislatures from re-
sponding to the unprecedented challenges associated with managing an
advanced, industrial capitalist society. Many of these discussions echoed

larger debates in the political system over the extent to which it was necessary for the American state to adjust or jettison long-standing traditions and practices. The justices of the Supreme Court, as the institutional guardians of the state's authoritative ideology, responded consistently in the years prior to and immediately following *Lochner* by defending the framers' vision, albeit not without some difficulty in the application of that vision. But it would not be long before an issue arose that led some justices to question the continued virtue and efficacy of traditional police powers jurisprudence.

CHAPTER FOUR

The Constitution Besieged

Our philosophy rests upon the dual postulate that there is a minimum of economic independence and comfort that must obtain if an individual is to be measurably free, and that this minimum can only be secured by the state assuming the obligation to see that it is in no case violated. It holds that liberty and law are correlative terms: that the first can truly exist only through, and by virtue of, the second. Remove all legal restraint on the manner in which industry shall be carried on and we invite but a merciless exploitation of the weak and their subjection to a condition of dependence.—William F. Willoughby (1914)[1]

The decision in *Lochner v. New York* triggered a minor adjustment in the way the Court went about elaborating the long-standing distinction between valid public-purpose legislation and invalid class legislation. Prompted by the Harlan block of dissenters and by members of the legal community who called for less common wisdom and more realism in judicial decision making—that is, for a more sociological jurisprudence—some members of the Court became more willing to attend to "expert" social science data which attested to the existence of unhealthful or unsafe working conditions and to the relationship between legislation and the mitigation of those harms. By the time the Court handed down its decision in *Bunting v. Oregon* twelve years after *Lochner*, it had become axiomatic in police powers jurisprudence that limits on working hours were reasonably related to a valid public interest in maintaining healthy and safe working environments.[2] Still, while this adjustment led the judiciary to accept some innovative forms of social legislation, it did not lead judges to abandon their allegiance to the jurisprudence that underlay the decision in *Lochner*. If anything, the new realism assumed that valid legislation had to promote health, safety, and morality; advocates simply added that new tools were available to help judges understand the social conditions that legislation was addressing. Through the 1910s a majority on the Court continued to do what previous majorities had been doing for decades: distinguish laws that seemed reasonably related to traditional police powers concerns from laws designed merely to impose unfair burdens or benefits on competing social classes.

The judiciary was able to sustain this long-standing distinction so long as it was assumed that promoting people's well-being was different from merely adjusting market relations. Around the turn of the century, however, increasing numbers of political, social, and legal elites began to argue that the framers' aversion to factional politics was anachronistic in an age that had witnessed the rise of the kind of European conditions of social dependency from which many of the framers believed the New World was immune. Taking up a theme that had been chanted by socially dependent classes since the beginning of the Republic, these advocates demanded the abandonment of the ethos of formal legal equality— which for them had resulted in a government whose passivity was linked to the interests of dominant classes—and the acceptance of a more progressive responsibility to manage a corporate economy by adjusting market relations that were harmful to classes that could no longer escape to the freedom of the freehold and were in no position to contract for their own well-being.

While in many respects the agenda of these progressive political and legal reformers represented a fundamental challenge to prevailing ideas about proper state-society relations, it was also the case that most progressives would have scoffed at the charge that their program was radical. This movement was made up mostly of businessmen, politicians, intellectuals, lawyers, and groups of middle-class, Eastern, urban, consumer-oriented reformers interested in preserving and defending existing power relationships by involving the state in the stabilization and rationalization of a tumultuous industrial economy. Their efforts—which took the form of municipal reform, civil service, zoning, ballot reform, antitrust legislation, railroad legislation, quality control in the manufacturing of food and drugs, and "scientific management" of the work force, natural resources, and the currency—were designed not to reconstruct society but rather to restore the sovereignty and legitimacy of existing political institutions (the reputation of which had been tarnished in the popular imagination by the routine disclosures of corporate corruption of state managers and the excesses of patronage), recover a competitive market from the powerful grip of monopoly capitalism, institutionalize a scheme of commercial planning so as to prevent a rapid depletion of scarce resources, mitigate the railroad's stranglehold on the distribution of goods, stabilize credit in the hope of breaking the cycle of boom and bust, establish quality control in production in order to permit American goods to enter foreign markets, and respond to some of the threats to the health and safety of consumers and workers arising out of unregulated production. There was also a strong sense that these reforms were necessary to stave off more radical movements—for example, although Herbert Croly supported unions as a moderating force in industrial relations, he attacked socialists for promoting a "class interest" rather than the "national interest."[3]

The battle between the so-called progressive movement and its conservative opponents represented an intraclass debate about the future of American politics, or at least it represented a debate among those who had little interest in reconstructing the social order;[4] therefore, the divisions separating participants in these debates should not be overstated. Nevertheless, many of the goals promoted by progressives required a reconceptualization of the role of the state in the management of social and economic relations, and consequently the debates entered into by traditionalists and progressives were viewed by the participants as very serious, even fundamental.[5] Stephen Skowronek has argued that turn-of-the-century American politics was preoccupied with the struggle over "building a new American state."[6] But before this new American state could be built, it was first necessary for political and social elites to come to grips with its legitimacy; and given the existence of a well-defined political tradition that had organized American politics since the time of the founding, the transformation from the old to the new was anything but smooth.

One prong of this systemwide debate over the virtue and efficacy of existing political tradition and practices took place in legal journals and judicial decisions and addressed the prevailing doctrines and distinctions relating to the nature and scope of the legislature's power to regulate social and economic relations. By the second decade of the twentieth century more and more judges and lawyers were drawing on the progressive notion that the general welfare in the age of industry required the government to expertly adjust and manage tumultuous market relations as a way to argue for the removal of the linchpin of traditional police powers jurisprudence—the distinction between valid public-purpose legislation and invalid social and economic legislation. As it came to pass, the issue they believed best exposed the futility of maintaining this distinction was the minimum wage. The ability of urban workers to earn a living wage was, for the framers, one of the key measures of social independence in a commercial republic. In explaining why they believed commercial development in the United States would be different from development in Europe, the framers placed great emphasis on how the availability of a vast freehold in the New World would act to inflate urban wages at least to a subsistence level (since wage earners who could not earn a subsistence living theoretically would choose to become self-sufficient yeoman farmers). However, progressive reformers claimed that a hard look at new social facts demonstrated that a free market and a neutral government had combined to create a class of wage earners who were not self-sufficient. These paupered laborers could no longer count on the freehold to "naturally" inflate their wages, and so it was the responsibility of the government to "artificially" inflate their wages through minimum wage legislation. The final chapter in the reign of the ethos of government neutrality involved a pitched legal battle over the constitutionality of this innovative social policy.

The Assault on Government Neutrality and Traditional Police Powers Jurisprudence

When in the 1890s Seymour Thompson and others in the *American Law Review* began arguing that courts should allow legislatures to protect vulnerable classes from their oppressors, they used arguments about the rise of social dependency that presaged a type of rhetoric that within a decade would become commonplace in national politics. The worldview from which legal reformers in the second decade of the twentieth century would launch a more sustained assault on traditional police powers jurisprudence was made respectable by figures outside legal culture like Teddy Roosevelt and Herbert Croly.

What distinguished Roosevelt from other progressives who decried "the tyranny of the bosses and the special interests"[7] was his belief that it was necessary not only to eradicate corruption in the institutions of government—through reforms like the direct primary and the recall, prohibitions on the use of corporate funds for political purposes, and an extended policymaking role for "expert" commissions—but also to tackle a more widespread and basic problem, the unequal distribution of social and economic power in society. Roosevelt argued that in order to check the extraordinary private power accumulated since the advent of industrialization, democratization of politics had to be linked with the positive use of public power on behalf of disadvantaged classes:

> The only way in which our people can increase their power over the big corporation that does wrong, the only way in which they can protect the working man in his conditions of work and life, the only way in which the people can prevent children working in industry or secure women an eight-hour day in industry, or secure compensation for men killed or crippled in industry, is by extending, instead of limiting, the power of government. There was once a time in history when the limitation of governmental power meant increasing liberty for the people. In the present day the limitation of governmental power, of governmental action, means the enslavement of the people by the great corporations who can only be held in check through the extension of governmental power.[8]

While not abandoning a liberal respect for preserving individual liberty, Roosevelt did suggest that an individual's opportunities for achievement, personal security, and happiness were becoming increasingly associated with collective action. This meant that ideological constructs which defined political legitimacy only in terms of the vocabulary of the individual or the welfare of every member of the community had to be disposed of—liberalism had to be able to accommodate, and not just control, the demands of groups: "[A] simple and poor society can exist as a democracy on a basis of sheer individualism," wrote Roosevelt in his *Autobiography*. "But a rich and complex industrial society cannot so exist; for some individuals, and especially those artificial individuals called corporations, become so very big that the ordinary individual is utterly dwarfed beside them, and cannot deal with them on terms of equality. It therefore becomes necessary for these ordinary individuals to combine in their turn, first in order to act in their collective capacity through the biggest of all combinations called the government, and second to act, also in their own self-defense, through private combinations, such as farmers' associations and trade unions."[9] In direct opposition to the goal of the framers, Roosevelt was proposing a rapprochement between government and factions; he wanted political elites to be willing to free government from the bondage of Madisonian notions of good government.

The revolutionary nature of this program was made explicit in 1909 by Roosevelt's ideological compatriot, Herbert Croly, in his influential *Promise of American Life*. Croly started with the observation that after industrialization the "earlier homogeneity of American society has been impaired." Specifically, the "experience of the last generation plainly shows that the American economic and social system cannot be allowed to take care of itself, and that the automatic harmony of the individual and the public interest, which is the essence of the Jeffersonian democratic creed, has proved to be an illusion." As a result, in order to prevent "such divisions from dissolving the society into which they enter," it had become necessary to substitute "a conscious social ideal for the earlier instinctive homogeneity of the American nation." Existing abuses could never be adequately addressed so long as reform was "considered to be a species of higher conservatism" and not a movement fundamentally to alter the political structure so that it was better able to respond to the exigencies of a new age.[10]

What precisely was it about the political system that was hampering reform efforts? At the most basic level it was the fact that "all Americans, whether they are professional politicians or reformers, 'predatory' millionaires or common people, political philosophers or schoolboys, accept the principle of 'equal rights for all and special privileges for none' as the absolutely sufficient rule of an American democratic system." Since the founding "the most sacred principle of democracy" was that no "citizen or any group of citizens" should enjoy "by virtue of the law any advantage over their fellow-citizens"; that society "is organized politically for the benefit of all the people." Clearly the "principle of equal rights has always appealed to its more patriotic and sensible adherents as essentially an impartial rule of political action—one that held a perfectly fair balance between the individual and society, and between different and hostile individual and class interests." However, in "its traditional form and expression," this principle "has concealed an extremely partial interest under a formal proclamation of impartiality"—the partiality of preserving patterns of social domination and dependency in an advanced industrial economy.[11]

In order to reestablish a balance among groups in society, to create a new harmony to replace the broken assumption of a naturally homogeneous social order, the "national government must step in and discriminate; but it must discriminate, not on behalf of liberty and the special individual [which only perpetuates private inequalities], but on behalf of equality and the average man." This is no more insidious than the prevailing belief that fairness is served when government is neutral, since the "practice of non-interference is just as selective in its effects as the practice of state interference. It means merely that the nation is willing to accept the results of natural selection instead of preferring to substitute the results of artificial selection." It was toward this end that Roosevelt won Croly's admiration as "the founder of a new national democracy," one that might "emancipate American democracy from its Jeffersonian bondage" (meaning the "Jeffersonian doctrine of equal rights"). Roosevelt's programs were "novel" and "radical" because they "in effect questioned the value of certain fundamental American ideas."[12]

Despite the efforts of progressives like Roosevelt and Croly, the political system's movement away from the fundamental American idea of equal rights could not be completed so long as courts continued to defend traditional conceptions of political legitimacy. The task of separating the judiciary from the manifestation of that idea in police powers jurisprudence was the responsibility of progressive lawyers. While most "professional" critics of *Lochner* era jurisprudence attempted merely to direct the Court's attention to the "real" relationship between working hours and worker health, some echoed the thoughts advanced by Seymour D. Thompson in the 1890s and argued for a new philosophy of American constitutionalism. In his presidential address before the American Association for Labor Legislation in 1914 William F. Willoughby noted, "It has been the fashion to characterize this change [to a new conception of the state's responsibilities] as one from individualism to collectivism or even socialism. Collectivistic it certainly is if by that we mean the recognition of social rights and duties and the use of social or collective action to meet them. That it is anti-individualistic in the sense of laying little, or less, emphasis upon the desirability of individual freedom and initiative is wholly incorrect." Willoughby referred to this new philosophy as "modern liberalism" because it "looks to state action as the means, and the only practical means, now in sight, of giving to the individual, all individuals, not merely a small economically strong class, real freedom. It holds that the so-called freedom of the dependant woman and child to work as long hours and under any conditions, no matter what the danger to health and limb is, in truth, but abject slavery masquerading under that name. Freedom means real liberty to choose."

The centerpiece of this new philosophy was a rather old and traditional concern—social independence, guaranteed by the state if necessary. In a passage that could have been written by the Knights of Labor—or even by Philadelphia's artisan community or the Working Men of New York or Jefferson or Paine, had they experienced the full brunt of industrialization—Willoughby asserted:

> Our philosophy rests upon the dual postulate that there is a minimum of economic independence and comfort that must obtain if an individual is to be measurably free, and that this minimum can only be secured by the state assuming the obligation to see that it is in no case violated. It holds that liberty and law are correlative terms: that the first can truly exist only through, and by virtue of, the second. Remove all legal restraint on the manner in which industry shall be carried on and we invite but a merciless exploitation of the weak and their subjection to a condition of dependence. We hold therefore that the refusal by the state . . . to prevent the exploitation of the weak and helpless through excessive hours of labor or the payment of inadequate compensation, and its refusal to ensure that due provisions be made . . . against the four great contingencies threatening the economic security of the individual—accident, sickness, old age and inability to find work, means its failure to meet that duty which it is the prime function of a constitutional government to perform; viz., the protection of the individual against oppression and the guaranteeing to him the fullest possible enjoyment of life, liberty and the pursuit of happiness.[13]

A year after the *Lochner* decision George W. Alger asked the New York State Bar Association directly to consider a new conception of the proper scope of government power:

> Has the State ever a clear duty to lend a hand to aid those who are obviously at a disadvantage in struggling with the forces of modern industry? Under our fundamental law and the principles declared in our Constitution, can our legislatures and courts recognize not only the facts of existing industrial inequality between men, but a duty to protect by law framed to meet new conditions the weaker against the stronger? When individual action alone cannot secure equalization of the conditions of competition, and where that failure is resulting in misery and distress, may the law intervene to protect the weak from the tyranny of the strong? Are the handicaps of life to be questions

solely for the individual, or are they at times and under special circumstances to be questions for the State itself to grapple with, and if not to solve, at least to create conditions under which the individual may solve them for himself?

Other "civilized countries" had accepted the new responsibility to protect dependent classes from the ravages of industrial inequality, but achieving this acceptance in the United States had been more difficult because "[o]ur fundamental law has for one of its principles that of equality—that before the law, men are equal in rights, privileges, and legal capacities." However, he pointed out that this principle was adopted when "[t]here was not a factory in the United States," when "[t]he artisan was his own master"; today the "*old theory of legal equality . . . finds itself in conflict with the facts of life.*" The new conception of the police power "must find its authority in the needs of the present and not solely in the traditions of the past."[14]

Louis Brandeis adopted a similar position in his discussion of the "living law." Changes in the relations of production had altered the traditional concerns of republican government. Within the last fifty years "we have passed through an economic and social revolution which affected the life of the people more fundamentally than any political revolution known to history. . . . [W]ith the introduction of the factory system and the development of the business corporation, [came] new dangers to liberty. . . . Ownership of the instruments of production passed from the workman to the employer. . . . The individual contract of service lost its character, because of the inequality in position between employer and employee." "Legal justice" in the United States was facing its greatest challenge because of "its failure to conform to contemporary conceptions of social justice."[15]

In response to *Lochner* and *Adair*, Judge Learned Hand insisted that, in light of contemporary industrial conditions, legislative power should be allowed to extend beyond traditionally accepted regulations to promote health and safety and prevent fraud. "For the state to intervene to make more just and equal the relative strategic advantages of the two parties to the contract, of whom one is under the pressure of absolute want, while the other is not, is as proper a legislative function as that it should neutralize the relative advantages arising from fraudulent cunning or from superior physical force. At one time the law did not try to equalize the advantages of fraud, but we have generally come to concede that the exercise of such mental superiority as fraud indicates, has no social value, but the opposite. It may well be that the uncontrolled exercise of the advantages derived from possessing the means of living of other men will also become recognized as giving no social benefit corresponding to the evils which result. If so, there is no ground for leaving it uncontrolled in the hands of individuals." As for the claim that the introduction of state power into the struggles between classes would open the door to factional politics, Hand responded: "That the legislature may be moved by faction, and without justice, is very true, but so may even the court. There is an inevitable bias upon such vital questions in all men, and the courts are certainly recruited from a class which has its proper bias, like the rest."[16]

Over and over the theme that echoed from the sharpest critics of the jurisprudence of *Lochner* was that it had become obsolete; the social and economic conditions that provided the foundations for its initial elaboration in the late eighteenth century had been swept away in the industrial tides of the late nineteenth century. Thomas Reed Powell noted that the problem underlying discussions of the constitutional status of labor legislation was not that the Court's jurisprudence was incoherent. "The majority opinions in the Adair case and the Coppage case set forth clear and definite ideas of liberty and of equality," he wrote. In those opinions it was considered "the essence of the liberty of employers that they be free to accept or reject employes for any reason they please," just as it was "of the essence of the liberty of employes that they be free to join unions or to keep aloof from them." From the majority's point of view, "equal freedom for employers and for employes is the watchword." However, this conception of freedom did not encompass "freedom from economic pressure." It was, rather, "freedom from legal restraint." By contrast, for workers, freedom from legal restraint guaranteed that they would have less economic liberty. In a sense a condition arose in which the protection of the "rights" of one class conflicted with the protection of the "rights" of the other; in such a condition, *it was simply not possible for the state to remain neutral*—the traditional notion that the police power cannot be used to remove "those inequalities that are but the normal and inevitable result [of exercising rights to property]" itself biased the system in the direction of owners of the means of production.[17] Or, as Louis M. Greeley put it, "the courts have said that this constitutional right freely to contract means that the workingman may not by law be prevented from accepting employment on any terms he may agree to, even though it may be notorious that those terms are disastrous to him, and that he is driven to accept them by his necessities, and has not any free choice. Some courts have even said that the disastrous consequences to the individual workingman afford no grounds of public welfare for a law to protect him from those consequences. Surely a perverse logic, this, which in the name of a theoretical freedom of contract which has no existence in fact, robs the workingman of the law which he requires for his well being, and which affords him the necessary protection he is powerless to secure for himself."[18]

The rise of industrial capitalism made it more and more difficult for people to conceive of a general welfare that somehow transcended the predicament of particular groups and classes; capitalist forms of production had also made it difficult to treat ownership of the means of production and the conditions of labor contracts as simply a proprietary concern of private individuals. "[W]hen we take into consideration the special legislation with which modern communities surround business, the protective tariffs, the corporation laws with their guaranties of individual immunity from the consequences of failure of mismanagement, the bankruptcy laws and receiverships by which the community wipes off at a stroke the results of particular business adversities and absorbs the loss by distributing it over the whole range of industry, the inappositeness of such expressions as '*his* business,' '*his* capital,' 'interference with *his* business' becomes all the more apparent." The vulnerable and dependent status of wage earners—how they "are subject to dismissal with or without cause, have no voice in management, no right to promotion, no right 'to see the books,' no right in fact but that of taking or refusing the wages . . . tendered them"—makes their special protection a matter of community concern. The bottom line is that the reconstitution of society has established "a multitude of new relationships between the members of the community, which it is the business of law . . . to recognize and adjust."[19]

But for more than a century this had not been the business of law; in fact, it had been the business of constitutional law to prohibit the state from adjusting the relationships between competing members of the community by advancing the interests of favored classes. By the end of the nineteenth century judges were willing to acknowledge that the more widespread condition of "unequal bargaining power" might help explain why workers were unable themselves to contract for safer and healthier working conditions, or for methods of payment that would prevent employers from fraudulently denying workers the wages they were due. Nevertheless, in the minds of many jurists, legitimate police power legislation still had to be designed specifically to promote health and safety and prevent fraud, and it could not be designed simply to improve the economic well-being of one class at the expense of another. New industrial conditions might broaden the need for health and safety legislation, and might make reasonable some innovative police power regulations, but for these judges the transformation of the economy did not necessitate the abandonment of this fundamental tenet of American constitutionalism. Consequently, up through the 1910s a majority of the justices continued to maintain the distinction between legitimate police powers, on the one hand (involving health, safety, or fraud), and arbitrary invasions into market relations, on the other (social and economic legislation); under this distinction, maximum hours laws and laws regulating the method of payment were upheld, while laws prohibiting yellow-dog contracts and banning profit-making employment agencies were struck down.

However, by the end of the decade the Court would begin to consider an issue that threatened to explode this traditional distinction once and for all.

The Minimum Wage and the Fateful Persistence of Traditional Police Power Limits

The logic supporting minimum wage legislation exposed a vulnerability in long-standing police powers jurisprudence. Judges had been primed to categorize legislation as either reasonably related to the advancement of health, safety, and morality (or the prevention of fraud) or as an illegitimate attempt to promote the economic well-being of one group or class at the expense of a competing group or class. But supporters of the minimum wage argued that, in light of prevailing industrial conditions, the health and general well-being of wage earners required the government to intervene on their behalf by forcing employers to pay a particular price for their labor. This claim was unprecedented. Previously, labor legislation had been considered acceptable only insofar as it applied to workers in particular kinds of industry for the purpose of providing a healthy and safe working environment or preventing fraud. While it was understood that the need for this kind of legislation was based in part on the assumption that workers were in no position to contract for these conditions on their own, the legislation was nevertheless linked to these conditions and not to the general goal of granting to workers an "unnatural" (non-market-based) economic advantage vis-à-vis their employers. The justification for minimum wage legislation extended the logic of maximum hours laws in such a way as to eviscerate the distinction between health and safety laws, on the one hand, and social and economic legislation, on the other. Whereas 1890s industrial conditions were such that workers in particular industries were unable to contract for a safe and healthy working environment, by the 1910s more people had come to see that workers were unable to contract for enough money to sustain themselves and their families.

The Constitution had been created largely to ensure that market competitors—debtors and creditors, employers and employees, producers and consumers—would be free not from all regulation but from government intrusions that amounted to unfair favoritism. From the beginning, though, this notion of unfair government favoritism made sense only if one assumed that in the absence of government favoritism relations among groups were essentially fair, and that individuals operating in the market would be self-sufficient and autonomous. Yet it was precisely these assumptions that were being challenged by many political and social elites in the early part of the twentieth century.

To accept the constitutionality of the minimum wage would be to abandon one of the oldest and most fundamental tenets of American constitutional law. However, those in favor of this revolution argued that the distinction upon which this tenet rested, between the promotion of health and safety, on the one hand, and arbitrary class legislation, on the other, was no longer tenable given the proliferation and intensification of social dependency under industrial capitalism. To reject the constitutionality of the minimum wage would be to commit to the founders' belief that the general welfare was something distinct from government disruption of "natural" market relations. In order for interested judges to maintain the distinction between legitimate police powers and arbitrary invasions into market relations, however, they were forced to make more explicit the assumptions about the inherent fairness of market relations that made the distinction meaningful in the first place—hence the emphasis starting in the early part of the twentieth century on the importance (not the inviolability) of liberty of contract, the right of individuals to compete in the market without arbitrary government interference. A necessary corollary of this defense was a denial of the charge that the maturation of capitalist forms of production had resulted in more coercive market relations and less freedom for vulnerable groups. In their attempt to maintain the long-standing distinction between legitimate police powers and illegitimate class politics, conservative judges were increasingly put into a position where they had to rely on outdated characterizations of social relations in American society.

At one and the same time the existing tradition provided arguments for its preservation and for its destruction. By the end of the second decade of the twentieth century the Supreme Court had reached a fork in the road: it could embrace the new realism and turn its back on the framers' vision of a republic free from the corruption of factional politics, or it could insist on the continued efficacy of this vision and turn its back on the extent to which industrialization had put an end to the kind of harmony in market relations that the framers had associated with infant capitalism.

The Court stood at that fork for some years. In *Stettler v. O'Hara* (1917) an equally divided Supreme Court, with Brandeis having recused himself because of prior involvement in the litigation, let stand an Oregon statute that set a minimum wage for women working in private employment.[20] The first section of the Oregon law provided: "It shall be unlawful to employ women or minors in any occupation within the State of Oregon for unreasonably long hours; and it shall be unlawful to employ women or minors in any occupation within the State of Oregon under such surroundings or conditions—sanitary or otherwise—as may be detrimental to their health or morals; and it shall be unlawful to employ women for any occupation within the State of Oregon for wages which are inadequate to supply the necessary cost of living and to maintain them in health; and it shall be unlawful to employ minors in any occupation within the State of Oregon for unreasonably low wages." An Industrial Welfare Commission, to be appointed by the governor, was authorized to determine appropriate standards for hours, wages, and working conditions. The commission eventually determined that women could not be made to work more than nine hours a day or fifty hours a week, that women had to be given a noon lunch period of no less than forty-five minutes, and that women had to be paid a weekly wage no less than $8.64, "any lesser amount being hereby declared inadequate to supply the necessary cost of living to such woman factory workers, and to maintain them in health."

When the state supreme court upheld the law in 1914, it noted that the constitutionality of a minimum wage was a question that was "practically new in the courts of this country." Minimum wage laws arose when legislatures determined that conditions had changed and that some "private enterprises ha[d] become so crowded that their demands amount[ed] to unreasonable exactions from women and children." Justice Robert Eakin's opinion made reference to the Supreme Court's determination in *Muller* "that woman's physical structure and her position in the economy of the race renders her incapable of competing with man either in strength or in endurance," and argued that this fact lies "at the foundation of all legislation attempted for the amelioration of woman's condition in her struggle for subsistence." The suggestion here was that it was appropriate to assure women a minimum wage because their inherent weakness and frailty made it more difficult for them to attract a price for the labor that was sufficient to sustain them. According to the court, "Every argument put forward to sustain the maximum hours law . . . applies equally in favor of the constitutionality of the minimum wage law as also within the police power of the state and as a regulation tending to guard the public morals and the public health." In order to clarify why exactly the public had a legitimate interest in the economic well-being of women, Justice Eakin cited with approval the position of the Massachusetts Commission on Minimum Wages, which indicated in 1912 that whenever "the wages of such a woman are less than the cost of living and the reasonable provision for maintaining the worker in health, the industry employing her is in receipt of the working energy of a human being at less than its cost, and to that extent is parasitic. The balance must be made up in some way. It is generally paid by the industry employing the father. It is sometimes paid in part by future inefficiency of the worker herself, and by her children, and perhaps in part ultimately by charity and the state."[21] By emphasizing *Muller*, the court attempted to link the minimum wage to existing justifications which permitted the state to extend favored treatment to classes of people who, because of their distinctive characteristics, were incapable of taking care of themselves, such as children and imbeciles (but, by implication, not able-bodied men), and whose resulting impoverishment placed a burden on the community. With this emphasis, the court sidestepped the more sweeping justification for a minimum wage, which would have tied the incapacity to obtain a living wage not to the frailty of particular classes but rather to the general conditions of social dependency created as a result of industrialization.

The editors of the *Harvard Law Review* offered a slight variation of the state court's position on the minimum wage. "As regards limiting the hours of work," they wrote, "the prevailing doctrine has come to be that reasonable restrictions may be placed upon the length of daily employment of all women and children and of men engaged in particularly dangerous and unhealthful occupations.... [The legislature] may constitutionally restrict the bargaining of employer and employee only to an extent determined by the harmful effects of the occupation upon the class of workers in question." From this firmly established principle, they noted that some would distinguish hours legislation from wage legislation on the grounds that the former is designed to protect employee health while the latter seems "rather like compelling [the employer] affirmatively to assist them [his employees] in order to correct social evils which, in a sense, he has not caused." But like the state court, they suggested that "such arguments . . . exaggerate the difference between the two methods of regulation" by neglecting how the "manufacturer who underpays is in fact affirmatively injuring his employees by utilizing the economic pressure for employment as a club." Still, they insisted that for the minimum wage to be constitutional, "it must also appear reasonably adapted to improve the welfare of the workers in question. . . . Whether the state control of wages is calculated to improve these conditions is for the courts to say. The question is obviously one of fact." The implication of this position was that minimum wage laws, like maximum hours laws, might or might not be constitutional, depending on how closely related they were to the promotion of health and safety. Apparently, then, a minimum wage law directed at particularly vulnerable groups and designed to provide the basic necessities of life would be all right; however, because these laws might be designed simply to enrich favored classes at the expense of their competitors, courts would have to carefully scrutinize each one to make sure it fell within acceptable constitutional guidelines.[22]

Others, however, were more persuaded by the argument (dismissed by the Harvard Law Review) that minimum wage laws were fundamentally different, and more insidious, than maximum hours laws. In 1917, after the U.S. Supreme Court deadlocked over the constitutionality of the Oregon statute, Rome G. Brown, who had participated in attempts to have the Oregon law struck down since 1914, wrote an article in which he outlined his objections to minimum wage legislation. He noted that these kinds of statutes "purport to be based upon the police-power regulation of occupations in the interest of 'public welfare, safety, health, and morals'" and that "their concrete object is to provide for working women a wage which shall not be less than that which is considered required to supply each female worker, as an independent supporter of herself, such full 'living wage' as will keep her in health and comfort." He then added, "The declaration by a state legislature that an attempted regulation of a business is enacted in promotion of the public health, safety or welfare, does not render the enactment valid as a police regulation"; in order to be valid a "public welfare statute must have a direct relation as a means to an end, and the end itself must be appropriate and legitimate." For example, "the regulation of hours is supported only because, and to the extent that, longer hours involve dangers to the safety and health of employees, arising out of hazards which are peculiar to the employment in question." Unlike regulation of working hours, minimum wage legislation was not designed to ameliorate hazardous working conditions. Brown was willing to admit that a woman's health and general well-being are promoted if she has "the full means of subsistence" (and are undermined when she does not), but argued that it is arbitrary to require the person "who happens to have that individual on his pay-roll" to provide that subsistence; if the state wants to promote the well-being of the poor, then it should do so through the enactment of general programs funded by the community as a whole. Brown referred to the opinion of the Court in *Coppage* that it was not an appropriate exercise of the police power for the legislature to attempt to remove those "inequalities of fortune" that "are but the normal and inevitable result of [the right of private property]" by helping some groups at the expense of others. "This sort of legislation is a new expression of the paternalistic and socialistic tendencies of the day. It savors of the division of property between those who have and those who have not, and the leveling of fortunes by division under government supervision. . . . [Such legislation] seems . . . to be a long step toward nullifying our constitutional guaranties."[23]

Brown's article prompted a response by Thomas Reed Powell. In it he quipped, "It may be doubted whether fortunes will be greatly leveled as a result of the administration of a statute which compels employers to pay normal employees at least $8.64 a week." His central point, however, was that these laws merely prevented an employer from taking advantage of his "superior bargaining power" and imposed "the burden of meeting the cost of producing the labor on those who voluntarily seek to enjoy the fruits of the labor" (rather than have an industry's production subsidized by others through poor relief that keeps workers alive). Powell insisted that Brown was wrong to suggest that minimum wage laws required employers to care for strangers, since every

> employer remains entirely free to say to any employee: "You are not worth to me that statutory minimum wage. Therefore I will not hire you." . . . It is plain that minimum-wage legislation does not compel employers to make any contract that in their judgment is not remunerative. It may, it is true, disable them from making as remunerative contracts as they might do if left free to bargain to their best advantage. The legislation is opposed to the theory that there is a constitutionally guaranteed right to make the most advantageous bargains which one's economic position permits. So is all usury legislation. . . . Standard rates of interest for loans, standard forms of insurance policies, a standard minimum of wages in certain employments—these are all indications of a public interest in the terms of individual bargains which outweighs the interest of individuals to make their bargains on the best or worst terms which they can get under unrestricted legal freedom of contract. They indicate the recognition that abstract legal freedom for each individual is deemed less precious than the adoption of general standards dictated by considerations of a wide social policy.[24]

This was exactly right—but it was also a serious challenge to longstanding assumptions about social independence in a commercial republic that had justified the neutral state since 1787. Usury, which had previously been understood to be a narrow exception to the regime of free contract, had now become the model of class relations in an industrial society. If people were no longer free "to make the most advantageous bargains" their economic position permitted, then apparently it was all right for the state to intervene on behalf of favored classes as they competed against other classes.

By 1917 four responses to minimum wage legislation had been elaborated: Brown's perspective insisted on treating the minimum wage as inherently violative of prevailing police power limits against purely social or economic legislation (the "leveling of fortunes"); Powell's perspective insisted on tearing down existing limits on the grounds that the assumptions about political economy that sustained them were no longer valid; the *Stettler* court's perspective was that minimum wage laws could be sustained on traditional grounds as an example of the state coming to the aid of groups that were vulnerable to a free-market regime because of their own distinctive weaknesses and incapacities; and the *Harvard Law Review*'s position was that the laws could be sustained on traditional grounds if it could be demonstrated that the purpose of the legislation was the promotion of public health and not the enrichment of favored classes.

Most state courts that addressed this issue followed the lead of the Oregon court and the *Harvard Law Review*. In *Williams v. Evans* (1917), the Minnesota Supreme Court, acknowledging that contractual liberty could be restrained only if the limitation was a "reasonable regulation to safeguard the public interest" and was not imposed "solely for the benefit of the individual," upheld the state's minimum wage act. The court noted that women were "not paid so well as men are paid for the same service" and that "in many cases the pay they receive for working during all the working hours of the day is not enough to meet the cost of reasonable living" (a condition that, among other things, leads "any number of them to accept the easy alternative of immorality to increase their income to meet their needs"). From this the justices concluded that women were not capable of looking after themselves, and that therefore it was perfectly appropriate for the legislature to protect them as they would children. In resting the decision on these grounds, the court did not speak to the question of whether "statutes of this kind applicable to men would be valid."[25]

That same year, Arkansas's highest court also used the logic of *Muller* to uphold a similar minimum wage law. The justices noted that "medical and other scientific experts" had indicated "that inadequate wages tend to impair the health of women in all cases and in some cases to injuriously affect their morals. Indeed, it is a matter of common knowledge that if women are paid inadequate wages so that they are not able to purchase sufficient food to properly nourish their bodies, this will as certainly impair their health as overwork. . . . The strength, intelligence and virtue of each generation depends to a great extent upon the mothers. Therefore, the health and morals of the women are a matter of grave concern to the public and consequently to the State itself." However, in a dissenting opinion joined by one other justice, Chief Justice Edgar A. McCulloch objected to the erosion of an important distinction in police powers jurisprudence. He admitted that "laws regulating [women's] hours of labor and the kind of labor in which they may engage, are valid because such regulations tend to the protection of health, not only of the women whose habits of labor are regulated, but the whole of humanity. The same may be said of child labor laws. The hours of labor of men in extra hazardous or arduous employments may be regulated by law because society at large is interested in the preservation of men's safety and morals." But, citing *Lawton v. Steele*, he noted that for police power legislation to be legitimate "it must appear, first, that the interests of the public generally, as distinguished from those of a particular class, require such interference; and, second, that the means are reasonably necessary for the accomplishment of the purpose and not unduly oppressive upon individuals." He referred his brethren to Freund's *Police Power*, in which the *Lochner* critic wrote, "The power to regulate the rate of wages, while freely exercised in former times, has not been claimed by any American state. . . . Considerations of health and safety which complicate the question of hours of labor do not enter into the question of rate. The regulation would be purely of an economic character. It would be closely analogous to the regulation of the price of other commodities or services." Adding what to him must have been an obvious point, the chief justice noted that "it may be truly said in a larger sense that the contentment which financial ease sometimes brings is conducive to health and morality, but, if so, that effect is not confined to either of the sexes." He agreed that it is "almost axiomatic that society would be better off . . . if there were no poor," but insisted that "unless the American conception of legal regulation of personal liberty has changed, and accepted theories of constitutional government are to be abandoned, it will scarcely be urged that the price of labor generally can or should be regulated by law."[26]

In light of these successive state victories for minimum wage laws, Charles K. Burdick predicted in 1922 that once the Supreme Court redirected its attention to this issue the legislation would be sustained "as an exercise of the police power for the protection of the physical and moral well-being of the workers involved . . . but also for the protection of the community against the burden of making up the deficit between the living wage and the wage received."[27] If history had been slightly different and the Court had resolved the issue in 1917, Burdick's position might have prevailed. But as it turned out, President Woodrow Wilson's selection of Brandeis in 1916, and Brandeis's decision to recuse himself from consideration of the Oregon minimum wage law, resulted in a deadlocked Supreme Court.[28] Had Brandeis not participated in earlier litigation over the minimum wage, or had Wilson picked another justice in 1916 who was sympathetic to minimum wage laws, the Court would have upheld this legislation in 1917. Instead, in 1923, after some significant personnel changes, a five-man majority struck down a District of Columbia minimum wage law for women and children in *Adkins v. Children's Hospital.*[29]

Justice George Sutherland began his opinion for the Court by noting that while there is "no such thing as absolute freedom of contract," at the same time, "[i]n making such contracts, generally speaking, the parties have an equal right to obtain from each other the best terms they can as the result of private bargaining," without the state interfering on behalf of one of the parties to this social competition. In holding that "generally speaking" one has a right to obtain the best terms possible in the course of private bargaining, Sutherland was rejecting Powell's suggestion that minimum wages laws were like usury and that there is no "constitutionally guaranteed right to make the most advantageous bargains which one's economic position permits." Sutherland preferred to treat usury as a traditional exception to what was otherwise a regime of private bargaining, where contractual relationship could be regulated but not interfered with for the purpose of extending special privileges to certain classes.

Sutherland reviewed those areas wherein the Court recognized the right of the state to regulate relations among competing social groups: in *Munn v. Illinois* (1877) the Court held that property "devoted to a public use . . . may be controlled by the public for the common good"; in a number of cases, such as *McLean v. Arkansas* (1908), the Court upheld statutes prescribing the character, methods, and time for payment of wages on the grounds that they were designed "to prevent unfair and perhaps fraudulent methods in the payment of wages" due to workers; and in cases such as *Holden v. Hardy* (1898) the Court upheld laws setting maximum hours for particular workers in particular occupations "on the ground that the legislature had [reasonably] determined that these particular employments, when too long pursued, were injurious to the health of the employees." According to Sutherland, these statutes "deal with incidents of the employment [that is, issues of health, safety, morality, and fraud] having no necessary effect upon the heart of the contract, that is, the amount of wages to be paid and received." Just as the government could regulate the proper packaging and handling of meat but (from Sutherland's perspective) not the price of the meat, so too could the government regulate the conditions of employment but not the price of labor. In fact, this distinction was acknowledged in *Bunting,* wherein the majority emphasized that in upholding a maximum hours law the Court was not in any way speaking to the status of legislation fixing wages, "thus recognizing an essential difference between the two."

Once one appreciated previous discussions of the police powers it was easy to see that minimum wage legislation differed from earlier cases "in every material respect. . . . It is simply and exclusively a price-fixing law, confined to adult women . . . , who are legally as capable of contracting for themselves as men." The decision in *Muller* upholding a maximum hours law for women workers in industry "proceeded on the theory that the difference between the sexes may justify a different rule respecting hours of labor in the case of women than in the case of men. . . . [T]hese consist in differences of physical structure, especially in respect of the maternal functions, and also in the fact that historically woman has always been dependent upon man, who has established his control by superior physical strength. . . . [W]hile the physical differences [between men and women] must be recognized in appropriate cases, and legislation fixing hours or conditions of work may properly take them into account, we cannot accept the doctrine that women of mature age require or may be subjected to restrictions upon their liberty of contract which could not lawfully be imposed in the case of men under similar circumstances." To extend the logic of *Muller* to uphold minimum wage laws it would be necessary to suggest that women not only were *less strong* than men but also that they were *less capable of making decisions* about the terms of employment than men. This argument might be acceptable if the law provided for a minimum wage for minors,[30] but to adopt such an argument in this case "would be to ignore all the implications to be drawn from the present day trend of legislation . . . by which woman is accorded emancipation from the old doctrine that she must be given special protection or be subjected to special restraint in her contractual and civil relationships."

Of course, another possible basis upon which one could argue that it was reasonable to treat men and women differently was the social fact that women as a class were poorer and thus more vulnerable to exploitation by greedy employers; it could also have been pointed out that women just entering the work force lacked the kind of training or experience that might empower them to attract a higher wage. This was the position adopted by Barbara N. Grimes, a critic of Sutherland's opinion: "Will the learned justices of the majority be pardoned for overlooking the cardinal fact that minimum-wage legislation is not and never was predicated upon political, contractual or civil inequalities of women? It is predicated rather upon evils to society, resulting from the exploitation of women in industry, who as a class labor under a tremendous economic hardship."[31] However, poverty, lack of training and experience, and vulnerability to industry exploitation made it difficult for *both* sexes to earn a living wage; focusing on these as the most relevant conditions would lend support for a minimum wage for all workers.[32] The majority was as unsympathetic to this argument as the framers were to wage- and price-fixing schemes and debtor-relief laws in the 1780s. "The feature of the statute which, perhaps more than any other, puts upon it the stamp of invalidity is that it exacts from the employer an arbitrary payment for a purpose and upon a basis having no causal connection with his business." Here, Sutherland was dismissing Powell's suggestion that a minimum wage law did not impose an unfair burden on employers because it did not require employers to hire anyone and therefore did not require them to pay someone a higher wage than she was worth; for the majority this was sophistry, since the same could be said for any regulation of the price of labor, services, or commodities designed to advance the interests of preferred classes (such as a regulation that required farmers to pay an "artificially" high minimum rate to ship their goods on railroads). Sutherland was also dismissing Powell's suggestion that employers who benefited from labor had a special obligation to pay the costs for maintaining the labor force; for Sutherland, this made as little sense as saying that producers or sellers had an obligation to support consumers at a minimally sufficient level. "In principle, there can be no difference between the case of selling labor and the case of selling goods. If one goes to the butcher, the baker or grocer to buy food, he is morally entitled to obtain the worth of his money but he is not entitled to more . . . simply because he needs more . . . and the shopkeeper, having dealt fairly and honestly in that transaction, is not concerned in any particular sense with the question of his customer's necessities. Should a statute undertake to vest in a commission power to determine the quantity of food necessary for individual support and require the shopkeeper, if he sell to the individual at all, to furnish that quantity at not more than a fixed maximum, it would undoubtedly fall before the constitutional test." In essence, the minimum wage "amounts to a compulsory extraction from the employer for the support of a partially indigent person, for whose condition there rests upon no peculiar responsibility, and therefore, in effect, arbitrarily shifts to his shoulders a burden which, if it belongs to anyone, belongs to society as a whole." Rather than burden one class with the responsibility to care for another (be it employers for poor employees, producers for poor consumers, or creditors for poor debtors), the society as a whole should bear the burden by passing poor-relief laws.

Sutherland acknowledged the "mass of reports" which indicated that women's earnings had increased, but he dismissed them as "only mildly persuasive" because the statistics were collected during a time when "earnings everywhere in all occupations have greatly increased—not alone in States where the minimum wage law obtains but in the country generally—quite as much or more among men as among women and in occupations outside the reach of the law as in those governed by it." But refuting these reports was not Sutherland's main concern. Even if minimum wage laws helped eliminate poverty, they would still be constitutionally deficient as a matter of principle; after all, debtor-relief laws certainly helped impoverished debtors in the years leading up to the creation of the Constitution. The framers created a system designed to prevent particular classes from using the powers of government to advance their interests at the expense of other classes. Sutherland ended his opinion with a warning about the kind of class warfare that might be unleashed if this sort of law was upheld. "If, for example, in the opinion of future lawmakers, wages in the building trades shall become so high as to preclude people of ordinary means from building and owning homes, an authority which sustains the minimum wage will be invoked to support the maximum wage for building laborers and artisans, and the same argument which has been here urged to strip the employer of his constitutional liberty of contract in one direction will be utilized to strip the employee of his constitutional liberty of contract in the opposite direction. . . . [T]he good of society as a whole cannot be better served than by the preservation against arbitrary restraint of the liberties of its constituent members." Sutherland's opinion is cold, unsympathetic, formalistic, and "progressive" in all the wrong ways (in suddenly treating working women as morally deserving of the same lack of concern and compassion as working men), but the constitutional vision embodied in the opinion is not unprecedented; it may be anachronistic, but it is also traditional and, in its own way, principled.

Chief Justice William Howard Taft and Justices Edward T. Sanford and Oliver Wendell Holmes dissented from Sutherland's opinion, with Brandeis once again recusing himself from the case. (His daughter was secretary of the minimum wage board involved in the case.)[33] Taft and Holmes wrote separate dissents. In his solo dissent, Holmes suggested, first, that the "degree of interference with [contractual] liberty" between employers and employees is the same whether one regulates hours or wages, and second, that "[i]t will take more than the Nineteenth Amendment to convince me that there are no differences between men and women, or that legislation cannot take those differences into account." Neither point was particularly responsive to the majority's argument. The question in police power cases was not whether liberty was being interfered with; it was whether a legislative interference with liberty was reasonably related to a legitimate government interest, an interest distinct from a desire to intervene in social conflicts on behalf of favored groups. In the opinion of the majority, regulations limiting the number of hours one could be forced to work in certain industries were often related to traditional concerns about health and safety, but regulations setting wages were more like illegitimate class legislation. As for Holmes's second point, the majority did say that the legislature was free to take into account relevant differences between men and women in promoting public health, safety, and morality; the question, though, was what difference could there be between men and women that would justify minimum wage legislation for women? The traditional assumptions that the "natural and proper timidity and delicacy of which belongs to the female sex evidently unfits it for many of the occupations of civil life" and that the "paramount destiny and mission of woman are to fulfil the noble and benign offices of wife and mother" had in the past been used to justify laws preventing women from entering certain occupations;[34] the belief that women are more frail than men might justify laws that ensure less strenuous working conditions (such as maximum hours laws). But, from the point of view of the majority, "the ancient inequality of the sexes, otherwise than physical, as suggested in the *Muller Case* ha[d] continued 'with diminishing intensity' " in light of the "present day trend of legislation," and the concern about female physical frailty seemed unrelated to the imposition of a minimum wage. Assuming that it was becoming more acceptable for women to enter the work force, on the basis of what assumption about the distinctive characteristics of women could one justify assuring them but not men a certain price for their labor? The majority was unwilling to suggest that women did not have the same intelligence or judgment as men and therefore could not be counted on to look after their own interest ("we cannot accept the doctrine that women of mature age require or may be subjected to restrictions on their liberty of contract which could not lawfully be imposed in the case of men under similar circumstances"), and Holmes suggested no alternative basis. He did, however, reassert his belief that the justices should stop asking themselves whether, in their judgment, legislation advanced a public purpose and just defer to the popular will.[35]

Taft's opinion was more to the point. If Sutherland's argument rested on a vision of market relations that treated free bargaining as the norm and inappropriate coercion as unusual and anomalous ("freedom of contract is . . . the general rule and restraint the exception," he said, appropriate only in isolated cases like usury), Taft's argument rested on the assumption that economic coercion and social dependency had become commonplace in industrial America. "Legislatures in limiting freedom of contract between employee and employer by a minimum wage proceed on the assumption that employees, in the class receiving the least pay, are not upon a full level of equality of choice with their employer and in their necessitous circumstance are prone to accept pretty much anything that is offered. They are peculiarly subject to the overreaching of the harsh and greedy employer. The evils of the sweating system and of the long hours and low wages which are characteristic of it are well known." (These sentiments echoed Taft's statements as president that the government should be "more sensitive to the inequality of conditions that exist among the people" and should consider changes in the "legal relations between the social classes, and in the amelioration of oppressive conditions.")[36] In a sense, the traditional justification for usury had become the norm, not the exception. For Taft, the important precedent was not the aversion to class legislation; it was the acceptability of legislation that promoted health and safety. And under current conditions, with many workers burdened by their "necessitous circumstance," minimum wage legislation was a reasonable attempt to promote their well-being and prevent their exploitation by heartless employers. He acknowledged that "it is a disputable question in the field of political economy how far a statutory requirement of maximum hours or minimum wages may be a useful remedy for these evils, and whether it may not make the case of the oppressed employee worse than it was before. But," he added, "it is not the function of this Court to hold congressional acts invalid simply because they are passed to carry out economic views which the Court believes to be unwise or unsound."

Taft went on to note that, since *Lochner*, the Court had upheld maximum hours laws in *Muller* and *Bunting*. In the latter case, "this Court sustained a law limiting the hours of labor of any person, whether man or woman, working in any mill, factory or manufacturing establishment to ten hours a day. . . . The law covered the whole field of industrial employment and certainly covered the case of persons employed in bakeries. Yet the opinion in the *Bunting Case* did not mention the *Lochner Case*. . . . It is impossible for me to reconcile the *Bunting Case* and the *Lochner Case* and I have always supposed that the *Lochner Case* was thus overruled *sub silentio*." Taft was correct that *Bunting* and *Lochner* cannot be reconciled on the question of the legitimacy of maximum hours laws for bakers. But the decision in *Bunting* did not necessarily support the claim for a minimum wage; this was emphasized by the majority in *Bunting*. Taft did say that in light of his discussion of *Lochner* and *Bunting*, "I assume that the conclusion in this case rests on the distinction between a minimum of wages and a maximum of hours in the limiting of liberty to contract"; he then went on to reject this distinction by pointing out that when it comes to wages and hours in the employment contract, "one is the multiplier and the other the multiplicand." However, Taft incorrectly formulated the basis for the majority's distinction between wage and hours legislation: the distinctions drawn by the Court in these kinds of cases were never based on the scope or intensity of the interference with contractual liberty (whether one regulation interfered more than another). The distinctions were based on considerations of whether there was a sufficient relationship established between the regulation and a legitimate government interest in health, safety, or the prevention of fraud; or whether, by contrast, the legislation seemed to be an arbitrary or class-based interference in market relations. The majority was not suggesting that liberty of contract was limited more when wages were regulated than when hours were regulated (or, for that matter, when method of payment was regulated); the majority simply concluded that there were better, more traditional reasons to accept limits on working hours in some circumstances (reasons relating to the health and safety issues associated with exhaustion or extended exposure to dangerous materials), while it appeared as though wage regulation was primarily designed to improve the economic condition of one class at the expense of a competing class. Taft, however, was willing to abandon the vision of a neutral state out of a belief that the promotion of health and safety could only be accomplished if government was free to intervene in social conflicts on behalf of vulnerable classes. He insisted that "there is very respectable authority from close observers" that long working hours and low wages are "equally harmful" to the employee.

In most respects the positions adopted by Sutherland and Taft were mutually exclusive: Sutherland adopted the logic of Brown's perspective, that minimum wage laws were unconstitutional as a matter of principle, and Taft adopted the logic of Powell's perspective, that they were legitimate efforts to correct for coercive market mechanisms. Sutherland addressed and dismissed the kind of analysis suggested by the state court in *Stettler*; Taft flirted with the idea of resting his conclusion on *Muller* but did not fully develop exactly what it was about the character or physique of women that qualified them for this special protection. Neither Sutherland nor Taft seemed particularly interested in engaging in the kind of careful, case-by-case, "new realism" scrutiny of minimum wage legislation suggested by the *Harvard Law Review*, although Taft did gesture in that direction when he made it a point to say that evidence indicated that minimum wage laws promoted the well-being of women (at the same time he indicated that he felt he should defer to the legislature), and Sutherland did attempt to show that there were reasons to be suspicious of that evidence (at the same time he indicated that the evidence would not be determinative of the outcome).

The debate had deadlocked. Unlike the divisions that surfaced in the Court in the latter part of the nineteenth century and the earlier part of the twentieth, in cases such as *Slaughterhouse, Powell, Ellis, Matthews,* and even *Lochner*, where it was clear that the justices by and large were in agreement over the relevant constitutional standards but disagreed over their proper application, the controversy over the minimum wage had provoked a dispute over the continued efficacy of traditional police powers jurisprudence. The new realism of sociological jurisprudence was successful at getting some justices to set aside their common understanding of the hazards of the work environment and rely instead on data indicating how certain legislation eased the burden of workers on the job, but it did not weaken the determination of those justices who felt compelled to maintain the distinction between valid health and safety legislation and illegitimate social and economic legislation.

It should be emphasized, though, that this was the specific compulsion of the *Adkins* majority, not some ill-defined commitment to laissez-faire in the abstract. A year after *Adkins* these justices had a chance to prove that they would be willing to uphold legislation that interfered with a woman wage earner's freedom to contract as long as the regulation proceeded on relevant differences between the sexes and was reasonably related to traditional police power concerns regarding health, safety, and morality. In *Radice v. New York* (1924), a unanimous Court, in an opinion written by Sutherland, upheld a state law prohibiting owners of restaurants located in big cities from hiring women to work between the hours of ten in the evening and six in the morning. "[C]onsidering their more delicate organism," the legislature determined that the "injurious consequences" of losing a "restful night's sleep"—which could "not be fully made up by sleep in the day time, especially in busy cities, subject to the disturbances incident to modern life"—"bear more heavily against women than men." Sutherland distinguished *Adkins* by arguing that the statute in that case "was a wage-fixing law, pure and simple. It had nothing to do with the hours or conditions of labor. . . . [We also said] that 'the physical differences [between men and women] must be recognized in appropriate cases, and legislation fixing hours or conditions of work may properly take them into account.' "[37]

The Collapse of Traditional Police Powers Jurisprudence

Reaction to the *Adkins* decision among constitutional scholars was mixed. When Edward Corwin reviewed the case for the *American Political Science Review* he agreed with Taft that *Lochner* and *Bunting* were inconsistent. But he continued by asking, "Is it true . . . that hour-laws and wage-laws rest on the same basis constitutionally? Chief Justice Taft and Justice Holmes contend in effect that they do; but Justice Sutherland's argument to the contrary is fairly convincing from the point of view of precedent."[38] A commentator for the *Illinois Law Review* expressed concern that the "dissenting opinions appear to favor an almost absolute surrender to legislative discretion, and argue that there is no material difference between the statute at bar and those which regulate the hours of labor or the methods of payment of wages and the weighing of coal in the mining industries"; he also expressed the hope that the case signaled the Supreme Court's willingness to reconsider its "surrender" to unbridled police powers (which he traced back to *Powell v. Pennsylvania*).[39] A writer for the *Virginia Law Review* expressed satisfaction with the result, explaining that while "it is true that special legislation governing the employment of women has been sustained," nevertheless "[i]n all cases *a real need for protection must be shown*, which need was conspicuously absent in the instant case." The argument that the Court should defer to Congress's determination about the public welfare "was merely a polite way of saying that the constitutional restrictions upon Congress should no longer operate."[40] Minor Bronaugh understood how people who had become used to social legislation might be upset with the decision, but they needed to remember that there was a well-recognized distinction in constitutional law between hours legislation and wage regulation; if the people wanted to free the states from the burdens of police power jurisprudence they should work for "a general social justice amendment to the Constitution."[41]

By contrast, George W. Goble, writing for the *American Law Review*, declared that the "case seems close" and that "[m]uch can be said to support either view," but suggested that because there was evidence that minimum wage laws contributed to the health and morals of women, the dissenters' views were the more accurate.[42] Other critics misleadingly implied that the Court had struck down the act simply because the state had interfered with liberty of contract. Writing in the *New York Law Journal*, I. Maurice Wormser called the decision "unsound," "unfortunate," and inconsistent "with the long line of recent federal decisions which interfere with liberty of contract quite as seriously and directly as the minimum-wage laws."[43] Charles Grove Haines characterized opinions like Sutherland's as "good examples of the specious methods of reasoning involved in declaring void legislative acts under such a vague phrase as due process of law."[44]

Perhaps the most extensive criticism of *Adkins* came from Thomas Reed Powell, who had grown tired of the extent to which Court conservatives seemed willing to falsify or ignore people's commonplace experiences in order to sustain what, in his judgment, had become indefensible distinctions in police powers jurisprudence. Whereas his first article provided an extended discussion of "The Constitutional Issue in Minimum-Wage Legislation," this time around he felt that the central issue was no longer the proper constitutional interpretation but rather the obstinacy of particular justices, hence his title "The Judiciality of Minimum-Wage Legislation." He opened by reviewing the various changes in Court personnel between 1917 and 1923 and concluded "that minimum wage legislation is now unconstitutional, not because the Constitution makes it so, not because its economic results or its economic propensities would move a majority of judges to think so, but because it chanced not to come before a particular Supreme Court bench which could not muster a majority against it and chanced to be presented at the succeeding term when the requisite, but no more than requisite, majority was sitting. In the words of the poet, it was not the Constitution but a 'measureless malfeasance which obscurely will it thus'—the malfeasance of chance and of the calender. . . . Literary interpretation of the Constitution has nothing whatever to do with it. . . . Arguments *pro* and arguments *contra* have no compelling inherent power. The issue was determined not by the arguments but by the arbiters." Powell then proceeded to characterize Sutherland's opinion as "indefensible" and "a flagrant instance of insufficient reasons," based not on the Constitution (which, he pointed out, nowhere mentions "liberty of contract") but rather on the justice's "personal views of desirable governmental policy."

Powell was certainly right to suggest that there was an unreal and unconvincing quality to the majority opinion; but he was wrong to suggest that the opinion can be understood only as a function of the idiosyncratic policy preferences of the majority. This "realist" account of judicial decision making underappreciated the extent to which Sutherland's argument flowed, not inevitably but understandably, from an overarching set of well-established legal doctrines and principles governing the legitimate exercise of police powers. The majority could be faulted for their continued loyalty to these standards and to the tradition of judicial enforcement of the public-purpose limit on legislation, but the problem faced by supporters of the minimum wage had as much to do with these well-established standards and traditions as the personnel on the Court.[45]

Powell did spend some time reviewing his earlier arguments in favor of a minimum wage. He once again characterized the issue as "whether an employer may be compelled to pay the cost of maintaining the employee whose full services he voluntarily uses in the conduct of his enterprise." Framing the question in this way allowed Powell to suggest that liberty of contract was not being restrained.[46] It also enabled him to challenge Sutherland's analogy between a minimum wage and a requirement that grocers give impoverished customers enough food to eat even if they cannot pay for it. "Differences in fact are obvious. A housewife who buys a can of peas from a grocer does not thereby devote to his enterprise the whole of her working hours. The nexus between grocer and customer is casual and spasmodic. Grocers are in no such position to drive hard bargains with customers as are employers to drive hard bargains with women employees. The effect of high prices for groceries tends to bring prices down more quickly than the effect of low prices for labor tends to raise them." Powell offered an alternative analogy which he considered to be closer to the mark: "If a construction company took workmen to a remote place where the only shelter, food, and clothing were what the company would furnish, there can be little doubt that a court would sustain a statute requiring that such supplies should be adequate to decent human requirements. Under different conditions the minimum-wage law says substantially the same thing." Few analogies could better dramatize the conditions of social dependency that made the call for a minimum wage so compelling; and few analogies could better dramatize the dissimilarity between contemporary industrial conditions and the vision of a neutral and liberty-loving commercial republic that sustained police power jurisprudence for almost a century and a half.[47]

Commenting on these various responses to *Adkins*, Roscoe Pound predictably rejected the realists' suggestion that the justices were merely imposing their policy preferences on the country. He preferred to think that "in the best of faith judges might [be referring] all twentieth-century social legislation to an ideal picture of the rural, agricultural, pioneer society of one hundred years ago, when our law was formative," the consequence of which was to "give a fixed content to the idea of reasonableness which is not necessarily reasonable in the urban, industrial society of to-day." To correct for this problem he urged against the recall of judges or referenda on judicial decisions and in favor of "a better apparatus of informing the courts as to the social background of the statutes on which they pass, so that instead of viewing them consciously or unconsciously on the background of the pioneer society of the formative era of our institutions, . . . they may be judged with reference to the actual environment of the industrial society of to-day."[48]

In his review of *The Supreme Court and Minimum Wage Legislation* (a compilation of a number of law review articles on the *Adkins* case), Ray A. Brown agreed with Pound's suggestion that judges should evaluate the basis for legislation with reference to contemporary industrial conditions but rushed to add that "much may pass in the name of the public good, which is simply the attempt of one class to aggrandize itself at the expense of another. . . . The judiciary should be better suited to detect these masqueraders than a popularly elected representative body."[49] Brown did not indicate whether he believed minimum wage laws were examples of class aggrandizement or regulation promoting the public good, but a few years later, on the eve of the Great Depression, he did offer an opinion in an article on the Court's police powers jurisprudence.

Writing in the *Harvard Law Review*, he reiterated the central questions in these kinds of cases: "Is there, in fact, a danger to the health or safety of the members of the state in the existing situation? Will the method adopted by the state guard against it?" With respect to minimum wage laws, Brown noted that the labor hours cases did not necessarily furnish a precedent for fixing wages; while both were related to liberty of contract as protected by the due process clause, "[i]n the realm of the police power, . . . differences between cases are usually factual and not legalistic." Nevertheless, as a factual matter Brown was willing to concede that the "same principle by which the state may penalize the proprietor of a business for utilizing his superior economic position to exact injurious hours of labor from his employees, may be employed to prohibit him from utilizing it to compel them to accept insufficient wages. It cannot be denied that starvation wages contribute to sickness and immorality, and it must be proclaimed that these are evils with which the state should grapple." He called the minimum wage case "the only unrepudiated decision in which, the facts being undisputed and the factors of health and safety apparent, the Court has denied to the state the power to do what it deemed necessary for the protection of the health and safety of its people. In that case, an instinctive dread of price fixing as an economic measure may easily have obscured in the Court's mind the health aspects of the legislation."[50]

Maybe more to the point, the majority's "dread" had to do with the implications for traditional limits on legislative power of establishing a precedent allowing a state to interfere in class relations on behalf of a favored class for the purpose of promoting the general well-being of that class, as opposed to promoting the welfare of a group through class-neutral legislation (such as poor-relief laws) or interfering in class relations for the purpose of protecting a particular group against dangerous, unhealthy, or fraudulent practices at the workplace. It is telling that Brown initially responded to minimum wage legislation by insisting that there was a meaningful difference between class aggrandizement and public health and safety, but he nevertheless concluded that, in light of existing evidence, it was not illegitimate to require employers to pay a higher price for labor than they would otherwise pay in the hope of transferring some wealth to poor workers; if this was not class politics as traditionally understood, it was hard to imagine what that category referred to anymore. Brown's conclusion demonstrates how the recommendation that judges should pay attention to the actual circumstances that gave rise to this new breed of legislation could not help but put pressure on a majority opinion that was more concerned about maintaining existing legal distinctions than acknowledging existing social conditions; and in the 1920s this advice was being offered with increasing frequency by members of the bar.[51]

Still, despite changes in the Court's personnel,[52] and despite the catastrophic exacerbation of the social conditions that gave rise to the minimum wage, neither the balance of power nor the terms of the debate changed much in the ten years following *Adkins*. The Court continued to shape its decisions on the assumption that there was a meaningful difference between public-purpose legislation and legislation that "arbitrarily" adjusted social and economic relations. The persistence of this ethos can be seen in a case that is sometimes used to illustrate the beginning of the collapse of the old jurisprudence. In *Nebbia v. New York* (1934) the Court considered a New York law that prohibited milk sellers from charging less than a specific amount for the price of milk. The ostensible purpose of the law was to ensure that milk producers and dealers would receive a "reasonable return" and thus continue production and distribution of the product. More than a half a century earlier, in *Munn v. Illinois* (1877),[53] the Court had held that the prices charged by businesses could be regulated only if the business affected the public interest; the Court in general worried that if the power to set prices on products or services was not linked to the public interest, it would create a factional free-for-all as businesses, workers, and consumers vied to gain "unnatural" advantages over their competitors. In order to preempt this free-for-all the Court subsequently held in a number of cases that only a few types of businesses affected the public interest and thus were proper objects of rate regulation—businesses such as utilities, railroads, grain elevators, insurance companies, and a small number of "traditionally" regulated activities like innkeeping.[54] However, in *Nebbia*, a bare majority of the Court upheld the price-fixing scheme, announcing at the same time that "there is no closed class or category of businesses affected with the public interest." This has been taken to mean that the Court had decided to defer to the legislature's judgment with respect to the wisdom of economic policies regarding price-fixing. But there is no indication in this opinion that the majority meant anything so sweeping by that declaration. Certainly Harlan F. Stone, Louis Brandeis, and Benjamin N. Cardozo were sympathetic to that argument, but Owen J. Roberts and Charles E. Hughes maintained an (admittedly ambivalent) attachment to the old distinctions; two years earlier, in *New State Ice Company v. Liebmann* (1932), they had joined with the conservatives in holding that the ice business did not sufficiently affect the public interest to make it a valid object of regulation.[55] A more likely interpretation of the result in *Nebbia* is that a few justices who were more or less committed to the public-purpose limit on legislative power concluded that there was a good reason to think that this law promoted the health of the community as a whole, and was not merely designed to enrich milk producers and large milk dealers; other justices who were also committed to the public-purpose limit disagreed with that conclusion.

In his opinion for the majority, Justice Roberts—who would soon vote to strike down a law fixing the price of labor—reiterated that the reasonableness of this kind of regulation depended on whether the facts demonstrated a relationship between the law and the well-being of the public; in the absence of such facts a law would be merely "arbitrary and discriminatory" and therefore unconstitutional. Roberts emphasized that milk was "an essential item of diet" and that the legislature had determined that "destructive and demoralizing competitive conditions and unfair trade practices . . . resulted in retail price cutting and reduced the income of the farmer below the cost of production," thus threatening the supply of milk to the community. On this basis more than any other the majority was able to conclude that it was a legitimate public purpose "to prevent ruthless competition from destroying the wholesale price structure on which the farmer depends for his livelihood, *and the community for an assured supply of milk.*" The four dissenters—McReynolds, Van Devanter, Sutherland, and Pierce Butler—acknowledged that "regulation to prevent recognized evils in business has long been upheld as permissible legislative action" but nevertheless insisted that "fixation of the price at which 'A,' engaged in an ordinary business, may sell, in order to enable 'B,' a producer, to improve his condition, has not been regarded as within legislative power." Once again, note that theirs was not a laissez-faire argument; their example of illegitimate legislation conjured up the image of class politics, not of unreasonably strong government burdens on free enterprise. For the dissenters this law represented little more than an attempt by farmers and large milk dealers to protect themselves against distributors' price-cutting practices, much to the disadvantage of "impoverished customers." The law "takes away the liberty of 12,000,000 consumers to buy a necessity of life in an open market" and "imposes direct and arbitrary burdens upon those already seriously impoverished with the alleged immediate design of affording special benefits to others." The same justices who viewed minimum wage laws as illegitimate efforts to provide special benefits (arbitrary and discriminatory advantages) to poor workers at the expense of employers also considered this act an illegitimate effort to provide special benefits to milk producers at the expense of poor consumers. They pointed out that this sort of class-based use of legislative power "conflicts with views of constitutional rights accepted since the beginning. . . . The Legislature cannot lawfully destroy guaranteed rights of one man with the prime purpose of enriching another, even if for the moment, this may seem advantageous to the public. And the adoption of any 'concept of jurisprudence' which permits facile disregard of the Constitution as long interpreted and respected will inevitably lead to its destruction."[56]

The divisions on the Court in this case echoed the divisions found in the *Slaughterhouse Cases* and *Powell v. Pennsylvania*,[57] in which the justices disagreed over whether a law was more properly interpreted as a public health measure or as an illegitimate grant of a special benefit to a favored class. What saved this example of price-fixing from the public-purpose limit on legislation was the accepted relationship between the rate scheme and the health of the community as a whole—the same conclusion that in the 1870s and 1880s saved the slaughterhouse monopoly and the ban on oleomargarine. However, the same public health argument was not available to advocates of the minimum wage. The best they could do was to say that a minimum wage would improve the health of a particular class. In the past, however, the Court was willing only to allow the legislature to impose a burden on one class (employers or railroads) in order to promote the health or well-being of another (employees or farmers) if the threat to the well-being of a particular class was caused by the class being burdened by the legislation (maintaining unhealthy working conditions or allowing sparks to fly from railroads onto someone's property). For the conservatives on the Court, employers who paid low wages were harming workers no more than store owners who charged prices that the poor could not afford. In light of the fact that the Court seemed determined to maintain these long-standing limits on legislative powers, supporters of the minimum wage either had to come up with some innovative arguments that fit into accepted police power categories or had to hope that a time would come when enough justices were willing to jettison the old jurisprudence.

Not wanting to wait for Godot, supporters of the minimum wage developed two new legal strategies to try to get their policy past the scrutiny of the judiciary. One strategy was to write statutes that required the minimum wage to be based not only on the subsistence needs of workers but also on the "value of the services rendered." This amendment to existing statutes was designed to address the complaint that minimum wage laws amounted to special favors for one group at the expense of another. If one could reasonably argue that the wage merely required employers to pay employees what they were worth, then in theory it was neither unjust enrichment for employees nor an arbitrary burden on employers. Moreover, while this was not the centerpiece of the *Adkins* case, in his opinion for the Court Sutherland did say that the minimum wage at issue did not take into account the value of the services rendered. Of course, this move had to be supported by an argument that the value of the services rendered could sometimes be better measured by the legislature than by the market, and some attempts at such an argument were offered.[58] But this aspect of the argument was usually finessed, kept implicit, for fear that it would be met with skepticism by judges who were on the lookout for class legislation and associated such legislation with efforts to substitute an "arbitrary" political judgment about wages and prices for the "natural" measure of the market. For judges who continued to believe that there was a difference between public-purpose legislation and legislation designed to impose unfair burdens and benefits on favored or despised classes, it was not sufficient for a legislature merely to declare that a certain price was the true value of some service or commodity. Judicial deference to that kind of declaration would amount to an abandonment of the responsibility to keep legislatures within the proper limits of their authority.

In any case, this strategy became commonplace, as Irene Osgood Andrews, the associate secretary for the American Association for Labor Legislation, noted in 1933 in an article entitled "Minimum Wage Comes Back!": "For a time it seemed that further legislation in this field was politically impossible. However, in 1925, two years after the District of Columbia case, Wisconsin, following the suggestion of the Court in regard to 'the value of the services rendered,' amended its minimum wage law to provide that 'no wage paid or agreed to be paid by any employer to any adult female shall be oppressive. Any wage lower than a reasonable and adequate compensation for the services rendered shall be deemed oppressive and is hereby prohibited.' . . . [Similar] legislation [elsewhere] specifically provides that 'an oppressive and unreasonable wage' shall mean 'a wage which is both less than the fair and reasonable value of the services rendered and less than sufficient to meet the minimum cost of living necessary for health.' "[59]

Another strategy adopted by supporters of minimum wage laws was primarily associated with the exigencies of the depression. This strategy involved linking the minimum wage to general economic recovery, and not just to the well-being of a particular class. According to one commentator writing in the *Yale Law Journal* in 1933, "Recent economic trends . . . have revealed a necessity for wage-fixing not appreciated at the time of the *Adkins* decision. It is now generally recognized that wage-cutting threatens the stability of industry. Reduced wages mean decreased purchasing power, and decreased purchasing power paralyzes trade. Moreover, unlimited ability to slash labor costs constitutes a vicious weapon for unscrupulous competition. These factors make minimum wage legislation essential to any program for economic recovery."[60] This conclusion was buttressed by a message issued on April 12, 1933, from FDR to the governors of thirteen industrial states urging the enactment of minimum wage laws "for protection of the public interest." He pointed out that the continual lowering of wages "is a serious form of unfair competition against other employers, reduces the purchasing power of the workers and threatens the stability of industry."[61]

In light of these two innovative arguments, a number of sympathetic commentators believed that the Supreme Court might respond more favorably to the "fair value" minimum wage law passed by the state of New York in 1933 than it had to the congressional statute that was struck down in *Adkins*. Unlike the District of Columbia act, the New York law did not "[quoting from *Adkins*] 'extract from the employer an arbitrary payment for a purpose and upon a basis having no causal connection with his business, or the contract or work the employee engages to do.' The basis for the computation of the minimum wage was 'not the value of the services rendered, but the extraneous circumstance that the employee needs to get a prescribed sum of money to insure her subsistence, health and morals.' . . . [Under the New York law] 'a fair wage' shall mean a wage fairly and reasonably commensurate with the value of the service or class of service rendered."[62] Still, while the writer took the position that these reasons made the New York law consistent with the Court's holding in *Adkins*, she nevertheless expressed hope that "the Court will repudiate the very premises of its former opinion. The theory that freedom of contract is the rule against which a specific statute must be proved a proper exception should now be accorded a 'deserved repose.' "[63]

On the eve of the Court's evaluation of the New York law a student note in the *Kentucky Law Journal* also emphasized two important changes that had taken place since *Adkins*. The first was the "current economic depression. . . . Whereas in earlier days the declared purpose of such statutes was the protection of the health and morals of woman workers, it is now the promotion of national economic recovery. . . . *This is significant because it means that minimum wage laws are no longer class legislation*; it cannot be said that the interests of only one party to the contract are considered." The other important change involved the Court's personnel. "Mr. Justice Sutherland and three of those who concurred with him in the *Adkins* decision remain on the bench. . . . The deciding votes are now those of Mr. Chief Justice Hughes and Mr. Justice Roberts, since there is no doubt about the sentiments of Justices Brandeis, Stone, and Cardozo. Mr. Hughes and Mr. Roberts have indicated in a number of cases their willingness to sustain state or federal statutes challenged on grounds of due process [such as the milk price-fixing scheme in *Nebbia*]. . . . [However,] I am instructed that Mr. Hughes is extremely reluctant to overrule a case expressly, especially when such action would result, as it almost certainly would here, in a five to four decision. Therefore, in order to placate the minority and to save the face of the court, it is my prediction that the Adkins case will be distinguished rather than directly overruled."[64] As it turned out, the student had offered a very savvy prediction of the actions of Chief Justice Hughes but was less in tune with Justice Roberts's sentiments and therefore with the outcome of the decision in *Morehead v. New York ex rel. Tipaldo* (1936).[65]

In his argument in favor of the state minimum wage law for women and children the solicitor general of New York emphasized that the wage "was based solely upon the fair value of the services rendered." In this respect the New York law met "every objection offered by this Court in the *Adkins* case." In response the lawyers challenging the statute pointed out that the New York Court of Appeals had held that the New York statute was not different from the one struck down by the Court in *Adkins* and argued that the "construction given by the New York Court of Appeals is controlling." As for the claim that the depression changed the social facts underlying the justification for the act, they responded that "the challenged Act is not an emergency statute." They then reiterated that these kinds of acts had to be related to the health of the public, and not simply to an interest in improving the social conditions of some classes, and "if it were a health measure, the wages paid to heads of families would most certainly be the first to be regulated." Moreover, while "there is a basis for saying that excessive hours of labor and night work for women directly affect the health of the worker, . . . the wages paid affect the health of the recipients only indirectly."

The opinion of the Court was written by Justice Butler. Given the fact that over the previous ten years the social and legal climate had become more hostile to the *Adkins* opinion, and that the commitment of some of the justices to the opinion was apparently becoming less assured, Butler attempted to avoid an unambiguous reaffirmation of the arguments against the minimum wage by emphasizing that the Court was considering a very narrow question: "The Adkins case, unless distinguishable, requires affirmance of the judgment below. The petition for the writ sought review upon the ground that this case is distinguishable from that one. No application has been made for reconsideration of the constitutional question there decided. The validity of the principles upon which that decision rests is not challenged. This court confines itself to the ground upon which the writ was asked or granted."[66] Despite the fact that the New York law required wages to reflect "the fair and reasonable value of the services rendered" and "sufficient to meet the minimum cost of living necessary for health," the majority chose instead to confine itself to the judgment of the New York Court of Appeals that there was "no material difference between the act of Congress [struck down in the *Adkins* case] and this act of the New York State Legislature. . . . The act of Congress had one standard, the living wage; this State act has added another, reasonable value. . . . [But forcing] the payment of wages at a reasonable value does not make inapplicable the principle and ruling of the *Adkins* case. The distinctions between this case and the *Adkins* case are differences in details, methods and time; the exercise of legislative power to fix wages in any employment is the same."[67] Butler noted that the petitioner argued that the New York court was mistaken in equating the two statutes; the solicitor general insisted in his brief that the "only basis for evaluating and arriving at the 'fair minimum wage' is the fair value of the services rendered." However, he responded that "petitioner's contention that the Court of Appeals misconstrued the Act cannot be entertained. This court is without power to put a different construction upon the state enactment from that adopted by the highest court of the

State."[68] Butler's opinion continues with five pages of extended quotations from the *Adkins* opinion, followed by a few pages that make the point that the reasons offered in support of minimum wage laws for women apply equally to men and thus form no basis for treating the sexes differently.

Only one member of the Court, Chief Justice Hughes, was willing to accept that a legislative declaration that a minimum wage should reflect the value of the services rendered distinguished this law from the act struck down in *Adkins*. Both then and now it has been the accepted wisdom to assume that his decision to walk a tightrope between *Adkins* and *Morehead* reflected his reluctance to overrule a case directly rather than a principled commitment to the distinctions he chose to emphasize; this might help explain his inability to offer a persuasive case for the distinction. Still, he tried, and in his separate dissent he began by attacking the majority's reluctance to even address the possibility that the law at issue in this case was different from the one struck down in *Adkins*. He observed that the New York court's decision was based not only on an interpretation of the state law but also on an interpretation of the meaning of *Adkins* as applied to that law, and he correctly pointed out that the state court's interpretation of *Adkins* "is not binding upon us."[69] He explained that the New York Court recognized in its opinion "that a wage is not denounced by the New York act as 'oppressive and unreasonable' unless it is less than the fair and reasonable value of the services rendered. . . . When the opinion of the state court goes beyond the statement of the provisions of the act, and says that the setting up of such a standard does not create a material distinction when compared with the Act of Congress in the Adkins case, the state court is not construing the state statute. It is passing upon the effect of the difference between the two acts from the standpoint of the Federal Constitution. It is putting aside an admitted difference as not controlling. . . . That, it seems to me, is clearly a federal and not a state question, and I pass to its consideration."[70]

Hughes then suggested that "the constitutional validity of a minimum wage statute like the New York act has not heretofore been passed upon by this Court." He argued, misleadingly, that the opinion in *Adkins* "contained a broad discussion of state power, but it singled out as an adequate ground for the finding of invalidity that the statute gave no regard to the situation of the employer and to the reasonable value of the service for which the wage was paid."[71] He also drew the Court's attention to the fact that the legislature in this case had made an uncontroverted finding of fact that minimum wage laws would promote the well-being of women workers, and added, somewhat disingenuously, "We are not at liberty to disregard these facts." Of course, a similar argument could have been made in response to the Court's decision in *Adkins*, the validity of which Hughes ostensibly was not calling into question. As for liberty of contract, he wrote that "while it is highly important to preserve that liberty from arbitrary and capricious interference, it is also necessary to prevent its abuse, as otherwise it could be used to override all public interests and thus in the end destroy the very freedom of opportunity which it is designed to safeguard."[72] In a subtle but important rewrite of the prevailing standards governing the police powers, Hughes asserted that "the test of validity [for this type of legislation] is whether the limitation upon the freedom of contract is arbitrary and capricious or one reasonably required in order appropriately to serve the public interest in the light of the particular conditions to which the power is addressed." This rewrite was important because it obscured the key distinction in these kinds of cases—one recognized in the traditional statement of the test found in *Lawton v. Steele* (1893)— which was that "to justify the State in thus interposing its authority in behalf of the public . . . it must appear, first, that the interests of the public generally, *as distinguished from those of a particular class*, require such interference, and second, that the means are reasonably necessary for the accomplishment of the purpose."[73] Toward the end of the opinion Hughes summarized his perspective on the New York law as follows: "The fact that the State cannot secure the benefit to society of a living wage for women employees by any enactment which bears unreasonably upon employers does not preclude the State from seeking its objective by means entirely fair both to employers and the women employed."[74]

Stone wrote a separate dissent, which was joined by Brandeis and Cardozo. They proclaimed their agreement with the Chief Justice's arguments but added that they "would not make the differences between the present statute and that involved in the Adkins case the sole basis of decision." Stone explained, "I attach little importance to the fact that the earlier statute was aimed only at a starvation wage and that the present one does not prohibit such a wage unless it is also less than the reasonable value of the service. Since neither statute compels employment at any wage, I do not assume that employers in one case, more than in the other, would pay the minimum wage if the service were worth less."[75] This observation makes it clear why the law at issue in this case was not different in kind from the one struck down in *Adkins*. The dissenters used this argument to support their conclusion that liberty of contract was not really being violated at all (since under either this scheme or the one at issue in *Adkins* employers were perfectly free either to hire workers or not, and theoretically they would hire workers only if they believed that the established wage was worth the value of the services rendered). It should be pointed out, though, that the same could be said about any price-fixing scheme—people are always free either to pay the established rate or to forgo the service—and besides, the important point for the majority was that this attempt to adjust the market relationship between employers and employees on behalf of a favored class was not supported by a legitimate concern about the health or safety of the community as a whole or by a legitimate concern about mitigating a harm caused by the burdened class. Still, "liberty of contract" had come to represent the Court's general attitude that market relationships should be free from government interference unless the legislature was promoting an acceptable public purpose, and so an attack on that phrase was the best way to make the rebuttal argument that the legislature should be free to adjust market relationships any time it wanted.

There is grim irony in speaking of the freedom of contract of those who, because of their economic necessities, give their service for less than is needful to keep body and soul together. . . . No one doubts that the presence in the community of a large number of those compelled by economic necessity to accept a wage less than is needful for subsistence is a matter of grave public concern, the more so when, as has been demonstrated here, it tends to produce ill health, immorality and deterioration of the race. The fact that at one time or another Congress and the legislatures of seventeen states, including Great Britain and its four commonwealths, have found that wage regulation is an appropriate corrective for serious social and economic maladjustments growing out of inequality in bargaining power, precludes, for me, any assumption that it is a remedy beyond the bounds of reason. It is difficult to imagine any grounds, other than our own personal economic predilections, for saying that the contract of employment is any the less an appropriate subject of legislation than are scores of others.[76]

Stone added, "I can perceive no more objection, on constitutional grounds, to [laws which require] an industry to bear the subsistence cost of the labor which it employs, than to the imposition upon it of the cost of its industrial accidents."[77] (Of course, the response to this point would be that traditional police powers jurisprudence had come to accept legislation that imposed special burdens on employers for the purpose of mitigating harmful working conditions for which they were responsible; the same tradition had not looked as favorably upon legislation that imposed special burdens on classes like employers or railroads in order to mitigate social harms that they did not directly cause.) He ended by saying, "We should follow our decision in the *Nebbia* case and leave the selection and the method of the solution of the problems to which the statute is addressed where it seems to me the Constitution has left them, to the legislative branch of the government."[78]

Should government adjustments in competitive relations between classes have to be justified to courts on the basis of some traditionally accepted distinctive public purpose, or should judges simply allow legislatures to correct "serious social and economic maladjustments growing out of inequality in bargaining power"? After *Morehead* it appeared as though a majority of the justices were still insisting on the first alternative. In fact, though, by 1936 five members of the Court had finally come to accept that the inability of workers to attract a living wage—that is, their inability to maintain their social independence in a commercial republic—meant that there was no longer any justification for maintaining the principle that legislation be class-neutral. Apparently, Justice Roberts, who had previously demonstrated an ambivalent attachment to the tradition, voted with the majority in *Morehead* because he believed (or found it convenient to believe) that the Court in that case was limited by the writ to address the narrow question of whether the New York law enjoyed a different constitutional standing from the law struck down in *Adkins*. Almost immediately, though, another case compelled the justices to review the wisdom of *Adkins*, and by the end of the year Roberts had decided to join the four *Morehead* dissenters in an opinion which ushered in a revolution in constitutional law.[79]

Unlike the legislation struck down in *Morehead*, the minimum wage law at issue in *West Coast Hotel v. Parrish* (1937)[80] did not require the wage to reflect the value of the services rendered; it merely required a wage adequate to maintain the well-being of an adult woman worker. The majority opinion was written by Chief Justice Hughes (who in *Morehead* had refused to say that he believed *Adkins* was wrongly decided). His opening assault on the liberty of contract doctrine was designed to make the point that it was no concern of judges if legislatures decided to make adjustments in the relationships among and between groups competing in the market. "The Constitution does not speak of freedom of contract. It speaks of liberty and prohibits the deprivation of liberty without due process of law. . . . [T]he liberty safeguarded is liberty in a social organization which requires the protection of law against the evils which menace the health, safety, morals and welfare of the people. . . . This power under the Constitution to restrict freedom of contract has many illustrations."[81] After offering a number of examples, including the decision in *Muller*, Hughes continued: "This array of precedents and the principles they applied were thought by the dissenting Justices in the *Adkins* case to demand that the minimum wage statute be sustained. The validity of the distinction made by the Court between a minimum wage and a maximum of hours in limiting liberty of contract was especially challenged. That challenge persists and is without any satisfactory answer."[82] Thus, "We think that . . . the decision in the Adkins case was a departure from true application of the principles governing the regulation by the State of the relation of employer and employed."[83]

This, of course, was not so—anyone interested in knowing the principles relating to the government's authority to regulate employer-employee relations need only look at the opinions and decisions of state and federal judges when they first began to address this issue at the end of the nineteenth century (and the almost unanimous concurrence in those decisions within the pages of law journals). But you can't blame the Chief Justice for claiming that he was merely correcting a mistake rather than jettisoning a constitutional tradition that was a century and a half old. He was less interested in clarifying the past than in forging a new conception of the role of the state in an industrial economy. He started in familiar territory, focusing on how the Court had always considered it a legitimate object of regulation for a state to extend special protections to women. "What can be closer to the public interest than the health of women and their protection from unscrupulous and overreaching employers? And if the protection of women is a legitimate end of the exercise of state power, how can it be said that the requirement of the payment of the minimum wage fairly fixed in order to meet the very necessities of existence is not an admissible means to that end? The legislature of the State was clearly entitled to consider the situation of women in employment, the fact that they are in the class receiving the least pay, that their bargaining power is relatively weak, and that they are the ready victims of those who would take advantage of their necessitous circumstance." However, Hughes was not satisfied to anchor the decision in a *Muller*-like argument; consequently, his opinion continued with a segue into a more expanded justification for legislative power. "The legislature was entitled to adopt measures to reduce the evils of the 'sweating system,' the exploiting of workers at wages so low as to be insufficient to meet the bare cost of living, thus making their very helplessness the occasion of a most injurious competition. . . . The adoption of [minimum wage laws] by many States evidences a deepseated conviction both as to the presence of the evil and as to the means adopted to check it. Legislative responses to that conviction cannot be regarded as arbitrary or capricious, and that is all we have to decide. Even if the wisdom of the policy is regarded as debatable and its effects uncertain, still the legislature is entitled to its judgment." As a general matter, "the exploitation of a class of workers who are in an unequal bargaining power and are thus relatively defenceless against the denial of a living wage is not only detrimental to their health and well being but casts a direct burden for their support on the community. . . . We may take judicial notice of the unparalleled demands for relief which arose during the recent period of depression and still continue to an alarming extent despite the degree of economic recovery which has been achieved. . . . The community is not bound to provide what is in effect a subsidy for unconscionable employers."[84]

After a decades-long assault the old regime had finally collapsed. The remaining four stalwart defenders, led by Sutherland, had no new arguments against a minimum wage upon which to rest an objection. Not surprisingly, Sutherland felt compelled to reiterate the points he had made in *Adkins*. He also reminded the majority that up until this case the question of whether a law was reasonable was a factual matter that each judge had to decide for himself and could not possibly depend on the law's popularity.[85] There was only one new objection that the dissenters could make, and that related to what they considered to be the majority's illegitimate and cowardly disregard for the established meaning of the Constitution:

It is urged that the question involved should now receive fresh consideration, among other reasons, because of "the economic conditions which have supervened"; but the meaning of the Constitution does not change with the ebb and flow of economic events. We frequently are told in more general words that the Constitution must be construed in the light of the present. If by that it is meant that the

Constitution is made up of living words that apply to every new condition which they include, the statement is quite true. But to say, if that be intended, that the words of the Constitution mean today what they did not mean when written—that is, that they do not apply to a situation now to which they would have applied then—is to rob that instrument of the essential element which continues it in force as the people have made it until they, and not their official agents, have made it otherwise. . . . The judicial function is that of interpretation; it does not include the power of amendment under the guise of interpretation.[86]

Sutherland was not wrong in saying that the majority had essentially amended the Constitution. But because the majority, understandably, did not feel free to proclaim that the judicial function included the power of amendment, their response to Sutherland's lament was not directly posed: Was it a greater evil to abandon this feature of the framers' Constitution or to maintain it despite the fact that the assumptions about social independence in a commercial republic that legitimized the tradition in the first place were no longer valid?

New social facts had finally brought down a century-old police powers jurisprudence. The central distinctions of this jurisprudence—distinctions based not on judgments about whether laws burdened free enterprise a lot or a little, but on judgments about whether interventions in market relations were related to a historically defined conception of the public purpose or instead were better understood as corrupt attempts by particular classes to gain unfair and unnatural advantages over their market adversaries—would no longer constitute the conceptual basis upon which the judiciary would determine the boundaries of legitimate legislative authority. Judges who wanted to continue to determine these boundaries would have to devise a new conceptual apparatus, and, in so doing, forge a new constitutional tradition with its own social origins, theoretical assumptions, distinctive language, peculiar preoccupations, historically informed categories, and internal tensions.

Afterword

The average Supreme Court judge, I believe, takes his constitutional theory very seriously. . . . To them such phrases as the separation of powers, checks and balance, judicial independence, national supremacy, states' rights, freedom of contract, vested rights, police power, not only express important realities, they are realities—they are forms of thought with a vitality and validity of their own.—Edward Corwin (1925)[1]

The *Lochner* era ushered in a change in the way American legal scholars thought about courts and judicial behavior. As people's experiences began to diverge from the assumptions underlying the jurisprudence of *Lochner*—assumptions about how individuals relate to one another in a free market and the possibility of class-neutral exercises of state power— members of the the legal community began to question whether judges were "really" basing their decisions on the principles they espoused, principles that to many seemed increasingly biased and detached from reality. It was not long before legal "realists" concluded that legal materials were merely rhetorical devices used by judges to mask (and hopefully legitimize) the exercise of raw power. Even some judges began to agree with the realists' conclusion that judges really decided cases on the basis of hunches and then justified them with whatever materials were handy.[2]

Realists sought to transform the legal community's conception of jurisprudence: what had been traditionally understood to be a legal science was now to be treated as a politically charged effort to impose an image of rationality and order on what in fact were exercises of political will and conditions of disorder. This belief in the theatrical, mystical, political, and arational role of jurisprudence in the legal process was eloquently advanced by Thurman Arnold in his *Symbols of Government* (1935). The "concern of jurisprudence," he wrote, is to prove that "unifying principles" exist in a society and then "to define them in general terms sufficiently broad so that all the little contradictory ideals appearing in the unending procession of particular cases will appear to be part of one great set of ideals." For example, "in the realm of the law the least favored members of society are comforted by the fact that the poor are equal to the rich and the strong have no advantage over the weak. The more fortunately situated are reassured by the fact that the wise are treated better than the foolish, that careless people are punished for their mistakes. . . . The dissatisfied minority is cheered by the fact that the law is elastic and growing. The conservative is convinced that it is becoming more and more certain. The industrial serf is told that no man, not even his great employers, is above the law. His employer, however, feels secure in the fact that his property is put above ordinary legislative law by the Constitution, which is the highest form of law there is. . . . It gives all people an equal chance for success, and at the same time protects those who have been born in more favored positions of privilege and power." Arnold concluded that these values (or reassurances) "are mutually so conflicting" that "no systematic set of doctrines can ever be used as either explanations or predictions concerning the habits of an institution."[3]

Constitutional adjudication during the *Lochner* era provided the impetus that would lead to many of the lessons taught by the realists: law is not above politics and power; decisions do not flow mechanically from abstract principles, and therefore reference to the language of law alone is insufficient as an explanation for judicial decisions; legal ideology represents an attempt to impose a politically charged image of coherence on social and political relations; the vision of society embodied in the law may contain contradictory elements or elements that are simply out of tune with many people's experiences. But however significant, even enduring, these lessons proved to be, many contemporaries of the legal realists disagreed with their ultimate conclusion that legal materials were not meaningful or important in understanding what judges did. Roscoe Pound was only one of many to reply to the realists that just as it was possible to overstate the extent to which legal materials are autonomous and completely directive of judicial behavior, so too can one overstate the extent to which they are meaningless and unworthy of scholarly attention, since, in his words, "received ideals are actual and everyday phenomena of the legal order."[4]

Among the best discussions arising out of these debates is Max Lerner's "The Supreme Court and American Capitalism." He noted how "the contemporary trend is to regard each judge as acting upon his own economic beliefs and his own preferences as to social policy, and as rationalizing or deliberately manipulating his legal views into conformity with his social views." This assumption led the realists to "treat all these legal factors in the judicial process less as rules than as techniques—fairly flexible and accordingly subservient to the more deeply rooted purposes of the judges." This trend "represents of course an extreme revulsion against the traditional views of the judge as objectively expounding a body of law that has some superior truth-sanction." However, Lerner argued that the realists did not take sufficient account of the fact that the judge's "mind is itself largely a social product, and that he is a judge within an economic system and an ideological milieu. Their influence is operative even when he is not applying the 'method of sociology,' or using law consciously as an instrument for social ends." Lerner believed that the essence of the judicial process was to be found in the relationship between these two structures, what he called "the world of social fact and the world of social ideas." He stressed that he was not advocating a belief in "a rigorous determinism" between economic and ideological structures: "The judicial process is not, as a too mechanical view might hold, powerless in the clutch of capitalist circumstance"; after all, "the same constitutional fabric that contains the absolute individualism of Justice Sutherland gives scope also to the humanistic individualism of Justice Holmes, and the social constructivism of Justice Brandeis." Still, "for an explanation of the main trend of constitutional decision we may therefore look to the institutional and ideological elements that exercise their compulsive force on the minds of the judges, and to the changes wrought in these elements principally by economic developments. For an explanation of the groupings within the Court, we may look to the variations in outlook and belief as between the individual members."[5]

Even Felix S. Cohen, in his discussion of the "transcendental nonsense" of legal materials, the "magic 'solving words' of traditional jurisprudence," acknowledged that scholars needed to come to grips with both the lessons of legal realism and the existence of legal culture. He agreed with the realists that "valuable as is the language of transcendental nonsense for many practical purposes, it is entirely useless when we come to study, describe, predict, and criticize legal phenomena" and that when "the vivid fictions and metaphors of traditional jurisprudence are thought of as reasons for decisions, rather than poetical or mnemonic devices for formulating decisions reached on other grounds, then the author, as well as the reader, of the opinion or argument, is apt to forget the social forces which mold the law and the social ideals by which the law is to be judged." But he nevertheless criticized "certain advocates of realistic jurisprudence" for conceptualizing "decisions as simply unanalyzable products of judicial hunches or indigestion." He warned that "magnifying the personal and accidental factors in judicial behavior, implicitly denies the relevance of significant, predictable, social determinants that govern the course of judicial decisions." While Cohen applauded the realists for performing "a real service in indicating the large realm of uncertainty in the actual law," he added that "actual experience does reveal a significant body of predictable uniformity in the behavior of courts" and that a "truly realistic theory of judicial decisions must conceive every decision as something more than an expression of individual personality, as concomitantly and even more importantly a function of social forces, that is to say, as a product of social determinants and an index of social consequences." Contrary to the realist image of a judge as an independent personality, "we know . . . that dominant economic forces play a part in judicial decisions, that judges usually reflect the attitudes of their own income class on social questions, . . . that judges are craftsmen, with aesthetic ideals, concerned with the aesthetic judgments that the bar and the law schools will pass upon their awkward or skillful, harmonious or unharmonious, anomalous or satisfying, actions and theories."[6]

A similar point was made by Edward S. Corwin. "A full explanation of the growth of American constitutional law must recognize that the relatively compact universe of constitutional theory is bathed in a vastly wider atmosphere of social and economic activity." However, "granting all this," Corwin then asked, "does constitutional theory"—by which he meant "those generalized, and often conflicting views of what the constitution is or ought to be"—"lose its significance?" His answer: "The average Supreme Court judge, I believe, takes his constitutional theory very seriously. . . . To them such phrases as the separation of powers, checks and balance, judicial independence, national supremacy, states' rights, freedom of contract, vested rights, police power, not only express important realities, they *are* realities—they are forms of thought with a vitality and validity of their own."[7]

In this study I have tried to reconstruct what I believe were the very real, socially constructed forms of thought within which many nineteenth- and early-twentieth-century jurists interpreted the events of their times. The hypothesis advanced in these pages—that the justices were by and large motivated by a principled commitment to the application of a constitutional ideology of state neutrality, as manifested in the requirement that legislation advance a discernible public purpose—explains a good deal more of the dependent variable (judicial behavior) than do hypotheses that suggest that the justices were basing decisions on a blind adherence to laissez-faire or on a desire to see members of their class win specific lawsuits or on an interest in imposing their idiosyncratic policy preferences on the country. Properly understood, the patterns of judicial decision making and the preoccupations of judicial opinions display a remarkable degree of coherence and consistency, down to the kinds of issues the justices faced with near unanimity and the kinds of issues on which they divided.

Contrary to neorealist explanations of the period, the story of the *Lochner* era is not about how reactionary justices in the late nineteenth century became more daring in their willingness to exploit legal materials in order to protect or promote their personal class or policy biases. Rather, the *Lochner* era is the story of how a changing social structure exposed the conservatism and class bias inherent in dominant ideological structures first formulated and institutionalized by the framers of the U.S. Constitution; it is the story of how an ideology that was fairly (albeit not completely) inclusive around the time of the founding became more and more exclusive as the century progressed and capitalist forms of production matured; and it is the story of how the Court, loyal to a historically defined conception of political legitimacy, struggled to maintain the coherence of this authoritative ideology in an era that witnessed an unprecedented intensification of class conflict. Focusing exclusively on judicial personalities, idiosyncratic belief systems, or personal policy preferences can lead us to overlook the continuities in nineteenth-century American political culture and the extent to which the justices of the late nineteenth century interpreted the social turmoil of the 1880s and 1890s through an ideological prism developed by another group of social elites in response to the social turmoil of the 1780s.

My argument is not intended as a general theory of judicial behavior, removable from the particular historical context toward which it is directed. It is likely that judicial behavior is shaped by many different factors: some judges may be highly principled and dedicated professional craftsmen; others may be savvy state managers who use their best political judgment to maintain both legitimacy and social order; others may be political hacks with (or without) a gift for fancy talk, interested only in promoting a particular political agenda; and still others may be opportunists who make themselves available for sale to the highest bidder. If there is a point to this study beyond its claim to identify the social origins and clarify the nature of constitutional adjudication during the *Lochner* era, it is that among those independent variables that scholars consider in their theories about judicial behavior there ought to be the autonomous influence of legal ideology as understood by interpretive communities existing in particular historical contexts.

The scope of this study makes it likely that I have overlooked some of the nuances of various judges' struggles to reconcile the constitutional ideology of classlessness with the intensification of class conflict. A more focused examination might discover that some jurists were more willing than others to accept the coercive effects of the market as justification for state protection of vulnerable groups; it might also be the case that some courts were more likely to defer to the reasons advanced by legislatures to justify special treatment or legislative classifications. But I believe that I have clarified the major patterns and preoccupations of constitutional jurisprudence at the turn of the century, enough, anyway, to appreciate that when the Court in *West Coast Hotel v. Parrish* (1937) gave "fresh consideration" to the question of police powers and finally permitted the establishment of a minimum wage on the grounds that "workers . . . in an unequal position with respect to bargaining power" were "exploited" by their employers and "relatively defenceless against the denial of a living wage,"[8] the United States underwent a true constitutional revolution. The significance of this case is not that it signaled the moment when a group of stubborn and reactionary judges finally abandoned fifty years of bad precedent; rather, it was the moment when a majority of the justices finally permitted a rapprochement between government and interests, when they expressed a willingness to allow government to intrude itself into market relations on the behalf of favored classes. Instead of requiring legislators to demonstrate that their policies were rationally related to a legitimate public purpose, the Court after 1937 was willing to assume that legislation was rational; as the majority stated in *United States v. Carolene Products* (1938; a case that, had it been argued at the turn of the century, might have prompted a good deal of debate about whether it involved illegitimate class favoritism or legitimate public health),[9] "[r]egulatory legislation affecting ordinary commercial transactions is not to be pronounced unconstitutional unless in the light of the facts made known or generally assumed it is of such a character as to preclude the assumption that its rests upon some rational basis within the knowledge and experience of the legislators."[10] As Martin Shapiro put it, "Congress need not justify intervention itself, . . . need not justify intervening to favor some participants in the economy over others, . . . [and] need not justify its choice of favorites."[11] In abandoning the principle that legislation had to be separated from the clash of interests among social groups, the Court re-created the Constitution so that it would accommodate the responsibilities demanded of a corporate liberal state.

Shapiro has also reminded us that the Supreme Court did not completely abandon the power to review the reasonableness or rationality of economic regulation; however, the modern Court's scrutiny of economic regulation tends to take place more in the realm of administrative law rather than constitutional law. Through administrative law, judges "have made themselves into major monitors of the reasonableness of the vast range of business regulation done through agency rulemaking. . . . The [Supreme] Court's opinions need not say that the agency has not done an adequate job of gathering and explaining its materials to allow the Court to decide whether its rule is reasonable. Clothed or not, however, the Court insists today that it is the ultimate decider of whether *rules* regulating business are reasonable, just as it used to claim that it was the ultimate decider whether *laws* regulating business were reasonable." There is, however, an important difference between the kind of review undertaken by the modern Court and the approach of *Lochner* era jurists: whereas the traditional approach evaluated the reasonableness of regulation in terms of its relationship to a narrow set of goals considered legitimate objects of public power, the determination of the reasonableness of contemporary regulation is usually a by-product of some kind of "marginal analysis, to the points at which the costs assigned to disfavored groups begin to climb sharply in return for increasingly smaller increments of benefit for the favored groups."[12] State power, legislative or administrative, is no longer filtered through the restrictions of *Lochner* era jurisprudence.

The "constitutional revolution of 1937" marked the moment when the founders' conception of a faction-free American Republic collapsed under the onslaught of corporate capitalism; their vision had survived as the organizing principle of American politics for exactly 150 years. The master principle of the neutral state was not the only aspect of the founding conception that buckled under the weight of the twentieth century, to be replaced by what Theodore J. Lowi referred to as the "Second American Republic." The presidency was fundamentally transformed into a "popular" branch that was expected to be a programmatic leader of an increasingly fragmented political system;[13] the Senate was formally democratized; the line separating the domains of national and state control over commerce, so carefully drawn by the founders and protected by the Court, was erased with the New Deal's extension of federal authority to include control over local manufacturing and production;[14] and long-standing standards regulating Congress's ability to delegate rule-making authority to executive agencies were set aside.[15] Other significant changes in the powers, practices, responsibilities, and organization of American politics—such as the expansion of the bureaucracy and the reliance on independent regulatory commissions—took place without the need for an explicit or implicit transformation of the fundamental law.[16] Like the collapse of the ethos of the neutral state, each of these changes occurred only after particular groups and individuals decided for particular reasons that prevailing practices were no longer convenient and appropriate and were able to win support for their alternative conception of the state. And each of these changes affected the way people thought about American politics. For example, in the aftermath of the demise of the neutral state, some have tried to link the general welfare to the interplay of social interests; these efforts to legitimize factional politics started early with Arthur Bentley's *Process of Government* in 1908 and continued through to the pluralists, some of whom attempted to transform Madison's *Federalist* no. 10 into a pluralist tract. In spite of these efforts, the breakdown of the barriers against special interest politics has taken its toll. It took a century and a half to move from "liberalism" to "corporate liberalism," and a lot less time to go from "corporate liberalism" to the "end of liberalism" and another "crisis of public authority."[17]

So far, though, the American state as a whole has been more successful at weathering the intellectual crises of the Second American Republic than has the Supreme Court. Having abdicated the responsibility of determining whether legislation was rationally related to a legitimate public purpose, judges created for themselves a new role in the political system, one that involved identifying those "preferred freedoms" or "suspect classifications" that might provide a basis for trumping the otherwise unrestrained power of the modern legislature. Previously, the Court had not been burdened with the task of identifying and giving weight to particular rights; in fact, for more than a century after the founding, the American constitutional tradition reflected the framers' nonchalance about specifying people's "rights and liberties." Since it was assumed that individual rights were subordinate to the general welfare, the prevailing belief in the eighteenth and nineteenth centuries was that rights and liberties were best protected by limiting the exercise of state power to those actions that advanced a general community interest; within this tradition, it was not necessary to define with precision precisely what rights and liberties people had in order for them to be protected. For the framers, this sensibility was manifested in the creation of a set of institutional structures that would be unresponsive to the corrupt pressures of factional politics (thus, in their judgment, making a bill of rights unnecessary if not downright dangerous), and for courts it was manifested in the development of a theory of the general welfare that was used as the basis for evaluating whether legislatures were acting within the proper scope of their authority. During the formative years of American constitutionalism, most disputes over the nature and scope of state power were treated as essentially empirical, not metaphysical: the Court's task was to determine whether the exercise of power advanced the general welfare, a determination that was filtered through historically defined ideological structures that recognized some justifications as legitimate (those that contributed to community health, safety, and morality) and others as not (those that seemed impartial, unequal, special, class based, or just arbitrary).

Industrialization undermined the social foundations that supported this constitutional methodology; that is to say, it made it more difficult to argue that one could discern a constitutionally recognized "general welfare" distinct from the interests of particular groups and classes, and it made it reasonable for some to argue that individual liberty was sometimes enhanced by the exercise of public power. The justices eventually accepted the idea that the corporate liberal state needed more leeway in rationalizing an advanced industrial economy and governing a heterogeneous social order. However, after the "switch-in-time," the justices were left with a serious problem. The demise of the public purpose limit on legislative power meant that the Court either would have to give up its traditional role of protecting individuals against arbitrary or oppressive government power or would have to develop, for the first time, some method of identifying a specific set of rights and liberties that could be asserted by individuals as a trump against the state. Some justices (like Holmes) had suggested earlier in the century that the Court might want to settle for the less active (almost invisible) role, but when the time came to abandon the old constitutionalism most members wasted no time suggesting in footnote 4 of *United States v. Carolene Products* (1938) a new source of constitutional limitations, rooted in a jurisprudence of "preferred freedoms" (such as those specified in the Bill of Rights) and supplemented by a judicial commitment to maintaining open and unprejudiced democratic processes.[18]

While it is generally recognized that footnote 4 of *Carolene Products* signaled a substantive redirection of the Court's role in the political system, it is not often recognized that this shift also required the Court to do something unprecedented; that is, to enumerate the specific freedoms and privileges that should be considered virtually inviolate even in a regime of expanded powers. In the nineteenth century it was assumed that government should leave individuals alone unless the state could convince a court that the exercise of power advanced a valid public purpose. By contrast, under the contemporary model, it has been assumed that the government's power should be left undisturbed unless an individual can convince a court that the law infringed on a discrete fundamental right.

Unlike the experience of nineteenth-century judges with the public purpose standard, however, the modern Court has been plagued by an inability to forge a consensus within the legal community in support of its authority to enforce a preferred freedoms limit on legislation.[19] The same skepticism that called into question the ability of judges to discern true public purposes has been deployed against judges who struggle to identify fundamental rights. This skepticism has been nurtured by the inability of partisans of preferred freedoms to agree on which rights are fundamental, or even on what it is that makes a right fundamental in the first place. (Among the more familiar candidates: the "traditions and collective conscience of the people," the text of the Constitution, the intent of the framers, the "reasoning spirit" of the Constitution, the obligations that emerge from a core commitment to the equal dignity of all individuals, the privileges and immunities that make self-government possible, the need to protect those whose interests are not served by the political process, and early liberalism's belief in the relationship between property and freedom.)[20] As a result, some conservative opponents of the modern Court have argued that judges should interfere in the political process only when such interference is inescapably justified, with the condition of inescapability being produced by some ostensibly obvious indicator, such as the literal language of the Constitution or the discoverable intent of the framers.[21] It is because an increasing number of justices embrace a frighteningly nihilistic—or, more generously, overly positivistic—conception of individual rights that the Supreme Court today seems prepared to find fewer and fewer reasons to block the exercise of power. For conservatives this kind of "restraint" represents the triumph of democracy over an imperial judiciary. For others it represents the sacrifice of the individual to the overarching power of the modern state.

Conservatives have used the lore of *Lochner* as a weapon in their struggle against the modern Court's use of fundamental rights as a trump on government power. If nothing else I hope this study helps remove that weapon from their hands. They argue that *Lochner* teaches us what happens when judges stray from the foundations of their legitimate authority and review legislation on the basis of their policy preferences rather than the law. But the real lesson of *Lochner* is that those foundations are no longer available as a basis for determining the proper role of the judiciary in American politics. The story of the *Lochner* era is a story about judicial fidelity to crumbling foundations, not judicial infidelity to recoverable foundations. The *Lochner* Court was following the law when it required the government to demonstrate the public purpose being served by interferences with liberty. In the wake of the collapse of that tradition, and as part of a general reconstitution of American politics, the modern Court was forced to devise innovative answers to some novel questions. Should the Court continue to erect liberty-barriers to the legislative power? If so, which liberties deserve protection against what is now presumed to be a regime of general powers rather than carefully circumscribed powers? If not, at what point does judicial deference to the political process amount to a betrayal of liberalism's twin commitment to representative government and individual liberty? *Any* answer to these questions would have represented a political choice, not in the sense of satisfying narrow policy preferences, but rather in the sense of establishing new constitutional foundations for a new Republic—foundations that represent (to paraphrase an earlier quote from Lerner) the ideological elements that should exercise their compulsive force on the minds of our judges. The lingering debates over the best answers to these inescapable questions will inevitably continue, but they should go forward unfettered by the fanciful claim that our burden is to rediscover ancient answers rather than forge agreement on the answers that seem best for us.

Notes

Introduction

1 Smith, "The Future of Public Law Scholarship," 95.
2 Slaughterhouse Cases, 16 Wallace 36 (1873); Munn v. Illinois, 94 U.S. 113 (1877); Mugler v. Kansas, 123 U.S. 623 (1887); and Powell v. Pennsylvania, 127 U.S. 678 (1888).
3 See Chicago, Milwaukee and St. Paul Railway Co. v. Minnesota, 134 U.S. 418 (1890).
4 Pollock v. Farmers' Loan and Trust Co., 158 U.S. 601 (1895); In re Debs, 158 U.S. 564 (1895); United States v. E. C. Knight Co., 156 U.S. 1 (1895); Lochner v. New York, 198 U.S. 45 (1905); and Adair v. United States, 208 U.S. 161 (1908).
5 Lochner v. New York, 198 U.S. 45 (1905).
6 Swisher, *American Constitutional Development*, 393, 341, 520–21.
7 Kelly and Harbison, *The American Constitution*, 498, 513–15, 518, 522–23.
8 Among the works that followed the lead established by Holmes, Swisher, and Kelly and Harbison: Jacobs, *Law Writers and the Courts*, 24 ("The development of the liberty of contract as a limitation upon the powers of both the state and national governments was a judicial answer to the demands of industrialists in the period of business expansion following the Civil War"); Haines, *Revival of Natural Law Concepts*, 179–80, 207, 230–31 (discussing "judge-made constitutional doctrines supported by the conservative groups of the country and fostered by the extreme individualism of leaders of industry and finance"); Paul, *Conservative Crisis and the Rule of Law*, 233, 237 (arguing that the Court's increasingly active conservative jurisprudence was part of a "traditional conservatism fearful of restless majorities upsetting the social order and the rights of property" and leading the Court to "exaggerat[e] its powers beyond all proportion"); A. S. Miller, *Supreme Court and American Capitalism*, 50, 57 (arguing that between the Civil War and the New Deal "the High Bench, under the leadership of Justice Stephen J. Field and such luminaries of the American bar as Roscoe Conkling, constructed principles of laissez faire and

read them into the Constitution to protect both the individual and corporate eco-nomic activity from adverse governmental regulation," principles and opinion that "are singularly devoid of rational reasons for the decisions"); Swindler, *Court and Constitution in the Twentieth Century*, 35–37 (arguing that the "jurisprudence of the new industrialism" centered on "the doctrine that private commercial activity should be confronted with a minimum of public interference"); Roche, *Sentenced to Life*, 206 ("The Constitution [was adapted] . . . to the exigent needs of the [robber barons]"); Jacobsohn, *Pragmatism, Statesmanship, and the Supreme Court*, 25–28 (describing Field as a "sort of hybrid of John Locke and Charles Darwin" who believed that the uninhibited accumulation of property was an "inalienable right" and arguing that *Lochner* constituted the "high-water mark of judicial reinterpreta-tion of the due process clause").

One of the most recent additions to this mischaracterization of *Lochner* era jurisprudence can found in Kens's otherwise very useful *Judicial Power and Reform Politics*: "The Lochner decision was, and remains, important because it signaled the Court's adoption of . . . laissez-faire social Darwinism, at a time when attachment to that philosophy was waning" (4–5). Kens attempts to defend this characterization in "The Source of a Myth."

9 Wiecek, *Liberty under Law*, 123–25.
10 Warren, "Progressiveness of the United States Supreme Court," and "A Bulwark to the State Police Power." In the first piece he argued that aside from *Lochner* there were only two cases in which a state law had been held unconstitutional. One was Connolly v. Union Sewer Pipe Co., 184 U.S. 540 (1902), which struck down an Illinois antitrust law because it illegally discriminated in favor of certain classes; and the other was Allgeyer v. Louisiana, 165 U.S. 578 (1897), which he viewed as of minor importance. For Warren, the evidence overwhelmingly supported the conclu-sion that the justices were far from reactionary; rather, they upheld virtually all progressive state legislation. To illustrate the point, Warren provided a list of cases wherein the justices upheld state regulations. A sample follows.

Wage legislation: eight-hour day for miners in Utah, Holden v. Hardy, 169 U.S. 366 (1898); Arkansas law requiring payment of all unpaid wages to railroad employees when discharged, St. Louis, etc., R.R. v. Paul, 173 U.S. 404 (1899); Tennessee law requiring redemption in money of store orders, etc., given to em-ployees for wages, Knoxville Iron Co. v. Harbison, 183 U.S. 13 (1901); Illinois coal-mining classification, coal miner's liability, and coal mine inspection law, Consoli-dated Coal Co. v. Illinois, 185 U.S. 203 (1902), and Wilmington Star Mining Co. v. Fulton, 205 U.S. 60 (1907); Kansas eight-hour law for labor on public works, Atkin v. Kansas, 191 U.S. 207 (1903); Ohio mechanics' lien law, Great Southern, etc., Co. v. Jones, 193 U.S. 532 (1904); eight-hour working day for women of Oregon, Muller v. Oregon, 208 U.S. 412 (1908); Arkansas law preventing contracting for wages on basis of screened coal mined, McLean v. Arkansas, 211 U.S. 539 (1909); full train-crew law of Arkansas, Chicago, etc., R.R. v. Arkansas, 219 U.S. 453 (1911); Iowa law forbidding railroads to deduct insurance benefits from the wages due employees for injury, C.B. & Q. R.R. v. McGuire, 219 U.S. 549 (1911).

Employees' injuries: Regulations with respect to the fellow-servant doctrine were upheld in Missouri Pacific Railway v. Mackey, 127 U.S. 205 (1888); Minnesota, etc., R.R. v. Herrick, 127 U.S. 210 (1888); Chicago, etc., R.R. v. Pontius, 157 U.S. 209 (1895); Tullis v. Lake Erie, etc., R.R., 175 U.S. 348 (1899); Louisville & Nashville R.R. v. Melton, 218 U.S. 36 (1910); Mobile, etc., R.R. v. Turnipseed, 219 U.S. 35 (1910); C. B. & Q. R.R. v. McGuire, 219 U.S. 549 (1911); Aluminum Co. v. Ramsey, 222 U.S. 251 (1911); and Minnesota Iron Co. v. Kline, 199 U.S. 593 (1905).

Sales of merchandise and conduct of business: Oleomargarine laws were upheld in Powell v. Pennsylvania, 127 U.S. 678 (1888); Plumley v. Massachusetts, 155 U.S. 461 (1894); and Capital City Dairy Co. v. Ohio, 183 U.S. 238 (1902); pure food laws in Arbuckle v. Blackburn, 191 U.S. 406 (1903); and Crossman v. Lurman, 192 U.S. 189 (1904); sanitary milk laws in New York v. Van DeCarr, 199 U.S. 552 (1905); and St. John v. New York, 201 U.S. 633 (1906); law restricting oyster dredging in Lee v. New Jersey, 207 U.S. 67 (1907); law requiring paint labels to show ingredients in Heath Co. v. Voist, 207 U.S. 338 (1907); fertilizer inspection in Patapsco Guano Co. v. North Carolina, 171 U.S. 345 (1898); laws forbidding sales of merchandise in bulk without notice to creditors in Lemieux v. Young, 211 U.S. 489 (1909); law forbidding drumming or soliciting business on railway trains in Williams v. Arkansas, 217 U.S. 79 (1910); law restricting private markets in Natal v. Louisiana, 139 U.S. 621 (1891); law requiring gaugers on coal and coke boats in Pittsburgh, etc., Coal Co. v. Louisiana, 156 U.S. 590 (1895); law forbidding pumping out natural mineral spring in Lindsley v. Natural Carbonic Gas Co., 220 U.S. 61 (1911); law forbidding gift and trading-stamp enterprises in Sperry, etc., Co. v. Rhodes, 220 U.S. 502 (1911); law regulating the weight of grain, seed, and hay and forbidding deductions in House v. Mayes, 219 U.S. 270 (1911); fish and game restriction laws in Lawton v. Steele, 152 U.S. 133 (1899); New York v. Hesterberg, 211 U.S. 31 (1909); and Geer v. Connecticut, 161 U.S. 519 (1896).

Restricting freedom of contract: The Court upheld laws providing for the licensing of physicians in Dent v. West Virginia, 129 U.S. 114 (1889); licensing of druggist in Gray v. Connecticut, 159 U.S. 74 (1895); registration of physicians in Reetz v. Michigan, 188 U.S. 505 (1903); and Watson v. Maryland, 218 U.S. 173 (1910); carrying concealed weapons in Miller v. Texas, 153 U.S. 535 (1894); licensing for speaking in public places in Davis v. Massachusetts, 167 U.S. 43 (1897); prohibiting waste to flow in gas and oil in Ohio Oil Co. v. Indiana, 177 U.S. 190 (1900); setting geographical limits on houses of ill fame in L'Hote v. New Orleans, 177 U.S. 587 (1900); regulating barber shops in Petit v. Minnesota, 177 U.S. 164 (1900); supporting a quarantine in Compagnie Française v. State Board of Health, 186 U.S. 360 (1902); setting limits on cow stables in Fischer v. St. Louis, 194 U.S. 361 (1904); requiring vaccinations in Jacobson v. Massachusetts, 197 U.S. 11 (1905); granting exclusive right to dispose of garbage in California Reduction Co. v. Sanitary Reduction Works, 199 U.S. 306 (1905), and Gardner v. Michigan, 199 U.S. 325 (1905); requiring keepers of places of amusement to admit all ticket holders in Western Turf Assn. v. Greenberger, 204 U.S. 359 (1907); prohibiting use of flag for advertising purposes in Halter v. Nebraska, 205 U.S. 34 (1907); restricting height of building in Welch v. Swasey, 214 U.S. 91 (1909); forbidding loans for more than 15 percent in Griffith v. Connecticut, 218 U.S. 563 (1910); restricting burials in city in Laurel Hill Cemetery v. San Francisco, 216 U.S. 358 (1910); forbidding advertising on street vehicles in Re Gregory, 219 U.S. 210 (1911); forbidding unauthorized use of portraits for advertising in Fifth Ave. Coach Co. v. New York, 221 U.S. 467 (1911); regulating assignments of wages in Mutual Loan Co. v. Martell, 222 U.S. 225 (1911); imposing liability for damages from riots in municipalities in Chicago v. Sturgis, 222 U.S. 313 (1911); and restricting pilots in Olsen v. Smith, 195 U.S. 332 (1904).

Warren also listed laws upholding antitrust legislation, gambling legislation, liquor and cigarette legislation, cattle legislation, regulation of railroad rates, corporate rates (grain elevators, water rates, telephone rates, gas rates), the banking industry, insurance and telegraph corporations, public improvements, and taxation laws. In the second article he continued with a list of decisions upholding antilottery laws, antitrust laws, laws regulating public service corporations (banks, railroad, grain, gas, electric light, and water companies), statutes imposing new liability on stockholders, inspection acts, and so on.

For other contemporaneous arguments in support of the proposition that the Court was not governed strictly by laissez-faire sensibilities, see Greeley, "The Changing Attitude of the Courts toward Social Legislation"; Hough, "Due Process of Law—To-Day"; and Cushman, "Social and Economic Interpretation of the Fourteenth Amendment."

11   Pound, "Liberty of Contract."

12   Hurst, *Law and the Conditions of Freedom*; and Levy, *Law of the Commonwealth*. Hurst's and Levy's discussions came at a time when other scholars were beginning to take note of the extent of government involvement in economic regulation during the nineteenth century. Handlin and Handlin, *Commonwealth*; and Hartz, *Economic Policy and Democratic Thought*, uncovered in early American thought and practice a neomercantilist sensibility that expected and encouraged government to play an active and interventionist promotional and regulatory role in the direction and management of productive enterprises. Other works followed the lead of Hartz and the Handlins. See Pierce, *Railroads of New York*; Heath, *Constructive Liberalism*; Primm, *Economic Policy in the Development of a Western State*; N. Miller, *The Enterprise of a Free People*; and other works cited in Pisani, "Promotion and Regulation."

13   Scheiber, *Ohio Canal Era*, "The Road to *Munn*;" "Law and the Imperatives of Progress;" and "Public Rights and the Rule of Law in American Legal History." Scheiber's book came out the same year that the Handlins' study of the concept of "commonwealth" was reissued. That same year Gordon Wood offered his forceful reinterpretation of early American political thought, *The Creation of the American Republic*, arguing that the nearly exclusive attention paid to the emphasis of Locke and liberalism on the founding prevented scholars from noting that generation's embrace of a "republican" tradition and its concerns with fostering civic virtue and promoting the general welfare of the community.

14   McCloskey, *American Supreme Court*, 104–5, 151–52; see also Semonche, *Charting the Future*, ix, 95, 432, 434 ("from 1890 to 1920 the surprising fact is not that the Court placed some obstacles in the path of the popular will but rather that these inhibitions were so relatively few"), and Urofsky, "Myth and Reality."

15   Beth, *The Development of the American Constitution*, xxi, xxiii, 41–42, 141, 182, 190; see also Mendelson, *Capitalism, Democracy, and the Supreme Court*, 1–3, 59,

63, 72 (acknowledging that state legislatures at the turn of the century vigorously exercised their police powers, but nevertheless characterizing the late-nineteenth-century Court's orientation as a kind of robber baron—inspired "pseudo-laissez-faire" which, while not completely hostile to legislation, was careful to limit it to "judge-approved" boundaries); Urofsky, *A March of Liberty*, 514, 543 (arguing that turn-of-the-century judges had a "probusiness, laissez-faire attitude" while admitting that courts did not really oppose and frustrate most protective legislation); Hall, *The Magic Mirror*, 238–43 (the "new doctrine of freedom or liberty to contract . . . echoed the laissez-faire and property rights sentiments of the era. . . . [However,] in the vast majority of cases [judges left protective legislation] and the police powers upon which they rested intact"); Currie, *The Constitution in the Supreme Court*, 45–50 (declaring that the Court's "liberty of contract" jurisprudence was driven into the Constitution "by bald fiat" and that judges attempted to use the due process clause to justify efforts to substitute their "opinion" about the reasonableness of legislation for that of the legislature, while at the same time noting that most social legislation manuevered its way successfully through this ostensibly unrestrained judiciary).

16   See E. Foner, "Abolitionism and the Labor Movement in Antebellum America"; McCurdy, "The Roots of Liberty of Contract Reconsidered"; Nelson, "The Impact of the Antislavery Movement"; D. M. Gold, "Redfield, Railroads, and the Roots of 'Laissez-Faire Constitutionalism' "; and Forbath, "The Ambiguities of Free Labor."

17   Forbath, "The Ambiguities of Free Labor," 783. The abolitionists' conception of free labor was much more narrow than Lincoln's. "Abe Lincoln talked about Northern labor's freedom in terms of economic independence, being able to own one's own shop or farm." While Lincoln's vision was "rooted in a regime of artisanal and petty entrepreneurial production," abolitionists "looked forward, as it were, to the emerging factory and wage labor regime."

The antebellum South had a very different view of the abolitionist conception of free labor. See E. Foner, "Abolitionism and the Labor Movement in Antebellum America," 57–58: "Standing outside the emerging capitalist economy of the free states (although also providing the raw material essential for its early development), the South gave birth to a group of thinkers who developed a striking critique of northern labor relations. The liberty of the northern wage earner, according to George Fitzhugh, John C. Calhoun, and the others, amounted to little more than the freedom to sell his labor for a fraction of its true value, or to starve. In contrast to the southern slave, who was ostensibly provided for in sickness and old age, and regardless of the vicissitudes of prices and production, the free laborer was the slave of the marketplace, and his condition exceeded in degradation and cruelty that of the chattel slave."

18   Scheiber, "Economic Liberty and the Constitution," 92.

19   Jones, "Thomas M. Cooley and 'Laissez-Faire Constitutionalism,' " 752, 755, and "Thomas M. Cooley and the Michigan Supreme Court," 103, 105.

20   McCurdy, "Justice Field and the Jurisprudence of Government-Business Relations"; Kay, "The Equal Protection Clause in the Supreme Court."

21   Benedict, "Laissez-Faire and Liberty," 298; D. M. Gold, *The Shaping of Nineteenth-Century Law*, 137, 139.

22   Nelson, *The Fourteenth Amendment*, viii, 14, 115, 149, 192.

23   Hall, *Magic Mirror*, 232–33, recognized that, in state judiciaries, substantive due process "was a means of voiding special legislation that aided one group over another," but he did not explore how this principle manifested itself in federal courts.

24   Nelson, *Fourteenth Amendment*, 8. Nelson by and large limited his close reading of cases to those in the 1870s and 1880s.

25   For example, I believe it is possible to trace the nineteenth-century judiciary's concern about market liberty and political equality to the founding of the Constitution, and not just to the antislavery movement or to the period of Jacksonian democracy. I also take issue with Nelson's claim that *Lochner* signaled a change in late nineteenth-century jurisprudence and that, in the decades following *Lochner*, many judges and commentators "read the case as authority for the federal courts to immunize fundamental rights from all legislative regulation." (*Fourteenth Amendment*, 198–99). One more example: McCurdy, in "Roots of Liberty of Contract Reconsidered," correctly noted that judges did not consider it legitimate for legislatures to interfere in labor contracts simply to address alleged disparities in bargaining power, and that this had something to do with the assumption in free labor ideology that the market provided wage earners with the opportunity to quit the wage-earning class. However, given the focus of his article, he leaves the impression that judges by and large were deferential to legislatures except when the motivation was to improve the bargaining status of workers vis-à-vis employers. I will attempt to show that this hostility was directed at all kinds of legislation that seemed designed to advance the interests of some players in the market at the expense of their competitors.

26   See Siegan, *Economic Liberties and the Constitution*; Porter, "*Lochner* and Company: Revisionism Revisited."

27   See Sunstein, "*Lochner*'s Legacy," 882: "We may thus understand *Lochner* as a case that failed because it selected, as the baseline for constitutional analysis, a system [of common-law rules and market relations] that was state-created, hardly neutral, and without prepolitical status. . . . Once the common law itself was seen to allocate entitlements and wealth, and the allocation seemed controversial [primarily because, as I will try to show, it led to conditions of social dependency—H.G.], a decision to generate a new pattern of distribution could not be for that reason impermissible."

28   This study builds on the theoretical and methodological assumptions shared by those associated with the "new institutionalism." See Orren and Skowronek, *Studies in American Political Development*; Block, *Revising State Theory*; Evans et al., eds., *Bringing the State Back In*; Dearlove, "Bringing the Constitution Back In"; Skocpol, ed., *Vision and Method*; Wolfe, *Limits of Legitimacy*; March and Olsen, "The New Institutionalism." For examples of this kind of approach in legal studies see Smith, "Political Jurisprudence"; Gordon, "Critical Legal Histories"; E. P. Thompson, *Whigs and Hunters*; E. D. Genovese, *Roll, Jordan, Roll*; Tomlins, *State and the Unions*.

29   See Bowles and Gintis, *Democracy and Capitalism*, 48–51. Hovenkamp, "Political Economy of Substantive Due Process," noted that in Great Britain political econo-

mists began to question the market's ability to harmoniously structure social relations early in the nineteenth century, while in the United States the same challenge
did not arise until almost the end of the century. He explained the difference as a by-
product of the different historical experiences of political economists on either side
of the Atlantic. Specifically, Americans enjoyed a sustained period of economic
growth throughout most of the nineteenth century; there was little concern about
Malthus's warnings regarding society's capacity to produce the food necessary to
sustain the population; there was virtually no concern about Ricardo's warnings
with respect to the monopoly tendencies associated with scarce land; and, in general,
(free) labor was perceived to be in short supply.

These changes in the structure of economic and social relations triggered a
sweeping period of transition in political and social thought and practice in the
United States. This study looks at the transformation in police powers jurispru-
dence. For accounts of other transformations see Barrow, *Universities and the
Capitalist State*; Fine, *Laissez-Faire and the General-Welfare State*; Forcey, *The
Crossroads of Liberalism*; Garraty, *The New Commonwealth*; Hays, *The Response
to Industrialism*; Hofstadter, *Social Darwinism in American Thought*; Kolko, *The
Triumph of Conservatism*; Lustig, *Corporate Liberalism*; McCloskey, *American
Conservatism in the Age of Enterprise*; Purcell, *The Crisis of Democratic Theory*;
Sklar, *The Corporate Reconstruction of American Capitalism*; Skowronek, *Building
a New American State*; Weibe, *The Search for Order*; Weinstein, *The Corporate
Ideal in the Liberal State*; and M. White, *Social Thought in America*.

30 See McCurdy, "Justice Field and the Jurisprudence of Government-Business Relations," 265: "Field's government-business jurisprudence perished, however, not
because it had been internally inconsistent or had failed to reflect the ideological
commitments of post-Civil War Americans, but rather because his doctrinal system
proved to be incongruent with the rapidly changing needs of an ever-expanding
capitalist society." While I reject the functionalist language of the "needs" of a
changing capitalist society I admire his early recognition of the fact that the important change occurring at the end of the nineteenth century was not in the Court's
jurisprudence but rather in the society.

31 P. L. Berger and Luckman, *Social Construction of Reality*.

32 See Sumner, *Reading Ideologies*.

33 See Geertz, *Interpretation of Cultures*, 5, 46, 314: "Ideas—religious, moral, practical, aesthetic—must, as Max Weber, among others, never tired of insisting, be
carried by powerful social groups to have powerful social effects; someone must
revere them, celebrate them, defend them, impose them."

34 In the United States, judges create, re-create, and defend their ideological constructs
by making reference to a very flexible set of concepts that run through liberal
jurisprudence. See Kennedy, "Form and Substance," and "Distributive and Paternalistic Motives in Contract and Tort Law"; Unger, "Critical Legal Studies."

35 Hunt, "The Ideology of Law," 16–17. In Roberto Unger's words, "In societies with a
heavy commitment to the rule of law, people often act on the belief that the legal
system possesses a relative generality and autonomy. To treat their understandings
and values as mere shams is to assume that social relations can be described and
explained without regard to the meanings of the men who participate in those

relations attributed to them" (Unger, *Law in Modern Society*, 56–57; see also his discussion in "Critical Legal Studies," 582).

36   See Gadamer, *Truth and Method*; Bleicher, *Contemporary Hermeneutics*; Hekman, "Beyond Humanism"; S. L. Carter, "Constitutional Adjudication," 821–27.

37   See Fish, *Is There a Text in This Class?*

38   See Fiss, "Objectivity and Interpretation"; and Dworkin, *A Matter of Principle*, chap. 6, "How Law Is Like Literature," and chap. 7, "On Interpretation and Objectivity." Like the response within literary criticism to the deconstructionists, these scholars have attempted to avoid the apparent nihilism of critical theory by suggesting that, while neither texts nor doctrine lead necessarily to decisions in specific cases, the existence of an "interpretive community" can establish and/or clarify authoritative standards of interpretation which act to corral the subjective dimension of interpretation. Ironically, Fiss borrowed this idea from the deconstructionist Stanley Fish, see Fish, *Is There a Text in This Class?* While this response adequately explains how judicial decision making is stabilized, it ultimately fails as an attempt to shore up traditional defenses of judicial power because it merely suggests that at some time in history a group of people were successful at imposing a contestable interpretation on particular legal texts or concepts. See Brest, "Interpretation and Interest"; and Fish, "Working on the Chain Gang," and "Wrong Again."

39   Kelman, "Trashing"; and Freeman and Schlegel, "Sex, Power and Silliness." As Stanley Fish almost never tires of pointing out, the mere act of demonstrating that a person's beliefs are historically contingent rather than transcendent, or partial and political rather than neutral and universal, cannot dislodge a person from the webs of meaning within which he or she operates and does not necessarily lead a person to alter her or his beliefs or behavior. See Fish, *Doing What Comes Naturally*.

40   Yablon, "The Indeterminacy of the Law," 919–20 (emphasis in original).

41   The argument that judges sometimes shape the law to service the needs and interests of favored classes, implied in discussions such as Friedman's *The Legal System* and Horwitz's *The Transformation of American Law*, is designed to appeal to our intuitive sense that powerful interests can and do manipulate state power. However, these kinds of instrumentalist arguments frequently suffer from what Stephen L. Carter has called "trivial interest analysis," the improbable or unsubstantiated assertion that a judge's decision is guided by a conscious intention to benefit his or her class ("Constitutional Adjudication and the Indeterminate Text," 828); see also Tushnet, "The Dialectics of Legal History," 1297. Not only does such a starting point vastly oversimplify judicial motive, it also exaggerates both the homogeneity of elite interests and the extent to which state institutions in general (and courts in particular) are amenable to their direct manipulation. Sugarman, "Law, Economy and the State in England," 213–66, 237, doubts that ruling-class theorists can explain, for example, how Parliament and the courts balanced "the property rights of the landed to enjoy their land with the necessity of factory owners and railway contractors to develop their land in a manner likely to affect that enjoyment? What role did the law play in mediating and legitimizing disputes between, say, insurers and those requiring cover against risks; company directors and promoters as against shareholders and creditors; large firms at odds with small firms?" See also Cham-

bliss and Seidman, *Law, Order, and Power*, 142. While some judges may at times cynically and consciously manipulate legal doctrine to advance the well-being of particular groups or classes, there is reason to believe that when used incautiously this kind of instrumentalist conception of judicial politics cannot be reconciled with the experiences of most members of the legal community.

42   Functionalist theories posit that judicial decisions respond to or fulfill certain political functions or social "needs." In the Marxist tradition there are arguments that link, for example, tort law, contract law, and the absolute right to property to economic needs of capitalism as well as arguments about the way law serves a political function by "mystifying" people into believing that capitalism is not exploitive. See Abel, "Torts"; Gabel and Abel, "Contract Law as Ideology"; Gabel, "Reification in Legal Reasoning"; Kairys, "Legal Reasoning"; Freeman, "Antidiscrimination Law"; and the references in Sugarman, "Law, Economy, and the State in England," 223–30. Among non-Marxist scholars there are similar arguments about how negligence principles, caveat emptor, and the fellow-servant rule lowered the cost of production and therefore are said to have been required by early industrialization; how the corporate structure and a variety of ad hoc rules were necessary to maximize efficiency; how a general system of rational rules offered capitalism the predictable structure it needed to encourage investment and contractual arrangements; and how the role of the Supreme Court is to confer legitimacy on political decisions. See the works cited by Gordon, "Critical Legal Histories," 75–87; Dahl, "Decision-Making in a Democracy," 294; C. Black, *The People and the Court*; Bickel, *The Least Dangerous Branch*, 29–30. Others talk generally about how the function of law is to foster development or "modernization" or to keep up with the degree of "complexity" associated with particular stages of development. See Nonet and Selznick, *Law and Society in Transition*, 14–15, 18, 25; D. Black, *The Behavior of Law*.

These theories deserve credit for reminding us that there is some relationship between legal rules and social structures that is more or less "objective," a relationship that one ought to be able to predict without reference to the self-conscious acts of particular groups or individuals; for example, feudal societies require institutions that specify and protect social relations organized around land tenures just as capitalist societies require institutions that promote and protect capital accumulation. In the absence of such institutions these societies would cease to be feudal or capitalist. However, these functionalist observations seem compelling only to the extent that they draw our attention to the fact that the labels we use to describe particular *social* arrangements are actually the by-product of a recognizable set of *legal* arrangements; in discussing capitalism and feudalism, law and society are part of an undifferentiated whole—if anything, the social relations identified as capitalist or feudal are produced by a particular regime of law. As we move away from a discussion of the essential institutional arrangements that make particular social structures possible, and toward a discussion of particular legal forms or particular judicial decisions, it becomes more and more difficult to say convincingly that the objects of our study were "required" by anything (much less by our own theoretical constructs). Robert Gordon has noted that one can find a great deal of variability in legal forms among similar socioeconomic structures, that there are "highly evolved dynamic capitalist societies that got that way through (despite?) radically different governmental policies towards capitalist enterprise: refusal of subsidies for transport ventures, intolerance towards the corporate form, state-sponsored insurance of workers against the risks of unemployment and industrial accidents, coordination of major investment decisions through central bureaucracies, and promotion of social and political stability through legal *reinforcement* of the 'feudal' rights of great agricultural proprietors. Of course, a nimble mind can invent a functional explanation for *anything*." (Gordon, "Critical Legal Histories," 82, citations omitted [emphasis in original]). Functionalist explanations also cannot account for the possibility that legal forms develop that might actually fail to perform expected functions or turn out to be dysfunctional in that they destabilize existing social relationships or work against the interests of dominant classes. Adamany, in "Legitimacy, Realignment Elections, and the Supreme Court," pointed out (as have many others) that people are not mystified by judicial pronouncements; Friedman, *History of American Law*, 233, argued that many legal rules did not contribute to certainty and predictability in market relations; Crouch, "The State, Capital and Liberal Democracy," 13–54, argued that because of the dominance of the financial sector it was possible that state policies in Britain operated to the detriment of capital as a whole. In general, the definitional relationships that may or may not exist between social and political structures are simply inadequate explanations for the existence of specific features of a legal system. See D. A. Gold et al., "Recent Developments in Marxist Theories of the Capitalist State," 38; G. Ross, "Nicos Poulantzas, Eurocommunism, and the Debate on the Theory of the Capitalist State," 155–56. For a critical review of instrumentalist and functionalist explanations of the New Deal, see Skocpol, "Political Response to Capitalist Crisis."

43   See Trubek, "Where the Action Is"; and Hunt, "Emile Durkheim," 27–29, for a discussion of Durkheim's treatment of those "ways of acting, thinking, and feeling, external to the individual" as "social facts" that are amendable to rigorous investigation—particularly when they take the form of law.

44   See Wirth, "Preface," xix, xxii: "It may be true that there are some social phenomena and, perhaps, some aspects of all social events that can be viewed externally as if they were things. But this should not lead to the inference that only those manifestations of social life which find expression in material things are real. It would be a very narrow conception of social science to limit it to those concrete things which are externally perceivable and measurable. . . . [S]ocial life and hence social science is to an overwhelming extent concerned with beliefs about the ends of action." See also Schutz, "Concept and Theory Formation in the Social Sciences," 15: "If the social sciences aim indeed at explaining social reality, then . . . [they] must include a reference to the subjective meaning an action has for the actor." Schutz's quote was cited by Ashcraft in the introduction to *Revolutionary Politics*. Ashcraft added that ideological structures "are understandable only in reference to a specific context, wherein the concepts, terminology, and even the internal structure of the theory itself are viewed in relation to the comprehensive ordering of the elements of social life" (11). See also Pocock, *Politics, Language, and Time*.

45   Geertz, *The Interpretation of Cultures*, 16. Or in the words of Stewart Macauley, "Law and the Behavioral Sciences," 158: "Many researchers bring the tool-kit of

methods fashionable in their social sciences and look for problems where those methods can be used. . . . Research techniques may be impeccable, but a rigorous answer to a silly question is still a rigorously silly answer. . . . [W]e must choose methods appropriate to questions worth asking about legal systems in their full social context."

46   E. P. Thompson, *Whigs and Hunters*, 262–63.

CHAPTER ONE   *The Origins of* Lochner *Era Police Powers Jurisprudence*

1   H. Mark Roelofs, quoted in Beth, *Development of the American Constitution*, 2fn.
2   Appleby, "Social Origins of American Revolutionary Ideology," 938; Matson and Onuf, *A Union of Interests*, 14–15. This tradition had found recent expression overseas in the "Country" opposition to the rise of Walpole's "Court" and his policies of promoting government credit, public debt, central banking, and a standing army. Walpole's executive-centered mercantilist regime threatened to transform the social foundations of British society and in so doing to undermine the landed aristocracy's status as England's traditional leaders. In response, they argued that Walpole's policies would undermine (a) the cultural cement of republican government, "civic virtue," the selfless attachment to the "public good" expected of all citizens, by encouraging the gluttonous pursuit of private gain; and (b) the structural safeguard of republican government, the "balanced" English Constitution, by creating an artificial "monied interest" among the people which would be inextricably linked to the designing ministries. These ministries would in turn seduce members of Parliament through bribery, patronage, and deceit and eventually burden the people with taxes, a public debt, and a standing army. For some Americans this tradition provided a compelling vocabulary with which to interpret events leading up to the revolution: the Stamp Act and the Townsend Duties were depicted as attempts to concentrate power in the hands of royal executives, the existence of patronage and plural officeholding was evidence for the deterioration of balanced government, and British troops in Boston and the subsequent "massacre" illustrated the potential oppression of standing armies. See Kramnick, *Bolinbroke and His Circle*; Pocock, *Machiavellian Moment*; Appleby, "Social Origins"; Bailyn, *Ideological Origins*, 48, 22–54.
3   Nash, *Urban Crucible*, 343–46.
4   Appleby, "Social Origins," 939. See generally Appleby, *Economic Thought and Ideology in Seventeenth-Century England*, and *Capitalism and a New Social Order*, 14–15; Matson and Onuf, *A Union of Interests*, 15ff.; McCoy, *Elusive Republic*, 77; Kramnick, "Republican Revisionism Revisited," 660, and "Great National Discussion," 8–9, 15–23.
5   Ashcraft, *Revolutionary Politics*, 176, 181–285. His summary of the early Whig position: "Because people have unequal amounts of property and accumulated capital (money), because there are controversies over titles and property rights and disputes arising out of contractual arrangements established by bargain and money, because trade and commerce now play an important role in the advancement of civilization, power *must* shift away from the monarch into the hands of a representative assembly in order to provide that security and protection for property which is the rationale for the institution of civil society" (221).

6   Kramnick, "Great National Discussion," 4, identified at least four distinctive idioms of politics—republicanism, Lockean liberalism, work-ethic Protestantism, and
state-centered theories of power and sovereignty—and invited scholars to explicate
"other less discernible idioms" such as "scientific whiggism" and the "moral sentiment" schools of the Scottish Enlightenment.

7   Nash, Urban Crucible, 340; Lynd, "Governing Class on the Defensive," 111.

8   Nash, Urban Crucible; 148.

9   Ibid., 161, 341–42. See also Nash, "Transformation of Urban Politics," and "Urban
Wealth and Poverty in Prerevolutionary America." Appleby wrote of these middling
classes that "their loyalties lay with future possibilities. A return to the good old days
of prescribed place and uncorrupted virtue held little appeal for them" ("Social
Origins," 949). See also Kramnick, "Republican Revisionism Revisited," 637.

10 Nash, "Social Change and the Growth of Prerevolutionary Urban Radicalism,"
"Artisans and Politics in Eighteenth Century Philadelphia," and Urban Crucible,
148–49; E. Foner, Tom Paine; Countryman, American Revolution, 77–78; Lynd,
Class Conflict, Slavery, and U.S. Constitution, pt. 1; Wilentz, Chants Democratic;
E. P. Thompson, "Moral Economy." Bogin, "Petitioning and the New Moral Economy of Post-revolutionary America," 392: "[S]mall farmers and marginal artisans . . . made recurrent demands for specific measures to diminish the spread
between the bottom and top economic levels and to protect weaker economic groups
from exploitation." After independence, the Philadelphia artisans made it a point to
include as part of the Pennsylvania Declaration of Rights the statement that good
government was inconsistent with "the particular emolument of advantage of any
single man, family, or set of men, who are a part only of that community" and that
all free men should have some calling by which they may honestly subsist. The
constituting documents also contained an article declaring that the concentration of
property in a few hands was dangerous to the common good and should be discouraged by the state.

The traditions of the moral economy should not be idealized. See E. F. Genovese,
"Many Faces of the Moral Economy"; Simpson, "Fourteenth Amendment Concepts." The Tudor Industrial Code allowed for the setting of minimum wages and the
protection of workers from wrongful dismissal, but it also provided for maximum
wages, the compulsory labor of all able-bodied persons, declared illegal any combination of workmen to secure higher wages, and provided that no workman was to
depart before the end of his agreed term. The code "sought to assure a profit to the
agricultural or industrial proprietor by guaranteeing him an adequate low-wage
labor supply and, at the same time, to safeguard the worker against undue and
unrestrained exploitation" (Rayback, History of American Labor, 12). See also
Morris, Government and Labor, 3–35.

11 See Banning, "James Madison and the Nationalists"; Stourzh, Alexander Hamilton;
Ferguson, "Political Economy, Public Liberty, and the Formation of the Constitution."

12 McCoy, Elusive Republic, 51, 68; see also his "Benjamin Franklin's Vision."

13 For a review of Madison's writings on the political economy of social dependency,
see McCoy, The Last of the Fathers, chap. 5. See also Bogin, "Petitioning and the
New Moral Economy in Post-Revolutionary America," 404–7.

14 McCoy, *The Last of the Fathers*, 297, 294–97.

15 Jefferson, *Notes on the State of Virginia*, "Query XIX: The present state of manufacturers, commerce, interior and exterior trade," 157. See Morgan, " 'Time Hath Found Us,' " 33 ("The mobs of the cities were to be feared because of their dependence upon others for their bread, opinions, and political leadership"); Liddle, " 'Virtue and Liberty' "; and Appleby, "Commercial Farming and the 'Agrarian Myth.' "

16 Bowles and Gintis, *Democracy and Capitalism*, 47–50. They go on to point out that there was a certain sleight of hand to this vision of an America without a propertyless working class because "although perhaps only one in five freeborn male household heads did not own land or tools of their trade in the late eighteenth century, slaves constituted about a third of the total economically active population. Propertyless workers—slave and freeborn—thus constituted roughly half of the labor force, certainly a larger portion than in any European nation at the time except England."

17 Appleby, "Republicanism in Old and New Contexts," 32; see also Appleby, *Capitalism and a New Social Order*, 97; and "What Is Still American," 299, 308. Appleby noted that Jefferson preferred the writings of the French philosopher Antoine Louis Claude Destutt de Tracy over Adam Smith because Tracy's *Treatise of Political Economy* more than Smith's *Wealth of Nations* "gave to human beings their own harmonizing qualities of good sense and moderation."

18 Bogin, "Petitioning and the New Moral Economy of Post-Revolutionary America," 403.

19 Appleby, *Capitalism and a New Social Order*, 40–43, 49, 92, 97.

20 See Kennedy, "The Structure of Blackstone's Commentaries"; Horwitz, *The Transformation of American Law*.

21 Bogin, "Petitioning and the New Moral Economy of Post-Revolutionary America."

22 Matson and Onuf, *A Union of Interests*, 38.

23 Rayback, *History of American Labor*, 41–42; Morris, *Labor and Government*, 92–135.

24 Lynd, "Mechanics in New York Politics," 82, 85, 104–5. In "Who Should Rule at Home?" 58, Lynd characterized many popular leaders as representing the "entrepreneurial" element: "Whereas Robert R. Livingston . . . stood for the 'politics of privilege,' the Smiths, Platts, and Brinckerhoffs of Dutchess politics represented the 'politics of opportunity.' " Simpson, "Fourteenth Amendment Concepts," 536–38, discussed how growing confidence in market mechanisms undermined enthusiasm for the traditions of the "moral economy."

25 Morris, *Government and Labor*, 42–51; Bowles and Gintis, *Democracy and Capitalism*, 49; Main, *Anti-Federalists*; Rayback, *History of American Labor*, 21; P. Foner, *History of Labor Movement*, 1:24–26. Lynd, "Mechanics in New York Politics," 83–84, noted how the "prevailing mode of production in colonial towns was a small workshop in which a master employed one to four journeymen and apprentices" and added that the "mechanic of the American Revolution was well-paid when compared to his European counterpart." He also noted, however, that "post-war economic trends—the shift from custom-made to wholesale order work, the decline of apprenticeship and indentured servitude, the emergence of a factory

district in the suburb which is now New York's lower east side—coincided with the influx of poor immigrants to intensify the conflict between employers and employees, as well as between the mechanics *en masse* and the city's merchants."

26   E. Foner, *Tom Paine*, 145–82. For more on how the development of capitalist relations led to the demise of the "moral economy" in England, see E. F. Genovese, "Many Faces of the Moral Economy."

27   Matson and Onuf, *A Union of Interests*; Kramnick, "Great National Discussion," 30.

28   Madison, "Memorial and Remonstrance," point 4, reprinted in Alley, *Supreme Court on Church and State*, 20.

29   Madison to Jefferson, October 24, 1787, quoted in Wood, *Creation of the American Republic*, 467.

30   Madison, cited in Conniff, "On the Obsolescence of the General Will." See also Kramnick, "Great National Discussion," 6 ("Government for Madison, much as for Locke, was a neutral arbiter among competing interests"). For more on Madison's remarks concerning the problem of local majorities see Jillson and Eubanks, "Political Structure of Constitution Making." On the ideological consensus of the delegates at Philadelphia, see Roche, "The Convention as a Case Study in Democratic Politics"; and Riker, "Gouverneur Morris in the Philadelphia Convention," 37–38.

31   *Federalist*, no. 10, 56–58, 54. Two interpretations of the Federalist Papers that highlight the concern with creating a "disinterested" or "faction-free" political system are Agresto's " 'A System without Precedent' " and Wills's *Explaining America*. The discussions in the Federalist Papers over the problem of factions and democracy reflect the concerns expressed by the delegates during the Constitutional Convention. See, for example, the exchanges among Sherman, Gerry, Mason, Wilson, and Madison on Thursday, May 31, over the question of whether the people ought to be able directly to elect the representatives of the first branch of the legislature.

32   *Federalist*, no. 10, 59; *Federalist*, no. 35, 215–16. See also Kramnick, "Great National Discussion," 14: "The class focus of the Federalists' republicanism is self-evident. Their vision was of an elite corps of men in whom civic spirit and love of the general good overcame particular and narrow interests. Such men were men of substance, independence, and fame who had the leisure to devote their time to public life and the wisdom to seek the true interests of the country as opposed to the wicked projects of local and particular interests."

33   *Federalist*, no. 10, 62, 57.

34   Ibid., no. 27, 167.

35   Ibid., no. 68, 444.

36   Ibid., no. 51, 339.

37   Ibid., no. 78, 509. If Madison had had his way, this structural attempt at resolving the problem of class-based politics would have culminated in giving the neutral national legislature the power to "negative" state laws that were contrary to his faction-free republican ideal. However, his fellow delegates at the convention believed this task would be more prudently placed in the federal judiciary, which could exercise this power under the authority of the supremacy clause. See Hobson, "Negative on State Laws." Madison believed that the convention's rejection of his negative very seriously undermined the value of the new national government.

38   For example, Edward Erler made Madison a "modern liberal" by ascribing to him
     the position that the public good is a mere "by-product of private acquisitiveness"
     ("Problem of the Public Good"). Conniff wrote that the Federalists replaced classical
     republicanism with "what we have come to call pluralist politics. . . . A society . . . is
     an artificial combination of a number of groups . . . since they do not have a common
     will, it is idle to seek it. . . . Thus, the state must become an arbitrator of interests, not
     a seeker of wisdom" ("On the Obsolescence of the General Will," 52–53). See
     Bourke, "Pluralist Reading of James Madison's Tenth *Federalist*."

39   Wills, *Explaining America*, 205.

40   Madison to Jefferson, October 24, 1787, cited in Schmitt and Webking, "Revolu-
     tionaries, Antifederalists, and Federalists," 228 (emphasis added).

41   Kenyon, *The Antifederalist*, xxxvii.

42   See Main, *Anti-Federalists*, chap. 11. Virtually all groups that had come to put their
     faith in commercial development—including urban artisans, tradesmen, appren-
     tices, and journeymen—celebrated the ratification of the Constitution. In the great
     Philadelphia procession of July 4, 1788, "[e]very trade in the city, from ship carpen-
     ters to shoemakers, from coachmakers to weavers, from instrument makers to
     Paine's old craft of staymaking, took part in this extraordinary procession, each
     trade marching in its respective craft association, with elaborate floats, flags and
     mottoes. . . . Rush and other observers were particularly impressed by the great float
     with carding and spinning machines for the manufacture of cotton, and the banner,
     'May the Union Government Protect the Manufacturers of America,' sponsored by
     the Society for the Promotion of Manufacturers" (Foner, *Tom Paine*, 296–97). See
     also Lynd, "Governing Class on the Defensive," 122–23, 130–31. On the civic
     humanist sensibilities of some Antifederalists see Kramnick, "Great National Dis-
     cussion," 10–12.

43   Ferguson, "Political Economy, Public Liberty, and the Formation of the Constitu-
     tion," 406.

44   In a letter to Jefferson, Madison lamented how members of Congress scrambled for
     subscriptions to the Bank of the United States in order to profit from Hamilton's
     policies and raised serious doubts "about the capacity of Congress to remain an
     independent branch of government." See Banning, *Jeffersonian Persuasion*, 204–5.
     See also Benedict, "The Jeffersonian Republicans," 29: "Republicans perceived
     government policies benefiting particular groups as violating the principle of 'equal
     rights.' A national bank, a protective tariff, a program to pay off state and national
     debts now in the hands of mere 'speculators' instead of the original holders—all
     these proposals were designed to benefit a small, influential portion of the commu-
     nity at the expense of the rest."

45   Banning, *Jeffersonian Persuasion*, chap. 10; McCoy, *Elusive Republic*, 185–235;
     Appleby, *Capitalism and New Social Order*, 103–4; Pangle, *Spirit of Modern
     Republicanism*, 100–101.

46   See Wilson, "Republicanism and the Idea of Party in the Jacksonian Period."

47   McCoy, *Elusive Republic*, 209–35; and Schlesinger, *Age of Jackson*, 8–9, 31.
     Schlesinger reported that between 1820 and 1840 the number of people engaged in
     manufacturing increased 127 percent, while agricultural labor increased only 79
     percent. Correspondingly, the number of city dwellers also increased (9). For more
     on the Jacksonian ideology of political equality see Meyers, *Jacksonian Persuasion*;

and Remini, *Andrew Jackson*. For a discussion of the inequality of social conditions in Jacksonian America, see Pessen, *Jacksonian America*, 77–100.

48 Hofstadter, *American Political Tradition*, 78; see also Blau, "Introduction," xiii–xiv.

49 Hofstadter, *American Political Tradition*, 70.

50 See Shefter, "Party, Bureaucracy, and Political Change," 218; and Hofstadter, *American Political Tradition*, 70–72. Jackson's standard explanation for why "the planter, the farmer, and mechanic, and the laborer" were "in constant danger of losing their fair interest in the Government" was that "the mischief springs from the power which the moneyed interest derives from a paper currency, which they are able to control, from the multitude of corporations with exclusive privileges which they have succeeded in obtaining in the different States" (ibid., 73–74). Hofstadter argued that as an enterpriser of middling success, Jackson saw things from the standpoint of Americans eager to advance in a democratic game of competition: "the master mechanic who aspired to open his own shop, the planter or farmer who speculated in land, the lawyer who hoped to be a judge, the local politician who wanted to go to Congress, the grocer who would be a merchant" (ibid., 74). As we shall see, this empathy did not extend to the working poor.

51 Shefter, "Party, Bureaucracy, and Political Change," 219. With respect to the spoils system, Schwartz, in "Liberty, Democracy, and the Origins of American Bureaucracy," argued that rotation in office had as much to do with the removal of a privileged elite from government as it did with party building. See also Crenson, *Federal Machine*. Remini reported that Jackson probably removed only 919 persons out of 10,093 during the first eighteen months of his administration. For the entire eight years of his presidency he dismissed a little more than 10 percent of all officeholders, "which is certainly not the record of a spoilsman when these figures are considered in the light of normal replacements due to death and resignations plus those removed for incompetence and dishonesty" ("Introduction," in Remini, *Age of Jackson*, ix–xxviii, xiifn).

52 As George Henry Evans put it for the Working Men in 1829, "The laws for private incorporations are all partial in their operations; favoring one class of society to the expense of the other, who have no equal participation" (reproduced in P. Foner, *We, the Other People*, 49). See also Diggins, *Lost Soul of American Politics*, 117–18; and Handlin and Handlin, *Commonwealth*.

53 Schlesinger, *Age of Jackson*, 336–37. At one Racine County mass meeting a resolution was adopted that demanded "that all exclusive privileges and monopolies, whereby the few may be enabled to amass wealth at the expense of the many, are contrary to the spirit of a government of true equality. . . . [Corporations] should be regulated by general laws for the privileges of which none can be excluded who comply with their provisions" (quoted in Hyman and Wiecek, *Equal Justice under Law*, 29).

54 Quoted in Pessen, *Jacksonian America*, 209. On the emerging Whig conception and its linkages to the founding tradition, see Howe, *Political Culture of the American Whigs*. For a discussion on how Jackson's democratized political support stimulated renewed fears of factionalism among elites, see Mayo, "Republicanism, Antipartyism, and Jacksonian Party Politics"; see also Cain, "Return of Republicanism."

55 John W. Vethake, "The Doctrine of Anti-Monopoly," from the *New York Evening Post*, October 21, 1835, reprinted in Blau, *Social Theories of Jacksonian Democracy*, 212.

56 Remini, *Age of Jackson*, 78–82, 81–82.

57 Ibid., xvi–xvii. Remini discovered that this ethos can be found in some very strange places: "Catherine E. Beecher published a book in 1847 entitled *Treatise on Domestic Economy for the Use of Young Ladies at Homes and at School* and touched on it in an offhanded way. 'Every man may aim at riches,' she wrote, 'unimpeded by any law or institution which secures privileges to a favored class, at the expense of another. Every law, and every institution, is tested by examining whether it secures equal advantages to all'" (xvii–xviii). Of course, this test was not considered necessary when laws were used by white men against slaves and Indians.

58 The inflation that hit New York City in 1834 fueled the argument of the anti-monopolists that the special chartering of banks had resulted in the devaluation of the currency. The next year supporters ran a slate of candidates in opposition to Tammany; they were the Equal Rights party, dubbed "Locofocos" by the Whig press when they responded to the Tammany practice of turning out the gaslights in order to quiet raucous meetings by lighting candles with new friction matches popularly known as "locofocos." The Locofoco Declaration of Principles denounced "all monopolies and all partial and unequal legislation"; they had become convinced that the "leaders of the two great political parties under which the people have arrayed themselves are selfish and unprincipled; the objects of both are power, honors, and emolument; they are the enemies of the equal rights of the citizen; be therefore no longer deceived; let us withdraw ourselves from both." And with that they resolved to "divest ourselves of all party feeling, party prejudices, and attachments to party leaders." (Rayback, *History of American Labor*, 84–86; P. Foner, *History of the Labor Movement*, 1:153–66; Hugins, *Jacksonian Democracy and the Working Class*, 37–43).

59 Sedgwick, "What Is a Monopoly? reprinted in Blau, *Social Theories of Jacksonian Democracy*, 220–36.

60 Schlesinger, *Age of Jackson*, 190, 188–89, 314–17.

61 William Leggett, "Democratic Editorials from the *New York Evening Post*," November 21, 1834, reprinted in Blau, *Social Theories of Jacksonian Democracy*, 75.

62 Rayback, *History of American Labor*, 3–4, 47.

63 "A series of technological innovations after Independence left America poised on the threshold of the Industrial Revolution: the factory (Samuel Slater built the first water-powered cloth mill in Pawtucket, Rhode Island, 1790); the factory system of production (Eli Whitney devised a system of assembling precision-made interchangeable parts in the manufacture of muskets, 1800); a new source of power (Oliver Evans perfected a high-pressure steam engine in 1787); an expanded market for the products of the industrial system (John Fitch and Robert Fulton devised steam-powered vessels, 1787–1807, and Peter Cooper built the first railroad in America in South Carolina, 1830)" (Hyman and Wiecek, *Equal Justice under Law*, 25).

64 As markets expanded, the shopkeeper's "goods were now sold in large lots; he found it necessary to increase his supply of raw materials, to increase his stock of finished goods, and to increase storage space. Since his goods were sold to country store-

keepers who must in turn sell them before payment could be expected, he had to extend long-term credit. The shopowner ceased to be a workman with close knowledge of his employees' problems; he became an executive and a merchant interested fundamentally in costs and markets" (Rayback, *History of American Labor*, 48); see also P. Foner, *History of the Labor Movement*, 1:67–68.

65   Hugins, *Jacksonian Democracy and the Working Class*, 53, 55; E. Foner, "Abolitionism and the Labor Movement," 58; and Haines and Sherman, *Role of the Supreme Court in American Government*, 500–502. On the response to the wage system, note Orestes Augustus Brownson, "The Laboring Classes," *Boston Quarterly Review* (July 1840): 358–95, reprinted in Blau, *Social Theories of Jacksonian Democracy*, 301–19, 306, 309: "All over the world this fact stares us in the face, the workingman is poor and depressed, while a large portion of the non-workingmen . . . are wealthy. . . . Wages is a cunning device of the devil, for the benefit of tender consciences, who would retain all the advantages of the slave system, without the expense, trouble, and odium of being slave-holders. . . . The actual condition of the workingman today, viewed in all its bearings, is not so good as it was fifty years ago." The repeated connection drawn between the northern wage system and the southern slavocracy is discussed in E. Foner, "Abolitionism and the Labor Movement."

For more on the experiences of working people during early industrialization, see Wilentz, *Chants Democratic*, and "Against Exceptionalism"; Prude, *Coming Industrial Order*, and "The Social System of Early New England Textile Mills"; and Dawley, *Class and Community*.

66   See S. J. Ross, *Workers on the Edge*.

67   See Wilentz, *Chants Democratic*; Bogin, "Petitioning and the New Moral Economy of Post-Revolutionary America"; Montgomery, *Beyond Equality*, and "Workers' Control of Machine Production"; Goodwyn, *Populist Moment*; Hahn and Prude, *Countryside in the Age of Capitalist Transformation*; Kulikoff, "Transition to Capitalism in Rural America." For a discussion of the literature addressing these alternative visions and the ideological barriers historical participants faced as they struggled to gain acceptance, see Lears, "The Concept of Cultural Hegemony."

68   Wilentz, *Chants Democratic*, 245. E. Foner, "Abolitionism and the Labor Movement in Antebellum America," 58: "The emergence of the nation's first labor movement in the late 1820s and 1830s was, of course, a response to fundamental changes taking place in the work patterns and authority relationships within traditional artisan production." This included the factory system, dilution of craft skill, the imposition of labor discipline, the growing gap between masters and journeymen, and the stratification of the social order. "Workingmen responded to these developments within the context of an ideology dating back to the Paineite republicanism of the American Revolution. The central ingredients of this ideology were a passionate attachment to equality (defined not as the leveling of all distinctions, but as the absence of large inequalities of wealth and influence), belief that independence—the ability to resist personal or economic coercion—was an essential attribute of the republican citizenry, and a commitment to the labor theory of value." See also McPherson, "Lincoln and Liberty," 62–63: "A man who depended on another for his living was not truly free—he was subject to the authority, to the orders and manipulation, of the man who paid his wages and who therefore dictated

the terms of his existence. Independence—and therefore liberty—could be achieved only by the ownership of productive property: a farm, a business, or a trade in which the skilled artisan owned his tools and was paid directly by the purchaser for the fruits of his labor rather than paid wages for his work. . . . Of course, with the rise of industrialization and immigration after 1820, a substantial wage-earning class of white men grew up owning little if any property." It was around this time that workers began composing alternative "Declarations of Independence." See P. Foner, *We, the Other People.*

69 Schlesinger, *Age of Jackson*, 313.

70 Quoted in Hugins, *Jacksonian Democracy and the Working Class*, 53–54, 56.

71 Berthoff, "Independence and Attachment, Virtue and Interest," 114.

72 Schlesinger, *Age of Jackson*, 153, 157. Schlesinger also quoted from a July 4, 1834, speech by Frederick Robinson, Democratic member of the New York legislature: "There always exists, in every community, two great interest[s]—that of the producer, whose interest it is to secure to himself, as much as he can of the fruit of his labor, of his own hands; and that of the capitalist, whose interest it is to take from the producer as much as he possibly can of the productions of his industry. A contest between these two classes is always going on in every country, where the capitalist has not completely reduced the producer to a state of slavery. . . . In whatever way the wealth of the community can be absorbed into few hands, the end must always be the same; it must be slavery for the masses" (168).

73 See Wilentz, *Chants Democratic*, and "Against Exceptionalism," 8–9; Pessen, "Thomas Skidmore, Agrarian Reformer," 281; Rayback, *History of American Labor*, 65–66, 69; P. Foner, *History of the Labor Movement*, 1:123–26, 130–40; Hugins, *Jacksonian Democracy and the Working Classes*, 13, 137–42, 145. According to Philip Foner, it was estimated that in 1829 more than seventy-five thousand persons were in prison in the United States because of debts, more than half for sums of less than twenty dollars. In New York City alone, nearly a thousand people were in jail for debts of five dollars or less.

74 Rayback, *History of American Labor*, 69–70; Hugins, *Jacksonian Democracy and the Working Class*, 16–17. Pessen, "Thomas Skidmore, Agrarian Reformer," 284–86: "[Aristocrats] succeeded by the use of money, inner party intrigue, extra-legal tactics, and newspaper excoriation. At the same time they accomplished the real destruction of the party as well as of its influence at the polls." These "aristocrats" could tolerate the educational reforms put forth by Frances Wright and Robert Dale Owen; in fact, it was a suggestion that was winning favor with more and more employers. See Schlesinger, *Age of Jackson*, 142–43, 183–84.

75 Schlesinger, *Age of Jackson*, 316. It is interesting to compare Van Buren's promise with the pamphlets of Mathew Carey, a rich Philadelphia businessman who believed that the poor were no more depraved than the other classes. He put together a list of the "erroneous opinions" that people had about the poor: "1. That every man, woman, and grown child able and willing to work may find employment. 2. That the poor, by industry, prudence, and economy, may at all times support themselves comfortably. . . . 3. That their sufferings and distresses chiefly, if not wholly, arise from their idleness, their dissipation, and their extravagance. 4. That taxes for the support of the poor, and aid afforded them by charitable individuals, or benevolent

societies, are pernicious, as by encouraging the poor to depend on them, they foster their idleness and improvidence, and thus produce, or at least increase, the poverty and distress they are intended to relieve" (ibid., 133).

76   William Leggett, "Democratic Editorials from the *New York Evening Post*," November 21, 1834, reprinted in Blau, *Social Theories of Jacksonian Democracy*, 77–78.

77   Frederick Robinson, "An Oration delivered before the Trades' Union of Boston and Vicinity, July 4, 1834," reprinted in Blau, *Social Theories of Jacksonian Democracy*, 326.

78   Theophilus Fisk, "An Address delivered at Julien Hall before the Mechanics of Boston, May 20, 1835," reprinted in Blau, *Social Theories of Jacksonian Democracy*, 201–2 (emphasis in original).

79   Wilentz, *Chants Democratic*, 285; S. J. Ross, *Workers on the Edge*, 55–57; Schlesinger, *Age of Jackson*, 270–71.

80   Hugins, *Jacksonian Democracy and the Working Class*, 222. Sean Wilentz argued that "the Working Men were the first to confront the frustrating power of a professional American party politics just then emerging—the first to learn how, with the many misrepresentations and machinations of American party competition, a popular yet radical challenge could be turned into its opposite" (*Chants Democratic*, 213).

81   Wilentz, *Chants Democratic*, 214.

82   Hugins, *Jacksonian Democracy and the Working Class*, 60.

83   Ely Moore, "Address delivered before the General Trades' Union of the City of New York at the Chartham Street Chapel, December 2, 1833," reprinted in Blau, *Social Theories of Jacksonian Democracy*, 292.

84   Hugins, *Jacksonian Democracy and the Working Class*, 61–62. See also Schlesinger, *Age of Jackson*, 194–98. Tomlins, *State and the Unions*, detailed the response of American courts to the efforts of working people to organize.

85   Frederick Robinson, "An Oration delivered before the Trades' Union of Boston and Vicinity, July 4, 1834," reprinted in Blau, *Social Theories of Jacksonian Democracy*, 338.

86   Hugins, *Jacksonian Democracy and the Working Class*, 63.

87   Commons, "Horace Greeley and the Working Class Origins of the Republican Party," 478–79; P. Foner, *History of the Labor Movement*, 1:183–88; see also E. Foner, "Abolitionism and the Labor Movement," 72–73.

88   McCoy, *The Last of the Fathers*, 175–78, 185–87, citing a letter Madison sent to Thomas Cooper, March 22, 1824.

89   Brownson, "The Laboring Classes," reprinted in Blau, *Social Theories of Jacksonian Democracy*, 309–10. See also E. Foner, "Abolitionism and the Labor Movement," 72–73: "the labor movement, devastated by the depression of 1837–42, was turning toward more individualist and self-help-oriented solutions to the problems of northern workingmen. Evans's own emphasis on the land question, which linked social justice so closely to individual ownership of private property, while seemingly abandoning the cooperative thrust of the labor movement of the 1830s, reflected the change. Evans . . . still insisted that true freedom required economic independence, but he appeared to be abandoning his critique of the wage system itself. Land reform, not a change in the system of production and labor relations, would solve

the problem of urban poverty and offer every workingman the opportunity to achieve economic independence, in the form of a homestead."

90   See E. Foner, *Free Soil, Free Labor, Free Men.*

91   E. Foner, "Abolitionism and the Labor Movement," 73–74.

92   From Godwin's *Life of William Cullen Bryan* (1883), 253–54, cited in Benedict, "Laissez-Faire and Liberty."

93   *Federalist,* no. 78, 509.

94   Calder v. Bull, 3 U.S. 386, 388 (1798).

95   Marbury v. Madison, 1 Cranch 137 (1803); McCulloch v. Maryland, 4 Wheaton 316 (1819); Gibbons v. Ogden, 9 Wheaton 1 (1825); Fletcher v. Peck, 6 Cranch 87, 139 (1810).

96   Dartmouth College v. Woodward, 4 Wheaton 518 (1819). See Campbell, "John Marshall, the Virginia Political Economy, and the Dartmouth College Decision." In his concurring opinion, Story conceded that while an existing charter was a contract binding on legislatures, it was possible for legislatures to reserve for themselves certain powers over the behavior of the corporations in the original charter. As the hostility to corporate privilege became more widespread, so too did the practice of including reserving clauses in special charters of incorporation and later in general incorporation laws. See Providence Bank v. Billings, 4 Peters 514 (1830). On the Marshall Court's recognition of corporate rights of property, see Story's opinion in Terrett v. Taylor, 9 Cranch 43 (1815).

97   Currie's Administrators v. The Mutual Assurance Society, 4 Hen. & Munf. 315 (Va. 1809). See Hyman and Wiecek, *Equal Justice under Law,* 26.

98   The justices did split over whether prospective bankruptcy statutes also violated "eternal and unalterable principles of justice" governing debtor-creditor relations. Still, the level on which the debate took place reflected the desire to put into practice the tenets of the framing ideology. Johnson's majority opinion (echoed by Thompson) focused on how "both the debtor and the society have their interests in the administration of justice, and in the general good; interests which must not be swallowed up and lost sight of while yielding attention to the claim of the creditor." In dissent, Marshall, concerned about keeping all such powers out of the hands of the more dangerous state legislatures, emphasized the historical conditions leading to the creation of the Constitution, noting how both prospective and retrospective efforts to change "the relative situation of debtors and creditors . . . had been used to such an excess by the State legislatures, as to break in upon the ordinary intercourse of society, and destroy all confidence between man and man. . . . To guard against the continuation of the evil was an object of deep interest with all the truly wise, as well as the virtuous, of this great community, and was one of the important benefits expected from reform of the government" (Ogden v. Saunders, 12 Wheaton 213 [1827], 282–83, 312, 354, 357).

99   Charles River Bridge Co. v. Warren Bridge Co., 36 U.S. 420 (1837). See Newmeyer, "Justice Joseph Story, The Charles River Bridge Case and the Crisis of Republicanism"; and Horwitz, *Transformation of American Law,* 130–39.

100 See Friedman, *History of American Law;* Horwitz, *Transformation of American Law;* Hurst, *Law and the Conditions of Freedom;* Scheiber, "Property Law, Expropriation, and Resource Allocation by Government."

101   See Pisani, "Promotion and Regulation," 742–43.
102   Barron v. Baltimore, 7 Pet. (32 U.S.) 243 (1833) and Scheiber, "Federalism and the American Economic Order."
103   See Hyman and Wiecek, *Equal Justice under Law*, 25–29; Friedman, *History of American Law*, 166–78. Pisani, "Promotion and Regulation," 751–54: the success of the corporation "derived from unique American economic conditions that included a relatively dispersed population . . . , a decentralized system of government that had very limited power to collect the capital needed to finance industrialization, and the absence of those great landed, commercial, or banking interests that supplied investment capital in Europe. Instead, the corporate form [initially] tapped a massive pool of small investors." Pisani also noted that corporations were considered a more democratic and less bureaucratic means by which the state could satisfy certain community needs; they also allowed the states to keep taxes low. While at the beginning virtually all corporate activity was heavily regulated, this began to erode around the 1830s with the advent of more capital-intensive ventures (like railroads) and with the depression at the end of the decade, which dried up investment capital. Over the decades restrictions were dropped one by one—general incorporation laws were followed by the removal of restrictions on maximum capitalization, the abandonment of efforts to protect stockholders, and permission to allow corporations to do all their business outside the state in which they were chartered. See also Tomlins, *State and the Unions*, 24–29.
104   See Friedman, *History of American Law*, 157–78; Holt, "Recovery by the Worker Who Quits"; Scheiber, "Road to *Munn*," and "Public Rights and the Rule of Law"; and Levy, *Law of the Commonwealth*. Chief Justice Shaw of Massachusetts permitted the use of eminent domain to aid any project that he felt created sufficient economic benefits. "Flooding to create a head of water to power a factory was a public use because it was 'an object of great public interest, especially since manufacturing has come to be one of the great public industrial pursuits of the commonwealth'" (from Hyman and Wiecek, *Equal Justice under Law*, 31–32, citing Shaw's opinion in Hazen v. Essex Co., 12 Cush. [66 Mass.] 475 [1853], at 478). Others interpreted this forced aid to commercial development as simply another use of public power to advance the interests of private groups or individuals. Note the disagreement among the justices in Taylor v. Porter, 4 Hill (4 N.Y.) 140 (1843). See also the discussion of Cooley below.
105   See Maltz, "Fourteenth Amendment Concepts in the Antebellum Era," 316–17; L. J. Howe, "The Meaning of 'Due Process of Law' Prior to the Adoption of the Fourteenth Amendment."
106   Portland Bank v. Apthorp, 12 Tyng (12 Mass.) 252 (1815), 253–54, 256–58. In the early nineteenth century, courts began to devise rules and principles to ensure that state taxation would be "uniform and equal." A review of this specific aspect of nineteenth-century constitutionalism is beyond the scope of this study; Newhouse's review, entitled *Constitutional Uniformity and Equality in State Taxation*, is over 2,400 pages long.
107   Vadine's Case, 6 Pick (23 Mass.) 187 (1828), 187–92. The Court also turned back the challenge that the act should not operate on Vadine because he was not a resident of Boston.
108   Three years after *Vadine's Case* the court used this same standard to uphold a bylaw

that required people who wanted to sell at market produce that was not from their farm to get the prior permission of the clerk of the market. The act was challenged on the grounds that it was "partial, and does not operate upon all the citizens of the commonwealth equally," but the court—in an interpretation that was quite generous to local producers—called it a "wholesome regulation" of trade "to prevent the market from being unnecessarily thronged and incumbered" (Nightingale's Case, 11 Pick [28 Mass.] 167 [1831], 168, 171).

109   Hewitt v. Charier, 16 Pick (33 Mass.) 353 (1835), 354–56. For a similar discussion, see Jordan v. Overseers of Dayton, 4 Ohio 295 (1831). Corwin discussed these cases in "The Basic Doctrine of American Constitutional Law," 42–43.

110   Commonwealth v. Blackington, 24 Pick (41 Mass.) 352 (1837), 358. Shaw is perhaps best known for his decision in Commonwealth v. Alger, 7 Cush. (61 Mass.) 53 (1851), 84–85, in which he defined the police power as "the power vested in the legislatures to make . . . all manner of wholesome and reasonable laws . . . not repugnant to the constitution, as they shall judge to be for the good and welfare of the commonwealth. . . . [In a] well ordered civil society . . . every holder of property, however absolute and unqualified may be his title, holds it under the implied liability that his use of it may be so regulated, that it shall not be injurious to the equal enjoyment of others having an equal right to the enjoyment of their property, nor injurious to the rights of the community. . . . Rights of property, like all other social and conventional rights, are subject to such reasonable limitations in their enjoyment, as shall prevent them from being injurious, and to such reasonable restraints and regulations established by law, as the legislature [may impose]" (from Hyman and Wiecek, *Equal Justice under Law*, 24–25).

111   From Wally's Heirs v. Kennedy, 2 Yerger (10 Tenn.) 554 (1831) 555–56 (emphasis in original); see also Vanzant v. Waddel, 2 Yerger (10 Tenn.) 260 (1829), 269–70. In striking down the act in *Wally's Heirs*, Judge Catron argued that had it been general, "it is confidently believed that such a law would not have found a single advocate in the legislature" (ibid).

112   Bank v. Cooper, 2 Yerger (10 Tenn.) 599 (1831), 606–7 (emphasis added). In striking down the act, Green wrote, "This law only acts upon individual cases, and is the same in principle, as if a law had been passed in favor of some one merchant, enabling him, by the method therein prescribed, to take judgment against his debtors without the right of appeal" (ibid).

113   For virtually identical interpretations of "law of the land," see Janes et al. v. Reynolds's Adm'rs, 2 Texas 250 (1847), 252 (" 'laws of the land' . . . are now, in their most usual acceptance, regarded as general public laws, binding all the members of the community under similar circumstances, and not partial or private laws, affecting the rights of private individuals, or classes of individuals"); Sears v. Cottrell, 5 Mich. (1 Cooley) 251 (1858), 254 ("The words 'due process of law,' mean the law of the land, and are to be so understood in the Constitution. . . . By 'the law of the land' we understand laws that are general in their operation, and that affect the rights of all alike; and not a special Act of the Legislature, passed to affect the rights of an individual against his will, and in a way in which the same rights of other persons are not affected by existing laws"); and the cases cited in Durkee v. City of Janesville, 28 Wis. 464 (1871), discussed below.

Sometimes this theme governed the most unlikely cases. *Ervine's Appeal* (1851) arose out of Patrick Ervine's efforts to make sure that his blind son Daniel would be taken care of after his death. In his last will and testament Patrick directed that his land be rented so that the proceeds could be used for Daniel's support; he further directed that his real estate not be sold during Daniel's lifetime. Upon Daniel's death, the land would then be sold for his remaining children to "receive share and share alike." Unfortunately, after the death of Patrick and his wife it was discovered that the proceeds from the rent were insufficient to care for the "suffering" and "totally helpless" Daniel. Daniel attempted to get the orphan's court to agree to have the land sold so that he might be supported by the interest, but this was rejected on the grounds that it violated both the expressed desire of Daniel's father not to have the land sold until after Daniel's death and the rights of Daniel's siblings to benefit from the proceeds of the sale. The legislature got wind of this unfortunate turn of events and enacted a statute ordering the orphan's court to appoint a court-supervised trustee to sell the real estate and invest the proceeds for the support of Daniel, but the orphan's court still refused. When the issue came before the Pennsylvania Supreme Court the judges struck down the state law for the same reasons offered by the orphan's court. At the end of the decision the majority instructed the state legislature on how to avoid having the court strike down laws in the future. "In closing this opinion," wrote Judge Coulter, "I may say that when, in the exercise of proper legislative powers, general laws are enacted, which bear or may bear on the whole community, if they are unjust and against the spirit of the constitution, the whole community will be interested to procure their repeal by a voice potential. And that is the great security for just and fair legislation." However, when the legislature departs from this practice and instead involves itself in particular disputes, the courts become "the only secure place for determining conflicting rights by due course of law" (Ervine's Appeal, 4 Harris [16 Pa. St.] 256 [1851], 268). See also Bagg's Appeal, 43 Pa. St. 512 (1862), 515: "Any form of direct government action on private rights, which, if unusual, is dictated by no imperious public necessity, or which makes a special law for a particular person, or gives directions for the regulation and control of a particular case after it has arisen, is always arbitrary and dangerous in principle, and almost always unconstitutional. But that is not arbitrary nor unconstitutional which, within the sphere of politics, makes general laws for all cases in the class that is at the time the subject of legislation."

114   See Aleinikoff, "Constitutional Law in the Age of Balancing."

115   In Bronson v. Kinzie, 1 Howard 311 (1843), 320, the Supreme Court struck down a law that deprived a party of his preexisting right to foreclose a mortgage by selling the premises, in part because the law applied only to "a particular class of contracts" and therefore was "not a general one."

116   Scheiber, "Road to *Munn*"; Newhouse, *Constitutional Uniformity and Equality in State Taxation*.

117   Benedict, "Laissez-Faire and Liberty," 312–13, 327–30. Between 1845 and 1872 eight states barred stock subscriptions, loans, or pledges of credit; and five barred all state aid to private enterprise (ibid., 322). See also Maltz, "Fourteenth Amendment Concepts in the Antebellum Era," 334–35.

118   Scheiber, "Government and the Economy," 137; Friedman, *History of American Law*, 157–66.

119 Benedict, "Laissez-Faire and Liberty," 321–22.
120 Jones, "Cooley and 'Laissez-Faire Constitutionalism,'" 755.
121 People v. Salem, 20 Mich. 487 (1870) (emphasis added), cited in Jones, "Cooley and the Michigan Supreme Court," 104–5.
122 Jones, "Cooley and the Michigan Supreme Court," 105.
123 Cooley, *Treatise on the Constitutional Limitations*. Cooley's was not the only work in the aftermath of the war that drew on the founding vision. Timothy Farrar's *Manual of the Constitution*, Francis Lieber's *Civil Liberty and Self-Government*, and John A. Jameson's *Treatise on Constitutional Conventions* echoed the arguments advanced by the Federalists in the late 1780s. See Larsen, "Nationalism and States' Rights in Commentaries on the Constitution After the Civil War."
124 Cooley, *Constitutional Limitations*, 736.
125 Ibid., 745.
126 Ibid., 1224, 1226, 1228fn (emphasis added). The same is true for limits on freedom of contract. "Freedom of contract is not absolute. It is subject to reasonable legislative regulation in the interests of public health, safety and morals, and, in a sense not resting merely on expediency, the public welfare. But restraints upon such freedom must not be arbitrary or unreasonable. Freedom is the general rule and restraint the exception" (ibid., 1236–37).
127 Ibid., 580.
128 Ibid., 802–10, 812. The section on "Unequal and Partial Legislation" is on pp. 802–45.
129 Ibid., 813, 824ff. (emphasis added).
130 Durkee v. City of Janesville, 28 Wis. 464 (1871), 465–70 (last emphasis added). Dixon then went on to note that "the clause '*law of the land*,' is held to mean a general public law, equally binding upon every member of the community" (470).
131 Correspondence between the House of Representatives of the State of Maine and the Supreme Judicial Court, 58 Maine 590 (1871), 593, 609. For an excellent discussion of police powers jurisprudence in Maine state courts, see D. M. Gold, *The Shaping of Nineteenth-Century Law*.

CHAPTER TWO   *The Master Principle of Neutrality and the Rise of Class Conflict*

1 Butchers' Union v. Crescent City, 111 U.S. 746, 758–59 (1883), Justice Field concurring.
2 In addition, the Congress passed the most extensive statutory extensions of the federal judiciary's jurisdiction in American history. The Judiciary Act of 1875 expanded federal judicial power to the limit: between 1862 and 1866 the Supreme Court's docket averaged 240 cases per term; from 1878 to 1882 that number had jumped to 855, and from 1886 to 1890 the Supreme Court was averaging 1,124 cases a year on its docket. See Keller, *Affairs of State*, 356–57; Wiecek, "The Reconstruction of Federal Judicial Power, 1863–1876."
3 Nelson, *Fourteenth Amendment*, 115, 149, citing Donnell v. State, 48 Miss. 661, 677–78 (1873); and State v. Gibson, 36 Ind. 389, 393 (1871).
4 The nationalization of antebellum police powers jurisprudence was not entirely unforeseen, although neither was it the principal agenda of the Republicans. Harold

Hyman, *More Perfect Union*, 368, concluded that the postwar constitutional reforms were motivated largely by a desire to make it more difficult for states to
"overfavor some individuals and groups and fetter others." More recently, William
Nelson, *Fourteenth Amendment*, 115, pointed out that in defending these new
constitutional restrictions on state behavior, Republicans argued that "the only
effect of the amendment was to prevent the states from discriminating arbitrarily
between different classes of citizens." Similarly, in his December 1865 State of the
Union message, Andrew Johnson emphasized that "monopolies, perpetuities, and
class legislation are contrary to the genius of free government, and ought not to be
allowed. Here there is no room for favored classes or monopolies; the principle of
our Government is that of equal laws and freedom of industry" (cited in Nelson,
Fourteenth Amendment, 91).

5   Montgomery, *Beyond Equality*, 25, 30, and *Fall of the House of Labor*, 46–47. In
Beyond Equality, 41, Montgomery noted that the *New York Times*' February 24,
1869, article "Our Working Classes" clustered the laboring force of New York City
into three income groups. "The most select class, composed of building tradesmen
and printers on daily papers, averaged over $26 a week. Below them stood those
paid around $20 a week, a group equal in size to the first. Included here were
blacksmiths, book printers, and painters, among others. The bottom group, three
times the size of the other two combined, was composed of those earning a meager
subsistence wage or less, ranging from boiler makers at $18 a week through iron
molders at $15 to shoemakers and waiters at $12 and $7, respectively. Their families
crowded the slum apartments and boardinghouses of the cities, and even the middle
bracket found the comforts of life eluding them." Each of these groups suffered
enormously during the spasmodic downturns in the economy.

6   Montgomery, *Beyond Equality*, x.

7   Slaughterhouse Cases, 83 U.S. 36 (1873).

8   Most of what follows is based on Franklin's extensive discussion in "The Foundations and Meaning of the Slaughterhouse Cases."

9   Durbridge v. Slaughterhouse Co., 27 La. Ann. 676 (1875) (calling the monopoly "a
wholesale bribery concern"). See also John A. Campbell's argument to the Court in
83 U.S. 36, 56.

10   Franklin, "The Foundation and Meaning of the Slaughterhouse Cases," 225.

11   83 U.S. 36, 78.

12   See Forbath, "The Ambiguities of Free Labor," 773–74.

13   83 U.S. 36 (emphasis added).

14   Nelson, *Fourteenth Amendment*, 159–60. This opinion was reiterated twenty years
later by William D. Guthrie in his *Lectures on the Fourteenth Amendment*, 20.

15   Chicago, Milwaukee, and St. Paul Railway Co. v. Minnesota, 134 U.S. 418 (1890).
His positions were not contradictory. In *Slaughterhouse* Bradley did not believe that
the legislature was acting for the general welfare; he felt that the monopoly was an
example of illegitimate and corrupt legislative favoritism. In the *Minnesota Rate
Case*, Bradley believed that railroads, like grain elevators, did affect the public
interest, and in those circumstances the concern with preventing the imposition of
special burdens or benefits was no longer relevant. The majority in that case felt
compelled to hold on to the power to review rate schemes in order to ensure that

they in fact served the general welfare and were not merely the result of discriminatory or factional politics.

16   83 U.S. 36 (emphasis added).

17   83 U.S. 36, 80. A few years after *Slaughterhouse* Justice Miller would reflect more on the nature of the police powers and the limitations embodied in the fourteenth amendment. In Davidson v. New Orleans, 96 U.S. 97, 102, 104 (1877), he bemoaned the fact that "it would seem, from the character of many of the cases before us, and the arguments made in them, that the clause under consideration is looked upon as a means of bringing to the test of the decision of this court the abstract opinions of every unsuccessful litigant in a State court." However, he also observed that the fourteenth amendment had to mean something. "[C]an a State make any thing due process of law which, by its own legislation, it chooses to declare such? To affirm this is to hold that the prohibition to the States is of no avail, or has no application where the invasion of private rights is effected under the forms of State legislation." To illustrate the limits on legislative power he used the classic example of illegitimate factional politics first elaborated by Justice Chase in *Calder v. Bull*: "It seems to us that a statute which declares in terms, and without more, that the full and exclusive title of a described piece of land, which is now in A., shall be and is hereby vested in B., would, if effectual, deprive A. of his property without due process of law, within the meaning of the constitutional provision."

18   Loan Assn. v. City of Topeka, 87 U.S. 655, 659, 664–65 (1874). See also Durach's Appeal, 62 Pa. St. 491 ("To lay with one hand the power of the government on the property of the citizen and with the other to bestow it on favored individuals to aid private enterprises, and build up private fortunes, is none the less a robbery because it is done under the forms of law and taxation"). For a contemporaneous discussion of the issue see Spahr, "The Taxation of Labor," 425 ("The principle of democracy is this: Equality before the laws for industries as well as men. To exempt one industry from taxation is to abandon democratic justice and to establish an industrial aristocracy").

The other side of this issue involved ensuring that the taxing power not be used as a class weapon which would single out certain groups for special burdens. In 1883, while riding the California circuit, Justice Field was asked to consider an equal protection challenge brought by railroad companies to California's property tax valuation rule, which exempted railroads from the practice of allowing the taxable value of property to be reduced by the amount of any mortgage on the property. (Railroads were usually mortgaged for all they were worth and could therefore escape all tax liability if they were permitted to "reduce" their burden.) Field acknowledged the established principle that different kinds of property could be taxed at different rates due to differences in their value or utility. But he stressed that there was a constitutional difference between unequal treatment based on dissimilarities in the types of property (which was legitimate) and unequal treatment based on discrimination against certain types of property owners (which was not). "Strangely, indeed, would the law sound in case it read that in the assessment and taxation of property a deduction should be made for mortgages thereon if the property be owned by white men or by old men, and not deducted if owned by black men or by young men; deducted if owned by landsmen, not deducted if owned by sailors; deducted if owned by married men, not deducted if owned by bachelors; . . . and so on, making a discrimination whenever there was any difference in the character or pursuit or condition of the owner." Field decided that the California taxing scheme amounted to an unconstitutional discrimination. County of Santa Clara v. Southern Pacific Railway Co., 18 F. 385, 396 (C.C.D. Cal. 1883). See Kay, "The Equal Protection Clause in the Supreme Court," 701–3.

19 "Brief and Argument for Plaintiffs in Error," submitted by W. C. Goudy in the case of Munn v. Illinois, 94 U.S. 113 (1877), 39–41, 48, 50.

20 Munn v. Illinois, 94 U.S. 113 (1877) (last emphasis in original). The decision by the majority to characterize grain elevators as "affected with a public interest" was no doubt a by-product of the central role played by these storage facilities in farm communities. This conclusion might also have been bolstered by the social effects of the brutal and debilitating deflation in farm prices brought on by the postwar effort on the part of the financial community to retire greenbacks and resume specie payments, an effort that culminated on January 2, 1879, when the United States went back on the gold standard. As Goodwyn explained in *The Populist Moment*, after the war the banking community and other creditor-bondholders had an interest in resuming specie payments. The currency had become depressed during the war years due to the issue of greenbacks; having purchased government bonds during the war, banks could look forward to windfall profits from redeeming them in gold valued at prewar levels. The taxpayers would pay the difference between the fifty-cent wartime dollars and the one-hundred-cent postwar dollars. In the decades following the war farmers were crushed by the falling farm prices and seasonal lack of credit (needed to get crops to market); the disaster led eventually to the Populist movement and the (unsuccessful) attempt to reform the nation's financial system so that it would cater to the interests of producers and not financial elites.

The debate over the issue of what kinds of business regulations were justifiable given the standard of the public interest did not end with *Munn*. In 1890, when railroads challenged the rates set by a commission on the grounds that they were oppressive, the Court granted relief. "The power to regulate is not the power to destroy, and limitation is not the equivalent of confiscation." The majority stressed that legislatures had the power to set rates and could do so through a commission, but in exercising that power states could not unreasonably punish railroads (through confiscatory rates) or unreasonably favor them (by setting extravagantly high rates). See Justice Samuel Blatchford's majority opinion and Miller's concurring opinion in Chicago, Milwaukee, and St. Paul Railway Co. v. Minnesota, 134 U.S. 418 (1890). On Bradley's dissent, see n. 15 above. Similar issues were raised when the Court reaffirmed its commitment to *Munn* in Budd v. New York, 143 U.S. 517 (1892).

21 Civil Rights Cases, 109 U.S. 3, 24 (1883). The special significance of this case lies not in the majority's interpretation of the equal protection clause per se, but rather in the Court's narrow interpretation of Congress's enforcement power under the fourteenth amendment.

In this study I chose to focus on the judiciary's treatment of government regulation of market relations; I have not examined how racism and sexism affected the judiciary's conception of "general welfare" legislation that placed special burdens on women and blacks. Certainly the belief that there were "good reasons" why it was appropriate to treat women differently helps explain not only the Court's willingness to allow legislatures to prohibit women from practicing professions (see Bradwell v. Illinois, 83 U.S. 130 [1873]) but also the judiciary's willingness to allow legislatures to extend special protections to working women (and children and "imbeciles") but not to working men (see Muller v. Oregon, 208 U.S. 412 [1908] and other state cases discussed later this chapter). The attitude toward blacks was more ambivalent, as William E. Nelson recently noted in *The Fourteenth Amendment*. When legislatures were so bold as to impose special and unique burdens on blacks explicitly in statutes, courts were willing to strike down those laws, as the Supreme Court did when it invalidated a law that forbade blacks from serving on juries, in Strauder v. West Virginia, 100 U.S. 303 (1880). But less explicit attempts to deny blacks equal rights through the use of standards or practices that, on their face, were race-neutral were generally upheld, as was the case when the justices refused to strike down literacy tests in Williams v. Mississippi, 170 U.S. 213 (1898). And as Nelson shows (124–36), political elites and judges were deeply divided over the question of whether segregation amounted to the imposition of unique burdens on blacks or whether they represented the imposition of equal burdens on blacks and whites for the good of both races.

22   Butchers' Union v. Crescent City, 111 U.S. 746, 758–59 (1883).

23   111 U.S. 746, 761.

24   Barbier v. Connolly, 113 U.S. 27, 31–32 (1884).

25   Yick Wo v. Hopkins, 118 U.S. 356, 366–68 (1885). The Court also quoted from a decision by the Court of Appeals of Maryland in the case of City of Baltimore v. Radecke, 49 Md. 217 (1878), which had struck down a scheme whereby city officials could revoke permits for the operation of steam engines on the grounds that the requirement was in no way calculated to promote "safety and security" and that it was more likely to proceed on the basis of "enmity or prejudice, from partisan zeal or animosity, from favoritism and other improper influences and motives easy of concealment and difficult to be detected and exposed" (118 U.S. 356, 372).

26   Kay, "The Equal Protection Clause in the Supreme Court," 695–96.

27   In Crowley v. Christensen, 137 U.S. 86 (1890), the Court upheld a San Francisco ordinance prohibiting the retail sale of liquor without a license, with Field explaining that the use of liquor was potentially harmful to the community and that there was probably a good reason to deny the license in this case.

28   Mugler v. Kansas, 123 U.S. 623, 661, 663 (1887).

29   Keller, *Affairs of State*, 413–14.

30   Cited in 45 *Albany Law Journal* 468 (June 4, 1892).

31   "Brief for the Plaintiff in Error," submitted by D. T. Watson for the case of Powell v. Pennsylvania, 127 U.S. 678 (1888), 37, 41.

32   "Brief for Defendant in Error," submitted by A. H. Wintersteen and Wayne Mac-Veagh for the case of Powell v. Pennsylvania, 127 U.S. 678 (1888), 5.

33   Powell v. Pennsylvania, 127 U.S. 678, 683–84 , 687 (1888).

34   People v. Marx, 99 N.Y. 377 (1885).

35   127 U.S. 678, 694. In *Marx*, the New York court continued by noting that the counsel for the state had all but admitted at oral argument that the law was not

intended as a health measure but rather was designed "to protect those engaged in the manufacture of dairy products, against the competition of cheaper substances" (99 N.Y. 377, 385).

36   "Notes," 37 *Albany Law Journal* 325 (April 28, 1888). The *Albany Law Journal* represented the point of view of legal conservatives. For a similar denouncement of oleomargarine laws from an occasionally progressive legal journal, see "Notes: New York's Oleomargarine Law," 18 *American Law Review* 677 (1884).

37   Bannard, "The Oleomargarine Law," 545–57.

38   Montgomery, *Fall of the House of Labor*, 167. As one contemporary explained, "The farmers boldly asserted that the 'iron kings' [of industry] were so protected that they are obliged to pay tribute for their clothing and farm machinery. . . . So the iron kings, out of the kindness of their hearts, decided that the honest farmer should be allowed to get even by plucking some other poor devil. In this instance it happens to be the poor laboring man. On this highly moral platform of 'you tickle me, I'll tickle you,' the iron king and honest farmer joined hands and worked together for favorable legislation. . . . [I]t seems to us that our Legislatures, in their tendency to protect favorite classes under the pretense of police regulation, are acting unwisely and unjustly, and should 'stop and listen' to the complaints of those who are depressed by these legislative attempts to elevate others" (45 *Albany Law Journal* 468 [June 4, 1892]).

39   The Republican party was made up of a coalition of conservatives (such as Secretary of the Treasury Hugh McCulloch and Secretary of State William H. Seward), who represented northern social and economic elites like import-export merchants, shippers, and bankers; so-called radicals (such as Thaddeus Stevens), who were disdainful both of the "mercantile elite" and the propertyless masses and supportive of an egalitarian entrepreneurial vision; and labor reformers (such as Andrew Cameron, editor of the *Workingman's Advocate*, and William H. Sylvis), who were trying to foster and protect workingmen's associations. In the years immediately following the war this coalition began to unravel. Conservatives were interested in a return to specie and in reducing both internal taxes and the tariff; radicals supported expansionist monetary policies and tariff protection; and labor reformers were struggling to obtain better wages and shorter hours and to maintain control over production. See Montgomery, *Beyond Equality*, 59–101. Oftentimes workers found themselves aligned with radicals. Philadelphia Republican congressman William D. Kelly, a disciple of Henry C. Carey, espoused a tariff to protect American industry and wage scales, a mildly inflationary paper currency to stimulate expansion, a federal eight-hour work law, and government-sponsored development of the Northwest. He rejected the view that government could not contribute to the well-being of wage earners: "The theory that labor . . . is merely a raw material, and that the nation which pays the least for it is wisest and best governed, is inadmissible in a democracy." Horace Greeley's *Political Economy* (1871) "attacked free trade, defended government subsidies for internal improvements, and endorsed labor unions" (Keller, *Affairs of State*, 162–63).

40   See S. Cohen, "Northeastern Business and Radical Reconstruction," 85–106.

41   Noble, *The Progressive Mind*, 4, 7, 8. Donnelly later helped to write the Populist Platform of 1892. Donnelly's view of finance capitalism was shared by Andrew

Johnson. "The aristocracy based on $3,000,000,000 of property in slaves . . . has disappeared; but an aristocracy, based on over $2,500,000,000 of national securities, has arisen in the Northern states, to assume that political control which the consolidation of great financial and political interest formerly gave to the slave oligarchy of the late rebel states." Kenneth M. Stampp called him the "last Jacksonian," decrying "monopolies, perpetuities, and class legislation" (cited in Stampp, *Era of Reconstruction*, 57–58).

42 E. Foner, *Reconstruction*, 18–34.

43 Montgomery, *Beyond Equality*, 7; Ross, *Workers on the Edge*, 94–140; Litwack, *American Labor Movement*, 3; McCurdy, "American Law and the Marketing Structure of the Large Corporation, 1875–1890." McCurdy's piece discusses the role that the Supreme Court played in breaking down protective barriers and special privileges in the forging of a truly national market. For example, see Welton v. Missouri, 91 U.S. 275 (1876); and Webber v. Virginia, 103 U.S. 344 (1880).

44 The practice of "conspicuous consumption" among America's new aristocracy does not need documentation, but some illustrations are instructive. William K. Vanderbilt spent a quarter of a million dollars on a single fancy-dress ball; the hostess wore an elegant white dress that matched trained live doves which fluttered around her throughout the evening. At another ball a sand trough filled with diamonds, emeralds, and rubies was placed at the center of the banquet table. Each guest was given a little sterling silver pail and shovel and told to dig. In Philadelphia, a debutante ball was enlivened with the presence of thousands of live butterflies; they flew around the room in their exquisite beauty, until, tired, "they fell to their glamorous deaths drowned in champagne glasses and crushed beneath satin slippers" (Schlesinger, *Almanac of American History*, 354).

45 Keller, *Affairs of State*, 373.

46 Ibid., 402.

47 Moody, "Workingmen's Grievances," 503.

48 Ibid., 186, 386–88.

49 The Strong quote is from Noble, *Progressive Mind*, 20. Turner argued that the "transformations through which the United States is passing in our own day are so profound, so far-reaching that it is hardly an exaggeration to say that we are witnessing the birth of a new nation in America. . . . The familiar facts of the massing of population in the cities and the contemporaneous increase in urban power, and the massing of capital and production in fewer and vastly greater industrial units, especially attest the revolution." He believed that the Populists saw "the sharp contrast between their traditional idea of America, as the land of opportunity, the land of the self-made man, free from class distinctions and from the power of wealth, and the existing America, so unlike the earlier ideal" (ibid., 25–26).

50 Testimony taken by the Senate Committee upon the Relations between Labor and Capital, 1833, reproduced in Garraty, *Labor and Capital in the Gilded Age*, 156, 158–60.

51 E. Foner, *Reconstruction*, 477; McCurdy, "Roots of Liberty of Contract," 27–29.

52 "The Labor Crisis," 105 *North American Review* 177, 212, 184, 188, 207–8, 213 (1867), cited in Forbath, "The Ambiguities of Free Labor," 787–88. Forbath went on to note that within a decade, as class conflict became more pronounced, Godkin

would come to view the labor movement as "communistic." What turned Godkin's opinion about labor was the observation that "the people were behaving in a manner no Radical could have anticipated. They were using their power to pursue class interests" (Montgomery, *Beyond Equality*, 336).

53   Forbath, "The Ambiguities of Free Labor," 802, 804, 806. One labor paper insisted a few years after the war that "independence, intelligence, and moral development of the masses are the only sure foundation of our Republican System of Government" (*Daily Evening Voice*, April 3, 1867, cited in Montgomery, *Beyond Equality*, 126). In Eric Foner's words, the "transformation of labor relations and the emergence of widespread tension between capital and labor" became "the principal economic and political problem" in the United States in the last quarter of the nineteenth century ("Reconstruction and the Crisis of Free Labor," 98).

54   Hays, *Response to Industrialism, 1885–1914*, 48. See also Garraty, *New Commonwealth, 1877–1890*, xiii.

55   E. Foner, *Reconstruction*, 477.

56   Montgomery, *Beyond Equality*, 176–96, 239, 252–53.

57   Ibid., 232, 238, 249–60. On the sham of market liberty there is the testimony of George McNeill before the Labor Committee of the Massachusetts legislature: "The laborer's commodity perishes every day beyond the possibility of recovery." Unlike the commodities of owners, workers "must sell to-day's labor to-day, or never." Hence the terms of the sale would always be made by the employer (ibid., 252).

58   Chapin, "The Relations of Labor and Capital," cited in Benedict, "Laissez-Faire and Liberty," 308. Chapin continued by arguing that "the era of social justice will not be ushered in by those who have nothing better to urge than the old strife of classes for supremacy." Benedict also cited the position of Charles Sumner, who complained that "whether they are paper-money schemes, tariff schemes, subsidy schemes, internal improvement schemes, or usury laws, they all have this in common with the most vulgar of the communist projects . . . and the errors of this sort in the past which have been committed in the interest of the capitalist class now furnish precedents, illustration and encouragement for the new category of demands" (ibid., 313).

59   Fink, "Labor, Liberty, and the Law," 912; see also Forbath, "American Labor Movement," 1121–23.

60   Garlock, "The Knights of Labor Courts," 17–18.

61   Powderly, "The Organization of Labor," 125–26 (emphasis added).

62   Hays, *Response to Industrialism*, 36.

63   Avrich, *Haymarket Tragedy*.

64   Fink, "Labor, Liberty, and the Law," 914–15; see also Forbath, "American Labor Movement," 1122–24.

65   Fink, "Labor, Liberty, and the Law," 921–22. Swindler drew a distinction between the "class-consciousness" of the Knights and the "wage-consciousness" of the AFL in *Court and Constitution in the Twentieth Century*, 51.

66   Goodwyn, *Populist Moment*. The quoted material is on pp. 50, 53, 111.

67   In 1893 Senator William Peffer of Kansas wrote that the motto of the Populist party was "Equal rights to all; special privileges to none" and identified as one of its missions the promotion of the "general welfare" through the abolition of "class legislation" ("The Mission of the Populist Party," 665–78).

68   Wilentz, "Against Exceptionalism," 15.
69   C. V. Woodward, *Reunion and Reaction*; E. Foner, "Reconstruction and the Crisis of
        Free Labor," 126.
70   The phenomenon of sympathy strikes is the best evidence of a growing class con-
        sciousness on the part of workers. Strikes swelled in frequency between 1886 and
        1888 during events like the Southwest railway strikes of 1886, the New York freight
        handlers dispute of 1887, and the Lehigh coal and railroad stoppages of 1888.
        "[T]he number of establishments shut by sympathetic strikes rose from an average
        of 166 yearly between 1886 and 1889 to 732 in 1890, 639 in 1891, and 738 in
        1892. . . . Eugene V. Debs was to extoll this extreme manifestation of mutuality as
        the 'Christ-like virtue of sympathy,' and to depict his own Pullman boycott, the
        epoch's most massive sympathetic action, as an open confrontation between that
        working-class virtue and a social order which sanctified selfishness" (Montgomery,
        "Workers' Control of Machine Production," 123–24). When embattled workers
        faced large, impersonal corporations or absentee owners they won substantial
        public support. See Keller, *Affairs of State*, 398.
71   Schlesinger, *Almanac of American History*, 336.
72   Keller, *Affairs of State*, 394.
73   Montgomery, "Workers' Control of Machine Production," 126–27.
74   Schlesinger, *Almanac of American History*, 374.
75   Swindler, *Court and Constitution in the Twentieth Century*, 52.
76   Shefter, "Regional Receptivity to Reform"; and Burnham, "The Changing Shape of
        the American Political Universe."
77   From Tiedeman, *The Unwritten Constitution*, 78–81:

> The so-called *laissez-faire* philosophy has, until lately, so controlled public opin-
> ion in the English-speaking world, that no disposition has been manifested by the
> depositaries of political power to do more than to control the criminal classes,
> provide for the care of the unfortunate poor and insane, and make public im-
> provements. . . . These general declarations of private rights were not then
> considered as important in controlling the power of government, because the
> government manifested no disposition to violate them. But a change has since then
> come over the political thought of the country. Under the stress of economical
> relations, the clashing of private interests, the conflicts of labor and capital, the
> old superstition that government has the power to banish evil from the earth, if it
> could only be induced to declare the supposed causes illegal, has been revived; and
> all these so-called natural rights, which the framers of our constitutions declared
> to be inalienable, and the violation of which they pronounced to be a just cause for
> rebellion, are in imminent danger of serious infringement. The State is called on to
> protect the weak against the shrewdness of the stronger, to determine what wages
> a workman shall receive for his labor, and how many hours he shall labor. Many
> trades and occupations are being prohibited, because some are damaged inciden-
> tally by their prosecution, and many ordinary pursuits are made government
> monopolies. The demands of the Socialists and Communists vary in degree and in
> detail, but the most extreme of them insist upon the assumption by government of
> the paternal character altogether, abolishing all private property in land, and
> making the State the sole possessor of the working capital of the nation.

Contemplating these extraordinary demands of the great army of discontents, and their apparent power, with the growth and development of universal suffrage, to enforce their views of civil polity upon the civilized world, the conservative classes stand in constant fear of the advent of an absolutism more tyrannical and more unreasoning than any before experienced by man—the absolutism of a democratic majority.

In these days of great social unrest, we applaud the disposition of the courts to seize hold of these general declarations of rights as an authority for them to lay their interdict upon all legislative acts which interfere with the individual's natural rights, even though these acts do not violate any specific or special provision of the Constitution.

For a discussion of Tiedeman's jurisprudence see Mayer, "The Jurisprudence of Christopher G. Tiedeman." Mayer recognized (at 142) that "courts did not uniformly follow his analysis." (The major exception was the Illinois Supreme Court. See the discussion of *Ritchie v. People*, below.)

78 Urofsky, "State Courts and Protective Legislation during the Progressive Era," 67.
79 Ex parte Westerfield, 55 Cal. 550, 551, 553 (1880).
80 From the editorial notes in 31 *Albany Law Journal* (January 31, 1885). See also "Notes: The New York Tenement House Cigar Law," 18 *American Law Review* 1021 (1884).
81 In re Jacobs, 98 N.Y. 98, 104, 110–15 (1885). Forbath, "American Labor Movement," 1134 fn 81, viewed the opinion as

an eloquent, if ironic, statement of the Gilded Age courts' vision of "free labor" and workers' dignity and independence. The court envisioned each sweated out-worker as a self-employed artisan "who carr[ies] on a perfectly lawful trade in his own home." The inequitable statute hinders the artisan "in the application of his industry." It "deprives him of his property" in the disposition of his labor and skills and "of his personal liberty" by driving him out of his own shop to work in a factory "upon such terms as, under . . . the inexorable laws of supply and demand, he may be able to obtain from his employer." The opinion is an unconscious parody of the values and fears of mid-nineteenth century artisans. In fact, the income and working conditions of homeworkers in the sweated trades like cigar-making were significantly worse than those of factory workers in the same industries, and rarely was the homeworker actually self-employed. Nonetheless, a judge reared on Lincoln's "Free Labor" ideology readily could have construed the homeworker's circumstances in that fashion. The homeworker was striving upward, hoping to become a propertied citizen and an entrepreneur. By the same Lincolnian lights, the anti-tenement law represented a tyrannical effort to hold Mr. Jacobs down, to reduce him to a factory wage-earner, and a cog in the union's and manufacturer's big machines.

See also Forbath, "Ambiguities of Free Labor," 796.
82 People v. Gillson, 109 N.Y. 389 (1888). This case involved a law which prohibited the practice of offering gifts or prizes along with the purchase of food. It was challenged on the grounds that its effect was to "oppress a certain class of citizen

traders, and to improperly discriminate against them in their business," and that "no abridgement of the rights by the legislature will be upheld or enforced, except as a regulation of police, operating to the benefit of all individuals of the community, equally." The court's opinion was written by Rufus W. Peckham, who rejected the state's claim that the law was intended to prohibit the practice of setting up lotteries: "there was no lottery or pretense of lottery in the transaction upon which the defendant was convicted of a violation of the act. There was not the slightest element of chance in the case. A counter had upon it various articles of crockery, all of which were in full view of the purchaser at the time he purchased the coffee in question. He was told that he could have any of those articles on that counter, to be picked out by himself, if he purchased two pounds of the coffee mentioned" (109 N.Y. 389, 390–91, 402).

83   Millett v. People, 117 Ill. 294, 296–97, 301–2 (1886). For "want of capacity" women and children were treated as a protected class, and laws regulating their labor were generally approved. It was also by virtue of this exception that courts upheld usury laws and the regulation of contracts entered into by seamen. As the Illinois court explained in Frorer v. People, 141 Ill. 171, 185–86 (1892), "Usury laws proceed upon the theory that . . . the borrower's necessities deprive him of freedom in contracting, and place him at the mercy of the lender," and because of the master-mariner relationship on board ship, seamen "constituted a servile class, as distinctly marked, and as dependent and helpless . . . as that of infants." However, most political leaders refused to acknowledge the possibility that this condition of servitude might exist in society at large, since such an admission would undermine the constitutional keystone, the faction-free republic. The Constitution and its supporting ideology had been founded on the promise that a person could maintain his or her autonomy and social independence in a market economy.

In "Distributive and Paternalistic Motives in Contract and Tort Law," Duncan Kennedy argued, correctly I think, that the attempt in contract law to treat certain contractual relationships differently on the basis of a concept such as "unequal bargaining power" is essentially arbitrary. But an ideological construct can be exposed as incoherent at some theoretical level and still be meaningful for its advocates; the social visions people use to interpret their world are chock-full of contradictions and arbitrary distinctions, but they are still used. Kennedy noted in that same article that the concept of unequal bargaining power may be easily deconstructed but nevertheless be ideologically significant to the extent that it allows liberals to argue that market relations in a capitalist economy are fundamentally fair (equal) but can use some adjustment on the margins. Identifying particular cases of unequal bargaining power "has no direct reference either to equality in the actual division of transaction surplus between buyer and seller, or to the actual division of social product among the warring groups of civil society. It nonetheless gives a very good feeling" (ibid., 621).

84   State v. Goodwill, 33 W.Va. 179, 182–83 (1889). Virtually all of the first wage regulations involving manner of payment fell in the face of the prohibition against class legislation. See Godcharles v. Wigeman 113 Pa. St. 431 (1886); Commonwealth v. Perry, 148 Mass. 160 (1889); State v. Fire Creek Coal and Coke Co., 33 W.Va. 188 (1889); State v. Loomis, 115 Mo. 307 (1893); Johnson v. Goodyear

Mining Co., 127 Cal. 5 (1899); State v. Missouri Tie and Timber Co., 181 Mo. 536 (1904). The *Albany Law Journal* labeled efforts to force companies to pay their employees once a week "class legislation" (41 *Albany Law Journal* 426 [May 31, 1890]). See also Stimson's contemporaneous *Handbook to the Labor Law of the United States*, 12–14, 89–90; Brannon, *Treatise on the Fourteenth Amendment*, 203–4. As Urofsky has pointed out, starting in the 1890s many states began upholding manner of payment legislation, usually after the justification was changed from one that asserted a vague health concern to one that asserted a specific interest in protecting the currency as the principal mode of exchange ("State Courts and Protective Legislation," 78–79).

85 Frorer v. People, 141 Ill. 171, 177–79, 185–87 (1892) (emphasis added).

86 State v. Loomis, 115 Mo. 307, 316 (1892). See also In re House Bill No. 203, 21 Colo. 27 (1895).

87 Ritchie v. People, 155 Ill. 98, 105, 111 (1895). Stimson, in his *Handbook to the Labor Law of the United States*, 64–65, commented a year after *Ritchie*: "It seems clear that, under the modern view that women are citizens, capable of making their own contracts, particularly in states where they have the right of suffrage, such legislation restricting their hours of labor is unconstitutional . . . as class legislation of the worst sort." However, the *Yale Law Journal* disagreed with the Illinois court's reasoning, as did many other courts. The editors argued that "the incessant jar and rumble of machinery" could diminish a woman's ability to bear children, and "it cannot be doubted that it is the duty of the State to protect posterity" ("Comment," 4 *Yale Law Journal* 200–201 [1895]). Most state courts agreed. Between *Ritchie* in 1895 and Muller v. Oregon, 208 U.S. 412, in 1908, only two state courts struck down similar statutes. In Burcher v. People, 41 Colo. 495 (1907), the Colorado court struck down the law on technical grounds having to do with the drafting of the statute; and in People v. Williams, 189 N.Y. 131 (1907), the New York court struck down the law on the same grounds used in *Ritchie*. More favorable treatment was received in Commonwealth v. Beatty, 15 Pa. Super. 5 (1900); Wenham v. State, 65 Neb. 394 (1902); State v. Buchanan, 29 Wash. 602 (1902); and State v. Muller, 48 Ore. 252 (1906), usually on the grounds that women were physically inferior and needful of assistance. "Surely an act which prevents the mothers of our race from being tempted to endanger their life and health by exhaustive employment can be condemned by none save those who expect to profit by it" (Commonwealth v. Beatty, 15 Pa. Super. 5, 8 [1900]). *Ritchie* itself was overturned in Ritchie v. Wayman, 244 Ill. 509 (1910), after Judge John P. Hand argued that the previous statute failed to draw the court's attention to the legislature's concern with the health of women. See Urofsky, "State Courts and Protective Legislation," 73–74.

88 Anonymous, "Some Restrictions upon Legislative Power," 25–27. The author went on to argue that statutes which forbade discrimination against Negroes in public accommodations violated the Constitution because they extended special protections to one class; that is to say, a restauranteur could exclude any white man he wished but not any black man. This application of the principle prompted the editor to note at the end of the article that "the foregoing is from a Southern contributor. It is perhaps hardly necessary to say that we do not assent to all his views."

89 Stimson, *Handbook to the Labor Law of the United States*, 12–13, 147–48.

90   L. Parker and Worthington, *Law of Public Health and Safety*, 6–7, 22–23. As examples of reasonable ordinances they included (citations omitted) those

> providing that no person shall keep combustible materials in large quantities, unless secured in a fire-proof structure; prohibiting the sale of milk without a license; prohibiting the adulteration of milk; requiring all imitations of lacteal products to be plainly marked; prohibiting the sale of meat except in specified places; requiring butchers to be licensed; declaring that private markets shall not be established, continued, or kept open, within twelve squares of a public market; prohibiting the slaughtering of animals within certain specified portions of the city, or anywhere within the limits of the city; restricting the slaughtering of animals to certain localities; regulating the construction and management of new slaughter-houses; prohibiting the making of soap and candles, contrary to the mode prescribed; prohibiting hog-pens, and the keeping of hogs, except for temporary purposes; providing that cattle shall not be permitted to go at large; prohibiting the keeping of hogs within certain limits, and providing that they shall not be permitted to run at large; prohibiting any person, not duly licensed, from removing refuse or contents of privies; providing that garbage shall be removed in water-tight carts; providing that intoxicating liquors shall not be used or kept in restaurants; prohibiting the sale of liquors during certain hours of the night; requiring the closing of saloons on Sundays; prohibiting the deposit in the streets or on private premises of garbage and refuge; prohibiting all persons, except undertakers, from removing dead bodies to the place of burial, and requiring bonds from undertakers; prohibiting the establishment of new cemeteries; prohibiting burials in certain localities; prohibiting the obstruction of streets by railroad trains; prohibiting persons, other than passengers, from getting on or off trains; regulating the speed of railroad trains; compelling boats laden with produce likely to become putrid to anchor until examined and passed by a health officer; declaring dense smoke from steamboats and chimneys of buildings a nuisance, and providing for abatement; prohibiting public laundries, except in certain localities; prescribing conditions under which laundries may be operated; regulating the driving or riding through the streets at a faster rate than six miles per hour, and requiring that speed shall be slackened at crossings, even in the case of ambulances; providing that hoistways shall be guarded by railings and supplied with trap-doors; prohibiting the erection of livery-stables, except with the consent of the adjoining property-owners; prohibiting the playing of musical instruments in the streets without a license. (Ibid., 70–72).

91   Binney, "Restrictions upon Local and Special Legislation in the United States" 613–32, 721–45, 816–57, 1019–33, 1109–61 (1892), 618–19, 722–24, 730, 816–17, 825 fn 2, 828. (The *American Law Register* later became the *University of Pennsylvania Law Review*.) Binney cited some early state court cases that expressed hostility to "special" legislation, including Morrison v. Bachert, 112 Pa. 322; Ayars' Appeal, 122 Pa. 266; Evans v. Job, 8 Nev. 322; Ex parte Stout, 5 Colo. 509; Cass v. Dillon, 2 Ohio St. 607; Mayor v. Shelton, 1 Head (Tenn.) 24 (ibid., 619). A less helpful discussion of the same issue was provided in a three-part article by Thomas Raeburn White, "Constitutional Prohibition of Local and Special Legislation in Pennsylva-

nia." (The constitutional issues surrounding "local" legislation are separate from the issues involved in "special" laws.)

92   The success of this campaign was anticipated and bemoaned by Edward Atkinson, who in 1886 argued that maximum hours laws would be an "obnoxious meddlesome interference by statute with the liberty of contract on the part of adults" ("The Hours of Labor," 509).

93   Earlier eight-hour movements had usually gone no further than to ask the government to set an example for employers by making eight hours the norm for government hiring practices. As Montgomery noted, in the years after the Civil War "workers were no more prepared ideologically to ask for the expansion of state activities . . . than their employers" (*Beyond Equality*, 334). Some eight-hour laws were passed after the Civil War, but their effectiveness was undermined by clauses that allowed employers and employees to avoid the restriction if they so contracted; most of these laws were repealed in the wake of the depression of the 1870s. See E. Foner, *Reconstruction*, 480–81.

94   Low v. Rees Printing Co., 41 Neb. 127, 135–36, 145 (1894). For a favorable review of the opinion, which praises its careful reasoning and its exhaustive review of the authorities, see "Comment," 4 *Yale Law Journal* 35 (1894). See also In re Eight Hour Bill, 21 Colo. 29 (1895); Stimson, *Handbook to the Labor Law of the United States*, 44–50.

95   Republic Iron & Steel Co. v. State, 160 Ind. 379, 385 (1902).

96   Guthrie, *Lectures on the Fourteenth Amendment*, 76, 106.

97   Labatt, "State Regulation of the Contract of Employment," 859, 868, 874–75. To prevent workers from concluding that "courts are a mere stronghold of capital" Labatt suggested that judges give more leeway to exercises of the police power designed to address the concerns of labor.

98   Cooley, "Labor and Capital before the Law," 507–8, 510–11, 514–15.

99   Jones, "Cooley and 'Laissez-Faire Constitutionalism,'" 770–71.

100   "A Century Old To-Day! New York's Splendid Celebration of the United States Judiciary," *New York Mail and Express*, February 4, 1890.

CHAPTER THREE   *The Old Constitutionalism and the New Realism*

1   Teichmueller, "The Province of Government," 29.

2   Foltz, "Should Women Be Executed?" 310.

3   From a reproduction of a Memorial Day address by former lieutenant governor of New York Charles T. Saxton, 55 *Albany Law Journal* 391–92 (June 12, 1897), 392.

4   Rose, "Strikes and Trusts," 713.

5   H. B. Brown, "The Distribution of Property," 660 (originally delivered before the ABA meeting at Milwaukee, August 31, 1893). Brown went on to suggest that "these conflicts between capital and labor are not of recent date. . . . One of the earliest recorded annals of the race is that of the exodus of the Israelites from Egypt, which seems to have been a national protest against the oppression of capital, and to have possessed the substantial characteristics of a modern strike. How far this revolt was due to the order of Pharaoh that the Israelites should provide their own straw to make bricks, and how far to the hereditary aversion of the Jewish race to manual

labor, we shall never know, at least until we hear the Egyptian side of the story" (ibid., 657). Always the fair-minded jurist.

6   Justice Brown's commencement is reproduced in 52 *Albany Law Journal* 18–21 (July 13, 1895), 20. Brown argued that corporations combined in order to get rid of competition, whereas labor (which began the process of consolidation more slowly "because less intelligent and alert to its own interests") combined in order to dictate "the terms upon which the productive and transportation industry of the country shall be carried on." For Brown, it was class conflict that presented the most serious challenge to the society, not growing inequities in the distribution of wealth. "With no reward for industry and no punishment for idleness, what would be the proportion of the industrious to the idle? Where would be the incentive to labor? What would become of the hundreds of thousands who are engaged in providing luxuries for the rich, and in ministering to their pleasures?" (ibid., 19).

Brown may have fretted less than others over the novelty of class conflict and may have been less self-conscious about the growing inequities in the distribution of wealth, but his admonitions that the law needed to remain above the fray and neutral with respect to the factionalization of American politics was reflective of the dominant assumptions of contemporaneous American constitutionalism.

7   Judson, "Liberty of Contract under the Police Power," 872.

8   Ibid., 876.

9   Dillon, "Property—Its Rights and Duties in Our Legal and Social Systems," 173–74. The article was originally delivered as an address before the New York State Bar Association meeting at Albany, January 25, 1895.

10   Lawton v. Steele, 152 U.S. 133, 137 (1893). See also Dent v. West Virginia, 129 U.S. 124 (1889): "Legislation is not open to the charge of depriving one of his rights without due process of law, if it be general in its operation upon the subjects to which it relates."

11   See Barbier v. Connolly, 113 U.S. 27 (1884); Yick Wo v. Hopkins, 118 U.S. 356 (1885); and Mugler v. Kansas, 123 U.S. 623, 661, 663 (1887), and the discussion of these cases in chapter 2 of this volume.

12   "Brief for Plaintiff in Error," submitted by Eppa Hunton in the case of Minneapolis and St. Louis Railway Co. v. Beckwith, 129 U.S. 26 (1888), 5, 12.

13   Ibid., 28–29, 31. See also the note on "Construction of Statutes Giving Double Damages against Railroad Companies for Failure to Fence," 25 *American Law Review* 114–16 (1891).

14   Missouri Pacific Railway Co. v. Mackey, 127 U.S. 205 (1888).

15   Bell's Gap R.R. v. Pennsylvania, 134 U.S. 232, 238 (1890).

16   "Brief and Argument for Plaintiff in Error," submitted by E. D. Kenna and J. W. Terry in the case of Gulf, Colorado and Santa Fe Railway Co. v. Ellis, 165 U.S. 150 (1896), 1–84, 7, 55–56, 74–75 (italics removed). The reference in the brief to laws closing barber shops on Sundays was meant to bring to mind the kind of discussion offered in the case notes of the *Harvard Law Review* that same year, which pointed out that such laws represented "an arbitrary discrimination against a special class," one that was not "actuated by some rational public reason" ("Special Legislation—Closing Barber Shops on Sunday," 9 *Harvard Law Review* 425–26 [1896], 425).

17   Taft, "Criticisms of the Federal Judiciary," 650. Taft argued that the responsibility of

the federal judiciary was to protect "the interest of the whole country against the temporary interest of the part" (651). His discussion was part of an explosion of interest in the question of the legitimacy of judicial review that arose in the aftermath of the Supreme Court's fateful 1895 term, which saw the justices strike down the income tax (Pollock v. Farmers' Loan and Trust Co., 158 U.S. 601) and the first antitrust suit (United States v. E. C. Knight Co., 156 U.S. 1) and uphold the use of the injunction against Debs's boycott in support of the Pullman strike (In re Debs, 158 U.S. 564). The discussions really began with an article written by Oregon governor Sylvester Pennoyer, "The Income Tax Decision, and the Power of the Supreme Court to Nullify Acts of Congress." The *American Law Review* kept the issue alive for years to come. For a start, see Allen, "The Income Tax Decision: An Answer to Gov. Pennoyer"; Pennoyer, "A Reply to the Foregoing"; J. Parker, "The Supreme Court and Its Constitutional Duty and Power"; Rosenberger, "The Supreme Court of the United States as Expounder of the Constitution"; Pennoyer, "The Case of Marbury v. Madison"; Akin, "Aggressions of the Federal Courts"; Winchester, "The Judiciary—Its Growing Power and Influence"; Trickett, "The Great Usurpation"; Meigs, "Some Recent Attacks on the American Doctrine of Judicial Power" (Meigs had written one of the only discussions of the origins of the power of judicial review to predate the crisis of the 1890s; see "The Relation of the Judiciary to the Constitution"); Esterline, "The Supreme Law of the Land"; Street, "The Irreconcilable Conflict"; Trickett, "Judicial Dispensation from Congressional Statutes"; McDonough, "The Alleged Usurpation of Power by the Federal Courts"; Meigs, "The American Doctrine of Judicial Power, and Its Early Origin"; Hallam, "Judicial Power to Declare Acts Void"; and Sargeant, "The American Judicial Veto."

The *American Law Review* was not the only forum for these debates. For more on the interest in judicial review around the turn of the century, see Alan F. Westin's introduction to Beard's *The Supreme Court and the Constitution*.

18 Gulf, Colorado and Santa Fe Railway Co. v. Ellis, 165 U.S. 150 (1896), 153–56, 158–59.

19 Ibid., 167–68.

20 "Argument and Brief for Plaintiff in Error," submitted by Robert Dunlap and E. D. Kenna in the case of Atchison, Topeka and Santa Fe R.R. Co. v. Matthews, 174 U.S. 96 (1898), 1–109, 14, 45–46, 49–50, 58.

21 Ibid., 98.

22 Ibid., 107, 112.

23 Ibid., 103–6.

24 Cotting v. Kansas City Stock Yards Co. and the State of Kansas, 183 U.S. 79, 105–9 (1901). The brief for the appellants, submitted by B. P. Waggener and Albert Houton, was 231 pages. They followed their first brief with a brief for reargument in which they asserted (at 58–59) that "security of property rights and confidence in the impartial administration of equal laws have been the true source of our marvelous prosperity during the last three decades, which is the wonder and envy of the world. It is the principle of equality which has given us stability and immense effective force. Whatever temporary local interest or prejudice or blindness may be—whether populism or communism or collectivism—the people of Kansas and other states must inevitably realize that the disregard of the principle of equality and

the restraint which it imposes is in conflict with their own vital and permanent welfare, and cannot be tolerated if we are to remain a free people under the rule of constitutional guaranties, restraining all arbitrary and despotic exercise of the powers of government."

25   Connolly v. Union Sewer Pipe Co., 184 U.S. 540, 564 (1901). Justice McKenna, who in *Ellis* took the position that it was inappropriate to treat railroads differently in actions involving fires, was the lone dissenter. He argued that the legislative classification in this case made sense in that it was

> the expression of the purpose of the State to suppress combinations to control the prices of commodities, not, however, in the hands of the producers, but in the hands of traders, persons or corporations. Shall we say that such suppression must be universal or not at all? . . . [A]re there not, between the classes which the statute makes, distinctions which the legislature had a right to consider? Of whom are the classes composed? The excluded class is composed of farmers and stock-raisers while holding the products or live stock produced or raised by them. The included class is composed of merchants, traders, manufacturers, all engaged in commercial transactions. That is, one class is composed of persons who are scattered on farms; the other class is composed of persons congregated in cities and towns, not only of natural persons but of corporate organizations. In the difference of these situations, and in other differences which will occur to any reflection, might not the legislature see difference in opportunities and powers between the classes in regard to the prohibited acts?" (Ibid., 571).

The opinion rested on the same principles that animated the majority, but it demonstrated a greater willingness to accept as legitimate and essentially neutral the motives underlying legislative classifications.

For another example of the judicial line drawing going on during this period, see American Sugar Refining Co. v. Louisiana, 179 U.S. 89 (1900). For examples at the state level, see State v. Sheriff of Ransey County, 48 Minn. 236 (1892), striking down a statute that exempted manufacturing establishments from a prohibition on the emission of dense smoke within the city; and Commonwealth v. Snyder, 38 Atl. Rep. (Pa.) 356 (1897), striking down an act requiring persons peddling in a certain county to take out a local license but exempting merchants, peddlers who sell to merchants, and citizens who sell the products of their own growth and manufacture. The *Harvard Law Review* reported on a state case (State v. Wise, 72 N.W. Rep. [Minn.] 843) which upheld an act forbidding the sale of liquor to any Indian on the grounds that "the Indians as a race are less civilized than the whites, less subject to moral restraint, more liable to acquire the liquor habit, and more dangerous when intoxicated. . . . The statute, in this view, does not make an arbitrary race discrimination, but rests on the mental and physical peculiarities of the Indians" ("Recent Cases: Constitutional Law—Class Legislation—Indians," 11 *Harvard Law Review* 414 [1898]).

26   "Notes of Recent Decisions: Constitutional Law: Fourteenth Amendment—Equal Protection of the Laws—Invalidity of the Illinois Anti-Trust Act of 1893, Which Exempted Agricultural Products from Its Provisions," 36 *American Law Review* 308–10 (1902), 310.

27   While there had always been some willingness to extend special protections to groups that found themselves unusually vulnerable (hence usury laws or laws protecting contracts made by sailors on ships) or who lacked the capacity to care for themselves in a harmonious market (hence laws regulating contracts involving minors), these were understood to be exceptions to the general assumption, exceptions that did not embody a principle that would permit the extension of these special protections to other groups.

28   "Notes of Recent Decisions: Constitutional Law: Police Regulations for the Protection of Laborers," 24 *American Law Review* 328–29 (1890).

29   S. D. Thompson, "Abuses of Corporate Privileges," 169–70, 199, 201, 203. The article was originally an address delivered before the Bar Association of the State of Kansas at Topeka, January 26, 1892.

30   Reno, "Arbitration and the Wage Contract," 837–38, 855.

31   Rose, "Strikes and Trusts," 713, 717–19. This was also the argument made by Clarence Darrow in his defense of Eugene Debs. "The whole industrial world has been made over in the last fifty years," he wrote in his brief to the justices. "It has practically been made anew in the last quarter of a century[.] And rules and regulations which concerned the interest and welfare of the small communities of the middle ages, with their isolated farms, their small shops and mills and their primitive tools can not equally [serve] the changed industrial conditions of today" in which "the whole relation of employer and employe, has been completely changed. . . . With a constant tendency in their business to replace man with machines, to replace skilled labor with unskilled, to replace men with women, and women with children, for women and children can feed machines as well as men, the tendency must constantly be to limit the demand for labor and increase its supply. The old political economists were wont to teach that where labor is displaced by machinery, the energies of the unemployed could be turned in some other direction. But the facts of life and business show that this theory can not prevail under the conditions of the present. . . . The refusal to work has been the only way that the laborer has thus far found to regulate the supply of the commodity that he has to sell" ("Brief and Argument for Petitioners," submitted by Clarence S. Darrow in the case of In re Debs, 158 U.S. 564 [1895], 88, 92).

32   F. C. Woodward, "Statutory Limitations of Freedom of Contract between Employer and Employe," 236–37, 244, 250, 255–56.

33   "Notes of Recent Decisions: Constitutional Law: Freedom of Contract: Validity of 'Store Order' Legislation," 27 *American Law Review* 141–43 (1893), 143. After noting that in response to earlier pronouncements on this topic the editor of the *Albany Law Journal* had dubbed the *Review* "the Great Corporation Killer," the *Review* commented that "Jesus pitied the poor; but his followers of the type of that editor seem to pity only the poor corporation" (ibid).

34   "Notes of Recent Decisions: Constitutional Law: Unconstitutionality of a State Statute Prohibiting Corporations from Paying Their Employees in Anything Except Lawful Money," 34 *American Law Review* 446–47 (1900), 447.

35   "Notes of Recent Decisions: Constitutional Law: Police Regulations—Validity of Statute Limiting the Hours of Female Labor," 29 *American Law Review* 766–68 (1895), 768. Even though the title of the note suggests that the discussion deals with laws protecting women workers, the article focuses on truck order laws.

36   See the discussion and the accompanying notes at the beginning of this chapter.

37   From the editor's notes in 56 *Albany Law Journal* 19–20 (July 10, 1897).

38   From the editor's notes in 61 *Albany Law Journal* 337 (June 2, 1900). The *Harvard Law Review* also commented some years later in connection with an identical case from Wisconsin: "As the legislation in the principal case can hardly be deemed necessary for the welfare of the community, the decision seems correct" (Recent Cases, "Constitutional Law—Police Power—Statute Forbidding Discharge of Employee Because Member of Labor Union," 16 *Harvard Law Review* 221 [1903]). While the *Yale Law Journal* was able to muster some lukewarm support for legislation protecting union labor members from arbitrary discharge—the contention "that the statute was a special law conferring a special privilege on some out of a class, is not free from doubt" and "perhaps does not strictly fall within special legislation" since "whatever privilege this gives to union men was enjoyed by nonunion already, and it rather equalizes their positions so far as discharge is concerned"—they did recognize that state court decisions showed "that paternal legislation in behalf of labor organizations, so far, at least, has not been considered by the courts to come within the scope of the police regulating power of the State" (Comment: Labor Union Legislation—Employer's Right to Discharge," 10 *Yale Law Journal* 256–57 [1901], 257, discussing Gillespie v. People, 58 N.E. [Ill.] 1009). See also "Recent Cases: Constitutional Law—Liberty of Contract—State v. Kreutzberg, 90 N.W. 1098 (Wis.)," 12 *Yale Law Journal* 44 (1902).

39   Justice Field never had a chance to speak directly to the issue of the state regulation of labor because he had already retired from the bench by the time *Holden* came around.

40   Reproduced in Holden v. Hardy, 169 U.S. 366, 369, 371, 376–79 (1897).

41   Much too much has been made of the importance of Allgeyer v. Louisiana, 165 U.S. 578, 590 (1896), on the development of the jurisprudence of the *Lochner* era. The case was briefly mentioned in *Holden* and in Peckham's *Lochner* opinion in order to establish the proposition that people have a general right to make contracts, subject to reasonable state regulations. *Allgeyer* itself is often misinterpreted as some kind of radical departure from previous doctrine. At a time when the justices found themselves occasionally disagreeing over the proper application of the standards governing the scope of the police power, they were in *unanimous* agreement in *Allgeyer* that there were limits over the extent to which Louisiana could regulate the kinds of contracts citizens of Louisiana entered into while they were *outside the state*.

> We are not alluding to acts done within the State by an insurance company or its agents doing business therein, which are in violation of the state statutes. . . . When we speak of the liberty to contract for insurance or to do an act to effectuate such a contract already existing, we refer to and have in mind the facts of this case, where the contract was made outside the State, and as such was a valid and proper contract. . . . This does not interfere in any way with the acknowledged right of the State to enact such legislation in the legitimate exercise of its police or other powers as it may seem proper. . . . [I]t may be conceded that this right to contract in relation to persons or property or to do business within the jurisdiction of the State may be regulated and sometimes prohibited when the contracts or business conflict with the policy of the State as contained in its statutes, yet the power does

not and cannot extend to prohibiting a citizen from making contracts of the nature involved in this case outside the limits and jurisdiction of the State, and which are also to be performed outside of such jurisdiction. . . . [T]he contract was valid in the place where made and where it was to be performed. (165 U.S. 578, 590–92)

In the course of this decision the justices did underscore Harlan's position in *Powell* that a person's "enjoyment upon terms of equality with all others in similar circumstances of the privilege of pursuing an ordinary calling or trade, and of acquiring, holding, and selling property, is an essential part of his rights of liberty and property as guaranteed by the Fourteenth Amendment" (ibid., 590). But, as the opinion makes clear, that statement does not and was not intended to establish a blanket right to contract that immunized people from state regulation. The central thrust of the decision is essentially jurisdictional—Louisiana can't tell one of its citizens traveling to New York that he cannot do something while in New York that it is legal to do in New York (like drink or buy a lottery ticket); the fourteenth amendment was simply the vehicle through which the federal court was empowered to protect that general "liberty."

42 This point is also made by McCurdy, "The Roots of Liberty of Contract Reconsidered."

43 Holden v. Hardy, 169 U.S. 366, 382–83, 390–98 (1897) (citations omitted). With respect to the issue of unequal bargaining power, Brown wrote, "It may not be improper to suggest in this connection that although the prosecution in this case was against the employer of labor, . . . his defence is not so much that his right to contract has been infringed upon, but that the act works a peculiar hardship to his employes, whose right to labor as long as they please is alleged to be thereby violated. The argument would certainly come with better grace and greater cogency from the latter class" (ibid., 397).

In another case, the Court also upheld an act that provided for the cashing of coal orders when presented by the miner to the employer, on the grounds that it served the state's interest in protecting the currency. See Knoxville Iron Co. v. Harbison, 183 U.S. 13.

44 In re Morgan, 26 Colo. 415 (1899).

45 See Harper, "Due Process of Law in State Labor Legislation," 620–21.

46 "Comment: The Constitutionality of the Minimum Wage Law," 13 *Yale Law Journal* 92–94 (1903), 92–93; see also "Recent Cases: Constitutional Law—Regulating the Rate of Wages—Class Legislation—Street v. Varney Electrical Supply Co., 66 N.E. 895 (Ind.)," 12 *Yale Law Journal* 509 (1903). The comment notes that the Indiana court struck down an act that required a minimum wage of twenty cents an hour to be paid to unskilled labor employed in public works as "class legislation." The same fate met similar acts in People v. Coler, 166 N.Y. 1; and State v. Norton, 5 Ohio N.P. 183.

47 "Comment: Constitutionality of Laws Regulating Hours of Employment," 12 *Yale Law Journal* 499–502 (1903), 500, 502.

48 "Comment: Legislative Restraint upon Hours of Labor as a Health Regulation," 13 *Yale Law Journal* 313–16 (1904), 315–16.

49   A history of the eight-hour movement in New York is provided in Groat, "The Eight Hour and Prevailing Rate Movement in New York State":

> Among the special trades that have at various times received consideration at the hands of the legislature are plumbers, railway employees, brick makers, stone cutters, bakers, barbers, horseshoers, engineers and drug clerks. As a rule the laws passed have been in the direction of restricting the number of hours of work in these trades, and in some cases provision has been made for licensing the workmen or granting certificates after an examination by a specially constituted board. The bakers' law provided for inspection of bake shops, in addition to limiting the number of hours to work. . . . The attitude of the courts toward this line of legislation, as indicated by recent decisions, has tended to check the zeal with which the bills have been urged. In 1904 the law pertaining to horseshoers was held to be unconstitutional. . . . The law required that all journeymen or master horseshoers should be examined by a state board . . . [which would] issue a certificate which served as evidence of fitness. . . . This law was annulled by the unanimous vote of the appellate division of the Supreme Court. . . . "It is difficult indeed to see how the regulation of shoeing horses has any tendency to promote the health, comfort, safety and welfare of society." (Ibid., 423–24)

50   See Kens, *Judicial Power and Reform Politics*, which provides some very interesting background on the origins of the act and on the subsequent case, and also argues that the New York attorney general dropped the ball in this case because he was distracted by the need to prepare for another big case before the Supreme Court involving franchise tax law. Ken's discussion of turn-of-the-century police powers jurisprudence, however, tends to give too much credence to the claim that judges (particularly Field) were laissez-faire ideologues enamored with the ethos of social Darwinism, and that doctrines like liberty of contract were unprecedented.

51   "Argument and Brief for Plaintiff in Error," submitted by Frank Harvey Field and Henry Weismann in the case of Lochner v. New York, 198 U.S. 45 (1905), 13, 26.

52   Ibid., 9, 14, 19–20, 23, 28–30, 36, 39–40.

53   Ibid., 33, citing Judge O'Brien's opinion in People ex re. Cossey v. Grout, 179 N.Y. 417, 434. He continued by concluding that the problem was that "there is nothing on the face of the law or in its manifest operation to show that it has any relation to the public health" (ibid., 23). Sidney Tarrow has argued convincingly that the statute in *Lochner* was intended not to promote public health but to bring nonunion bakeries into compliance with union shops. See Tarrow, "Lochner versus New York: A Political Analysis."

54   Three justices had been appointed to the Court between the time of *Holden* and *Lochner*: McKenna in 1898 (virtually contemporaneously with the *Holden* decision), Holmes in 1902, and Day in 1903. The majority was made up of the two *Holden* dissenters, Brewer and Peckham, plus two justices who were in the *Holden* majority, Brown and Fuller, plus McKenna. The dissenters included two members of the *Holden* majority, Harlan and White, and the two justices who had been appointed by Teddy Roosevelt—Holmes and Day.
      Semonche, *Charting the Future*, 181–82:

Apparently the Justices in conference decided to agree with the lower court and uphold the legislation; with Fuller in dissent, Harlan accepted the task of writing the Court's opinion. Peckham agreed to write for the dissenters. When the opinions were read on April 17, 1905, however, the New York Justice began with the majority opinion. Harlan dissented for White and Day, and Holmes filed a separate dissent. From their internal construction, especially taking into account Harlan's unusual style, the opinions were apparently reversed. Someone had switched sides. . . . Since Peckham and Brewer were the strongest advocates of freedom of contract, their positions seemed fixed, and the Chief had shown himself a recent convert. Excluding the final four dissenters leaves Brown and McKenna. Since in the past both Justices had expressed their belief that the police power afforded the states wide latitude, their presence in the Lochner majority is surprising. Without further evidence . . . the selection of the "vacillating jurist" defies resolution.

(Actually, it is "surprising" only if one attempts to characterize the justices as either sympathetic to police powers in the abstract or hostile to police powers in the abstract.) Beth, in *Development of the American Constitution*, 185–86 suggested that Justice Brown was swayed by the fact that Henry Weismann, a baker and self-taught lawyer, argued the case on behalf of Lochner. On the other hand, Kens suggested that McKenna might have been influenced by an overly romanticized conception of the bakers' life; his father had been a successful baker in a small frontier town in California. Kens, *Judicial Power and Reform Politics*, 132.

55   198 U.S. 45, 53–55, 56–59, 64 (1905).

56   Ibid., 66, 69–70, 72–73.

57   Ibid., 75–76. As a matter of his own policy preferences, Holmes was skeptical about wage and hours laws. Note his letter to Harold J. Laski, *Holmes-Laski Letters*, 1:51–52, cited in Bickel and Schmidt, *The Judiciary and Responsible Government*, 597 fn 148.

58   For an extensive bibliography of articles prompted by *Lochner*, see Warren, *Supreme Court in United States History*, 2:713–14fn. See also Warren's "The Progressiveness of the United States Supreme Court" and "A Bulwark to the State Police Power"; and Belz, "The Realist Critique of Constitutionalism in the Era of Reform."

59   Shatto, "Notes on Current Legislation: Hours of Labor."

60   Andrews, "Tendencies of the Labor Legislation of 1910."

61   Dean, "The Law of the Land," 654, 673. According to Dean, the "Law of the Land" means more than that notice and hearing shall be given before rights are determined. . . . It means that private property cannot be taken for private use . . . [or for] public use without just compensation . . . and that one class cannot be taxed for the benefit of the entire public . . . and that . . . discrimination against any man to freely labor, to contract with reference to that labor, or to enjoy the results of his labor, cannot be made. . . . It means that rates charged by a public utility corporation, which will prevent a fair income on the capital invested, cannot be established; and that regulations prescribed in court procedure must be uniform in their operation, and not favor one litigant as against another litigant or class of litigants" (672–73).

62   Browne, "The Super-Constitution," 342. In this piece Browne argued that America's courts were becoming too tolerant of state police powers. "As long as the exercise of

the police power was restrained by constitutional limitations, and legislation upheld only when its purpose was clearly, unequivocally and directly to protect the public (not the private) health, safety and morals it worked no special harm, but in view of the modern tendency of the courts we can see that it [the doctrine of the police powers] was always a torpedo under the ark." He argued that the unwillingness of American courts to sufficiently restrain democratic state legislatures contributed to the Bolshevik revolution. The people of Russia "set up a government that they call a democracy; the very kind of government that most of those who shout loudest for a democracy in this country, mean; and perhaps it is nearer to a pure democracy than any that has been essayed in modern times. . . . Perhaps Trotsky when living in the United States read some of our legislative enactments and the decisions of our courts sustaining them . . . and was inspired thereby to embody them in the Russian law" (ibid., 330, 335, 337).

63   "Notes: Legislative Minimum Wage for Women and Minors," 28 *Harvard Law Review* 89–91 (1914), 89–90. In an earlier volume published one year before *Lochner*, the editors wrote, "If judicial knowledge fails to disclose whether a statute is a legitimate exercise of the police power, evidence should be introduced to enlighten the judicial mind. The abuse of power depends on facts, which can be determined as well as any other facts. Only by this means can adequate protection be extended to newly discovered industries, and a line of decisions, unsound in the light of later experience, be avoided by the courts." The "unsound decision" referred to was *Powell*, upholding the regulation of oleomargarine. See "Notes: Power of the Courts to Review Police Regulations," 17 *Harvard Law Review* 269–70 (1904). Two years after *Lochner* the review reported approvingly that a New York court, in People v. Williams, 116 N.Y. App. Div. 379, had voided an act that restricted women from working at night on the grounds that "no evidence was offered showing the injurious effect on women of a reasonable amount of night work in factories" ("Recent Cases: Police Power—Regulation of Business and Occupations—Prohibition of Night Work by Women in Factories," 20 *Harvard Law Review* 653 [1907]). See also Swayze, "Judicial Construction of the Fourteenth Amendment," 12: "A state legislature may prescribe an eight-hour day for miners; the hours during which women are allowed to work may be limited; and the right to restrict the ordinary liberty of contract by legislation for the protection of workmen where the legislation bears some reasonable relation to the public health, the public safety, or public morals is thoroughly established."

64   Dunscomb, "The Police Power and Civil Liberty," 94–95. Dunscomb also recognized that it was legitimate for the state to set a standard for a day's labor (a) when there was no contract between the parties and (b) for those "persons not fully *sui juris*, as minors, or in some States women of all ages" (ibid., 95).

65   Green, "Judicial Censorship of Legislation," 97–99. Green also discussed the disappointment caused by the New York court's decision in the Workman's Compensation Case, Ives v. South Buffalo Railway Co., 201 N.Y. 271:

> They [who were disappointed] deemed the establishment of employer's liability for accidental injury a necessary step toward relieving a situation productive of social injustice and economic loss, disastrous to the workman and mischievous to the community. . . . In order to see the question as judges saw it, let us assume for

the moment that the legislature, activated by sympathy for the injured workman, looked around to find the nearest rich man on whom to shift the burden of the loss, and found him in the employer. The motive is commendable, but unquestionably, if that is all, the act is not due process. . . . It is evident . . . that one of the things intended to be accomplished by the fourteenth amendment was to prevent the former slave states from resorting to oppressive and discriminatory methods of maintaining order and working out their social problems. . . . Whatever that "prevailing morality or strong and preponderant opinion," of which Judge Holmes has spoken, "may hold" two centuries hence "to be greatly and immediately necessary to the public welfare," it is certain that for some time to come severely whipping at discretion for an offense by a negro against a white man, not so punished when committed by a white man or against a negro, will be deemed an illegitimate method of preserving racial purity, and that for as long a time taking property from a person who is supposed to be prosperous in order to give it to one in adversity will have to be justified by further reasons other than that it is a method of preventing economic waste and establishing social justice. (Ibid., 101)

See also Wickersham, "The Police Power, a Product of the Rule of Reason," 307–9, 316:

[A]ny law which the legislature may choose to enact for the avowed purpose of protecting public health, public safety, or public morals, or of providing for the general public welfare, shall be valid, notwithstanding any effect which such law may have upon the rights guaranteed by the Constitution. . . . [However, if] the views of Mr. Justice Holmes, in dissenting from the majority opinion in Lochner v. New York, should prevail, and courts be held to have "nothing to do with the right of a majority to embody their opinion in law," written constitutions had better be avowedly and formally abolished. . . . [W]hen the judiciary no longer shall feel at liberty to construe the provisions of the fundamental law "in the light of reason," constitutional government, in the sense in which it has been understood for a century and a half, will be at an end, and the doctrine of the police power will have been swallowed up in the capacious maw of unrestrained democracy.

66 McLaughlin, *The Courts, the Constitution, and Parties*, 3–4, 276–78. The book is a collection of five essays. The earlier quotes are from an essay entitled "The Power of a Court to Declare a Law Unconstitutional," 3–107; and the latter are from an essay entitled "A Written Constitution in Some of its Historical Aspects," 245–91.

67 Freund, "Limitation of Hours of Labor and the Federal Supreme Court." A month later the same point was made by Frederick Pollock in "The New York Labour Law and the Fourteenth Amendment": "The legal weakness of this reasoning, if we may say so, is that no credit seems to be given to the State legislature for knowing its own business. . . . How can the Supreme Court at Washington have conclusive judicial knowledge of the conditions that affected bakeries in New York?" After the decision Samuel Gompers remarked that "if the majority of the court who signed the opinion had visited modern bakeries in this state, and had seen the conditions that prevail, even under the ten hour law, they would have believed that it was within the police

powers of this state to regulate the hours" (*New York Tribune*, April 19, 1905, cited in Kens, *Judicial Power and Reform Politics*, 132). In an exchange of letters in 1910, Elihu Root and President Taft agreed that the decision was wrong, with Root arguing that the result would have been different if the facts had been made plainer to the justices. Ibid., 207fn.

68   Frankfurter, "Hours of Labor and Realism in Constitutional Law," 353–73; Pound, "The Need of a Sociological Jurisprudence," "The Scope and Purpose of Sociological Jurisprudence," and "Mechanical Jurisprudence."

69   For a contemporary discussion of the intrusion of "new information" into twentieth-century legal culture, see Johnson, *American Legal Culture.*

70   Pound, "Liberty of Contract," 454–55, 457–58, 462, 471, 480–81.

71   For a contemporary evaluation of the evidence and arguments presented in the brief, see Bryden, "Brandeis's Facts."

72   Muller v. Oregon, 208 U.S. 412 (1908). The only change in the Court's personnel between *Lochner* and *Muller* was William H. Moody's replacement of Henry B. Brown in 1906.

73   McLean v. Arkansas, 211 U.S. 539 (1908), 548–50. Brewer and Peckham, the *Holden* dissenters, dissented without explanation. The position adopted by the majority had been advanced twelve years earlier by a commentator who was very sensitive to the distinction between class legislation and the general welfare. In his *Handbook to the Labor Law of the United States*, 112, Stimson wrote, "If it be true that coal miners are as a class in danger of being fraudulently imposed by their employers as to the amount due them for wages when paid by the ton, owing to the peculiar nature of the business, it would seem that their contracts for wages might reasonably be regulated under the police power in order to prevent a general fraud."

74   Adair v. United States, 208 U.S. 161 (1908). Holmes (in an opinion joined by McKenna, who was in the *Lochner* majority) did better in dissent here than he did in *Lochner*. Against the majority challenge that the act bore no relation to a federal interest in interstate commerce, he argued that the act should be upheld on the basis of a federal interest in industrial peace on the railroads. Besides, the act "simply prohibits the more powerful party to exact certain undertakings, or to threaten dismissal or unjustly discriminate on certain grounds against those already employed." Roscoe Pound criticized Harlan's position that "the public have no interest in bringing about a real equality in labor-bargainings" on the grounds that the community had a general interest in obviating "strikes and disorders" ("Liberty of Contract," 480–81).

75   Coppage v. Kansas, 236 U.S. 1 (1914), 16–18. In dissent, Day and Hughes argued that the law was designed to protect the right of association, which they claimed was promoting a neutral general interest. For more on the social vision represented in this case, see Casebeer, "Teaching an Old Dog Old Tricks."

76   Frankfurter, "Hours of Labor and Realism in Constitutional Law," 363–64, 370.

77   Freund, "Constitutional Limitations and Labor Legislation," 614, 619–20, 622.

78   Osgood, "A Review of Labor Legislation in the United States for the Year 1909," 165, 176.

79   Andrews, "Tendencies of the Labor Legislation of 1910," 224. (This is the same person cited in the previous note). In this piece she reiterated that "we must not

forget that labor legislation to be effective must be based upon careful investigation of the conditions pervading each particular industry, for this alone makes possible a standardization of occupations based upon actual needs of health and safety" (234).

80   In 1910 Hughes replaced Brewer (one of the two *Holden* dissenters); when he left the Court (for the first time) in 1916 to become the Republican presidential candidate he was replaced by John H. Clarke. Also in 1910 Van Devanter replaced White and Joseph R. Lamar replaced Moody; when Lamar died in 1916 he was replaced by Brandeis. In 1912 Pitney replaced Harlan, and in 1914 McReynolds replaced Horace H. Lurton. In all, only four of the justices who had been on the Court when *Muller* was handed down were still on the Court in 1917: McKenna (who was in the *Lochner* majority), Holmes, Day, and White (all *Lochner* dissenters). The other justices sitting on the Court in 1917 were Clarke, McReynolds, Pitney, Brandeis, and Van Devanter.

81   W. Lair Thompson and C. W. Fulton, for plaintiffs in error, reproduced in Bunting v. Oregon, 243 U.S. 426 (1917), 427–29.

82   Felix Frankfurter, George M. Brown, and J. O. Bailey, for defendant in error, ibid., 431–33.

83   Ibid., 435, 437, 438.

84   Adams v. Tanner, 244 U.S. 590 (1917), 593–94.

85   Ibid., 601–2, 606–7, 609, 615.

86   People v. Schweinler Press, 214 N.Y. 395, 412 (1915); see also Ritchie v. Wayman, 244 Ill. 509 (1910).

CHAPTER FOUR   *The Constitution Besieged*

1   Willoughby, "The Philosophy of Labor Legislation," 17, 19–20.

2   See Harper, "Due Process of Law in State and Labor Legislation," 622–25, for a review of the gradual acceptance by federal and state judges of the constitutionality of laws regulating hours of labor.

3   See Kolko, *The Triumph of Conservatism*; Weinstein, *The Corporate Ideal in the Liberal State*; Forcey, *The Crossroads of Liberalism*; Link, *Woodrow Wilson and the Progressive Era*; Lustig, *Corporate Liberalism*. The Croly quote is from Forcey, *Crossroads of Liberalism*, 47.

4   Some of those who struggled to give meaning to their changing life-styles elaborated social visions that directly challenged the power relationships embedded in industrial capitalism. Agrarian reformers attempted to redirect the class bias embedded in the system's prevailing structures of finance, production, and distribution away from the interests of bankers, railroads, and large commercial farmers and toward the interests of smaller producers by agitating for reform of the credit system and the creation of farm cooperatives; however, their efforts were permanently derailed in the 1890s with the co-optation of the Populists into the Bryan wing of the Democratic party. The Knights of Labor tried to reassert the tradition of artisan republicanism in the age of industrial capitalism, but their movement was eclipsed in the late 1880s and 1890s, to be replaced by the conservative American Federation of Labor, which accepted new forms of industrial production (thus turning away from the issue of workers' control of production) and instead worked to realize the best

wages and work environments possible under these circumstances. Many workers found a new alternative vision in the leadership of Eugene V. Debs and the Socialist party, but in spite of some significant accomplishments this movement also failed to realize any lasting gains. See Goodwyn, *The Populist Moment*; Montgomery, *Fall of the House of Labor*; and Weinstein, *The Corporate Ideal in the Liberal State*.

5   For a discussion of how this debate manifested itself in presidential politics in the first part of the century, see Gillman, "The Constitution Besieged."

6   Skowronek, *Building a New American State*.

7   Ibid., 21–22. In March 1912, candidate Roosevelt spoke before a crowd at Carnegie Hall and repeated the theme: The only tyrannies from which men, women, and children are suffering in real life are the tyrannies of minorities, and, as Harbaugh has recorded the event, TR proceeded to name them: "the coal trust, the water-power trust, the meat-packing trust." (Harbaugh, *Life and Times of Theodore Roosevelt*, 397–98).

8   Roosevelt, "Address at San Francisco, September 14, 1912," in Harbaugh, *The Writings of Theodore Roosevelt*, 288–91.

9   Roosevelt, *An Autobiography*, 276.

10 Croly, *Promise of American Life*, 139, 153, 139, 147.

11 Ibid., 151, 179–80, 185–86.

12 Ibid., 190–91, 170–71, 173–74. Roosevelt did question the continued efficacy of certain well-established principles of political legitimacy, but of course he was no "radical." The Republican Roosevelt thought it was possible to remedy the problem of privilege in government and society without replacing it with the traditional fear of conservatives, the "popular corruption" of active democratic politics. His solution can be found in the linkage he sought between more representative government and a larger governing role to be played by independent regulatory commissions, professional bureaucrats, and the president.

With respect to commissions, Roosevelt argued that on those types of issues that invited improper favors—such as tariff legislation, river and harbor acts, and pension laws—the people and their legislators had to realize that the general welfare would best be served by delegating policymaking to an independent body of experts, whose decisions would be closely scrutinized by a democratized legislature. A commission would perform the "difficult task of framing in outline the legislation that the country, as distinguished from the special interests, really needs." Majorities might do a good job of checking private privilege in government, but they are not very reliable when it comes to the "expert" and "efficient" "management" of an increasingly complex social order: "[T]here are certain matters, as to which the voters do not at present have the chance of thus acting directly, where it is important that the chance be given them. But they can only exercise such choice with wisdom and benefit where it is vitally necessary to exercise it, on condition of not being confused by the requirement of exercising it in the great multitude of cases where there is no such necessity, and where they can with advantage delegate the duty to the man they deem most fit to do the business" (Roosevelt, "A Remedy for Some Forms of Selfish Legislation," Harbaugh, *Writings*, 264–66). As Samuel P. Hays has pointed out, it was "the spirit of science and technology, of rational system and organization," that "shifted the location of decision-making continually upward so as to narrow the range of influences impinging upon it." Bureaucratic professionalism was becoming for Roosevelt the new measure of the general welfare; the politics of "pressure group action, logrolling in Congress, [and] partisan debate could not guarantee rational and scientific decisions." Hays also noted that Roosevelt's progressivism was not a struggle between the "people" and the "corporations." If anything it was believed that "the large corporation could more readily afford to undertake conservation practices, that they alone could provide the efficiency, stability of operations, and long-range planning inherent in the conservation idea." Roosevelt explicitly rejected western insurgency "because it expressed the aims of only one economic group in society which, if dominant, would exercise power as selfishly as did the Eastern business community." The goal of the movement was to break off patterns of inefficient exploitation of resources and to empower independent and expert professionals who, in any given case, would be able to balance or pick and choose between the interests of timber companies, environmentalists, small farmers, cattlemen, and settlers. Hays, *Conservation and the Gospel of Efficiency*, preface to the Atheneum edition, and 2–3, 266, 263, 267.

Roosevelt explained his "stewardship theory" of the presidency in his *Autobiography*, 388: "My view was that every officer, and above all every executive officer in high position, was a steward of the people. . . . I declined to adopt the view that what was imperatively necessary for the Nation could not be done by the President unless he could find some specific authorization to do it. My belief was that it was not only his right but his duty to do anything that the needs of the Nation demanded unless such action was forbidden by the Constitution or by the laws." The expansion of executive power was necessary because no other part of the federal government was capable of the kind of selective involvement that Roosevelt expected of his new republic.

As summarized by Skowronek, the rise of the independent regulatory commission, the professional public servant, and the active national executive "merged hopes for a responsible new democracy with hopes for a responsive new political economy. . . . By transforming ideological conflicts into matters of expertise and efficiency, bureaucrats promised to reconcile the polity with the economy and to stem the tide of social disintegration. . . . [For Roosevelt], the position of the President as a nationally elected officer was to be coupled with the professional discipline of the bureaucrat to ensure that special interests would be kept at an arm's length and that the national interest would be raised above private power" (Skowronek, *Building a New American State*, 165–66).

13 Willoughby, "The Philosophy of Labor Legislation," 17, 19–20.

14 Alger, *The Old Law and the New Order* 237–38, 239–43 (from chap. 9, "The Law and Industrial Inequality," 237–61, originally a paper read before the New York State Bar Association at its annual meeting in 1906; emphasis added).

15 Brandeis, "The Living Law," 463.

16 Hand, "Due Process of Law and the Eight-Hour Day," 506, 508.

17 Powell, "Collective Bargaining before the Supreme Court," 408, 413.

18 Greeley, "The Changing Attitude of the Courts toward Social Legislation," 223. At the time he was writing, Greeley expressed the hope that the courts were receding from their "extreme view."

19 Adler, "Labor, Capital, and Business at Common Law," 242–43, 264–65.

20 Stettler v. O'Hara, 243 U.S. 629 (1917). Frankfurter submitted a brief on behalf of the act. For an account of Brandeis's role in the earlier litigation, see Bickel and Schmidt, *The Judiciary and Responsible Government*, 593–95. When the Court first heard the case a few years earlier the decision apparently went against the statute. Holmes prepared a dissent in which he essentially reiterated the objections he had raised in his *Lochner* dissent; namely, that a reasonable man would believe that the statute advanced the public welfare, and that the Court had upheld many other laws that interfered with contractual freedom. He was driven to add: "The earlier decisions on the Fourteenth Amendment began within the time of some Justices still upon the Bench and went no further than an unpretentious assertion of the liberty to follow the ordinary callings. I think that the expansion of that platitude into the dogma of liberty of contract is extravagant and mistaken" (ibid., 596–98). The dissent was never delivered because the majority opinion never saw the light; for some reason, either because the majority was shaky or because the writer was not ready to deliver it, the case was held off for a year. The following year, Lamar became ill; he died in January 1916. Hughes retired a few months later. The case was reargued later that year. Ibid., 598–99.

21 Stettler v. O'Hara, 69 Ore. 519 (1914), 521–26, 535, 538.

22 "Notes: Legislative Minimum Wage for Women and Minors," 28 *Harvard Law Review* 89–91 (1914), 90–91.

23 R. G. Brown, "Oregon Minimum Wage Cases," 472–73, 479, 482, 486.

24 Powell, "The Constitutional Issue in Minimum-Wage Legislation," 3, 6, 10, 18. Powell recognized that minimum wage laws might put people out of work: the "only employees who can complain of minimum-wage legislation are those whom the employer rejects." Powell considered it a "serious defect" in legislation such as this that it included no "special provision for caring for the unemployables." He added, though, that "a statute is not invalid because it takes only the first step in dealing with a situation and leaves other steps to be adopted as experience shall advise" (18).

25 Williams v. Evans, 139 Minn. 32 (1917), 34, 39–40. Another challenge was turned back in G. O. Miller Telephone Co. v. Minimum Wage Commission, 145 Minn. 262 (1920). The Supreme Court of the State of Washington upheld a minimum wage law for women and children in Larsen v. Rice, 100 Wash. 642 (1918). The justices did not elaborate their own rationale for the outcome: "The reasoning of the justices of the Oregon court [in *Stettler v. O'Hara*] appeals to us as sound and conclusive, and we are content to rest our judgment on the authority of the cases as there determined" (ibid., 646).

26 State v. Crowe, 130 Ark. 272 (1917), 281–85. In his dissent, McCulloch expressed the view that it was not poor wages that drove women to "immorality." The failure to attain wealth "often brings discontent and unhappiness, but I am unwilling to say that woman's health or virtue is dependent upon financial circumstances so as to justify the State in attempting to regulate her wages. Her virtue is without price, in gold. She may become the victim of her misplaced affections and yield her virtue, but sell it for money—no. When she falls so low as that it is only from the isolated helplessness of her shame and degradation" (ibid., 285).

27 C. K. Burdick, *Law of the American Constitution*, 582.

28   Back in 1917, in their respective discussions of the Oregon minimum wage act, both
     Rome Brown and Thomas Reed Powell surmised that McKenna, Holmes, Clarke,
     and Day voted to uphold the act, and White, Van Devanter, McReynolds, and Pitney
     voted to strike it down. See Brown, "Oregon Minimum Wage Cases," 485; Powell,
     "Constitutional Issue in Minimum-Wage Legislation," 1–2. Over the next six years,
     two of the justices considered sympathetic to the legislation, Clarke and Day, were
     replaced by two who turned out to be not as sympathetic, Sutherland and Butler,
     respectively. On the other side, however, two of the justices thought to be hostile to
     the minimum wage, White and Pitney, were replaced by two others who eventually
     upheld the regulation, Taft and Sanford. When McKenna finally took a public
     position on the issue he surprised the earlier surmisers by voting against the mini-
     mum wage.

29   Adkins v. Children's Hospital, 261 U.S. 525 (1923). Of course, had things worked
     out a bit differently, the minimum wage would have been struck down in 1914,
     when the Court first heard the *Stettler* case. See fn. 20, above.

30   In a case decided a year after *Adkins*, Stevenson v. St. Clair, 201 N.W. 629 (Minn.),
     the high court of Minnesota upheld a minimum wage law for minors, arguing that,
     unlike adult women, minors as a class did not have the capacity to fend for
     themselves in wage negotiations. This distinction between *Adkins* and *Stevenson*
     was recognized by the editors of *Harvard Law Review*. See "Recent Cases," 38
     Harvard Law Review 980–81 (1924).

31   From 11 *California Law Review* 353 (1923), 357, cited in Powell, "The Judiciality
     of Minimum-Wage Legislation," 558–59fn. Grimes called for "a movement for the
     appropriate amending of the law of our land to require some such modification as
     that no statute shall be declared unconstitutional by the Supreme Court of the
     United States without a seven to two majority of the Court."

32   This point was made by Minor Bronaugh: "[I]t is difficult to see how a low or high
     wage can affect women as a class to a greater extent than men. Undernourishment
     due to the lack of a living wage is the misfortune of man and woman alike. The
     physical difference between the sexes which renders the female less capable of
     arduous labor for long continued periods would not seem to differentiate the sexes
     when it comes to a matter of wages" ("Minimum Wage Laws," reproduced in
     National Consumers' League, *The Supreme Court and Minimum Wage Legislation*,
     207–19, 214–15).

33   Bryden, "Brandeis's Facts," 304.

34   Bradwell v. Illinois, 16 Wall. 130 (1873) (Bradley's concurring opinion), in which the
     Court upheld Illinois's policy of prohibiting women from practicing law.

35   In Holmes's judgment, "the power of Congress seems absolutely free from doubt.
     The end—to remove conditions leading to ill health, immorality, and the deteriora-
     tion of the race—no one would deny to be within the scope of constitutional
     legislation. The means are the means that have the approval of Congress, of many
     states, and of those governments from which we have learned our greatest lessons.
     When so many intelligent persons, who have studied the matter more than any of us
     can, have thought that the means are effective and are worth the price, it seems to me
     impossible to deny that the belief reasonably may be held by reasonable men."
     Adkins v. Children's Hospital, 261 U.S. 525 (1923).

36 Taft, *Popular Government*, 229.

37 Radice v. New York, 264 U.S. 292 (1924). For other examples of the Court's determination to maintain the distinction between valid health and safety legislation and illegitimate interferences in the market, see Jay Burns Baking Co. v. Bryan, 264 U.S. 504 (1924) (striking down a statute regulating the size of bread loaves as unrelated to the prevention of consumer fraud); Weaver v. Palmer Bros., 270 U.S. 402 (1926) (striking down a law forbidding the use of shoddy in quilt manufacturing on the ground that sterilization removed the dangers of shoddy); and Louis K. Liggett Co. v. Baldridge, 278 U.S. 105 (1928) (striking down a requirement that drugstores be owned by licensed pharmacists on the ground that "mere stock ownership in a [drug store] can have no real or substantial relation to the public health"). Other cases are discussed by Currie, *The Constitution in the Supreme Court*, 143–46.

38 Corwin, "Constitutional Law in 1922–1923," 56.

39 Bruce, "Constitutional Law—Due Process of Law—Minimum Wage Act."

40 W. C. H., "District of Columbia Minimum Wage Case," reproduced in National Consumers' League, *The Supreme Court and Minimum Wage Legislation*, 197–206, 205 (emphasis in original).

41 Bronaugh, "Minimum Wage Decision," 218–19.

42 Goble, "The Minimum Wage Decision," 424. For a similar conclusion, see Borchard, "The Supreme Court and the Minimum Wage," 134–37.

43 Reproduced in National Consumers' League, *The Supreme Court and Minimum Wage Legislation*, 224–34, 224, 226.

44 Haines, "Minimum Wage Act for District of Columbia Held Unconstitutional." He added that the majority's unwillingness to expand the legitimate scope of government power was rooted in "a spirit of individualism and *laissez faire* characteristic of the pioneer conditions which prevailed in a large part of the country more than a generation ago" and complained that this spirit "is ill suited to the industrial conditions now prevailing in many American communities" (592).

Haines apparently could not be convinced that the "vague" due process clause could have a relatively clear tradition behind it. In 1926, Rodney L. Mott explained in his exhaustive discussion of the concept (*Due Process of Law*, 277, 295), that it had been long understood that this concept included an aversion to "special and partial laws," that most legal writers recognized the relationship between the due process clause and the equal protection clause, and that the "ultimate result [in constitutional law] would probably have been much the same whether the 'equal protection of the law' had been inserted in the constitution or not." Mott also argued that the Supreme Court had never made an effort to carefully distinguish between the due process and equal protection clauses until Truax v. Corrigan, 257 U.S. 312 (1921), in which the Court struck down a law that prevented judges from issuing injunctions against ex-employees whose picketing of a former employer resulted in a loss of business, but which allowed injunctions to be issued against others who might picket a business and drive away customers. Among other things, the Court, in an opinion by Taft, announced that "the equal protection clause was aimed at undue favor and individual or class privilege, on the one hand, and at hostile discrimination or the oppression of inequality on the other; it secures equality of protection not only for all, but against all, similarly situated; it is a pledge of the protection of equal laws. . . . Immunity granted to a class, however limited, having the effect to deprive another class, however limited, of a personal or property right, is just as clearly a denial of equal protection of the laws to the latter class as if the immunity were in favor of, or the deprivation of right permitted worked against, a larger class." It is likely that the Court decided to rest this old sensibility more explicitly on the equal protection clause because it did not want to challenge the validity of the Clayton Act, which, of course, was not covered by the equal protection clause.

45   "Professor Thomas Reed Powell's argument that the decision is without explanation; that it was determined by the chance which brought it before these particular judges; that it was decided, 'not by the arguments but by the arbiters' is more clever than profound. One may admit that different judges will decide the same case differently, but one certainly may seek for some further explanation for the varying decisions under the Fourteenth Amendment than that of 'malfeasance of chance and of the calender'" (R. A. Brown, "Book Review," 910).

46   He also rejected the suggestion in the majority opinion that the statute "compels the employer to choose between charity or the abandonment of his enterprise. . . . No mention is made of the third possibility that the employer may secure male employees not subject to the act, though this, in fact, is what the employer did in the case at bar." This alternative, of course, did very little to help impoverished working women in the District of Columbia.

47   Powell, "The Judiciality of Minimum-Wage Legislation." See also Groat, "Economic Wage and Legal Wage," 500: "[M]any changes have come about in industry since 1787. . . . These changes are especially evident in that successor to the master and servant relation[,] the employer and employee relation—which expresses a new industrial era quite revolutionary in the extent of the changes. An eighteenth century constitution cannot, without change, be fitted to these twentieth century conditions."

48   Pound, Introduction to *The Supreme Court and Minimum Wage Legislation*, comp. National Consumers' League, xxii, xxvii. For a similar opinion see Frank M. Parrish, "Minimum Wage Law for Women as a Violation of the Fifth Amendment," reproduced in ibid., 159–69 (originally published in the *Michigan Law Review*). Pound was not the only one impatient with criticism based on realist assumptions. The editors of the *New York Law Journal* chose to reproduce one discussion of the *Adkins* case because the author "does not in any respect criticize the personalities, motives or intelligence of the majority of the learned Court, but merely criticizes their reasoning and result. The more criticism of that sort there is, the better for the future of the Republic" (ibid., 196). Ray A. Brown was also impatient with the legal realists' approach to this problem. "Such considerations," he noted, "almost persuade one to abandon the further study of the cases in this field to the biographer and the psychoanalyst. But the author, perhaps at the risk of being deemed fatuous, believes that an attempt should be made to render somewhat more orderly, understandable, and shall it be said juristic, the work that the Court has done." He noted that it was not always possible to tie a judge's decision to an assumption about his preference toward certain kinds of legislation: the conservative Justice Brewer wrote

the opinion in *Muller v. Oregon*, while Brown, "whose opinion in *Holden v. Hardy* is a monument of liberalism, was found with the majority in the much criticized *Lochner v. New York*." Moreover, he pointed out that a good number of police power decisions had been unanimous. So, "in the aggregate of cases decided by the Court on due process and police power, the individual views of the judges enter and play their role, and yet in the mass merge and become but parts outlining and shading the whole body of the law" (Ray A. Brown, "Police Power—Legislation for Health and Personal Safety," 42 *Harvard Law Review* 866–98 [1929], 868–69).

49 R. A. Brown, "Book Review," 912.

50 R. A. Brown, "Police Power," 887, 897–98.

51 Pound's call for better judicial information about the social facts underlying legislation was echoed by Fowler Vincent Harper, who in the course of the exhaustive survey "Due Process of Law and Labor Legislation" for the *Michigan Law Review* came out in favor of a special "legal research bureau" which would "conduct researches [*sic*] in the legal and economic or other fields concerned in legislation under review by the courts, and upon request or suggestion of the court furnish valuable studies to those tribunals in the performance of their delicate and difficult task." Harper argued that this kind of bureau was made necessary by virtue of the importance in police powers jurisprudence of factual determinations about whether legislation actually promoted public health, safety, and morality; he also suggested that this reform would get around the problem of the unreliability of decisions based on a judge's "general knowledge" and "common understanding" and the overly partisan character of most "sociological briefs," like the one used by Brandeis (Harper, "Due Process of Law and Labor Legislation," 890–96). See also Bikle, "Judicial Determinations of Questions of Fact Affecting the Constitutional Validity of Legislative Action."

52 All of the justices who voted to sustain the act in *Adkins* were gone from the Court by the time the issue of the minimum wage was reconsidered (Brandeis having recused himself from the original decision). Taft was replaced by Hughes in 1930, Sanford was replaced by Roberts in 1930, and Holmes was replaced by Cardozo in 1932. One of the justices who voted to strike down the law in *Adkins*, McKenna, was replaced by Stone in 1925. By the early 1930s it was clear that Brandeis, Stone, and Cardozo were solidly in favor of the minimum wage; Hughes and Roberts proved to be more ambivalent.

53 See chapter 2.

54 See Wolff Packing Co. v. Court of Industrial Relations, 262 U.S. 522 (1923); Tyson & Brothers v. Banton, 273 U.S. 418 (1927); Ribnik v. McBride, 277 U.S. 350 (1928); and New State Ice Co. v. Liebmann, 285 U.S. 262 (1932).

55 Apparently, both Hughes and Roberts struggled with the application of traditional police powers jurisprudence. Hughes's biographer reported that the Chief Justice considered these close cases; Roberts "is said to haved paced the floor . . . until the early morning hours" before deciding how to vote in *Nebbia* (Pusey, *Charles Evans Hughes*, 700; Currie, *The Constitution in the Supreme Court: The Second Century*, 210).

56 Nebbia v. New York, 291 U.S. 502 (1934) (emphasis added). McReynolds's opinion closely resembles the argument offered by Robert A. Maurer, a law professor at

Georgetown University. Writing in 1934, Maurer observed that many "critics" had argued that "Constitutional limitations upon the exercise of governmental power . . . should not stand in the way of what is at the time thought to be desirable, socially or economically. . . . In this atmosphere, any attempt to revaluate [sic] what has been heretofore considered an accepted canon of constitutional law, is faced with the peculiar, one might say the extraordinary, responsibility of assuming the defensive." Undeterred, Maurer insisted that since the early 1870s the Supreme Court had consistently maintained that individual liberties could be subordinated to the public interest if legislation bore a "real and substantial relation . . . to the accomplishment of a legitimate police power purpose." He acknowledged that the Court at the end of the nineteenth century voided fewer state regulations than the modern Court, but that was because "there was in those decades of our history, a dearth of state regulatory legislation of that character"; the regulations that were in place were largely "elementary and unobjectionable" and presented no "ground for contention that they were arbitrary and bore no real and substantial relation to legitimate governmental regulatory purposes." He went on to argue that the rise of more experimental legislation in the twentieth century, quite naturally, evoked less sympathetic judicial pronouncements. See "Due Process and the Supreme Court," 710–11, 715, 729, 731. More recently, Sutherland's characterization of the law has been seconded by Siegan, *Economic Liberties and the Constitution*, 143.

57   See chapter 2.

58   See Groat, "Economic Wage and Legal Wage."

59   Andrews, "Minimum Wage Comes Back!" 104–5.

60   "Comments: Constitutionality of the New York Minimum Wage Law," 42 *Yale Law Journal* 1250–58 (1933), 1251–52.

61   Andrews, "Minimum Wage Comes Back!" 103.

62   Ibid., 1255.

63   Ibid., 1258.

64   Macbeth, "Student Notes: The Present Status of the Adkins Case," 65–66.

65   Morehead v. N.Y. ex rel. Tipaldo, 298 U.S. 587 (1936).

66   Ibid., 604–5.

67   Ibid., 607–8.

68   Ibid., 609.

69   Ibid., 621.

70   Ibid., 622.

71   Ibid., 622–23.

72   Ibid., 627.

73   Lawton v. Steele, 152 U.S. 133, 137 (1893) (emphasis added).

74   298 U.S. 587, 629, 631. Hughes also addressed the point reasserted by the majority that the rationale behind these laws provides no basis upon which to treat men and women differently. "This separation and corresponding distinctions in legislation is one of the outstanding traditions of legal history. The Fourteenth Amendment found the States with that protective power and did not take it away or remove the reasons for its exercise. . . . We have not yet arrived at a time when we are at liberty to override the judgment of the State and decide that women are not the special subject of exploitation because they are women and as such are not in a relatively defenceless position."

75   Ibid., 631.
76   Ibid., 632–33.
77   Ibid., 635.
78   Ibid., 636.
79   Powell, *Vagaries and Varieties in Constitutional Interpretation*, 81 n. 89: "Mr. Justice Roberts's position in the two cases can be harmonized as the view of one who was unable to distinguish the Adkins case but who would accept an opportunity to overrule it." It is also common wisdom that the decision in West Coast Hotel v. Parrish, 300 U.S. 379 (1937), which was handed down March 29, 1937, less than two months after FDR unveiled his Court-packing plan, was actually made some time before the plan and therefore was not a response to a threat. See Currie, *The Constitution in the Supreme Court: The Second Century*, 210; Frankfurter, "Mr. Justice Roberts."
80   West Coast Hotel v. Parrish, 300 U.S. 379 (1937).
81   Ibid., 391–92.
82   Ibid., 395.
83   Ibid., 397.
84   Ibid., 398–99.
85   He wrote: "Undoubtedly it is the duty of a member of the court, in the process of reaching a right conclusion, to give due weight to the opposing views of his associates; but in the end, the question which he must answer is not whether such views seem sound to those who entertain them, but whether they convince him that the statute is constitutional or engender in his mind a rational doubt upon that issue. The oath which he takes as a judge is not a composite oath, but an individual one" (ibid., 401).
86   Ibid., 402–4.

Afterword

1   Corwin, "Constitution v. Constitutional Theory: The Question of the States v. the Nation," 104–5.
2   See Hutcheson, "The Judgment Intuitive: The Function of the 'Hunch' in Judicial Decisions."
3   Arnold, *The Symbols of Government*, 10, 35, 49–51. Arnold wrote: "Human institutions inevitably gather around themselves burning idealists seeking to attract unprincipled practices, even when they are producing humanitarian results; dignified conservatives willing to defend the worst social abuses because even human suffering is preferable to the adoption of unsound principles; stern realists intent in showing that society is a sham; and devoted scholars busy painting a rational, logical, and moral paradise for the comfort of those struggling in an irrational world" (ibid., 10).
4   See Pound, "The Call for Realist Jurisprudence."
5   Lerner, "The Supreme Court and American Capitalism," 697–701.
6   F. S. Cohen, "Transcendental Nonsense and the Functional Approach," 812, 820, 843, 854.
7   Corwin, "Constitution v. Constitutional Theory: The Question of the States v. the Nation," 104–5.

8 West Coast Hotel v. Parrish, 300 U.S. 379 (1937).

9 For an analysis that attempts to demonstrate that the Filled Milk Act was an example of special interest politics and did not advance the general welfare, see G. P. Miller, "The True Story of Carolene Products."

10 United States v. Carolene Products, 304 U.S. 144 (1938).

11 Shapiro, "The Supreme Court's 'Return' to Economic Regulation," 134.

12 Ibid., 138, 134.

13 See Tulis, "The Two Constitutional Presidencies." In Lowi's words, the presidency has become an institution at the head of a "plebiscitary republic" in which un-programmatic and unaccountable presidential power is based on a direct, unmediated relationship with powerful constituents who have high expectations that he will service their interests, thus making him incapable of "saying no to any important arguments," robbing him of any capacity "to establish priorities among claims for policies," and forcing him to "live on appearances and have contingency plans for deceit" (Lowi, *The Personal President*, 65, 96, 157, 174).

14 Up through the Civil War there was some dispute about whether states had the authority to nullify and resist federal laws that contravened state policy, but even the most fervent nationalists who participated in this debate over federal supremacy acknowledged limits on the authority of the federal government to intrude into purely intrastate matters. In Gibbons v. Ogden, 9 Wheaton 1 (1824), John Marshall noted that while Congress's power to regulate commerce "among the several states" implied the right to extend federal power into the interior of the states, it did not authorize the national government to regulate commerce "which is completely internal, which is carried on between man and man in a state, or between different parts of the same state, and which does not extend to or affect other states." Throughout most of the nineteenth century, this distinction between intra- and interstate commerce led to a relatively clear division of responsibility between the national government and the states: the national government focused its efforts almost exclusively on promoting commerce by establishing systems of credit and currency, sponsoring internal improvements, imposing tariffs, disposing of public lands, protecting patents, and preventing states from interfering with the free flow of commercial traffic; by contrast, the states regulated the day-to-day activities of commercial life, in particular manufacturing and production. See Skowronek, *Building a New American State*.

In bringing to life this principled distinction between intra- and interstate commerce, courts in the nineteenth century generally held that the regulation of manufacturing and production was a matter of local concern and could not be reached by the federal government, whereas the promotion of commerce and the regulation of distribution and transportation were essentially interstate activities and therefore the responsibility of the federal government. See The Daniel Ball, 77 U.S. 557 (1871); Kidd v. Pearson, 128 U.S. 1 (1888). When, in the late nineteenth century, Congress attempted to expand its authority beyond those activities traditionally understood to involve interstate commerce (such as railroads, waterways, or the distribution and processing of meat) and passed laws relating to production and sales, the Supreme Court struck them down as literally unprecedented. See United States v. E. C. Knight Co., 156 U.S. 1 (1895); Hammer v. Dagenhart, 247 U.S. 251

(1918); Schechter Poultry Corp. v. United States, 295 U.S. 495 (1935); Carter v. Carter Coal Co., 298 U.S. 238 (1936). After the "switch-in-time that saved nine" the justices for the first time allowed the federal government to take full control of manufacturing and production. See National Labor Relations Board v. Jones & Laughlin Steel Corp., 301 U.S. 1 (1937); United States v. Darby, 312 U.S. 100 (1941); Wickard v. Filburn, 317 U.S. 111 (1942).

15   The framers well understood that the concept of separation of powers was designed to prevent the concentration of the various responsibilities of government in one branch. At the same time, it had been assumed that the legislature might occasionally find it convenient to delegate certain decisions to another branch, so long as the *delegation* did not amount to a *surrender* of the legislative power. The Supreme Court determined that a delegation was appropriate if it was accompanied by some meaningful direction ("interstitial administration" or "fill in the details" legislation) or the assignment of a specific task triggered by a specific set of circumstances ("contingent legislation"); Congress's power to delegate was also limited by general constitutional prohibitions and by the belief that some specific congressional responsibilities must be performed by the Congress, like providing "advice and consent" for treaties, formulating admiralty law, or trying impeachments. See Wayman v. Southard, 23 U.S. 1 (1825); The Brig Aurora, 11 U.S. 382 (1813); also see Tribe, *American Constitutional Law*, 362.

In Panama Refining Co. v. Ryan, 293 U.S. 388 (1935), a near-unanimous Court struck down a provision of the National Industrial Recovery Act (NIRA) that authorized the president to prohibit the interstate transportation of oil produced in excess of state allowances. The justices concluded that the Congress had stated no policy, nor identified any triggering circumstance, to guide the president in deciding whether to authorize NIRA codes regulating interstate shipment of oil; the Chief Justice observed critically that "the Congress left the matter to the President without standard or rule, to be dealt with as he pleased." Later that year, in Schechter Poultry Corp. v. United States, 295 U.S. 495 (1935), the Court struck down section 3 of the NIRA as unprecedented: "It supplies no standards for any trade, industry, or activity. It does not undertake to prescribe rules of conduct to be applied to particular states of fact determined by appropriate administrative procedure. . . . [T]he discretion of the President in approving or prescribing codes, and thus enacting laws for the government of trade and industry throughout the country, is virtually unfettered." Even Cardozo, who dissented in *Panama Refining*, had to agree that the powers granted to the executive in the poultry code section of the NIRA represented "delegation running riot. . . . The delegated power of legislation which has found expression in this code is not canalized within banks that keep it from overflowing."

However, as Peter Woll has noted, "Since the beginning of World War II every instance of congressional delegation of legislative power to the President or the administrative branch has been upheld" (*American Bureaucracy*, 156). Congress began delegating to the executive branch "a grant of authority and jurisdiction that left each agency pretty much to its own judgment as to what to do and how to do it. . . . One administrative agency after another was given power to make important public policy decisions that had hitherto been reserved to legislatures or, in fact, not made at all" (Lowi, *Personal President*, 52). Of course, Congress is free to offer guidance and direction to its agents, but judges no longer link the legitimacy of delegation to the existence of meaningful standards; their focus is not on preventing overbroad delegation but rather on reviewing the essential fairness of administration procedures and on scrutinizing administrative decisions that affect "preferred freedoms" or fundamental rights. See United States v. Robel, 389 U.S. 258 (1967); Kent v. Dulles, 357 U.S. 116 (1958); Greene v. McElroy, 360 U.S. 474 (1960).

16 See Skowronek, *Building a New American State.*

17 See Lowi, *The End of Liberalism*; Lustig, *Corporate Liberalism*; McConnell, *Private Power and American Democracy*; and Purcell, *The Crisis of Democratic Theory.*

18 United States v. Carolene Products Co., 304 U.S. 144 (1938). Footnote 4 was attached to Justice Stone's declaration in the body of the opinion that "regulatory legislation affecting ordinary commercial transactions is not to be pronounced unconstitutional unless in the light of the facts made known or generally assumed it is of such a character as to preclude the assumption that it rests upon some rational basis within the knowledge and experience of the legislators." There are still echoes of the old constitutionalism in this declaration, in the inference that the justices used to pronounce legislation unconstitutional if they considered it irrational, but the clear signal is that this tradition is being laid to rest, to be replaced by the values identified in the footnote:

> There may be narrower scope for the operation of the presumption of constitutionality when legislation appears on its face to be within a specific prohibition of the Constitution, such as those of the first ten amendments, which are deemed equally specific when held to be embraced within the Fourteenth. . . . It is unnecessary to consider now whether legislation which restricts those political processes which can ordinarily be expected to bring about repeal of undesirable legislation, is to be subjected to more exacting judicial scrutiny under the general prohibitions of the Fourteenth Amendment than are most other types of legislation. . . . Nor need we enquire whether similar considerations enter into the review of statutes directed at particular religious . . . or national . . . or racial minorities . . . whether prejudice against discrete and insular minorities may be a special condition, which tends seriously to curtail the operation of those political processes ordinarily to be relied upon to protect minorities, and which may call for a correspondingly more searching judicial inquiry.

Martin Shapiro has argued that the post-New Deal Court often uses the language of "preferred freedoms" to protect a new set of economic rights that take the form of benefits to the clients of the New Deal: government jobs, food stamps, welfare, disability, social security, and the like; see "The Constitution and Economic Rights."

19 See Adamson v. California, 332 U.S. 46 (1947), particularly the debate between Frankfurter and Hugo L. Black; Dennis v. United States, 341 U.S. 494 (1951), particularly the debate between Frankfurter and William O. Douglas. Frankfurter launched his attack on the concept of preferred freedoms in Kovacs v. Cooper, 336 U.S. 77 (1949).

20 Many of these arguments are reviewed by Ackerman in *We the People*, 10–16.

21 Ibid., 12.

Bibliography

Abel, Richard. "Torts." In *The Politics of Law: A Progressive Critique*, ed. David Kairys, pp. 185–200. New York: Pantheon Books, 1982.

Ackerman, Bruce. *We the People: Foundations*. Cambridge: Harvard University Press, 1991.

Adamany, David. "Legitimacy, Realignment Elections, and the Supreme Court." *Wisconsin Law Review* 1973: 790.

Adams, Willi Paul. *The First American Constitutions: Republican Ideology and the Making of State Constitutions in the Revolutionary Era*. Chapel Hill: University of North Carolina Press, 1980.

Adler, Edward A. "Labor, Capital, and Business at Common Law." *Harvard Law Review* 29 (1916): 241–76.

Agresto, John T. "Liberty, Virtue, and Republicanism: 1776–1787." *Review of Politics* 39 (1977): 474.

———. " 'A System without Precedent'—James Madison and the Revolution in Republican Liberty." *South Atlantic Quarterly* 82 (1983): 129–44.

Akin, John W. "Aggressions of the Federal Courts." *American Law Review* 32 (1898): 669–700.

Aleinikoff, T. Alexander. "Constitutional Law in the Age of Balancing." *Yale Law Journal* 96 (1987): 943–1005.

Alger, George W. *The Old Law and the New Order*. Boston and New York: Houghton Mifflin, 1913.

Allen, Lafon. "The Income Tax Decision: An Answer to Gov. Pennoyer." *American Law Review* 29 (1895): 847–56.

Alley, Robert S., ed. *The Supreme Court on Church and State*. New York: Oxford University Press, 1988.

Andrews, Irene Osgood. "Minimum Wage Comes Back!" *American Labor Legislation Review* 23 (1933): 103–5.

———. "A Review of Labor Legislation in the United States for the Year 1909." *American Political Science Review* 4 (1910): 163–79.

———. "Tendencies of the Labor Legislation of 1910." *American Political Science Review* 5 (1911): 224–34.

Anonymous. "Some Restrictions upon Legislative Power." *Albany Law Journal* 43 (1891): 25–27.

Appleby, Joyce. "The American Heritage: The Heirs and the Disinherited." *Journal of American History* 74 (1987): 798–813.

———. *Capitalism and a New Social Order: The Republican Vision of the 1790s*. New York and London: New York University Press, 1984.

———. "Commercial Farming and the 'Agrarian Myth' in the Early Republic." *Journal of American History* 68 (1983): 848.

———. *Economic Thought and Ideology in Seventeenth-Century England*. Princeton, N.J.: Princeton University Press, 1978.

———. "Republicanism in Old and New Contexts." *William and Mary Quarterly* 43 (1986): 20–34.

———. "The Social Origins of American Revolutionary Ideology." *Journal of American History* 64 (1978): 935–58.

———. "What Is Still American in the Political Philosophy of Thomas Jefferson?" *William and Mary Quarterly* 39 (1982): 308.

Arnold, Thurman W. *The Symbols of Government*. 1935. Reprint. New York and Burlingame, Calif.: Harcourt, Brace and World, 1962.

Ashcraft, Richard. *Revolutionary Politics and Locke's Two Treatises of Government*. Princeton, N.J.: Princeton University Press, 1986.

Atkinson, Edward. "The Hours of Labor." *North American Review* 142 (1886): 507–15.

Avrich, Paul. *The Haymarket Tragedy*. Princeton, N.J.: Princeton University Press, 1984.

Bailyn, Bernard. *The Ideological Origins of the American Revolution*. Cambridge, Mass., and London: Belknap Press of the Harvard University Press, 1967.

Baldwin, Roger N. and Clarence B. Randall. *Civil Liberties and Industrial Conflict*. Cambridge, Mass.: Harvard University Press, 1938.

Bannard, Henry C. "The Oleomargarine Law: A Study of Congressional Politics." *Political Science Quarterly* 2 (1887): 545–57.

Banning, Lance. "James Madison and the Nationalists, 1780–1783." *William and Mary Quarterly* 40 (1983): 227–55.

———. *The Jeffersonian Persuasion: Evolution of a Party Ideology*. Ithaca, N.Y.: Cornell University Press, 1978.

Barrow, Clyde W. *Universities and the Capitalist State: Corporate Liberalism and the Reconstruction of American Higher Education, 1894–1928*. Madison: University of Wisconsin Press, 1990.

Beard, Charles. *An Economic Interpretation of the Constitution*. New York: Free Press, 1913.

———. *The Supreme Court and the Constitution*. 1912. Reprint. Englewood Cliffs, N.J.: Prentice-Hall, 1962.

Belz, Herman. "The Realist Critique of Constitutionalism in the Era of Reform." *American Journal of Legal History* 15 (1971): 288–306.

Benedict, Michael Les. "The Jeffersonian Republicans and Civil Liberty." In *Essays in the History of Liberty: Seaver Institute Lectures at the Huntington Library*, pp. 23–41. San Marino, Calif.: Henry E. Huntington Library, 1988.

———. "Laissez-Faire and Liberty: A Re-evaluation of the Meaning and Origins of Laissez-Faire Constitutionalism." *Law and History Review* 3 (1985): 293–331.

———. "Preserving the Constitution: The Conservative Basis of Radical Reconstruction." *Journal of American History* 61 (1974): 65–90.

Berger, Peter L., and Thomas Luckman. *The Social Construction of Reality: A Treatise on the Sociology of Knowledge*. New York: Anchor Books, 1966.

Berger, Raoul. "Ely's 'Theory of Judicial Review.' " *Ohio State Library Journal* 42 (1981): 87.

———. *Government by Judiciary*. Cambridge, Mass., and London: Harvard University Press, 1977.

Berthoff, Rowland. "Independence and Attachment, Virtue and Interest: From Republican Citizen to Free Enterpriser, 1787–1837." In *Uprooted Americans: Essays to Honor Oscar Handlin*, ed. Richard L. Bushman et al., pp. 99–124. Boston: Little, Brown, 1979.

Beth, Loren P. *The Development of the American Constitution, 1877–1917*. New York: Harper and Row, 1971.

Bickel, Alexander. *The Least Dangerous Branch*. Indianapolis: Bobbs-Merrill, 1962.

Bickel, Alexander M., and Benno C. Schmidt, Jr. *The Judiciary and Responsible Government, 1910–1921*. New York: Macmillan, 1984.

Bikle, Henry Wolf. "Judicial Determinations of Questions of Fact Affecting the Constitutional Validity of Legislative Action." *Harvard Law Review* 38 (1924): 6–27.

Binney, Charles Chauncey. "Restrictions upon Local and Special Legislation in the United States." *American Law Register* 41 (1892): 613–32, 721–45, 816–57, 1019–33, 1109–61.

Black, Andrew F., III. "Wages and Hours Laws in the Courts." *University of Pittsburgh Law Review* 5 (1939): 223–46.

Black, Charles. *The People and the Court*. New York: Macmillan, 1960.

Black, Donald. *The Behavior of Law*. New York: Academic Press, 1976.

Blau, Joseph L. "Introduction: Jacksonian Social Thought." In *Social Theories of Jacksonian Democracy: Representative Writings of the Period 1825–1850*, ed. Joseph L. Blau, pp. ix–xxviii. New York: Liberal Arts Press, 1954.

———, ed. *Social Theories of Jacksonian Democracy: Representative Writings of the Period 1825–1850*. New York: Liberal Arts Press, 1954.

Bleicher, Joseph. *Contemporary Hermeneutics*. London: Routledge and Kegan Paul, 1980.

Block, Fred. *Revising State Theory: Essays in Politics and Postindustrialism*. Philadephia: Temple University Press, 1987.

Blum, John Morton. *The Republican Roosevelt*. Cambridge, Mass., and London: Harvard University Press, 1977.

Bogin, Ruth. "Petitioning and the New Moral Economy of Post-Revolutionary America." *William and Mary Quarterly*, ser. 3 45 (1988): 391–425.

Borchard, E. M. "The Supreme Court and the Minimum Wage." In *The Supreme Court and Minimum Wage Legislation: Comment by the Legal Profession on the District of Columbia Case*, comp. National Consumers' League, pp. 134–37. New York: New Republic, 1925.

Bourke, Paul F. "The Pluralist Reading of James Madison's Tenth *Federalist*." *Perspectives in American History* 9 (1975): 271–95.

Bowles, Samuel, and Herbert Gintis. *Democracy and Capitalism: Property, Community, and the Contradictions of Modern Social Thought.* New York: Basic Books, 1986.

Brandeis, Louis D. "The Living Law." *Illinois Law Review* 10 (1916): 461–71.

Brannon, Henry. *A Treatise on the Rights and Privileges Guaranteed by the Fourteenth Amendment to the Constitution of the United States.* Cincinnati: W. H. Anderson, 1901.

Brest, Paul. "The Fundamental Rights Controversy: The Essential Contradictions of Normative Constitutional Scholarship." *Yale Law Journal* 90 (1981): 1063.

———. "Interpretation and Interest." *Stanford Law Review* 34 (1982): 765–73.

Bronaugh, Minor. "Minimum Wage Laws." In *The Supreme Court and Minimum Wage Legislation: Comment by the Legal Profession on the District of Columbia Case,* comp. National Consumers' League, pp. 207–19. New York: New Republic, 1925.

Brown, Henry B. "The Distribution of Property." *American Law Review* 27 (1893): 656–83.

Brown, Ray A. "Book Review." *Harvard Law Review* 39 (1926): 909–12.

———. "Due Process of Law, Police Power, and the Supreme Court." *Harvard Law Review* 40 (1927): 943–68.

Brown, Rome G. "Oregon Minimum Wage Cases." *Minnesota Law Review* 1 (1917): 471–86.

Browne, Jefferson B. "The Super-Constitution." *American Law Review* 54 (1920): 321–50.

Bruce, A. A. "Constitutional Law—Due Process of Law—Minimum Wage Act." *Illinois Law Review* 18 (1923): 118.

Bryden, David P. "Brandeis's Facts." *Constitutional Commentary* 1 (1984): 281–326.

Burdick, Charles K. *The Law of the American Constitution: Its Origin and Development.* New York and London: G. P. Putnam's Sons, 1922.

Burdick, Francis M. "Is Law the Expression of Class Selfishness?" *Harvard Law Review* 25 (1912): 349–71.

Burnham, Walter Dean. "The Changing Shape of the American Political Universe." *American Political Science Review* 59 (1965): 10–28.

Cain, Marvin R. "Return of Republicanism: A Reappraisal of Hugh Swinton Legare and the Tyler Presidency." *South Carolina Historical Magazine* 79 (1978): 264–80.

Campbell, Bruce A. "John Marshall, the Virginia Political Economy, and the Dartmouth College Decision." *American Journal of Legal History* 19 (1975): 40–65.

Carter, Lief H. *Contemporary Constitutional Lawmaking: The Supreme Court and the Art of Politics.* New York: Pergamon Press, 1985.

Carter, Stephen L. "Constitutional Adjudication and the Indeterminate Text: A Preliminary Defense of an Imperfect Muddle." *Yale Law Journal* 94 (1985): 821.

Casebeer, Kenneth M. "Teaching an Old Dog Old Tricks: *Coppage v. Kansas* and At-Will Employment Revisited." *Cardozo Law Review* 6 (1985): 765–97.

Chambliss, William, and Robert Seidman. *Law, Order, and Power.* 2d ed. Philippines: Addison-Wesley, 1982.

Chapin, A. L. "The Relations of Labor and Capital." *Transactions of the Wisconsin Academy of Sciences, Arts, and Letters* 1 (1870–1872).

Chessman, G. Wallace. *Theodore Roosevelt and the Politics of Power.* Boston: Little, Brown, 1969.

Cohen, Felix S. "Transcendental Nonsense and the Functional Approach." *Columbia Law Review* 35 (1935): 809–49.

Cohen, Stanley. "Northeastern Business and Radical Reconstruction: A Re-examination." In *Reconstruction: An Anthology of Revisionist Writings*, ed. Kenneth M. Stampp and Leon F. Litwack, pp. 85–106. Baton Rouge and London: Louisiana State University Press, 1969.

Collins, Charles Wallace. *The Fourteenth Amendment and the States.* Boston: Little, Brown, 1912.

Commons, John R. "Horace Greeley and the Working Class Origins of the Republican Party." *Political Science Quarterly* 24 (1909): 468–88.

Conniff, James. "On the Obsolescence of the General Will: Rousseau, Madison, and the Evolution of Republican Political Thought." *Western Political Quarterly* 28 (1975): 49–51.

Cooley, Thomas M. "Labor and Capital before the Law." *North American Review* 139 (1884): 503–16.

———. *A Treatise on the Constitutional Limitations Which Rest upon the Legislative Power of the States of the American Union.* 1868. 8th ed. Boston: Little, Brown, 1927.

Corwin, Edward S. *American Constitutional History: Essays by Edward S. Corwin.* Ed. Alpheus T. Mason and Gerald Garvey. New York, Evanston, Ill., and London: Harper Torchbooks, 1964.

———. "The Basic Doctrine of American Constitutional Law." In *American Constitutional History: Essays by Edward S. Corwin*, ed. Alpheus T. Mason and Gerald Garvey, pp. 25–45. New York, Evanston, Ill., and London: Harper Torchbooks, 1964. Originally published in *Michigan Law Review* 12 (1914).

———. "Constitution v. Constitutional Theory: The Question of the States v. the Nation." In *American Constitutional History: Essays by Edward S. Corwin*, ed. Alpheus T. Mason and Gerald Garvey, pp. 99–108. New York, Evanston, Ill., and London: Harper Torchbooks, 1964. Originally published in *American Political Science Review* 19 (1925): 290.

———. "Constitutional Law in 1922–1923." *American Political Science Review* 18 (1924): 49.

———. "Due Process of Law Before the Civil War." In *American Constitutional History: Essays by Edward S. Corwin*, ed. Alpheus T. Mason and Gerald Garvey, pp. 46–66. New York, Evanston, Ill., and London: Harper Torchbooks, 1964. Originally published in *Harvard Law Review* 24 (1911).

———. "The Supreme Court and the Fourteenth Amendment." In *American Constitutional History: Essays by Edward S. Corwin*, ed. Alpheus T. Mason and Gerald Garvey, pp. 67–98. New York, Evanston, Ill., and London: Harper Torchbooks, 1964. Originally published in *Michigan Law Review* 7 (1909).

Countryman, Edward. *The American Revolution.* New York: Hill and Wang, 1985.

Crenson, Matthew. *The Federal Machine: The Beginnings of Bureaucracy in Jacksonian America.* Baltimore: Johns Hopkins University Press, 1975.

Croly, Herbert. *The Promise of American Life.* 1909. Reprint. Indianapolis: Bobbs-Merrill, 1965.

Crouch, Colin. "The State, Capital and Liberal Democracy." In *State and Economy in Contemporary Capitalism*, ed. Colin Crouch. London: Croom Helm, 1979.

Currie, David P. *The Constitution in the Supreme Court: The Second Century, 1888–1986.* Chicago and London: University of Chicago Press, 1990.

Cushman, Robert E. "Social and Economic Interpretation of the Fourteenth Amendment." *Michigan Law Review* 20 (1922): 737.

Dahl, Robert. "Decision-Making in a Democracy: The Supreme Court as a National Policy-Maker." *Journal of Public Law* 6 (1957): 279.

———. *Who Governs? Democracy and Power in an American City.* New Haven, Conn., and London: Yale University Press, 1961.

Dawley, Alan. *Class and Community: The Industrial Revolution in Lynn.* Cambridge, Mass.: Harvard University Press, 1976.

Dean, Oliver H. "The Law of the Land." *American Law Review* 48 (1914): 641–75.

Dearlove, John. "Bringing the Constitution Back In: Political Science and the State." *Political Studies* 37 (1989): 521–39.

Diggins, John Patrick. *The Lost Soul of American Politics: Virtue, Self-Interest, and the Foundations of Liberalism.* New York: Basic Books, 1984.

Dillon, John F. "Property—Its Rights and Duties in Our Legal and Social Systems." *American Law Review* 29 (1895): 161–88.

Dunscomb, S. Whitney, Jr. "The Police Power and Civil Liberty." *Columbia Law Review* 6 (1906): 93–101.

Dworkin, Ronald. *Law's Empire.* Cambridge, Mass., and London: Harvard University Press, 1986.

———. *A Matter of Principle.* Cambridge, Mass., and London: Harvard University Press, 1985.

———. *Taking Rights Seriously.* Cambridge, Mass., Harvard University Press, 1978.

Ely, John Hart. *Democracy and Distrust.* Cambridge, Mass.: Harvard University Press, 1980.

Erler, Edward J. "The Problem of the Public Good in *The Federalist*." *Polity* 13 (1981): 649–67.

Esterline, Blackburn. "The Supreme Law of the Land." *American Law Review* 40 (1906): 566–79.

Evans, Peter B., Dietrich Rueschemeyer, and Theda Skocpol, eds. *Bringing the State Back In.* Cambridge: Cambridge University Press, 1985.

Ferguson, E. James. "Political Economy, Public Liberty, and the Formation of the Constitution." *William and Mary Quarterly* 40 (1983): 389–412.

Filler, Louis, ed. *Late Nineteenth-Century American Liberalism.* Indianapolis and New York: Bobbs-Merrill, 1962.

Fine, Sidney. *Laissez-Faire and the General Welfare State: A Study of Conflict in American Thought, 1865–1901.* Ann Arbor: University of Michigan Press, 1956.

Fink, Leon. "Labor, Liberty, and the Law: Trade Unionism and the Problem of the American Constitutional Order." *Journal of American History* 74 (1987): 904–25.

Fish, Stanley. *Doing What Comes Naturally: Change, Rhetoric, and the Practice of Theory in Literary and Legal Studies.* Durham, N.C., and London: Duke University Press, 1989.

———. *Is There a Text in This Class? The Authority of Interpretive Communities.* Cambridge, Mass.: Harvard University Press, 1980.

———. "Working on the Chain Gang: Interpretation in Law and Literature." *Texas Law Review* 60 (1982): 551–67.

——. "Wrong Again." *Texas Law Review* 62 (1983): 299–316.

Fiss, Owen M. "Foreword: The Forms of Justice." *Harvard Law Review* 93 (1979): 1.

——. "Objectivity and Interpretation." *Stanford Law Review* 34 (1982): 739–73.

Foltz, Clara. "Should Women Be Executed?" *Albany Law Journal* 54 (1896): 309–10.

Foner, Eric. "Abolitionism and the Labor Movement in Antebellum America." In *Politics and Ideology in the Age of the Civil War*, ed. by Eric Foner, pp. 57–76. New York and Oxford: Oxford University Press, 1980.

——. *Free Soil, Free Labor, Free Men: The Ideology of the Republican Party Before the Civil War*. London: Oxford University Press, 1970.

——. *Reconstruction: America's Unfinished Revolution, 1863–1877*. New York: Harper and Row, 1988.

——. "Reconstruction and the Crisis of Free Labor." In *Politics and Ideology in the Age of the Civil War*, ed. Eric Foner, pp. 97–127. New York and Oxford: Oxford University Press, 1980.

——. *Tom Paine and Revolutionary America*. London, Oxford, and New York: Oxford University Press, 1976.

Foner, Philip S. *History of the Labor Movement in the United States*. Volume 1: *From Colonial Times to the Founding of the American Federation of Labor*. New York: International Publishers, 1947.

——. *History of the Labor Movement in the United States*. Volume 2: *From the Founding of the American Federation of Labor to the Emergence of American Imperialism*. New York: International Publishers, 1955.

——. ed. *We, the Other People: Alternative Declarations of Independence by Labor Groups, Farmers, Women's Rights Advocates, Socialists, and Blacks, 1829–1975*. Urbana: University of Illinois Press, 1976.

Forbath, William E. "The Ambiguities of Free Labor: Labor and Law in the Gilded Age." *Wisconsin Law Review* 1985: 767–817.

——. "The Shaping of the American Labor Movement." *Harvard Law Review* 102 (1989): 1109–1256.

Forcey, Charles. *The Crossroads of Liberalism: Croly, Weyl, Lippmann, and the Progressive Era, 1900–1925*. New York: Oxford University Press, 1961.

Frankfurter, Felix. "Hours of Labor and Realism in Constitutional Law." *Harvard Law Review* 29 (1916): 353–73.

——. *Law and Politics: Occasional Papers of Felix Frankfurter, 1913–1938*. Ed. Archibald MacLeish and E. F. Prichard, Jr. New York: Harcourt, Brace and Co., 1939.

——. "Mr. Justice Roberts." *Pennsylvania Law Review* 104 (1955): 311.

Franklin, Mitchell. "The Foundations and Meaning of the Slaughterhouse Cases." *Tulane Law Review* 18 (1943): 1–88, 218–62.

Freeman, Alan. "Antidiscrimination Law: A Critical Review." In *The Politics of Law: A Progressive Critique*, ed. David Kairys, pp. 96–116. New York: Pantheon Books, 1982.

Freeman, Alan David, and John Henry Schlegel. "Sex, Power and Silliness: As Essay on Ackerman's Reconstructing American Law." *Cardozo Law Review* 6 (1985): 847.

Freund, Ernst. "Constitutional Limitations and Labor Legislation." *Illinois Law Review* 4 (1910): 609–23.

——. "Limitation of Hours of Labor and the Federal Supreme Court." *Green Bag* 17 (1905): 411–17.

Friedman, Lawrence M. *A History of American Law*. New York: Simon and Schuster, 1973.

———. *The Legal System: A Social Science Perspective*. New York: Russell Sage Foundation, 1975.

———. "Two Faces of Law." *Wisconsin Law Review* 1984: 13–35.

Friedman, Lawrence M., and Harry N. Scheiber, eds. *American Law and the Constitutional Order: Historical Perspectives*. Cambridge, Mass., and London: Harvard University Press, 1978.

Gabel, Peter. "Reification in Legal Reasoning." *Research in Law and Sociology* 3 (1980): 25.

Gabel, Peter, and Richard Abel. "Contract Law as Ideology." In *The Politics of Law: A Progressive Critique*, ed. David Kairys, pp. 172–84. New York: Pantheon Books, 1982.

Gadamer, Hans Georg. *Truth and Method*. New York: Seabury Press, 1975.

Garlock, Jonathan. "The Knights of Labor Courts: A Case Study in Popular Justice." In *The Politics of Informal Justice*. Volume 1: *The American Experience*, ed. Richard L. Abel, pp. 17–33. New York: Academic Press, 1982.

Garraty, John A., ed. *Labor and Capital in the Gilded Age: Testimony Taken by the Senate Committee upon the Relations between Labor and Capital—1883*. Boston: Little, Brown, 1968.

———. *The New Commonwealth, 1877–1890*. New York, Evanston, Ill., and London: Harper and Row, 1968.

Geertz, Clifford. *The Interpretation of Cultures*. New York: Basic Books, 1973.

Genovese, Elizabeth Fox. "The Many Faces of the Moral Economy: A Contribution to a Debate." *Past and Present* 58 (1973): 161–68.

Genovese, Eugene D. *Roll, Jordan, Roll*. New York: Pantheon Books, 1976.

Goble, George W. "The Minimum Wage Decision." *American Law Review* 58 (1924): 423–31.

Gold, David A., Clarence Y. H. Lo, and Erik Olin Wright. "Recent Developments in Marxist Theories of the Capitalist State." *Monthly Review* 27 (1975): 29–43.

Gold, David M. "Redfield, Railroads, and the Roots of 'Laissez-Faire Constitutionalism.'" *American Journal of Legal History* 27 (1983): 254–68.

———. *The Shaping of Nineteenth-Century Law: John Appleton and Responsible Individualism*. Westport, Conn.: Greenwood Press, 1990.

Goodnow, Frank J. "Book Reviews." *Columbia Law Review* 13 (1913): 87–92.

Goodwyn, Lawrence. *The Populist Moment: A Short History of the Agrarian Revolt in America*. Oxford, New York, and London: Oxford University Press, 1978.

Gordon, Robert W. "Critical Legal Histories." *Stanford Law Review* 30 (1984): 57.

Greeley, Louis M. "The Changing Attitude of the Courts toward Social Legislation." *Illinois Law Review* 5 (1910): 222–32.

Green, Frederick. "Judicial Censorship of Legislation." *American Law Review* 47 (1912): 90–110.

Groat, George Gorham. "Economic Wage and Legal Wage." *Yale Law Journal* 33 (1924): 489–500.

———. "The Eight Hour and Prevailing Rate Movement in New York State." *Political Science Quarterly* 21 (1906): 414–33.

Gunther, Gerald, ed. *Cases and Materials on Constitutional Law*, 10th ed. Mineola, N.Y.: Foundation Press, 1980.

Guthrie, William D. *Lectures on the Fourteenth Article of Amendment to the Constitution of the United States.* Boston: Little, Brown, 1898.

Hahn, Steven, and Jonathan Prude, eds. *The Countryside in the Age of Capitalist Transformation: Essays in the Social History of Rural America.* Chapel Hill and London: University of North Carolina Press, 1985.

Haines, Charles Grove. "Minimum Wage Act for District of Columbia Held Unconstitutional." *American Law Review* 58 (1924): 581–94.

———. *The Revival of Natural Law Concepts.* 1958. Reprint. New York: Russell and Russell, 1965.

Haines, Charles Grove, and Foster H. Sherman. *The Role of the Supreme Court in American Government and Politics, 1835–1864.* Berkeley: University of California Press, 1957.

Hall, Kermit L. *The Magic Mirror: Law in American History.* New York and Oxford: Oxford University Press, 1989.

Hallam, Oscar. "Judicial Power to Declare Acts Void." *American Law Review* 48 (1914): 85–114, 225–73.

Hamilton, Alexander, John Jay, and James Madison. *The Federalist.* New York: Modern Library.

Hand, Learned. "Due Process of Law and the Eight-Hour Day." *Harvard Law Review* 21 (1908): 495–509.

Handlin, Oscar, and Mary Flug Handlin. *Commonwealth: A Study in the Role of Government in the American Economy: Massachusetts, 1774–1861.* Rev. ed. Cambridge, Mass.: Harvard University Press, 1969.

Harbaugh, William H. *The Life and Times of Theodore Roosevelt.* London: Oxford University Press, 1975.

———, ed. *The Writings of Theodore Roosevelt.* Indianapolis and New York: Bobbs-Merrill, 1967.

Harper, Fowler Vincent. "Due Process of Law in State Labor Legislation." *Michigan Law Review* 26 (1928): 599 (pt. 1), 763 (pt. 2), 888 (pt. 3).

Hartz, Louis. *Economic Policy and Democratic Thought: Pennsylvania, 1776–1860.* Cambridge, Mass.: Harvard University Press, 1948.

Hays, Samuel P. *Conservation and the Gospel of Efficiency: The Progressive Conservation Movement, 1890–1920.* 1959. Reprint. New York: Atheneum, 1975.

———. *The Response to Industrialism, 1885–1914.* Chicago and London: University of Chicago Press, 1957.

Heath, Milton S. *Constructive Liberalism: The Role of the State in Economic Development in Georgia to 1860.* Cambridge, Mass.: Harvard University Press, 1954.

Hekman, Susan. "Beyond Humanism: Gadamer, Althusser, and the Methodology of the Sciences." *Western Political Quarterly* 38 (1983): 98–115.

Hobson, Charles F. "The Negative on State Laws: Madison, the Constitution, and the Crisis of Republican Government." *William and Mary Quarterly* 36 (1979): 215–35.

Hofstadter, Richard. *The American Political Tradition.* 1948. Reprint. New York: Vintage Books, 1974.

———. *Social Darwinism in American Thought.* Boston: Beacon Press, 1944.

Holt, Wyth. "Recovery by the Worker Who Quits: A Comparison of the Mainstream, Legal Realist, and Critical Legal Studies Approaches to a Problem of Nineteenth Century Contract Law." *Wisconsin Law Review* 1986: 677–732.

Horwitz, Morton. *The Transformation of American Law, 1780–1860*. Cambridge, Mass.: Harvard University Press, 1977.

Hough, Charles M. "Due Process of Law—To-Day." *Harvard Law Review* 32 (1919): 218–33.

Hovenkamp, Herbert. "The Political Economy of Substantive Due Process." *Stanford Law Review* 40 (1988): 379–447.

Howe, Daniel Walker. *The Political Culture of the American Whigs*. Chicago: University of Chicago Press, 1978.

Howe, Lowell J. "The Meaning of 'Due Process of Law' Prior to the Adoption of the Fourteenth Amendment." *California Law Review* 18 (1930): 583–609.

Hugins, Walter. *Jacksonian Democracy and the Working Class: A Study of the New York Workingmen's Movement, 1829–1837*. Stanford, Calif.: Stanford University Press, 1960.

Hull, N. E. H. "Reconstructing the Origins of Realist Jurisprudence: A Prequel to the Llewelleyn-Pound Exchange over Legal Realism." *Duke Law Journal* 1989: 1302–34.

Hunt, Alan. "Emile Durkheim: Towards a Sociology of Law." In *Marxism and Law*, ed. Piers Beirne and Richard Quinney, pp. 27–43. New York: John Wiley and Sons, 1982.

———. "The Ideology of Law: Advances and Problems in Recent Applications of the Concept of Ideology to the Analysis of Law." *Law and Society Review* 19 (1985): 11–37.

Hurst, James Willard. *Law and the Conditions of Freedom in the Nineteenth-Century United States*. Madison: University of Wisconsin Press, 1956.

Hutcheson, Joseph C., Jr. "The Judgment Intuitive: The Function of the 'Hunch' in Judicial Decisions." *Cornell Law Quarterly* 14 (1929): 285.

Hyman, Harold M. *A More Perfect Union*. New York: Alfred A. Knopf, 1973.

Hyman, Harold M., and William M. Wiecek. *Equal Justice under Law: Constitutional Development, 1835–1875*. New York: Harper and Row, 1982.

Jacobs, Clyde E. *Law Writers and the Courts: The Influence of Thomas M. Cooley, Christopher G. Tiedeman, and John F. Dillon upon American Constitutional Law*. Berkeley and Los Angeles: University of California Press, 1954.

Jacobsohn, Gary J. *Pragmatism, Statesmanship, and the Supreme Court*. Ithaca, N.Y., and London: Cornell University Press, 1977.

Jefferson, Thomas. *Notes on the State of Virginia*, introduction by Thomas Perkins Abernethy. New York: Harper Torchbooks, 1964.

Jernegan, Marcus Wilson. *Laboring and Dependent Classes in Colonial America, 1607–1783*. 1931. Reprint. New York: Frederick Ungar, 1965.

Jillson, Calvin C., and Cecil L. Eubanks. "The Political Structure of Constitution Making: The Federal Convention of 1787." *American Journal of Political Science* 28 (1984): 435–58.

Johnson, John W. *American Legal Culture, 1908–1940*. Westport, Conn.: Greenwood Press, 1981.

Jones, Alan. "Thomas M. Cooley and 'Laissez-Faire Constitutionalism': A Reconsideration." *Journal of American History* 53 (1967): 751–71.

―――. "Thomas M. Cooley and the Michigan Supreme Court: 1865–1885." *American Journal of Legal History* 10 (1966): 97–121.

Judson, Frederick N. "Liberty of Contract under the Police Power." *American Law Review* 25 (1891): 871–98.

Kairys, David. "Legal Reasoning." In *The Politics of Law: A Progressive Critique*, ed. David Kairys, pp. 11–17. New York: Pantheon Books, 1982.

Kay, Richard S. "The Equal Protection Clause in the Supreme Court, 1873–1903." *Buffalo Law Review* 29 (1980): 667–72.

Keller, Morton. *Affairs of State: Public Life in Late Nineteenth Century America*. Cambridge, Mass.: Belknap Press of the Harvard University Press, 1977.

Kelly, Alfred H., and Winfred A. Harbison. *The American Constitution: Its Origins and Development*. New York: W. W. Norton, 1948.

Kelman, Mark. *A Guide to Critical Legal Studies*. Cambridge, Mass., and London: Harvard University Press, 1987.

―――. "Trashing." *Stanford Law Review* 36 (1984): 293–348.

Kennedy, Duncan. "Distributive and Paternalistic Motives in Contract and Tort Law, with Special Reference to Compulsory Terms and Unequal Bargaining Power." *Maryland Law Review* 41 (1982): 563.

―――. "Form and Substance in Private Law Adjudication." *Harvard Law Review* 89 (1976): 1685.

―――. "The Structure of Blackstone's Commentaries." *Buffalo Law Review* 28 (1979): 205–382.

Kens, Paul. *Judicial Power and Reform Politics: The Anatomy of Lochner v. New York*. Lawrence: University Press of Kansas, 1990.

―――. "The Source of a Myth: Police Powers of the States and Laissez Faire Constitutionalism, 1930–1937." *American Journal of Legal History* 35 (1991): 70–98.

Kenyon, Cecelia M., ed. *The Antifederalists*. 1966. Reprint. Boston: Northeastern University Press, 1985.

Klare, Karl E. "Judicial Deradicalization of the Wagner Act and the Origins of Modern Legal Consciousness, 1937–1941." *Minnesota Law Review* 42 (1978): 265.

Kolko, Gabriel. *The Triumph of Conservatism*. New York: Free Press, 1963.

Kramnick, Isaac. *Bolinbroke and His Circle: The Politics of Nostalgia in the Age of Walpole*. Cambridge, Mass.: Harvard University Press, 1968.

―――. "The 'Great National Discussion': The Discourse of Politics in 1787." *William and Mary Quarterly*, ser. 3, 45 (1988): 3–31.

―――. "Republican Revisionism Revisited." *American Historical Review* 87 (1982): 629–64.

Kulikoff, Allan. "The Transition to Capitalism in Rural America." *William and Mary Quarterly*, ser. 3, 46 (1989): 120–44.

Labatt, C. B. "State Regulation of the Contract of Employment." *American Law Review* 27 (1893): 857–75.

Larsen, Charles E. "Nationalism and States' Rights in Commentaries on the Constitution After the Civil War." *American Journal of Legal History* 3 (1959): 360.

Lears, T. J. Jackson. "The Concept of Cultural Hegemony: Problems and Possibilities." *American Historical Review* 90 (1985): 567–93.

Leff, Arthur Allen. "Economic Analysis of Law: Some Realism about Nominalism." *Virginia Law Review* 60 (1974): 451.

———. "Unspeakable Ethics, Unnatural Law." *Duke Law Journal* 1979: 1229.

Lerner, Max. "The Supreme Court and American Capitalism." *Yale Law Journal* 42 (1933): 668–701.

Levy, Leonard W. *The Law of the Commonwealth and Chief Justice Shaw.* Cambridge, Mass.: Harvard University Press, 1957.

Liddle, William D. " 'Virtue and Liberty': An Inquiry into the Role of the Agrarian Myth in the Rhetoric of the Revolutionary Era." *South Atlantic Quarterly* 77 (1978): 15–38.

Link, Arthur S. *Woodrow Wilson and the Progressive Era, 1910–1917.* New York and Evanston, Ill.: Harper and Row, 1954.

Litwack, Leon, ed. *The American Labor Movement.* New York: Simon and Schuster, Touchstone edition, 1986.

Lowi, Theodore J. *The End of Liberalism: Ideology, Policy, and the Crisis of Public Authority.* New York: W. W. Norton, 1969.

———. *The Personal President: Power Invested, Promise Unfulfilled.* Ithaca, N.Y., and London: Cornell University Press, 1985.

Lustig, R. Jeffrey. *Corporate Liberalism: The Origins of Modern American Political Theory, 1890–1920.* Berkeley: University of California Press, 1982.

Lynd, Staughton, ed. *Class Conflict, Slavery, and the United States Constitution.* Indianapolis: Bobbs-Merrill, 1967.

———. "A Governing Class on the Defensive." In *Class Conflict, Slavery, and the United States Constitution,* ed. Staughton Lynd, pp. 109–32. Indianapolis: Bobbs-Merrill, 1967.

———. "The Mechanics in New York Politics, 1774–1785." In *Class Conflict, Slavery, and the United States Constitution,* ed. Staughton Lynd, pp. 79–108. Indianapolis: Bobbs-Merrill, 1967.

———. "Who Should Rule at Home? Dutchess County, New York, in the American Revolution." In *Class Conflict, Slavery, and the United States Constitution,* ed. Staughton Lynd, pp. 25–61. Indianapolis: Bobbs-Merrill, 1967.

Macauley, Stewart. "Law and the Behavioral Sciences: Is There Any There There?" *Law and Policy* 6 (1984): 149–87.

Macbeth, Norman, Jr. "Student Notes: The Present Status of the Adkins Case." *Kentucky Law Journal* 24 (1935): 59–68.

McClosky, Robert G. *American Conservatism in the Age of Enterprise, 1865–1919.* New York: Harper and Row, 1951.

———. *The American Supreme Court.* Chicago and London: University of Chicago Press, 1960.

McConnell, Grant. *Private Power and American Democracy.* New York: Vintage Books, 1960.

McCoy, Drew R. "Benjamin Franklin's Vision of a Republican Political Economy for America." *William and Mary Quarterly* 35 (1978): 605–28.

———. *The Elusive Republic: Political Economy in Jeffersonian America.* New York and London: W. W. Norton, 1980.

———. *The Last of the Fathers: James Madison and the Republican Legacy.* Cambridge: Cambridge University Press, 1989.

McCurdy, Charles W. "American Law and the Marketing Structure of the Large Corporation, 1875–1890." *Journal of Economic History* 38 (1978): 631–49.

———. "Justice Field and the Jurisprudence of Government-Business Relations: Some Parameters of Laissez Faire Constitutionalism, 1863–1897." *Journal of American History* 61 (1975): 970–1005.

———. "The Roots of Liberty of Contract Reconsidered: Major Premises in the Law of Employment, 1867–1937." *Supreme Court Historical Society* 1984: 20–33.

McDonough, James B. "The Alleged Usurpation of Power by the Federal Courts." *American Law Review* 46 (1912): 45–61.

McLaughlin, Andrew C. *The Courts, the Constitution, and Parties.* Chicago: University of Chicago Press, 1912.

McPherson, James M. "Lincoln and Liberty." In *Essays in the History of Liberty: Seaver Institute Lectures at the Huntington Library*, pp. 59–74. San Marino, Calif.: Henry E. Huntington Library, 1988.

Main, Jackson Turner. *The Anti-Federalists: Critics of the Constitution, 1781–1788.* Chapel Hill: University of North Carolina Press, 1961.

Maltz, Earl M. "Fourteenth Amendment Concepts in the Antebellum Era." *American Journal of Legal History* 32 (1988): 305–46.

Mannheim, Karl. *Ideology and Utopia: An Introduction to the Sociology of Knowledge.* New York and London: Harcourt Brace Jovanovich, 1936.

March, James G., and Johan P. Olsen. "The New Institutionalism: Organization Factors in Political Life." *American Political Science Review* 78 (1984): 734–49.

Matson, Cathy D., and Peter S. Onuf. *A Union of Interests: Political and Economic Thought in Revolutionary America.* Lawrence: University Press of Kansas, 1990.

Maurer, Robert A. "Due Process and the Supreme Court—A Reevaluation." *Georgetown Law Journal* 22 (1934): 710–49.

Mayer, David N. "The Jurisprudence of Christopher G. Tiedeman: A Study in the Failure of Laissez-Faire Constitutionalism." *Missouri Law Review* 55 (1990): 95–161.

Mayo, Edward L. "Republicanism, Antipartyism, and Jacksonian Party Politics: A View from the Capital." *American Quarterly* 31 (1979): 3–20.

Meigs, William M. "The American Doctrine of Judicial Power, and Its Early Origin." *American Law Review* 47 (1912): 683–96.

———. "The Relation of the Judiciary to the Constitution." *American Law Review* 19 (1885): 175–203.

———. "Some Recent Attacks on the American Doctrine of Judicial Power." *American Law Review* 40 (1906): 641–70.

Mendelson, Wallace. *Capitalism, Democracy, and the Supreme Court.* New York: Appleton-Century-Crofts, 1960.

Meyers, Marvin. *The Jacksonian Persuasion: Politics and Belief.* 1957. Reprint. New York: Vintage Books, 1960.

Miliband, Ralph. *Marxism and Politics.* Oxford: Oxford University Press, 1977.

———. *The State in Capitalist Society.* New York: Basic Books, 1969.

Miller, Arthur Selwyn. *The Supreme Court and American Capitalism.* New York: Free Press, 1968.

Miller, Geoffrey P. "The True Story of Carolene Products." *Supreme Court Review* 1987: 397–428.

Miller, Nathan. *The Enterprise of a Free People: Aspects of Economic Development of New York State during the Canal Period, 1792–1838*. Ithaca, N.Y.: Cornell University Press, 1962.

Montgomery, David. *Beyond Equality: Labor and the Radical Republicans, 1862–1872*. New York: Alfred A. Knopf, 1967.

———. *The Fall of the House of Labor*. Cambridge: Cambridge University Press, 1987.

———. "Workers' Control of Machine Production in the Nineteenth Century." *Labor History* 17 (1976): 485–505. Reprinted in *The Labor History Reader*, ed. Daniel J. Leab, pp. 107–31. Urbana and Chicago: University of Illinois Press, 1985.

Moody, William Godwin. "Workingmen's Grievances." *North American Review* 138 (1884): 502–10.

Morgan, Robert J. " 'Time Hath Found Us': The Jeffersonian Revolutionary Vision." In *200 Years of the Republic in Retrospect*, ed. William C. Harvard and Joseph L. Bernd, pp. 20–36. Charlottesville: University Press of Virginia, 1976.

Morris, Richard B. *Government and Labor in Early America*. New York: Octagon Books, 1965.

Mott, Rodney L. *Due Process of Law: A Historical and Analytical Treatise of the Principles and Methods Followed by the Courts in the Application of the Concept of the "Law of the Land."* Indianapolis: Bobbs-Merrill, 1926.

Nash, Gary B. "Artisans and Politics in Eighteenth Century Philadelphia." In *Race, Class, and Politics: Essays on American Revolutionary Society*, ed. Gary B. Nash, pp. 243–68. Urbana and Chicago: University of Illinois Press, 1986.

———. "Social Change and the Growth of Prerevolutionary Urban Radicalism." In *Race, Class, and Politics: Essays on American Revolutionary Society*, ed. Gary B. Nash, pp. 211–42. Urbana and Chicago: University of Illinois Press, 1986.

———. "The Transformation of Urban Politics, 1700–1764." In *Race, Class, and Politics: Essays on American Revolutionary Society*, ed. Gary B. Nash, pp. 141–70. Urbana and Chicago: University of Illinois Press, 1986.

———. *The Urban Crucible: Social Change, Political Consciousness, and the Origins of the American Revolution*. Cambridge, Mass., and London: Harvard University Press, 1979.

———. "Urban Wealth and Poverty in Prerevolutionary America." In *Race, Class, and Politics: Essays on American Revolutionary Society*, ed. Gary B. Nash, pp. 173–209. Urbana and Chicago: University of Illinois Press, 1986.

National Consumers' League, comp. *The Supreme Court and Minimum Wage Legislation: Comment by the Legal Profession on the District of Columbia Case*. New York: New Republic, 1925.

Nedelsky, Jennifer. "Confining Democratic Politics: Anti-Federalists, Federalists, and the Constitution." *Harvard Law Review* 96 (1982): 340–60.

———. *Private Property and the Limits of American Constitutionalism: The Madisonian Framework and Its Legacy*. Chicago and London: University of Chicago Press, 1990.

Nelson, William E. *The Fourteenth Amendment: From Political Principle to Judicial Doctrine*. Cambridge, Mass., and London: Harvard University Press, 1988.

———. "The Impact of the Antislavery Movement upon Styles of Judicial Reasoning in Nineteenth-Century America." *Harvard Law Review* 87 (1974): 513.

Newhouse, Wade J. *Constitutional Uniformity and Equality in State Taxation*, 2d ed. Buffalo: William S. Hein, 1984.

Newmyer, Kent. "Justice Joseph Story, The Charles River Bridge Case and the Crisis of Republicanism." *American Journal of Legal History* 17 (1973): 232–70.

Noble, David W. *The Progressive Mind, 1890–1917.* Rev. ed. Minneapolis, Minn.: Burgess Publishing, 1981.

Nonet, Phillippe, and Philip Selznick. *Law and Society in Transition: Toward Responsive Law.* New York: Harper and Row, 1978.

Orren, Karen, and Stephen Skowronek. *Studies in American Political Development: An Annual.* Volume 1. New Haven, Conn., and London: Yale University Press, 1986.

Osgood, Irene. "A Review of Labor Legislation in the United States for the Year 1909." *American Political Science Review* 4 (1910): 163–79.

Pangle, Thomas L. *The Spirit of Modern Republicanism: The Moral Vision of the American Founders and the Philosophy of Locke.* Chicago and London: University of Chicago Press, 1988.

Parker, Junius. "The Supreme Court and Its Constitutional Duty and Power." *American Law Review* 30 (1896): 357–64.

Parker, Leroy, and Robert H. Worthington. *The Law of Public Health and Safety, and the Powers and Duties of Boards of Health.* Albany, N.Y.: Matthew Bender, 1892.

Paul, Arnold M. *Conservative Crisis and the Rule of Law: Attitudes of Bar and Bench, 1887–1895.* Ithaca, N.Y.: Cornell University Press, 1960.

Peffer, William. "The Mission of the Populist Party." *North American Review* 157 (1893): 665–78.

Pennoyer, Sylvester. "The Case of Marbury v. Madison." *American Law Review* 30 (1896): 188–202.

——. "The Income Tax Decision, and the Power of the Supreme Court to Nullify Acts of Congress." *American Law Review* 29 (1895): 550–58.

——. "A Reply to the Foregoing." *American Law Review* 29 (1895): 856–63.

Pessen, Edward. *Jacksonian America: Society, Personality, and Politics.* 1969. Rev. ed. Urbana and Chicago: University of Illinois Press, 1985.

——. "Thomas Skidmore, Agrarian Reformer in the Early American Labor Movement." *New York History* 35 (1954): 280–96.

Pierce, Harry H. *Railroads of New York: A Study of Government Aid, 1826–1875.* Cambridge, Mass.: Harvard University Press, 1953.

Pisani, Donald J. "Promotion and Regulation: Constitutionalism and the American Economy." *Journal of American History* 74 (1987): 740–68.

Pocock, J. G. A. *The Machiavellian Moment: Florentine Political Thought and the Atlantic Republican Tradition.* Princeton, N.J.: Princeton University Press, 1975.

——. *Politics, Language, and Time: Essays on Political Thought and History.* New York: Atheneum, 1971.

Pollock, Frederick. "The New York Labour Law and the Fourteenth Amendment." *Law Quarterly Review* 21 (1905): 211–13.

Porter, Mary Cornelia. "*Lochner* and Company: Revisionism Revisited." In *Liberty, Property, and Government: Constitutional Interpretation Before the New Deal,* ed. Ellen Frankel Paul and Howard Dickman. Albany: State University of New York Press, 1989.

Posner, Richard. *The Economics of Justice.* Cambridge, Mass., and London: Harvard University Press, 1981.

———. *The Problems of Jurisprudence.* Cambridge, Mass., and London: Harvard University Press, 1990.

Poulantzas, Nicos. *Political Power and Social Classes,* trans. Timothy O'Hagen. London: New Left Books, 1973.

———. "The Problem of the Capitalist State." In *Ideology in Social Science,* ed. Robin Blackburn. New York: Vintage Books, Random House, 1973.

Pound, Roscoe. "The Call for a Realist Jurisprudence." *Harvard Law Review* 44 (1931): 697.

———. "Liberty of Contract." *Yale Law Journal* 18 (1909): 454–87.

———. "Mechanical Jurisprudence." *Columbia Law Review* 8 (1908): 605.

———. "The Need of a Sociological Jurisprudence." *Green Bag* 19 (1907): 607.

———. "The Scope and Purpose of Sociological Jurisprudence." *Harvard Law Review* 24 (1911): 591, continued at *Harvard Law Review* 25 (1912): 140, 489.

Powderly, T. V. "The Organization of Labor." *North American Review* 135 (1882): 118–26.

Powell, Thomas Reed. "Book Reviews." *Columbia Law Review* 13 (1913): 559–61.

———. "Collective Bargaining before the Supreme Court." *Political Science Quarterly* 33 (1918): 396–429.

———. "The Constitutional Issue in Minimum-Wage Legislation." *Minnesota Law Review* 2 (1917): 1–21.

———. "The Judiciality of Minimum-Wage Legislation." *Harvard Law Review* 37 (1924): 545–73.

———. *Vagaries and Varieties in Constitutional Interpretation.* New York: Columbia University Press, 1956.

Pressen, Edward. "Did Labor Support Jackson?: The Boston Story." *Political Science Quarterly* 64 (1949): 262–74.

Primm, James N. *Economic Policy in the Development of a Western State: Missouri, 1820–1860.* Cambridge, Mass.: Harvard University Press, 1954.

Prude, Jonathan. *The Coming Industrial Order: Town and Factory Life in Rural Massachusetts, 1810–1860.* Cambridge: Cambridge University Press, 1983.

———. "The Social System of Early New England Textile Mills: A Case Study, 1812–40." In *The New England Working Class and the New Labor History,* ed. Herbert G. Gutman and Donald H. Bell, pp. 90–127. Urbana and Chicago: University of Illinois Press, 1987.

Purcell, Edward A. *The Crisis of Democratic Theory: Scientific Naturalism and the Problem of Value.* Lexington: University Press of Kentucky, 1973.

Pusey, Merlo J. *Charles Evans Hughes.* 1951. Reprint. New York and London: Columbia University Press, 1963.

Ransom, William L. *Majority Rule and the Judiciary.* New York: Charles Scribner's Sons, 1912.

Rawls, John. *A Theory of Justice.* Oxford: Oxford University Press, 1971.

Rayback, Joseph G. *A History of American Labor.* New York: Macmillan, 1959.

Remini, Robert, ed. *The Age of Jackson.* Columbia: University of South Carolina Press, 1972.

———. *Andrew Jackson and the Course of American Freedom, 1822–1832.* New York: Harper and Row, 1981.

Reno, Conrad. "Arbitration and the Wage Contract." *American Law Review* 26 (1892): 837–56.

Ricci, David. "Receiving Ideals in Political Analysis: The Case of Community Power Studies, 1950–1970." *Western Political Quarterly* 33 (1980): 451–75.

Riker, William H. "Gouverneur Morris in the Philadelphia Convention." In *The Art of Political Manipulation*, ed. William H. Riker, pp. 34–51. New Haven, Conn., and London: Yale University Press, 1986.

Roche, John P. "The Convention as a Case Study in Democratic Politics." In *Essays on the Making of the Constitution*, ed. Leonard W. Levy, pp. 175–212. London and New York: Oxford University Press, 1969. Originally published as "The Founding Fathers: A Reform Caucus in Action." *American Political Review* 55 (1961): 799–816.

———. "Entrepreneurial Liberty and the Fourteenth Amendment." *Labor History* 4 (1963): 3–31.

———. *Sentenced to Life.* New York: Macmillan, 1974.

Roosevelt, Theodore. *An Autobiography.* New York: Charles Scribner's Sons, 1926.

———. *The New Nationalism.* New York: The Outlook Company, 1910.

Rose, U. M. "Strikes and Trusts." *American Law Review* 27 (1893): 708–40.

Rosenberger, J. C. "The Supreme Court of the United States as Expounder of the Constitution." *American Law Review* 30 (1896): 55–68.

Ross, George. "Nicos Poulantzas, Eurocommunism, and the Debate on the Theory of the Capitalist State." *Socialist Review* 44 (1979): 143–58.

Ross, Steven J. *Workers on the Edge: Work, Leisure, and Politics in Industrializing Cincinnati, 1788–1890.* New York: Columbia University Press, 1985.

Sargeant, Noel. "The American Judicial Veto." *American Law Review* 51 (1917): 663–710.

Saxton, Charles T. "Memorial Day Address." *Albany Law Journal* 55 (June 12, 1897): 391–92.

Scheiber, Harry N. "Economic Liberty and the Constitution." In *Essays in the History of Liberty: Seaver Institute Lectures at the Huntington Library*, pp. 75–99. San Marino, Calif.: Henry E. Huntington Library, 1988.

———. "Federalism and the American Economic Order, 1789–1910." *Law and Society Review* 10 (1975): 57–118.

———. "Government and the Economy: Studies in the 'Commonwealth' Policy in Nineteenth-Century America." *Journal of Interdisciplinary History* 3 (1972): 135–51.

———. "Law and the Imperatives of Progress: Private Rights and Public Values in American Legal History." In *Ethics, Economics, and the Law*, edited by J. Roland Pennock and John W. Chapman, pp. 303–20. New York and London: New York University Press, 1982.

———. *Ohio Canal Era: A Case Study of Government and the Economy, 1820–1861.* Athens, Ohio: Ohio University Press, 1969.

———. "Property Law, Expropriations, and Resource Allocation by Government: The United States, 1789–1910." *Journal of Economic History* 33 (1973): 232–51.

———. "Public Rights and the Rule of Law in American Legal History." *California Law Review* 72 (1984): 217–51.

———. "The Road to *Munn*: Eminent Domain and the Concept of Public Purpose in the State Courts." *Perspectives in American History* 5 (1971): 329–402.

Schlesinger, Arthur M., Jr. *The Age of Jackson.* Boston: Little, Brown, 1945.
———, ed. *The Almanac of American History.* New York: Perigee Books, 1983.
Schmitt, Gary J., and Robert H. Webking. "Revolutionaries, Antifederalists, and Federalists: Comments on Gordon Wood's Understanding of the American Founding." *Political Science Reviewer* 9 (1979): 195–229.
Schutz, Alfred. "Concept and Theory Formation in the Social Sciences." In *Sociological Theory and Philosophical Analysis* , ed. Dorothy Emmet and Alasdair MacIntyre, pp. 1–19. London: Macmillan, 1970.
Schwartz, Joel D. "Liberty, Democracy, and the Origins of American Bureaucracy." *Harvard Law Review* 97 (1984): 815.
Semonche, John E. *Charting the Future: The Supreme Court Responds to a Changing Society, 1890–1920.* Westport, Conn.: Greenwood Press, 1978.
Shalpole, Robert E. "Republicanism and Early American Historiography." *William and Mary Quarterly* 39 (1982): 334–56.
———. "Toward a Republican Synthesis: The Emergence of an Understanding of Republicanism in American Historiography." *William and Mary Quarterly* 20 (1972): 49–80.
Shapiro, Martin. "The Constitution and Economic Rights." In *Essays in the Constitution of the United States,* ed. M. Judd Harmon. Port Washington, N.Y.: Kennikat Press, 1978.
———. "The Supreme Court's 'Return' to Economic Regulation." In *Studies in American Political Development,* ed. Karen Orren and Stephen Skowronek, 1:91–141. New Haven, Conn.: Yale University Press, 1986.
Shatto, Edith. "Notes on Current Legislation: Hours of Labor." *American Political Science Review* 2 (1907): 57–60.
Shefter, Martin. "Party, Bureaucracy, and Political Change in the United States." In *Political Parties: Development and Decay,* ed. Louis Maisel and Joseph Cooper, pp. 211–65. Beverly Hills: Sage Publications, 1978.
———. "Regional Receptivity to Reform: The Legacy of the Progressive Era." *Political Science Quarterly* 98 (1983): 459–83.
Siegan, Bernard H. *Economic Liberties and the Constitution.* Chicago: University of Chicago Press, 1981.
Simpson, A. W. B. "Fourteenth Amendment Concepts in the Antebellum Era." *University of Chicago Law Review* 46 (1979): 533–601.
Sklar, Martin J. *The Corporate Reconstruction of American Capitalism, 1890–1916: The Market, the Law, and Politics.* Cambridge: Cambridge University Press, 1988.
Skocpol, Theda. "Political Response to Capitalist Crisis: Neo-Marxist Theories of the State and the Case of the New Deal." *Politics and Society* 10 (1980): 155–201.
———, ed. *Vision and Method in Historical Sociology.* Cambridge: Cambridge University Press, 1984.
Skowronek, Stephen. *Building a New American State: The Expansion of National Administrative Capacities, 1877–1920.* Cambridge: Cambridge University Press, 1982.
Smith, Rogers M. "Political Jurisprudence, the 'New Institutionalism,' and the Future of Public Law." *American Political Science Review* 82 (1988): 89–108.
Spahr, Charles B. "The Taxation of Labor: The American Theory." *Political Science Quarterly* 1 (1886): 400–436.

Stagner, Stephen. "The Recall of Judicial Decisions and the Due Process Debate." *American Journal of Legal History* 24 (1980): 257–72.

Stampp, Kenneth M. *The Era of Reconstruction, 1865–1877.* New York: Vintage Books, 1965.

Stimson, F. J. *Handbook to the Labor Law of the United States.* New York: Charles Scribner's Sons, 1896.

Storing, Herbert J., ed. *The Anti-Federalists: Writings by the Opponents of the Constitution,* selected by Murray Dry from *The Complete Anti-Federalist.* Chicago and London: University of Chicago Press, 1981.

Stourzh, Gerald. *Alexander Hamilton and the Idea of Republican Government.* Stanford, Calif.: Stanford University Press, 1970.

Street, Judge Robert G. "The Irreconcilable Conflict." *American Law Review* 41 (1907): 686–95.

Sugarman, David. "Law, Economy and the State in England, 1750–1914: Some Major Issues." In *Legality, Ideology, and the State,* ed. David Sugarman, pp. 213–66. London and New York: Academic Press, 1983.

Sumner, Colin. *Reading Ideologies: An Investigation into the Marxist Tradition of Ideology and Law.* London: Academic Press, 1979.

Sunstein, Cass. "*Lochner*'s Legacy." *Columbia Law Review* 87 (1987): 873–919.

Swayze, Francis J. "Judicial Construction of the Fourteenth Amendment." *Harvard Law Review* 26 (1912): 1–41.

Swindler, William F. *Court and Constitution in the Twentieth Century: The Old Legality, 1889–1932.* Indianapolis and New York: Bobbs-Merrill, 1969.

Swisher, Carl Brent. *American Constitutional Development.* Boston and New York: Houghton Mifflin, 1943.

Taft, William Howard. "Criticisms of the Federal Judiciary." *American Law Review* 29 (1895): 641–74.

———. *Popular Government: Its Essence, Its Performance and Its Perils.* New Haven, Conn.: Yale University Press, 1913.

Tarrow, Sidney. "Lochner versus New York: A Political Analysis." *Labor History* 5 (1964): 277–312.

Taylor, Hannis. *Due Process of Law and the Equal Protection of the Laws.* Chicago: Callaghan and Company, 1917.

Teichmueller, H. "The Province of Government." *American Law Review* 29 (1895): 21–31.

Thompson, E. P. "The Moral Economy of the English Crowd in the Eighteenth Century." *Past and Present* 50 (1971): 76–136.

———. *Whigs and Hunters: The Origins of the Black Act.* New York: Pantheon Books, 1975.

Thompson, Seymour D. "Abuses of Corporate Privileges." *American Law Review* 26 (1892): 169–203.

Tiedeman, Christopher G. *The Unwritten Constitution of the United States: A Philosophical Inquiry into the Fundamentals of American Constitutional Law.* New York and London: G. P. Putnam's Sons, 1890.

Tomlins, Christopher L. *The State and the Unions: Labor Relations, Law, and the Organized Labor Movement in America, 1880–1960.* Cambridge: Cambridge University Press, 1985.

Tribe, Laurence. *American Constitutional Law*, 2d ed. Mineola, N.Y.: Foundation Press, 1988.

———. *Constitutional Choices*. Cambridge, Mass., and London: Harvard University Press, 1985.

Trickett, William. "The Great Usurpation." *American Law Review* 40 (1906): 356–76.

———. "Judicial Dispensation from Congressional Statutes." *American Law Review* 41 (1907): 65–91.

Trubek, David M. "Where the Action Is: Critical Legal Studies and Empiricism." *Stanford Law Review* 36 (1984): 575.

Tulis, Jeffrey. "The Two Constitutional Presidencies." In *The Presidency and the Political System*, ed. Michael Nelson, pp. 59–84. Washington, D.C.: CQ Press, 1984.

Tushnet, Mark. "Darkness on the Edge of Town: The Contributions of John Hart Ely to Constitutional Theory." *Yale Law Journal* 89 (1980): 1037.

———. "The Dialectics of Legal History." *Texas Law Review* 57 (1979): 1295–1305.

———. "Truth, Justice, and the American Way: An Interpretation of Public Law Scholarship in the Seventies." *Texas Law Review* 57 (1979): 1307.

Unger, Roberto Mangabeira. "The Critical Legal Studies Movement." *Harvard Law Review* 96 (1983): 563.

———. *Law in Modern Society: Toward a Criticism of Social Theory*. New York: Free Press, 1976.

Urofsky, Melvin I. *A March of Liberty: A Constitutional History of the United States*. New York: Alfred A. Knopf, 1988.

———. "Myth and Reality: The Supreme Court and Protective Legislation in the Progressive Era." *Yearbook of the Supreme Court Historical Society* (1983): 53–72.

———. "State Courts and Protective Legislation during the Progressive Era: A Reevaluation." *Journal of American History* 72 (1985): 63–91.

Warren, Charles. "A Bulwark to the State Police Power—The United States Supreme Court." *Columbia Law Review* 13 (1913): 667.

———. "The Progressiveness of the United States Supreme Court." *Columbia Law Review* 13 (1913): 294.

———. *The Supreme Court in United States History, Volume Two, 1836–1918*. 1922. Rev. ed. Boston and Toronto: Little, Brown, 1926.

Wechsler, Herbert. "Toward Neutral Principles of Constitutional Law." *Harvard Law Review* 73 (1959): 1.

Weibe, Robert H. *The Search for Order, 1877–1920*. New York: Hill and Wang, 1967.

Weinstein, James. *The Corporate Ideal in the Liberal State, 1900–1918*. Boston: Beacon Press, 1968.

White, James Boyd. "The Judicial Opinion and the Poem: Ways of Reading, Ways of Life." *Michigan Law Review* 82 (1984): 1669.

White, Morton. *Social Thought in America: The Revolt against Formalism*. Boston: Beacon Press, 1947.

White, Thomas Raeburn. "Constitutional Prohibition of Local and Special Legislation in Pennsylvania." *American Law Register* [*University of Pennsylvania Law Review*] 49 (1901): 623–35, 687–707; 50 (1902): 27–49.

Wickersham, George W. "The Police Power, a Product of the Rule of Reason." *Harvard Law Review* 27 (1914): 297–316.

Wiecek, William M. *Liberty under Law*. Baltimore and London: Johns Hopkins University Press, 1988.

———. "The Reconstruction of Federal Judicial Power, 1863–1876." In *American Law and the Constitutional Order*, ed. Lawrence M. Freedman and Harry N. Scheiber. Cambridge, Mass.: Harvard University Press, 1978.

Wilentz, Sean. "Against Exceptionalism: Class Consciousness and the American Labor Movement, 1790–1920." *International Labor and Working Class History* 26 (1984): 1–24.

———. *Chants Democratic: New York City and the Rise of the American Working Class, 1788–1850*. New York and Oxford: Oxford University Press, 1984.

Willoughby, William F. "The Philosophy of Labor Legislation." *American Political Science Review* 8 (1914): 14–24.

Wills, Garry. *Explaining America: The Federalist*. New York: Penguin Books, 1981.

Wilson, Major. "Republicanism and the Idea of Party in the Jacksonian Period." *Journal of the Early Republic* 8 (1988): 419–42.

Winchester, Boyd. "The Judiciary—Its Growing Power and Influence." *American Law Review* 32 (1898): 801–13.

Wirth, Louis. "Preface." In *Ideology and Utopia*, by Karl Mannheim, pp. x–xxx. New York and London: Harcourt Bruce Jovanovich, 1936.

Wolfe, Alan. *The Limits of Legitimacy: Political Contradictions of Contemporary Capitalism*. New York: Free Press, 1977.

Woll, Peter. *American Bureaucracy*. 2d ed. New York: W. W. Norton, 1977.

Wood, Gordon S. *The Creation of the American Republic, 1776–1787*. New York and London: W. W. Norton, 1969.

———. "Democracy and the Constitution." In *How Democratic Is the Constitution?* ed. Robert A. Goldwin and William A. Schambra, pp. 1–17. Washington, D.C.: American Enterprise Institute for Public Policy Research, 1980.

Woodward, C. Vann. *Reunion and Reaction: The Compromise of 1877 and the End of Reconstruction*. Boston: Little, Brown, 1951.

Woodward, Frederic C. "Statutory Limitations of Freedom of Contract between Employer and Employe." *American Law Review* 29 (1895): 236–65.

Yablon, Charles M. "The Indeterminacy of the Law: Critical Legal Studies and the Problem of Legal Explanation." *Cardozo Law Review* 6 (1985): 917.

Table of Cases

Index

About the Author. Howard Gillman is Assistant
Professor of Political Science at the University of
Southern California.

Library of Congress Cataloging-in-Publication Data
Gillman, Howard.
The Constitution besieged : the rise and demise of
Lochner era police powers jurisprudence / Howard
Gillman.
p. cm.
Includes bibliographical references and index.
ISBN 0-8223-1283-2 (cloth : acid-free paper)
ISBN 0-8223-1642-0 (paper : acid-free paper)
1. Police power—United States—History.   2. Political
questions and judicial power—United States—History.
3. Judicial process—United States—History.
4. United States—Constitutional law—Economic
liberties—History.   5. Liberty of contract—United
States—History.   6. Social legislation—United
States—History.   7. Social conflict—United States—
History.   I. Title.
KF5399.G55 1993
342.73′0418—dc20
[347.302418]   92-15814 CIP